P9-BIN-805

Crossing Cultures

Crossing Cultures

Readings for Composition

Seventh Edition

Annie Knepler
University of Illinois, Chicago

Ellie Knepler

Myrna Knepler
Emeritus, Northeastern Illinois University

Houghton Mifflin Company

Boston • New York

For permission to use copyrighted material, grateful acknowledgment is made to the copyright holders on pp. 385–88, which are hereby made part of this copyright page.

Library of Congress Cataloging-in-Publication Data

Crossing cultures : readings for composition / Annie Knepler, Ellie Knepler, Myrna Knepler. -- 7th ed.
     p. cm.
  Includes bibliographical references and index.
  ISBN 0-321-41736-4
  1.   College readers. 2. Pluralism (Social sciences)--Problems, exercises, etc. 3. Report writing--Problems, exercises, etc. 4. Culture--Problems, exercises, etc. 5. English language--Rhetoric. 6. Readers--Social sciences. I. Knepler, Annie. II. Knepler, Ellie. III. Knepler, Myrna.
  PE1417.C75 2007
  808'.0427--dc22

           2006026289

Copyright © 2008 by Houghton Mifflin Company. All rights reserved.

No part of this work may be reproduced or transmitted in any form or by any means, electronic or mechanical, including photocopying and recording, or by any information storage or retrieval system without the prior written permission of Houghton Mifflin Company unless such copying is expressly permitted by federal copyright law. Address inquiries to College Permissions, Houghton Mifflin Company, 222 Berkeley Street, Boston, MA 02116-3764.

Printed in the U.S.A.

Instructor's examination copy
  ISBN-10: 0-618-91804-3
  ISBN-13: 978-0-618-91804-1

For orders, use student text ISBNs
  ISBN-10: 0-618-91806-X
  ISBN-13: 978-0-618-91806-5

1 2 3 4 5 6 7 8 9—DOC—11 10 09 08 07

Contents

PART IV   Working and Spending   157

PART V   Defining Ourselves   205

PART VI American Encounters 249

PART VII   Home and Away   307

PART VIII   Communicating   335

Rhetorical Contents

Narration (Observation and reporting)

Definition

Irony, Humor, and Satire

Poetry

Preface

Now in its 7th edition, *Crossing Cultures* has been in continual use in classrooms across America and beyond for almost 25 years. First conceived by Henry and Myrna Knepler in 1983 in response to what they saw as a need for dialogue between cultures and for a dialogue about culture, it was among the first of its kind to use issues of culture and multiculturalism as a jumping-off point for composition. With each edition, *Crossing Cultures* has been expanded, broadened, and updated not only to reflect changing notions about culture, but also to challenge what it means to "cross cultures."

Many scholars and academics have questioned the use of the word "culture," pointing out that cultures are not, and never have been, static or definable. Cultures are constantly in flux—they are hybrids of various histories, experiences, migrations, and other influences, which themselves are constantly changing. A definition of a particular culture also depends on the lens through which it is viewed, and who is looking through that lens. As its title implies, *Crossing Cultures* has always embraced and reflected this idea: cultural boundaries are fluid, and it is precisely the fact the cultures are constantly "crossing"—encountering, conflicting, interacting, mingling, incorporating, appropriating, and adapting one another—that makes them impossible to define.

NEW SELECTIONS AND FEATURES

As *Crossing Cultures* has grown, we have expanded our definition of culture to include, for instance, cultures created by class, sexual identity, technology, work, music, pop culture, fashion, and online communities. These newer ways of looking at culture shine a light on the fact that while traditional definers of culture like race, class, and ethnicity are essential starting points for talking about culture, they are only the beginning of the conversation.

The fifteen new pieces we have chosen for this edition reflect both new ways of thinking about culture and add new voices to this ongoing conversation. We have added more selections that deal with issues of class, including "The Field Trip," Cheri Register's narrative of an enlightening school trip to her town's meatpacking plant, and Kristin Kovacic's "'Proud to Work for the University,'" about her immigrant father's shifting pride in his job as his employer's loyalties also shift in a way that reflects changing labor conditions in America. David Leonhardt's essay "The College Dropout Boom" explores the reasons behind the low university retention rates of working-class students.

Other pieces reflect how changes in technology have affected our everyday lives. In "Love You, K2a2a, Whoever You Are," Amy Harmon uses her own response to her DNA testing results as a starting point to ponder the relationship between DNA testing and identity. The hazards of using and discarding technology are thoughtfully investigated and critiqued by Elizabeth Grossman in "High-Tech Wasteland." Clive Thompson's "Meet the Life Hackers" looks at how technology has led to living spaces and workplaces that are constantly open to interruption, while Rob Walker explores how our lives have become constantly open to advertisement and persuasion in "The Hidden (In Plain Sight) Persuaders."

New authors Emiene Shija Wright and Rasma Haidri both bring fresh perspectives to the ongoing discussion of what it means to grow up in a bicultural household. Other authors bring fresh takes on cultural interaction. In "No Kinda Sense," Lisa Delpit, an educator and educational theorist, examines her complicated feelings toward her own daughter's use of African-American English in the classroom. Ginia Bellafante investigates how new technologies have helped immigrant families both maintain and adapt their dating and marriage traditions. And David Sedaris, Uzodinma Iweala, and Rachel Louise Snyder all confront and describe aspects of their own identities that are only revealed to them when they go abroad.

Besides the new pieces, the most important new feature to the 7th edition of *Crossing Cultures* is that we have reorganized the chapters to make them more cohesive. In some cases we have moved pieces to chapters where we felt they were more appropriate, and provided more fruitful contexts for writing and discussion. We have also created two entirely new chapters, "Working and Spending" and "Home and Away," that reflect current important topics of discussion.

USING CROSS-CULTURAL THEMES

The success of this book and our experiences teaching with it have convinced us that cross-cultural subjects are ideal for a composition course. They provide strong and meaningful topics for discussion and writing both by broadening students' perspectives and by allowing them to draw on stories and themes from their own lives. *Crossing Cultures'* selections challenge accepted beliefs by asking students to consider the lives, ideas, aspirations, and prejudices of people who may be very different from them. At the same time, reading and having one's classmates read selections from one's own culture is likely to heighten students' self-assurance and prompt them to reflect on the meaning of their own experiences. This reflection and reaction to reading and class discussion can often be the starting point for writing that "belongs" to the student, yet extends beyond his or her own experience of the world.

The readings in *Crossing Cultures* have been collected from a variety of sources and are meant to reflect a broad range of perspectives, ideas, and rhetorical styles.

Each selection has also been chosen because it is a "good read" whose subject and style will engage college students and provide thought-provoking material for class discussion as well as compelling ideas for writing.

USING *CROSSING CULTURES* AS A COMPOSITION TEXT

Clearly, students produce stronger writing when they are motivated to write—engaged by content that is thematically interesting and challenging. However, more is needed to turn that interest into good writing. *Crossing Cultures* provides many tools to help students develop stronger reading and composition skills. The "Critical Reading" chapter helps students understand the essential connection between reading and writing, and guides students through strategies and techniques that will help them become more active and critical readers. Furthermore, each selection in the book is followed by a set of exercises that can be used for class discussions or as writing prompts. "Some of the Issues" aids students in careful reading by providing questions to help them clarify and analyze the content and meaning of an essay. The questions in "The Way We Are Told" ask students to examine the author's rhetorical strategies, and point out the significance and effect of stylistic choices we make when we compose. Each exercise section concludes with "Some Subjects for Writing," prompts that can be used for essays or journal entries. Asterisks indicate questions or writing topics that refer to more than one selection, often giving students the chance to compare and contrast two different views of the same subject. In response to reviewers' feedback, we have retailored some of the questions to prompt responses from students that are more analytical than narrative.

The arrangement of the book allows the instructor both flexibility and structure. *Crossing Cultures* contains selections of varying length, difficulty, and style. Selections are arranged thematically; each section begins with an accessible essay, moving on to more challenging and difficult readings. There is also a supplementary rhetorical table of contents that organizes the readings based on the writers' stylistic patterns.

Online Teaching Center

The Instructor Manual for this text is available on the book's accompanying Online Teaching Center located at college.hmco.com/pic/knepler7e. The manual includes some practical teaching tips and information about each reading as well as the answers to the exercises.

ACKNOWLEDGMENTS

We wish to thank our editor, Ginny Blanford, who devoted her considerable enthusiasm and expertise to seeing this project through from beginning to end. She knew when to gently nudge and when to offer valuable support and guidance. Rebecca Gilpin's meticulous attention to schedules and details was invaluable in making the entire editing process run smoothly. Jenny Bevington skillfully and efficiently navigated the complicated and time-consuming task of securing reprint permissions for each of the pieces in the book, and did it with an abundance of grace and cheer. Patrick Franzen expertly and deftly coordinated the many details involved in the production of this book.

Several readers and reviewers gave us expert advice and suggestions for improving the texts. We thank the reviewers arranged by the publisher: Anne Carr, Southeast Community College; Sylvia Cunningham, Guilford College; Jeremy Justus, University of Louisville; Charlene Knadle, Suffolk County Community College; Debra M. Rodriguez, Hiram College; and Donna Winchell, Clemson University.

Many colleagues and friends generously offered ideas, expertise, encouragement, and support at various stages throughout the book. A big thanks to Caryn Aviv, Martha Bayne, Joseph Berman, Helena Marie Carnes, Carla Cenker, Diane Chin, Ralph Cintron, Charlie Clements, Jennifer Cohen, Gilly Costello, Jamie Daniel, Eamon Dolan, Ann Feldman, Adam Fischler, Ellen Grimes, Jim Hall, Eileen Hess, Pennie Holmes-Brinson, Zabrin Inan, Malvin Jeffries, Tamar Kamionkowski, Julie Kleinman, Kate Kinast, Liz Knepler, Andrea Kuti, Jon Langford, Benay Lappe, Amy Ludwig, Diana Miller, Mary Moran, Dev Noily, Derek Owens, Candice Samjhana Rai, Rashmi Ramaswamy, David Schaafsma, Peter Sherman, Janet Smith, Christine Tarkowski, Amy Thesing, Helen Tsatsos, Bettina Van Pelt, Nadine Wasserman, Dinah Wayne, Sue Weinstein, Janice Witzel, and Ellen Youniss, for consistently keeping our spirits up and our minds active. Carrie Spitler, Evelyn Delgado, and Donna Kiser at the Neighborhood Writing Alliance, and all the writers in the *Journal of Ordinary Thought* groups, were a constant source of inspiration.

We have dedicated this book with much love to Shaina and Tobi Knepler-Foss. *Crossing Cultures* was born before they were, and they have grown up knowing their aunts and grandparents as editors of "the family book." They are now old enough to use it themselves.

Annie Knepler
Ellie Knepler
Myrna Knepler

INTRODUCTION

READING AND THINKING CRITICALLY

You might be asking yourself why a textbook for a writing class would begin with a chapter on reading. The answer is simple: reading and writing are connected in a fundamental way.

In your writing courses, you will be asked to respond to what you read and to use your reading as a source for ideas and information. Keep in *mind* that, in general, good writers are good readers. They read often and from a wide variety of sources. As they read, or after they finish a selection, they note down interesting passages or write a response to the reading in a journal. Good writers pay attention to the author's style and note the techniques the author uses to make his or her points. They think about where they agree and disagree with the author and why. And, they read to find new topics and ideas for their own writing.

For most of you, reading has become an essential part of your everyday life both in and out of school. However, we read differently depending on our purpose. We read a traffic sign to know which way to go, or an instruction manual to learn how to use a new software program. A newspaper is something we might read both to gather information and to begin to reflect on the events of the world around us. In this case, we process what we are reading with a more critical eye.

Sometimes we think of ourselves as reading simply for pleasure, such as when we read a novel, a short story, or a poem, but even then we are often making connections and analyzing, even if we don't realize that's what we're doing. A character's experience in a novel might help us think through a similar experience we've had, or to consider why someone we know acted in a particular way. By making those connections, we are reading critically, asking questions about what we've read and comparing the concepts in a reading to other ideas we've encountered.

As a student, it is important that you approach your academic readings as an *active* critical reader. Being an active critical reader generally means that you are taking more formal and deliberate steps to analyze what you read. Simply put, you should read the essays in this book differently than you would read your computer manual or a novel by your favorite writer. You will be encouraged to write down and think through your responses to the essays, stories, and poems in *Crossing Cultures*. Your primary goal in reading critically and actively should be to incorporate new ideas and perspectives into your own understanding of the world around you by engaging in a conversation with what you're reading. This in no way means that you should not find pleasure in the readings in this book, only that you are engaging with them on a different and deeper level.

WHAT DOES IT MEAN TO READ CRITICALLY?

In order to effectively incorporate ideas from what you read into what you write, you need to develop the strategies and skills to read critically. Critical readers ask questions as they read. They note down ideas and comparisons they find striking. They work to question and to figure out the author's perspective, keeping in mind what they know about the author's background and values. They consider the author's style of writing, and the writing techniques the author uses in order to develop his or her thesis.

Ultimately, critical readers attempt to form a clear and accurate understanding of what the author is trying to say in order to come up with their own purposeful analysis of what they've read.

You might think of your own writing, therefore, as a way to interact or converse with what you read. Even if what you write does not directly respond to something you've read, the essays you write should somehow reflect the way the reading has influenced your approach to a specific topic. Writing is generally a process of moving back and forth between your reading and your computer or pen and paper, particularly if you are incorporating specific ideas or quotations from your reading.

In order to fully absorb a reading and integrate it into your own writing, you generally need to read it more than once (perhaps several times). You will notice different aspects of the reading each time you look at it. New passages will stand out to you and ideas that didn't seem clear will come into focus. Even if the words on a page don't change, your reading of them does as your ideas evolve. Good writers often reread the material they're working with even after they've finished a draft of their paper.

LOOKING AHEAD

Many of us are taught to approach our reading as if it were a mystery novel. We come to think that looking ahead will spoil the reading somehow, and that we should only read something beginning to end. But good critical readers skim the entire piece before reading it carefully in order to develop a sense of what the piece is about and to get a glimpse of the author's perspective.

Before you sit down to read and take notes on your reading, take some time to read the headnote (the introductory information that precedes the selection), which will give you some background on both the author and the piece itself. Look through the piece, and read passages that stand out to you. Also take note of words or phrases that seem especially significant, or that are repeated throughout the reading. Then, ask yourself what you already know about the topic and what assumptions you might bring to the reading. Consider the title and ask yourself what it might tell you about the reading. Some titles are primarily descriptive, and will tell you a great deal about the topic of the piece. Others are more subtle. For example, consider the title of Emiene Shija Wright's "Saying Something in African." You may take note of the fact that African is not a language. Therefore, what might the author be trying to tell us? Also consider the phrase, "saying something." It can refer to the literal act of speaking. But it is also a term that people use when someone makes a significant point, as in, "Now you're really saying something!"

Once you have skimmed through the piece and have done some initial thinking about it, sit down in a comfortable setting with a pen or pencil and a notebook, and prepare to read closely and carefully.

IDENTIFYING THE THESIS

A thesis is the main point that the author wants to convey to the reader. Sometimes an author will state his or her thesis directly; in other cases, the thesis will be implied. You will see examples of both throughout this reader. You can think of the thesis as representing the author's purpose in writing the piece. Whether or not the author tells you straight out what he or she wants to convey, or implies his or her purpose through examples and illustrations, all good writers have something they want to say.

In many cases, the author will state a thesis within the first few paragraphs. A writer may set up the thesis in such a way that the reader is drawn into the piece and becomes curious about the author's topic or perspective. Sometimes an author will start with an anecdote, a question, or a brief scenario that relates to some aspect of their thesis. In other cases, the author will present an idea in order to argue against it. Below are the first five paragraphs of Stephanie Coontz's "Where Are the Good Old Days," an essay that traces the history of the American family. It appears in Part III of this book. As you read the paragraphs below, try to identify the author's thesis. Also consider how Coontz sets up her main point and guides the reader toward her thesis:

> The American family is under siege. To listen to the rhetoric of recent months, we have fallen down on the job. We're selfish; too preoccupied with our own gratification to raise our children properly. We are ungrateful; we want a hand-out, not a hand.
>
> If only we'd buckle down, stay on the straight and narrow, keep our feet on the ground, our shoulder to the wheel, our eye on the ball, our nose to the grindstone. Then everything would be all right, just as it was in the family-friendly '50s, when we could settle down in front of the television after an honest day's work and see our lives reflected in shows like Ozzie and Harriet and Father Knows Best.
>
> But American families have been under siege more often than not during the past 300 years. Moreover, they have always been diverse, both in structure and ethnicity. No family type has been able to protect its members from the roller-coaster rides of economic setbacks or social change. Changes that improve the lives and fortunes of one family type or individual often resulted in losses for another.
>
> A man employed in the auto industry, for example, would have been better off financially in the 1950s than now, but his retired parents would be better off today. If he had a strong taste for power, he might prefer Colonial times, when a man was the undisputed monarch of the household and any disobedience by wife, child, or servant was punishable by whipping. But woe betide that man if he wasn't born to property. In those days, men without estates could be told what to wear, where to live, and whom to associate with.
>
> His wife, on the other hand, might have been happier in the 1850s, when she might have afforded two or three servants. We can be pretty sure, though, that the black or Irish servants of that day would not have found the times so agreeable. And today's children, even those scarred by divorce, might well want to stay put rather than live in the late 19th century, when nearly half of them died before they reached their late teens.

In this case, Coontz states her thesis directly in the third paragraph. She questions the idea that the family is currently "in crisis" by arguing that there has never been such a thing as a "normal" or "ideal" family, and that families have always struggled, though with different issues at different times in history. Coontz sets up her thesis by playing on what she feels might be our assumptions. She mimics what she sees as commonly held perspectives on the contemporary family. Coontz goes on to provide evidence of these and we can assume that she will further develop this argument in her essay. A thesis often appears toward the beginning of an essay, but it doesn't have to.

Sometimes an author will imply the thesis rather than state it directly. In many of the narrative essays you will read in this text, the authors develop a point through recounting specific incidents or events. Instead of *telling* you what they want to say, they *show* you through illustrations and examples. Although an author may not tell you his or her purpose directly, he or she has an idea that he wants to get across. You might ask yourself why an author describes something in a specific way. What kinds of details does the author give? Does she present the subject in a positive or negative light? What language does she use? Authors' reasons for choosing whether to state their thesis directly or indirectly may depend on a number of factors: the audience they're writing for, the topic of their piece, the genre they prefer, as well as their own personal style of writing.

IDENTIFYING CLAIMS AND EVIDENCE

How the author develops the thesis determines how the piece is organized. In order to understand the organization and structure of the reading, you will need to identify the claims the author makes throughout the piece to support his or her thesis, and consider the kinds of evidence the author uses to back up those claims. Evidence can appear in various forms: Authors might use statistics or numbers to back up their points; they might relate an anecdote or story that serves as an example of their claim; or they might quote from another source or authority on the topic. In her essay "Less Is More: A Call for Shorter Work Hours," Barbara Brandt argues that Americans spend too much time at work compared to people in many industrialized countries where the standards of living are just as high, but where workers have more time to devote to community, leisure, family, and other pursuits.

In the following paragraph, which appears in the middle of Brandt's essay, try to identify both her claim and the evidence she uses to back it up:

> In our era, almost every other industrialized nation (except Japan) has fewer annual working hours and longer vacations than the United States. This includes all of Western Europe, where many nations enjoy thriving economies and standards of living equal to or higher than ours. Jeremy Brecher and Tim Costello, writing in *Z Magazine* (Oct. 1990), note that "European unions during the 1980s made a powerful and largely successful push to cut working hours. In 1987 German metalworkers struck and won a 37.5-hour week; many are now winning a 35-hour week. In 1990, hundreds of thousands of British workers have won a 37-hour week."

Brandt states her claim in the first sentence by telling us that we should look to other industrialized nations whose work hours are shorter. To back up her claim, she quotes from another source, one that provides statistical information confirming the fact that workers in other industrialized nations have successfully fought for a shorter work week.

IDENTIFYING PATTERNS AND TECHNIQUES

Depending on their purpose in writing a piece, authors apply various techniques in order to argue a point or convey a certain mood or feeling. Some authors rely a great deal on detailed description that allows the reader to "see" and "feel" the experiences they recount, while others might compare and contrast two people or events. Another technique is to demonstrate cause and effect by showing how one event influenced the outcome of another. Strong writing generally follows certain *patterns*, where an author uses identifiable techniques in order to support a thesis and develop an idea or argument. In other words, the piece follows a certain logic and there is a clear and thought-out reason for why the author has chosen to write that way.

One example of a technique that you may already be familiar with is "compare and contrast." We often use comparison and contrast to formulate arguments and make decisions in our daily lives. For example, you might try to persuade your parents that you should be allowed a certain privilege (staying out later, using the car) because your friends have that right, or you might compare one teacher to another in order to decide what class to take. Authors compare and contrast to demonstrate how both the differences *and* the similarities between two examples reveal something about the point they want to make. For instance, a writer might compare two cities with similar populations in order to show the impact of a specific regulation that one city has enacted but the other has not. If the author were to compare a large city with a small town or rural area, the comparison would not have the same effect.

In "Bikinis and Tieras: Quinceañeras" Vendela Vida uses the technique of comparing and contrasting throughout her essay. She uses it both to distinguish the contemporary quinceañera from that of the past, as well as to distinguish the quince from other teenage rites of passage. Toward the beginning of her essay, she compares the quinceañera to the debutante ball in order to call into question a common assumption that the two serve the same purpose:

> Although the *quince* is often considered akin to the debutante ball, there are some substantial differences between the two fêtes: Unlike the debutante ball, in which upper-middle- to upper-class girls are presented to society, *quinceañeras* can be of any class (tales of cars being sold and second mortgages taken out on homes to cover the cost of a *quince* are not uncommon), and while the debutante ball is usually held in honor of a group of girls, the *quince* party is typically thrown for one girl, who, as symbolized by her tiara, is queen for the day.

It is important to Vida's thesis that readers understand that, unlike the debutante ball, the quince is not only the province of the wealthier classes, but it is still very much connected to wealth and status, or at least to the perception of those attributes. Later in her essay, Vida uses compare and contrast to demonstrate the differences between current quinces and those of the past:

> "*Quinces* are different now," says Angela Lopez, a fifty-year old Miami woman who went through her *quince* in Havana, Cuba, before her family moved to America. "It used to be the *experience* of the day of your *quince* that was important," she says. "My parents kept me at home all the time before I turned

fifteen. My *quince* was a ritual that said I was allowed to start going out and be seen. I was allowed to start painting my lips and wear makeup in public."

"*Quince* parties today have turned into carnival theme shows with women in Marie Antoinette dresses pulling elaborate stunts," concurs Dulce Goldberg, a teacher at Miami High who went through her own *quince* in Cuba and is now regularly invited to her students' *quinces* in Miami. "I've been to *quinces* where the girls even make their entrance in a hot air balloon." She shakes her head. "Hot air balloons!"

Though it is the people she quotes who make the contrast, Vida's placement of the quotes together allows her to make her point.

Writers also control the tone and the language of their writing in order to demonstrate their point. Descriptive writing is a technique that allows the writer to show you what they want to say by giving you a visual image that sets a particular mood. The way an author describes an object or an incident can tell you a lot about how they feel about it. In "The Jacket," Gary Soto wants to convey the narrator's disappointment when, instead of giving him a tough leather jacket like "bikers wear," his mother presents him with a jacket several sizes too large and "the color of day-old guacamole." In the following passage, the author describes the first time he tries on the jacket:

> I put the jacket on. I zipped it up and down several times and rolled the cuffs up so they didn't cover my hands. I put my hands in the pockets and flapped the jacket like a bird's wings. I stood in front of the mirror, full face, then profile, and then looked over my shoulder as if someone had called me. I sat on the bed, stood against the bed, and combed my hair to see what I would look like doing something natural. I looked ugly. I threw it on my brother's bed and looked at it for a long time before I slipped it on and went out to the backyard, smiling a "thank you" to my mom as I passed her in the kitchen. With my hands in my pockets I kicked a ball against the fence, and then climbed it to sit looking into the alley. I hurled orange peels at the mouth of an open garbage can, and when the peels were gone I watched the white puffs of my breath thin to nothing.

How does the narrator feel about the jacket? Furthermore, how does the jacket make him feel about himself? If we picture the narrator with his hands in his pockets, looking down at the ground (how else would he see the ball that he kicks?) we can imagine a boy who feels far from "tough" in his new jacket.

Though you will be able to identify certain patterns, every writer is unique and uses different techniques in different ways. Furthermore, you are unlikely to find a piece of writing that relies solely on one technique. Ultimately, although one might be able to characterize a piece as primarily "descriptive" or "persuasive," most strong writing contains a number of identifiable patterns and techniques. It is important to look for and be able to identify these patterns and techniques since they are essential to understanding not only *what* the author's purpose is, but *how* the author chooses to convey his or her point. Most importantly, they provide examples and models for techniques you might apply in your own writing.

MAKING YOUR MARK

As a critical reader, it is important that you keep track of the observations and questions that come up as you read and reread. Though you may not be used to writing in your textbooks, making notes in pencil on the text itself is often the best way to keep track of your responses and keep your ideas flowing. Of course you cannot write in a library book or a book that you've borrowed from a friend or an instructor, but you can write in your own books.

Here is an example of how one reader marked the opening paragraphs by Stephanie Coontz that you saw earlier:

The American family is under siege. To listen to the rhetoric of recent months, we have fallen down on the job. We're selfish; too preoccupied with our own gratification to raise our children properly. We are ungrateful; we want a handout, not a hand.

when was this written?

does she believe this?

If only we'd buckle down, stay on the straight and narrow, keep our feet on the ground, our shoulder to the wheel, our eye on the ball, our nose to the grindstone. Then everything would be all right, just as it was in the family-friendly '50s, when we could settle down in front of the television after an honest day's work and see our lives reflected in shows like Ozzie and Harriet and Father Knows Best.

clichés

I think these are TV shows about families, but look them up. Maybe compare to Simpsons?

thesis?

But American families have been under siege more often than not during the past 300 years. Moreover, they have always been diverse, both in structure and ethnicity. No family type has been able to protect its members from the roller-coaster rides of economic setbacks or social change. Changes that improve the lives and fortunes of one family type or individual often resulted in losses for another.

what types is she talking about?

comparison and contrast

how does the author know this?

A man employed in the auto industry, for example, would have been better off financially in the 1950s than now, but his retired parents would be better off today. If he had a strong taste for power, he might prefer Colonial times, when a man was the undisputed monarch of the household and any disobedience by wife, child, or servant was punishable by whipping. But woe betide that man if he wasn't born to property. In those days, men without estates could be told what to wear, where to live, and whom to associate with.

when was this?

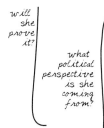

His wife, on the other hand, might have been happier in the 1850s, when she might have afforded two or three servants. We can be pretty sure, though, that the black or Irish servants of that day would not have found the times so agreeable. And today's children, even those scarred by divorce, might well want to stay put rather than live in the late 19th century, when nearly half of them died before they reached their late teens.

Notice that the reader circled words or phrases she didn't know and wrote a question mark in the margin. She also made notes to herself to look into references she wasn't sure about, so that she could ask the instructor about them in class. The reader identified the thesis and noticed that the author used comparison and contrast to begin to back up each point. She also questioned whether or not the evidence so far was substantial, which will help remind her to look for further evidence as she moves along. Finally, she started to think about the theme of families and the media, planting a seed for a possible writing topic.

Though you will ultimately develop your own style and strategies for making marks in your readings, here are some helpful guidelines

- Underline passages that stand out to you or ones in which the author makes key claims.
- Make notes in the margin when you have a reaction to a specific point or when a point relates to something else you've read.
- Identify unfamiliar words you need to look up and passages you do not fully understand.

READING NEW OR DIFFICULT MATERIAL

We all struggle when we read new and difficult material. Even college professors have a tough time understanding readings on a new subject or in a different field. A reading may be difficult not only because it contains difficult vocabulary or complicated sentence structures; a reading may be difficult to *you* because the subject itself is unfamiliar.

However, even if you don't fully understand what an author is trying to say, you can often pick out the writer's key claims. Once you identify these claims, a good strategy is to try and paraphrase these passages by putting them into your own words. After you gain a better understanding of certain key claims, you can try to fit these ideas into the larger point the author is trying to make.

USING THE QUESTIONS

The questions at the end of each selection will help you both comprehend and analyze the reading. The "Some of the Issues" questions help you to identify key issues in the reading and to consider how the ideas in the reading relate to one another. Often, these questions ask you to paraphrase or summarize a section of the reading in order to better understand the author's meaning. These questions may also ask you to analyze some of the author's ideas and think about why the author came to a certain conclusion or made a specific point. In other cases, the questions call for you to compare some aspect of the reading with a personal experience or with other readings.

The questions in the section called "The Way We Are Told" address issues of style and technique. These questions ask you to consider the author's specific writing choices. Essentially they call for you to think about why the author stated or organized something the way he or she did.

The section called "Some Subjects for Writing" offers ideas and topics for more extended writing. Your instructor may assign or ask you to choose one of these topics for a more formal essay, but you should also consider writing more informally in response to some of these prompts. If you keep a reading journal for your class, you should use some of the writing prompts to help develop your journal responses to each reading and to help you move from reading to writing.

PART **I**

GROWING UP

As we grow up, our awareness of the world around us gradually expands. The learning process begins at birth and never stops. We get to know our physical surroundings—a crib, perhaps, then a room, a house. We become aware of a parent and learn that if we cry, that parent will do something for us. We also learn that others want things from us; much of the time these demands are designed to stop us from doing what we want at that moment. Communication, we find, works in both directions.

What we learn depends, of course, on our environment, although we do not know that in our early lives. Then, we believe that our way of talking—our language—is the only one, and that the way things happen is the only way they can be done. For many Americans, these earliest experiences are confined to one culture. Sooner or later we learn, however, that we coexist with people whose experience or upbringing differs from ours. The discovery of that fact may come as a shock, particularly when we find at the same time that our culture is in some way not welcomed or accepted, that there is a barrier between "ours" and "theirs," a barrier that we cannot readily cross.

Each author in Part I confronts that barrier while growing up. Gary Soto's despised jacket, ugly, torn, and several sizes too large, becomes inflated in importance in the author's mind into a symbol of what keeps him from fitting in. In Harry Mark Petrakis's story "Barba Nikos," the narrator illustrates the conflict that often arises between first- and second-generation immigrants when the ways of the Old Country—and their parents' accented English—become a source of embarrassment. Maxine Hong Kingston, brought up in a Chinese environment, turns silent when she enters public school. In "Saying Something in African," Emiene Shija Wright struggles to negotiate her own sense of identity as the daughter of an African father and an African-American mother after she moves from Nigeria to Montgomery, Alabama following her parents' separation. In "Scents," Maria Laurino uses a humiliating incident from her high school gym class as a jumping-off point for examining how smells relate to culture, ethnicity, and class.

In the last essay, Vendela Vida investigates the world of the quinceañera, a coming of age ritual for many Latina girls, and explores its role and function in contemporary teenage culture. Finally, in his poem, "Incident," Countee Cullen speaks simply but tellingly of his first confrontation, at age eight, with prejudice.

The Jacket

Gary Soto

Gary Soto is a poet and prose writer influenced by his working-class Mexican-American roots. His writing style captures the particulars of everyday life and at the same time offers a glimpse of larger, more universal themes.

This selection takes a specific object, a jacket, and uses it to describe a feeling and mood at a particular time in the author's life. Most of us have shared the experience of having a piece of clothing take on a significance beyond its practical purpose.

Soto, born in 1952 in Fresno, California, has published numerous works of fiction and poetry for young adults and children, as well as several volumes of poetry for adults. He has chronicled his childhood in three volumes of memoirs: Living Up the Street *(1985),* Lesser Evils *(1988), and* Small Faces *(1986), from which this essay is taken. His most recent book, is a young adult novel,* Accidental Love *(2006). He lives in Berkeley, California.*

1   My clothes have failed me. I remember the green coat that I wore in fifth and sixth grade when you either danced like a champ or pressed yourself against a greasy wall, bitter as a penny toward the happy couples.

2   When I needed a new jacket and my mother asked what kind I wanted, I described something like bikers wear: black leather and silver studs, with enough belts to hold down a small town. We were in the kitchen, steam on the windows from her cooking. She listened so long while stirring dinner that I thought she understood for sure the kind I wanted. The next day when I got home from school, I discovered draped on my bedpost a jacket the color of day-old guacamole. I threw my books on the bed and approached the jacket slowly, as if it were a stranger whose hand I had to shake. I touched the vinyl sleeve, the collar, and peeked at the mustard-colored lining.

3   From the kitchen mother yelled that my jacket was in the closet. I closed the door to her voice and pulled at the rack of clothes in the closet, hoping the jacket on the bedpost wasn't for me but my mean brother. No luck. I gave up. From my bed, I stared at the jacket. I wanted to cry because it was so ugly and so big that I knew I'd have to wear it a long time. I was a small kid, thin as a young tree, and it would be years before I'd have a new one. I stared at the jacket, like an enemy, thinking bad things before I took off my old jacket, whose sleeves climbed halfway to my elbow.

4   I put the big jacket on. I zipped it up and down several times and rolled the cuffs up so they didn't cover my hands. I put my hands in the pockets and flapped the jacket like a bird's wings. I stood in front of the mirror, full face, then profile, and then looked over my shoulder as if someone had called me.

I sat on the bed, stood against the bed, and combed my hair to see what I would look like doing something natural. I looked ugly. I threw it on my brother's bed and looked at it for a long time before I slipped it on and went out to the backyard, smiling a "thank you" to my mom as I passed her in the kitchen. With my hands in my pockets I kicked a ball against the fence, and then climbed it to sit looking into the alley. I hurled orange peels at the mouth of an open garbage can, and when the peels were gone I watched the white puffs of my breath thin to nothing.

5   I jumped down, hands in my pockets, and in the backyard, on my knees, I teased my dog, Brownie, by swooping my arms while making bird calls. He jumped at me and missed. He jumped again and again, until a tooth sunk deep, ripping an L-shaped tear on my left sleeve. I pushed Brownie away to study the tear as I would a cut on my arm. There was no blood, only a few loose pieces of fuzz. Damn dog, I thought, and pushed him away hard when he tried to bite again. I got up from my knees and went to my bedroom to sit with my jacket on my lap, with the lights out.

6   That was the first afternoon with my new jacket. The next day I wore it to sixth grade and got a D on a math quiz. During the morning recess Frankie T., the playground terrorist, pushed me to the ground and told me to stay there until recess was over. My best friend, Steve Negrete, ate an apple while looking at me, and the girls turned away to whisper on the monkey bars. The teachers were no help: they looked my way and talked about how foolish I looked in my new jacket. I saw their heads bob with laughter, their hands half covering their mouths.

7   Even though it was cold, I took off the jacket during lunch and played kickball in a thin shirt, my arms feeling like braille from goose bumps. But when I returned to class I slipped the jacket on and shivered until I was warm. I sat on my hands, heating them up, while my teeth chattered like a cup of crooked dice. Finally warm, I slid out of the jacket but put it back on a few minutes later when the fire bell rang. We paraded out into the yard where we, the sixth graders, walked past all the other grades to stand against the back fence. Everybody saw me. Although they didn't say out loud, "Man, that's ugly," I heard the buzz-buzz of gossip and even laughter that I knew was meant for me.

8   And so I went, in my guacamole-colored jacket. So embarrassed, so hurt, I couldn't even do my homework. I received C's on quizzes and forgot the state capitals and the rivers of South America, our friendly neighbor. Even the girls who had been friendly blew away like loose flowers to follow the boys in neat jackets.

9   I wore that thing for three years until the sleeves grew short and my forearms stuck out like the necks of turtles. All during that time no love came to me—no little dark girl in a Sunday dress she wore on Monday. At lunchtime I stayed with the ugly boys who leaned against the chainlink fence and looked around with propellers of grass spinning in our mouths. We saw girls walk by alone, saw couples, hand in hand, their heads like bookends pressing air together. We saw them and spun our propellers so fast our faces were blurs.

10   I blame that jacket for those bad years. I blame my mother for her bad taste and her cheap ways. It was a sad time for the heart. With a friend I spent my sixth-grade year in a tree in the alley, waiting for something good to happen to me in that jacket, which had become the ugly brother who tagged along wherever I went. And it was about that time that I began to grow. My chest puffed up with muscle and, strangely, a few more ribs. Even my hands, those fleshy hammers, showed bravely through the cuffs, the fingers already hardening for the coming fights. But that L-shaped rip on the left sleeve got bigger; bits of stuffing coughed out from its wound after a hard day of play. I finally Scotch-taped it closed, but in rain or cold weather the tape peeled off like a scab and more stuffing fell out until that sleeve shriveled into a palsied arm. That winter the elbows began to crack and whole chunks of green began to fall off. I showed the cracks to my mother, who always seemed to be at the stove with steamed-up glasses, and she said that there were children in Mexico who would love that jacket. I told her that this was America and yelled that Debbie, my sister, didn't have a jacket like mine. I ran outside, ready to cry, and climbed the tree by the alley to think bad thoughts and watch my breath puff white and disappear.

11   But whole pieces still casually flew off my jacket when I played hard, read quietly, or took vicious spelling tests at school. When it became so spotted that my brother began to call me "camouflage," I flung it over the fence into the alley. Later, however, I swiped the jacket off the ground and went inside to drape it across my lap and mope.

12   I was called to dinner: steam silvered my mother's glasses as she said grace; my brother and sister with their heads bowed made ugly faces at their glasses of powdered milk. I gagged too, but eagerly ate big rips of buttered tortilla that held scooped-up beans. Finished, I went outside with my jacket across my arm. It was a cold sky. The faces of clouds were piled up, hurting. I climbed the fence, jumping down with a grunt. I started up the alley and soon slipped into my jacket, that green ugly brother who breathed over my shoulder that day and ever since.

EXERCISES

Some of the Issues

1. How does the narrator describe the jacket he wants? How does he describe the jacket his mother buys for him? What do these descriptions say about the narrator's self-image as an adolescent?
2. Why does the narrator call the jacket a "stranger whose hand I had to shake" in paragraph 2?
3. Why do you think the narrator's mother buys him such a large jacket?
4. How does the incident in paragraph 5 foreshadow events later in the story?
5. What problems or misfortunes does the narrator attribute to the jacket? To what extent do you think his perceptions differ from reality?

6. Although there is little or no direct discussion of class and ethnicity in the story, there is a sense that both are important. How is this apparent?

7. Throughout the essay, Soto refers to the jacket in different ways: "a stranger" (paragraph 2), "an enemy" (paragraph 3). Make a list of the various words and phrases he uses to describe the jacket. How do his perceptions of the jacket change? What does the jacket come to symbolize by the last line of the story?

*8. Read Malcolm X's "Hair" (page 232). Compare Malcolm's attitude toward his hair with Soto's view of the jacket. How do their approaches differ? How are they similar?

The Way We Are Told

9. Throughout the essay, Soto uses short, simple sentences in combination with longer, more complex ones. How or why are these short sentences effective?

10. Soto uses many similes and metaphors in the story. Find as many of them as you can and discuss which ones you feel are most effective. How do they work as a stylistic tool?

*11. Read Piri Thomas's "Alien Turf." Whereas Soto uses vivid images throughout the story, allowing the reader to visualize certain scenes or moments, Thomas uses dialogue that lets the reader "hear" the action. Discuss the difference between these two methods of description. Why might an author choose to emphasize one over the other?

Some Subjects for Writing

12. Soto uses the jacket to provide focus and continuity in his story. Write an essay or story in which, like Soto, you focus on one object and its significance in your life. What did this object mean to you? What metaphors and similes would you use to describe this object?

13. Some people feel that clothes make the person. How true is the statement, "You are what you wear"? What kinds of judgments do we make about individuals based on the way they dress? Write an essay in which you analyze the importance placed on clothing in our society. Depending on the focus of your essay, you may want to take into consideration some of the following issues: school uniforms; gang-related clothing and insignias; fashion magazines and the fashion industry; or the relationship between clothing and musical/artistic taste.

14. Keeping in mind Soto's use of visual imagery, create a comic book based on the story of the jacket. Which scenes would you illustrate? In what places would you use captions or bubbles for dialogue?

*Asterisks used in this context denote questions and essay topics that draw on more than one selection.

Barba Nikos

Harry Mark Petrakis

Harry Mark Petrakis was born in St. Louis in 1923 but has spent most of his life in and around Chicago. A novelist and short story writer, his books include Pericles on 31st Street *(1965),* A Dream of Kings *(1966), and* Stelmark: A Family Recollection *(1970), from which the following selection is an excerpt. Petrakis, himself of Greek descent, often sets the scene of his writing among Greek Americans and immigrants. The story Petrakis tells here describes the strains that can come between first- and second-generation immigrants.*

Located in the eastern Mediterranean, Greece has some eleven million inhabitants. It gained its independence in the nineteenth century after centuries of rule by the Turkish empire. It is a relatively poor country, many of whose people have sought their fortunes elsewhere, including the United States, which has a large population of Greek descent.

Ancient Greece, the Greece Barba Nikos talks about so proudly, has often been called "the cradle of Western civilization." Among its many small city-states, Athens stands out as the first representative democracy. Of the earliest philosophers, poets, historians, and scientists whose works have been preserved, most are Athenians. Achilles, whom Barba Nikos mentions, is a mythical warrior who plays a central role in Homer's Iliad, *the epic poem about the war between the Greek city-states and Troy. Alexander the Great, King of Macedonia, conquered the Middle East as far as India some 2,300 years ago. Marathon was not a footrace but a city in Greece where, in 490 B.C., the Athenians won a major battle against the invading Persians. According to legend, a Greek soldier ran from Marathon to Athens to carry the news of victory—before collapsing dead from the strain. He ran the same distance as the thousands who now run in marathons all over the world, except he ran it in full armor.*

1   There was one storekeeper I remember above all others in my youth. It was shortly before I became ill, spending a good portion of my time with a motley group of varied ethnic ancestry. We contended with one another to deride the customs of the old country. On our Saturday forays into neighborhoods beyond our own, to prove we were really Americans, we ate hot dogs and drank Cokes. If a boy didn't have ten cents for this repast he went hungry, for he dared not bring a sandwich from home made of the spiced meats our families ate.

2   One of our untamed games was to seek out the owner of a pushcart or a store, unmistakably an immigrant, and bedevil him with a chorus of insults

and jeers. To prove allegiance to the gang it was necessary to reserve our fiercest malevolence for a storekeeper or peddler belonging to our own ethnic background.

3   For that reason I led a raid on the small, shabby grocery of old Barba Nikos, a short, sinewy Greek who walked with a slight limp and sported a flaring, handlebar mustache.

4   We stood outside his store and dared him to come out. When he emerged to do battle, we plucked a few plums and peaches from the baskets on the sidewalk and retreated across the street to eat them while he watched. He waved a fist and hurled epithets at us in ornamental Greek.

5   Aware that my mettle was being tested, I raised my arm and threw my half-eaten plum at the old man. My aim was accurate and the plum struck him on the cheek. He shuddered and put his hand to the stain. He stared at me across the street, and although I could not see his eyes, I felt them sear my flesh. He turned and walked silently back into the store. The boys slapped my shoulders in admiration, but it was a hollow victory that rested like a stone in the pit of my stomach.

6   At twilight when we disbanded, I passed the grocery alone on my way home. There was a small light burning in the store and the shadow of the old man's body outlined against the glass. Goaded by remorse, I walked to the door and entered.

7   The old man moved from behind the narrow wooden counter and stared at me. I wanted to turn and flee, but by then it was too late. As he motioned for me to come closer, I braced myself for a curse or a blow.

8   "You were the one," he said, finally, in a harsh voice.

9   I nodded mutely.

10   "Why did you come back?"

11   I stood there unable to answer.

12   "What's your name?"

13   "Haralambos," I said, speaking to him in Greek.

14   He looked at me in shock. "You are Greek!" he cried. "A Greek boy attacking a Greek grocer!" He stood appalled at the immensity of my crime. "All right," he said coldly. "You are here because you wish to make amends." His great mustache bristled in concentration. "Four plums, two peaches," he said. "That makes a total of 78 cents. Call it 75. Do you have 75 cents, boy?"

15   I shook my head.

16   "Then you will work it off," he said. "Fifteen cents an hour into 75 cents makes"—he paused—"five hours of work. Can you come here Saturday morning?"

17   "Yes," I said.

18   "Yes, Barba Nikos," he said sternly. "Show respect."

19   "Yes, Barba Nikos," I said.

20   "Saturday morning at eight o'clock," he said. "Now go home and say thanks in your prayers that I did not loosen your impudent head with a solid smack on the ear." I needed no further urging and fled.

21   Saturday morning, still apprehensive, I returned to the store. I began by sweeping, raising clouds of dust in dark and hidden corners. I washed the windows, whipping the squeegee swiftly up and down the glass in a fever of fear that some member of the gang would see me. When I finished I hurried back inside.

22   For the balance of the morning I stacked cans, washed the counter, and dusted bottles of yellow wine. A few customers entered, and Barba Nikos served them. A little after twelve o'clock he locked the door so he could eat lunch. He cut himself a few slices of sausage, tore a large chunk from a loaf of crisp-crusted bread, and filled a small cup with a dozen black shiny olives floating in brine. He offered me the cup. I could not help myself and grimaced.

23   "You are a stupid boy," the old man said. "You are not really Greek, are you?"

24   "Yes, I am."

25   "You might be," he admitted grudgingly. "But you do not act Greek. Wrinkling your nose at these fine olives. Look around this store for a minute. What do you see?"

26   "Fruits and vegetables," I said. "Cheese and olives and things like that."

27   He stared at me with a massive scorn. "That's what I mean," he said. "You are a bonehead. You don't understand that a whole nation and a people are in this store."

28   I looked uneasily toward the storeroom in the rear, almost expecting someone to emerge.

29   "What about olives?" he cut the air with a sweep of his arm. "There are olives of many shapes and colors. Pointed black ones from Kalamata, oval ones from Amphissa, pickled green olives and sharp tangy yellow ones. Achilles carried black olives to Troy and after a day of savage battle leading his Myrmidons, he'd rest and eat cheese and ripe black olives such as these right here. You have heard of Achilles, boy, haven't you?"

30   "Yes," I said.

31   "Yes, Barba Nikos."

32   "Yes, Barba Nikos," I said.

33   He motioned at the row of jars filled with varied spices. "There is origanon there and basilikon and daphne and sesame and miantanos, all the marvelous flavorings that we have used in our food for thousands of years. The men of Marathon carried small packets of these spices into battle, and the scents reminded them of their homes, their families, and their children."

34   He rose and tugged his napkin free from around his throat. "Cheese, you said. Cheese! Come closer, boy, and I educate your abysmal ignorance." He motioned toward a wooden container on the counter. "That glistening white delight is feta, made from goat's milk, packed in wooden buckets to retain the flavor. Alexander the Great demanded it on his table with his casks of wine when he planned his campaigns."

35   He walked limping from the counter to the window where the piles of tomatoes, celery, and green peppers clustered. "I suppose all you see here are

some random vegetables?" He did not wait for me to answer. "You are dumb again. These are some of the ingredients that go to make up a Greek salad. Do you know what a Greek salad really is? A meal in itself, an experience, an emotional involvement. It is created deftly and with grace. First, you place large lettuce leaves in a big, deep bowl." He spread his fingers and moved them slowly, carefully, as if he were arranging the leaves. "The remainder of the lettuce is shredded and piled in a small mound," he said. "Then comes celery, cucumbers, tomatoes sliced lengthwise, green peppers, origanon, green olives, feta, avocado and anchovies. At the end you dress it with lemon, vinegar, and pure olive oil, glinting golden in the light."

36   He finished with a heartfelt sigh and for a moment closed his eyes. Then he opened one eye to mark me with a baleful intensity. "The story goes that Zeus himself created the recipe and assembled and mixed the ingredients on Mount Olympus one night when he had invited some of the other gods to dinner."

37   He turned his back on me and walked slowly again across the store, dragging one foot slightly behind him. I looked uneasily at the clock, which showed that it was a few minutes past one. He turned quickly and startled me. "And everything else in here," he said loudly. "White beans, lentils, garlic, crisp bread, kokoretsi, meat balls, mussels and clams." He paused and drew a deep, long breath. "And the wine," he went on, "wine from Samos, Santorini, and Crete, retsina and mavrodaphne, a taste almost as old as water . . . and then the fragrant melons, the pastries, yellow diples and golden loukoumades, the honey custard galatobouriko. Everything a part of our history, as much a part as the exquisite sculpture in marble, the bearded warriors, Pan and the oracles at Delphi, and the nymphs dancing in the shadowed groves under Homer's glittering moon." He paused, out of breath again, and coughed harshly. "Do you understand now, boy?"

38   He watched my face for some response and then grunted. We stood silent for a moment until he cocked his head and stared at the clock. "It is time for you to leave," he motioned brusquely toward the door. "We are square now. Keep it that way."

39   I decided the old man was crazy and reached behind the counter for my jacket and cap and started for the door. He called me back. From a box he drew out several soft, yellow figs that he placed in a piece of paper. "A bonus because you worked well," he said. "Take them. When you taste them, maybe you will understand what I have been talking about."

40   I took the figs and he unlocked the door and I hurried from the store. I looked back once and saw him standing in the doorway, watching me, the swirling tendrils of food curling like mist about his head.

41   I ate the figs late that night. I forgot about them until I was in bed, and then I rose and took the package from my jacket. I nibbled at one, then ate them all. They broke apart between my teeth with a tangy nectar, a thick sweetness running like honey across my tongue and into the pockets of my cheeks. In the morning when I woke, I could still taste and inhale their fragrance.

42   I never again entered Barba Nikos's store. My spell of illness, which began some months later, lasted two years. When I returned to the streets I had forgotten the old man and the grocery. Shortly afterwards my family moved from the neighborhood.

43   Some twelve years later, after the war, I drove through the old neighborhood and passed the grocery. I stopped the car and for a moment stood before the store. The windows were stained with dust and grime, the interior bare and desolate, a store in a decrepit group of stores marked for razing so new structures could be built.

44   I have been in many Greek groceries since then and have often bought the feta and Kalamata olives. I have eaten countless Greek salads and have indeed found them a meal for the gods. On the holidays in our house, my wife and sons and I sit down to a dinner of steaming, buttered pilaf like my mother used to make and lemon-egg avgolemono and roast lamb richly seasoned with cloves of garlic. I drink the red and yellow wines, and for dessert I have come to relish the delicate pastries coated with honey and powdered sugar. Old Barba Nikos would have been pleased.

45   But I have never been able to recapture the halcyon flavor of those figs he gave me on that day so long ago, although I have bought figs many times. I have found them pleasant to my tongue, but there is something missing. And to this day I am not sure whether it was the figs or the vision and passion of the old grocer that coated the fruit so sweetly I can still recall their savor and fragrance after almost thirty years.

EXERCISES

Some of the Issues

1. Why do the gang members attack immigrants of their own ethnic group?
2. What is the first sign that the narrator will change his mind about his deed?
3. What is the boy's first reaction to the olives? How does it set the scene for later reactions?
4. What does Barba Nikos mean when he says, "a whole nation and a people are in this store"?
5. In what way do the last two paragraphs sum up the theme of the essay?

The Way We Are Told

6. In the first four paragraphs the author uses a number of rather unusual words and phrases for simple events: *motley, repast, untamed, bedevil, malevolence, to do battle.* What effect is achieved by this choice?
7. Contrast the tone of the narrative frame at the beginning and end of the selection with the telling of the story through dialog in the middle. What is the effect?

8. Examine the various references to Barba Nikos throughout the selection. What impression do we have of him in the beginning? How does it change?
9. List the various references linking food and drink to mythology. What is their purpose?

Some Subjects for Writing

10. Write an essay about a traditional family celebration that was important to you as a child. Describe in detail the rituals, ceremonies, and foods associated with it. Was symbolism involved? What meaning did the ceremony have for you in early life? Has that meaning changed as you have grown older?
11. Interview several second-generation children of immigrants about their relationship to their family and their feelings about their identity. Using Petrakis as a starting point, write an essay in which you analyze and compare the similarities and differences between their experiences and beliefs.

Girlhood Among Ghosts

Maxine Hong Kingston

Maxine Hong Kingston's parents came to America from China in the 1930s. She was born in Stockton, California, in 1940 and graduated from the University of California at Berkeley.

The following selection comes from The Woman Warrior: Memories of a Girlhood Among Ghosts *(1976), for which Kingston received the National Book Critics Circle Award. The ghosts she refers to are of several kinds: the spirits and demons that Chinese peasants believed in, the ghosts of the dead, and, more significantly, the whole of non-Chinese America, peopled with strange creatures who seem very powerful but not quite human, and whose behavior is often inexplicable.*

Kingston continued her autobiography with China Men *(1981). Since then she has also written* Hawaii One Summer *(1981) and a novel,* Tripmaster Monkey *(1988). Her newest work is* The Fifth Book of Peace *(2003).*

1   Long ago in China, knot-makers tied string into buttons and frogs, and rope into bell pulls. There was one knot so complicated that it blinded the knot-maker. Finally an emperor outlawed this cruel knot, and the nobles could not order it anymore. If I had lived in China, I would have been an outlaw knot-maker.

2   Maybe that's why my mother cut my tongue. She pushed my tongue up and sliced the frenum. Or maybe she snipped it with a pair of nail scissors, I don't remember her doing it, only her telling me about it, but all during childhood I felt sorry for the baby whose mother waited with scissors or knife in hand for it to cry—and then, when its mouth was wide open like a baby bird's, cut. The Chinese say "a ready tongue is an evil."

3   I used to curl up my tongue in front of the mirror and tauten my frenum into a white line, itself as thin as a razor blade. I saw no scars in my mouth. I thought perhaps I had had two frena, and she had cut one. I made other children open their mouths so I could compare theirs to mine. I saw perfect pink membranes stretching into precise edges that looked easy enough to cut. Sometimes I felt very proud that my mother committed such a powerful act upon me. At other times I was terrified—the first thing my mother did when she saw me was to cut my tongue.

4   "Why did you do that to me, Mother?"

5   "I told you."

6   "Tell me again."

7   "I cut it so that you would not be tongue-tied. Your tongue would be able to move in any language. You'll be able to speak languages that are completely different from one another. You'll be able to pronounce anything. Your frenum looked too tight to do those things, so I cut it."

8   "But isn't 'a ready tongue an evil'?"

9   "Things are different in this ghost country."

10   "Did it hurt me? Did I cry and bleed?"

11   "I don't remember. Probably."

12   She didn't cut the other children's. When I asked cousins and other Chinese children whether their mothers had cut their tongues loose, they said, "What?"

13   "Why didn't you cut my brothers' and sisters' tongues?"

14   "They didn't need it."

15   "Why not? Were theirs longer than mine?"

16   "Why don't you quit blabbering and get to work?"

17   If my mother was not lying she should have cut more, scraped away the rest of the frenum skin, because I have a terrible time talking. Or she should not have cut at all, tampering with my speech. When I went to kindergarten and had to speak English for the first time, I became silent. A dumbness—a shame—still cracks my voice in two, even when I want to say "hello" casually, or ask an easy question in front of the check-out counter, or ask directions of a bus driver. I stand frozen, or I hold up the line with the complete, grammatical sentence that comes squeaking out at impossible length. "What did you say?" says the cab driver, or "Speak up," so I have to perform again, only weaker the second time. A telephone call makes my throat bleed and takes up that day's courage. It spoils my day with self-disgust when I hear my broken voice come skittering out into the open. It makes people wince to hear it. I'm getting better, though. Recently I asked the postman for special-issue stamps; I've waited since childhood for postmen to give me some of their own accord. I am making progress, a little every day.

18   My silence was thickest—total—during the three years that I covered my school paintings with black paint. I painted layers of black over houses and flowers and suns, and when I drew on the blackboard, I put a layer of chalk on top. I was making a stage curtain, and it was the moment before the curtain parted or rose. The teachers called my parents to school, and I saw they had been saving my pictures, curling and cracking, all alike and black. The teachers pointed to the pictures and looked serious, talked seriously too, but my parents did not understand English. ("The parents and teachers of criminals were executed," said my father.) My parents took the pictures home. I spread them out (so black and full of possibilities) and pretended the curtains were swinging open, flying up, one after another, sunlight underneath, mighty operas.

19   During the first silent year I spoke to no one at school, did not ask before going to the lavatory, and flunked kindergarten. My sister also said nothing for three years, silent in the playground and silent at lunch. There were other quiet Chinese girls not of our family, but most of them got over it sooner than we did.

I enjoyed the silence. At first it did not occur to me I was supposed to talk or to pass kindergarten. I talked at home and to one or two of the Chinese kids in class. I made motions and even made some jokes. I drank out of a toy saucer when the water spilled out of the cup, and everybody laughed, pointing at me, so I did it some more. I didn't know that Americans don't drink out of saucers.

20   I liked the Negro students (Black Ghosts) best because they laughed the loudest and talked to me as if I were a daring talker too. One of the Negro girls had her mother coil braids over her ears Shanghai-style like mine; we were Shanghai twins except that she was covered with black like my paintings. Two Negro kids enrolled in Chinese school, and the teachers gave them Chinese names. Some Negro kids walked me to school and home, protecting me from the Japanese kids, who hit me and chased me and stuck gum in my ears. The Japanese kids were noisy and tough. They appeared one day in kindergarten, released from concentration camp, which was a tic-tac-toe mark, like barbed wire, on the map.

21   It was when I found out I had to talk that school became a misery, that the silence became a misery. I did not speak and felt bad each time that I did not speak. I read aloud in first grade, though, and heard the barest whisper with little squeaks come out of my throat. "Louder," said the teacher, who scared the voice away again. The other Chinese girls did not talk either, so I knew the silence had to do with being a Chinese girl.

22   Reading out loud was easier than speaking because we did not have to make up what to say, but I stopped often, and the teacher would think I'd gone quiet again. I could not understand "I." The Chinese "I" has seven strokes, intricacies. How could the American "I," assuredly wearing a hat like the Chinese, have only three strokes, the middle so straight? Was it out of politeness that this writer left off strokes the way a Chinese has to write her own name small and crooked? No, it was not politeness; "I" is a capital and "you" is lowercase. I stared at the middle line and waited so long for its black center to resolve into tight strokes and dots that I forgot to pronounce it. The other troublesome word was "here," no strong consonant to hang on to, and so flat, when "here" is two mountainous ideographs. The teacher, who had already told me every day how to read "I" and "here" put me in the low corner under the stairs again, where the noisy boys usually sat.

23   When my second grade class did a play, the whole class went to the auditorium except the Chinese girls. The teacher, lovely and Hawaiian, should have understood about us, but instead left us behind in the classroom. Our voices were too soft or nonexistent, and our parents never signed the permission slips anyway. They never signed anything unnecessary. We opened the door a crack and peeked out, but closed it again quickly. One of us (not me) won every spelling bee, though.

24   I remember telling the Hawaiian teacher, "We Chinese can't sing 'land where our fathers died.'" She argued with me about politics, while I meant because of curses. But how can I have that memory when I couldn't talk? My mother says that we, like the ghosts, have no memories.

25   After American school, we picked up our cigar boxes, in which we had arranged books, brushes, and an inkbox neatly, and went to Chinese school, from 5:00 to 7:30 P.M. There we chanted together, voices rising and falling, loud and soft, some boys shouting, everybody reading together, reciting together and not alone with one voice. When we had a memorization test, the teacher let each of us come to his desk and say the lesson to him privately, while the rest of the class practiced copying or tracing. Most of the teachers were men. The boys who were so well behaved in the American school played tricks on them and talked back to them. The girls were not mute. They screamed and yelled during recess, when there were no rules; they had fistfights. Nobody was afraid of children hurting themselves or of children hurting school property. The glass doors to the red and green balconies with the gold joy symbols were left wide open so that we could run out and climb the fire escapes. We played capture-the-flag in the auditorium, where Sun Yatsen and Chiang Kai-shek's pictures hung at the back of the stage, the Chinese flag on their left and the American flag on their right. We climbed the teak ceremonial chairs and made flying leaps off the stage. One flag headquarters was behind the glass door and the other on stage right. Our feet drummed on the hollow stage. During recess the teachers locked themselves up in their office with the shelves of books, copybooks, inks from China. They drank tea and warmed their hands at a stove. There was no play supervision. At recess we had the school to ourselves, and also we could roam as far as we could go—downtown, Chinatown stores, home—as long as we returned before the bell rang.

26   At exactly 7:30 the teacher again picked up the brass bell that sat on his desk and swung it over our heads, while we charged down the stairs, our cheering magnified in the stairwell. Nobody had to line up.

27   Not all of the children who were silent at American school found voice at Chinese school. One new teacher said each of us had to get up and recite in front of the class, who was to listen. My sister and I had memorized the lesson perfectly. We said it to each other at home, one chanting, one listening. The teacher called on my sister to recite first. It was the first time a teacher had called on the second-born to go first. My sister was scared. She glanced at me and looked away; I looked down at my desk. I hoped that she could do it because if she could, then I would have to. She opened her mouth and a voice came out that wasn't a whisper, but it wasn't a proper voice either. I hoped that she would not cry, fear breaking up her voice like twigs underfoot. She sounded as if she were trying to sing though weeping and strangling. She did not pause or stop to end the embarrassment. She kept going until she said the last word, and then she sat down. When it was my turn, the same voice came out, a crippled animal running on broken legs. You could hear splinters in my voice, bones rubbing jagged against one another. I was loud, though. I was glad I didn't whisper. There was one little girl who whispered.

EXERCISES

Some of the Issues

1. After reading the selection, explain why Kingston says in the first paragraph, "In China, I would have been an outlaw knot-maker." Why does she call herself an outlaw? And, considering the legend she tells, why would she have been a knot-maker?

2. "Maybe that's why my mother cut my tongue." That startling sentence introduces a remembered conversation with her mother. Is it possible that the tongue-cutting never took place? What evidence do you find either way?

3. Kingston is silent in some situations but not in others. When is she silent and when is she not?

4. How did the American and the Chinese schools differ in the way they were run? In the way they affected the children?

The Way We Are Told

5. Kingston uses several symbols: the knot, the tongue, the Chinese word for *I*. Explain their meaning and use.

6. What is the effect of the first sentence of paragraph 2? Were you startled by it?

7. Kingston departs from strict chronological order in telling her story. What is the effect?

Some Subjects for Writing

8. Kingston describes times when she was embarrassed or "tongue-tied." Describe a time when you were afraid to speak. Include descriptions of your feelings before, during, and after the incident.

9. Kingston suggests that, in Chinese-American culture, girls are brought up very differently from boys. In your own experience of the culture in which you were raised does gender make an important difference in upbringing? Give examples in your answer.

*10. In Maxine Hong Kingston's story and in Emiene Shija Wright's "Saying Something in African," questions of voice and language play major roles. In an essay, compare and contrast the experiences of the two central characters.

Saying Something in African

Emiene Shija Wright

Emiene Shija Wright was born in Nigeria to an African father and an African-American mother. Her mother had fled the United States partly to escape the disillusionment she felt with the failures of the civil rights movement. Wright spent the first half of her childhood in a small village in Nigeria and the second half in Montgomery, Alabama—two very different worlds. In this essay, she takes us along on a journey of reconciliation between her African identity and her African-American one, finding in the end that the two are inseparable.

In doing so she also shows that neither identity can be defined precisely: Describing someone as "African," for example, ignores the vast diversity and complexity of cultures, languages, and traditions that make up that continent. The title of Wright's essay reflects this: Her American classmates pester her to "Say something in African." In reality, there are an estimated 1,800 different languages spoken in Africa. Some, such as Swahili or Yoruba, are spoken by millions of people; others are spoken by several hundred or fewer. Tiv, the language Wright learned growing up, is spoken by about 6 million people, mostly in Nigeria and Cameroon.

This essay is reprinted from the anthology Waking Up American: Coming of Age Biculturally *(2005).*

1   Emiene: No plan succeeds without God.
2   Shija: Come, let us go.
3   I used to wonder why my parents gave me these names. To me, these were warrior names, names for people who would face trials and uncertainty. In this light, my name was almost prophetic—but the biggest struggle I faced growing up was becoming comfortable in my own self.
4   Jos, Nigeria, mid-1970s. An African American woman lies in a hospital bed, hoping she has made the right decision to have this child. She has not been home in almost a decade, and her marriage is on the rocks. From the window, she looks out over the courtyard, and sees a dog loping across it with a human placenta in his mouth. Right then, her water breaks.
5   I was born to an African American mother and a Nigerian father. My mother taught at a school for girls, and my father was a bureaucrat within the

police department. For the first half of my childhood, my home was part of a large compound in the village of Adikpo. Despite the kerosene generator, it was a fairly modern house with a sunken living room, piano, and our own bedrooms. My grandfather, Buono, his two wives and children, my uncle and his family, my parents, my brother and two sisters, and three servants all lived together in the compound. Each family had a separate dwelling that faced the common yard. My parents ran a restaurant with rooms for rent in one of the unoccupied buildings, and my aunt and her family were frequent visitors. My home was filled with people, and I was the baby of them all.

6   Every morning, Uncle Tion came by for our walk. He would be angry if my mother didn't have me dressed and ready to go. I would ride on his shoulders to the local bar, and we would tarry for hours gossiping with neighbors and friends. After enough "hot drinks," someone was sure to slip me a few sips and then I would be tipsy, too, which amused Tion no end. It was our secret, and one of the reasons he was my favorite uncle. In the afternoon, my siblings and I biked around the village. I refused to ride with my oldest sister, who in my opinion could ride only slightly better than I could, opting instead for my big brother's handle-bars. We made a lot of good-natured mischief, from stealing cigarettes to spying on local politicians staying overnight with their mistresses. When it rained, we would play in the downpour while the adults put out receptacles to catch the water. In good times, a party at our home could last several days.

7   My mother and I conversed in English, but I spoke with a British accent, the way most English-speakers around me did. She never learned to speak Tiv, my father's ethnic language, very well. I didn't mind. I spoke Tiv with my dad, and didn't like it when my mother tried to join in. "That's our language," I would say in my four-year-old lisp. It was a rare intimacy between me and my dad, and I guarded it jealously.

8   Even as a young child, I got on with my father poorly. His middle daughter, a robust, active child, was his favorite. She was a fast runner, and could kick a soccer ball like a boy. I, on the other hand, was more introverted and shy. She loved for him to swing her through the air by her arms, but whenever he tried this with me, I invariably ended up with a bump on the head. His mustache always seemed to scratch my face when he kissed me, and his hands were harder than my mother's when he spanked me. But I was hungry for his attention. So I spoke Tiv, and when he and my mother argued, as they did often, I broke things on purpose. I blamed him for the strife, since when he was away things were peaceful. He in turn said my mother must have had bad thoughts about him when I was in her belly, and stopped swinging me through the air.

9   My mother was industrious and generally liked in the community. Having a restaurant/inn on the premises was her idea, and it was profitable. She was given the name Hemba Don, Glorious One, by my grandfather Buono. Their relationship was more affectionate than he and my father's. Buono was a respected elder known for making powerful medicines. He and my mother were both

early risers, and he compared her favorably with the other women in the compound. "Look at this," he would say, "Hemba Don has dressed the children, made me breakfast, and been to the market already, and you people are still about yawning and scratching your bottoms-o. Ah-ah!"

10   Though good-looking, my father was not so well liked. His mother, Bueh, was a junior wife, younger, and under the authority of Buono's earlier, more established wives. She produced only two children, my father and my aunt, another blow to their status in the household. As a youngster, he had to bribe the other kids with kola nuts to play with him—but those days were long behind him. By the time he and my mother met, he was a sophisticated man of the world. He had been educated in British schools and was a very stylish dresser. He drove luxury cars, shunned palm wine for imported Italian, and listened mainly to classical music. My father loved going out to clubs and parties, despite being an awful dancer. His real talent lay in impressing women. On their first date, he surprised my mother with a dress and a pair of shoes that fit her perfectly, without having to ask her size. They married less than six months later. It was a case of opposites attracting. Unfortunately, it didn't work.

11   Politically, the two were as different as night and day. My mother was a fierce idealist. In the States, she had been active in the protest movement, and studied nonviolent resistance. But seeing police dogs attack Southern children and the murder of Malcolm X, she sheared off her straightened hair and booked a flight on the first thing smoking to West Africa. She landed with a bachelor's degree and a friend's address in her pocket. She was probably more in love with Africa than with my dad. My father, on the other hand, was a budding conservative. He was scornful of those who weren't educated, including members of his own family.

12   My father's carefully cultivated manners hid a nasty surprise: self hate. Though he would not explicitly admit it, he believed Europeans superior to Africans in almost every way. "Look at that," he would say of his half-brother Gbayo, a beautiful dark boy our age with whom we often played, "the black sheep amongst the white." Upon learning of her membership in the Urban League, he accused my mother of plotting to overthrow the U.S. government, despite the league's reputation for being more moderate than the NAACP.

13   Their fights were epic and stingingly personal. "I do not want my children knowing that their mother descended from slaves!" he raged when she taught us American history. "Why not?" she replied. "Your people did the selling." Every so often, women my father said were "crazy" would show up at our door, shouting at him, or they would send angry letters in the mail. Some women were Nigerian, some African American, and once there was even a schoolgirl. I was not allowed to read the letters, but I guessed at their contents, because my mother reacted to the letters the same way she did after a visit—she would shake her head and laugh quietly to herself, all day long. But she looked like she wanted to cry.

14   Montgomery, Alabama, mid-1980s. After nine years, my parents divorced, and my mother returned with us children to her home in Alabama. Her mother had recently died, and my mother was too drained to fight the child-support settlement—an astonishing $150 a month for four children. She had been outside Alabama's social and political network for fifteen years, so even though she had risen to the level of principal in Africa, finding teaching work was difficult.

15   Mom took a night job, and sold Avon products out of a small grocery store on the side. We kids sold penny candy at school and cups of frozen Kool-Aid in the neighborhood during summer. Our clothes, though clean and neat, were never the latest styles, and when the car stopped working, there was no money to have it fixed. We simply took the bus and budgeted within an inch of our lives. Despite hardship, we had a close-knit family, and went to museums, patronized the library, and performed in a local children's theater my mother started. We had a lot of good times together.

16   At first, I was not used to seeing so many white people, and I thought something was wrong with them. "Oh Mommy," I said, upon seeing a popular shampoo commercial in which a woman repeatedly tossed her head, "what happened to that lady's hair? It's so messy! She can't even braid it!"

17   I attended a Catholic school on a need-based scholarship. Although it was an excellent private school, oftentimes I found myself speaking an English superior to that of my instructors. The kids were another story altogether. There is no place in Alabama for a little black girl with a British accent. It was as though I had dropped from the sky.

18   "Say something in African!" At recess, I was regularly swarmed by dozens of kids, all with this same demand. It baffled me. To them, Africa was one big jungle, not a continent broken up by thousands of languages. They laughed when I used British terms—referring to a car trunk as "the boot" and to french fries as "chips"—and when I didn't understand slang. Though I knew their behavior was more curious than malicious, I became very shy and self-conscious, and tried hard to lose my accent so I wouldn't feel so different from everyone.

19   Eventually, even the reduced tuition became too much of a burden, and I had to switch to public school. Not to be surmounted, my mother made provisions for me to participate in the "M-and-M" program, so called because it provided buses to transport kids from all-black neighborhoods to magnet schools across town, in mostly white areas. Again I stood out because of my accent and almost Victorian manners. I was tipped for gifted programs, and I excelled almost effortlessly. For some reason, these novelties enraged my new classmates.

20   Monkey. Tarzan. African booty-scratcher. I was called these names every day for the next four years. Although the school was predominantly white, the African American students were the ones who persecuted me relentlessly. The dark-skinned kids were especially cruel, quickest to disparage my African ancestry. My pointing out that they were darker than me was the quickest route to a fight. I learned to ignore the gaps around me in line, to avoid groups of unsupervised kids

in the halls, and to stay in the bathroom until lunchtime was almost over. Generally my tormenters had to settle for sneaking pushes, handling my homework between pinched fingers, and pretending that I stank. They behaved as though being African were a disease they did not want to catch.

21   Even by the late 1980s, most of the students' concepts of Africa were based on old Tarzan movies and images of starving Ethiopian children. They had a deep-seated hostility toward anything African. "I'm not black, I'm brown," the kids would say. During Black History Month, when images of dancing Africans wearing fringe and playing drums were shown, they were palpably embarrassed. These pictures, which featured dancers in unusual and grotesque contortions, took the Africans out of a cultural context and seemed designed to engender feelings of shame in black kids. The taunting was a little more pointed those days. The images contradicted the reality before them of a high-achieving, well-spoken African. Cognitive dissonance showed on their faces: Either they had been lied to about Africa or I was putting on an elaborate front to hide my true uncivilized nature. The depth of their anger suggests they believed the latter.

22   Despite the bullying, I clung to the belief that it was they who had the problem, not me. "Hey girl, is you a African?" "Yes," I would reply to hoots of laughter. The constant tormenting drummed into me that I was different. I was African. A defiant pride became my shield. The more I was called an African in epithet, the more obligated I felt to excel and contradict the notions of what an African was supposed to be.

23   One day on the playground, everything spun out of control. It started no different from any other recess: I was the last one picked, and my team was angry to get stuck with me. I think I missed a ball. My teacher, who regularly turned a blind eye to the abuse, found me surrounded by a ring of kids yelling, shoving, and kicking me. I was crying but fighting back. She scolded all of us, but asked only me to stay after class. "Why are you always the center of attention, Emiene? Why is everyone always picking on you?"

24   I considered her question. Since transferring to the school, I had done my best to avoid trouble. I got straight As, or the rare B in math. I hardly spoke to anyone, and I had only one friend, who was not in any of my classes. My throat tightened with the effort of holding back tears. There could be only one explanation. "Because I'm African." She looked at me for a long time with an impassive expression. Tears started rolling down my face. "Well," she said, "you'll just have to try harder to get along."

25   At home, my mother tried to keep me connected to my heritage, but it was difficult for her, since she wasn't Nigerian herself. She taught me to cook Nigerian dishes and attempted to transmit cultural knowledge based on her own experiences, but something within me started to change. I began tuning her out. Going to Africa had been the greatest adventure of her life, and at times it seemed Africa was the only thing my mother wanted to talk about. She introduced my siblings and me to strangers as her "African children."

26   More than anything the kids at school said, my mother's behavior embarrassed me. It was bad enough that others slapped "African" on my forehead to avoid seeing me as a person. It felt as though my mother was doing the same thing, though with a positive spin. More than anything, I just wanted to be allowed to be, the way it seemed other people just were.

27   I lost fluency in Tiv, since I saw my father only during vacations and we spoke English exclusively by then. Strangely, my mother began using Tiv with me in front of others. Perhaps she wanted to keep me connected, but it felt so unnatural—we still never spoke it in private. I felt like she was showing off, trotting me out like an exotic dog or life-size souvenir. I quietly rebelled by acting as though I couldn't understand her, or using the most substandard English I could muster. I was American, too, African American like her, and I refused to "say something in African" so she could set me apart.

28   In spite of my distaste for my mother's nostalgia for Africa, by junior high I too began exploiting my connection. I was shy, so it helped to be known for something other than nerdy good grades. I was known as "the girl from Africa," and I was popular. I learned to spin my story into something exotic and cool, dropping details that implied our servants were the starched and ironed type, not the barefoot, dusty house-boys that we treated like family. I was a fraud, but I rationalized my behavior, thinking it was about time being African actually benefited me somehow. I looked forward to college, and the day I would meet "people like me," people to whom the label "African" would not be a blessing or a curse, but simply a part of who I was.

29   I met other Africans my age for the first time at college in Michigan. Though I had some male friends who were African, the majority of my friends were African American. Still, I attended meetings of the African Student Union. I wanted to belong so badly I did the thing I'd hated the most: I fetishized them, seeing the African students as a group I wanted to belong to, rather than as individuals.

30   Sometimes I even found myself speaking with an accent I didn't possess. It broke my heart to hear the affectionate *o* caressing the ends of sentences, which I had nearly forgotten since moving away from my extended family. I couldn't resist adding it myself, and repeating, however slightly, their melodic cadence in my own speech. That quickly stopped when a few students broke into a round of Yoruba with me, and wanted to know why I couldn't respond. When pressed for details, it felt like an apology to say that my parents were divorced and I had been raised by my African American mother. I didn't want pity, I wanted acceptance. But my lack of cultural reference points was embarrassing—I didn't know the musicians, politicians, or historical events that were the touchstones of their lives. What I did know was food and clothes.

31   I made *ifo* stew worth fighting over, seasoned Nigerian style—if it didn't make the bridge of my nose sweat at the first taste, it wasn't hot enough. I could tie a head wrap better than many native Nigerian girls at school, and several

girls remarked that I owned more Nigerian clothes than they did. I began to read up on Nigeria's history, and talked to my mom about what it had been like for her over there. I wanted to fill in the gaps between my experiences as an African and the actual culture, of which I did not possess a deep understanding. Eventually I ran for office in the ASU. I dismissed the tinge of resentment I felt from some of the women as general female animosity until I overheard a group of them talking about me. "She's not really Nigerian," one girl said. "She doesn't even speak any language." "She's just mixed," another added. She said the last word like I was something dirty.

32   I was mad enough to fight, and sick to my stomach. In that instant I felt totally negated. Africa was the stick I had been beaten with for years. I had suffered for being African, and yet continued to rep Nigeria to the fullest. After all these years, now I wasn't Nigerian enough? Hadn't I earned the right to claim it, by my tears?

33   It had never occurred to me that none of that would count to culturally immersed, ethnically identified Nigerians. To them, I was an outsider, an impostor, an American with an African name.

34   I examined my heart, and found I still felt Nigerian. My first concepts of family and my self-worth all came from that source: my grandfather's songs, the gold hoops I had worn since infancy, my aunt peeling mangoes and placing each slice carefully on my tongue. But the soundtrack to my life was indelibly American, full of my grandmother's classic blues albums and then, later, hip-hop. I began to realize that I could not base my identity on what people said I was or wasn't. Being called an African booty-scratcher wasn't what made me African, and a couple of girls questioning my legitimacy couldn't undo my identity.

35   I still say, if asked, that I am Nigerian. It is my birthplace, my lineage, and it's the answer people are looking for when they wonder about the origin of my name or my physical features. But I am also as American as sweet potato pie. My existence adds to the possibilities of what can be: Nigerian girls can have Southern values and radical politics, and African American women can be personally invested in the global fight against sexism, ethnocentrism, and class prejudice.

36   In fact, being at the juncture of these two cultures has given me a fuller stake in this war than, I believe, either one alone would have. I am ready to see us advance. Come, let us go. Perhaps that was the plan all along.

EXERCISES

Some of the Issues

1. Why does Wright describe her names as "warrior names" (paragraph 3)? How does she feel about her names? Are there other names that have significance in Wright's narrative?

2. How does Wright describe her childhood home in Africa? What was her relationship with her family like?
3. What status did Wright's father hold in his family and what were his values (paragraph 10)? How were they different from her mother's?
4. Why does Wright say that her mother was probably "more in love with Africa" than with her father (paragraph 11)? What drew Wright's mother to Africa in the first place?
5. Why did Wright's father believe Europeans to be superior to Africans? What do you think fueled that hatred?
6. What image did Wright's classmates in the United States have of Africa and of Wright's accent (paragraphs 17–24)? Why were they unable to make sense of where she came from? On what do you think their image of Africa, and their attitude toward Wright, was based?
7. Why does Wright's mother's behavior embarrass her (paragraph 26)?
8. How does Wright's attitude toward her heritage begin to change? What is her initial view of the Africans she meets in college and how does she respond to them (paragraphs 29–33)?
9. How does Wright come to describe herself at the end of her narrative (paragraph 34)? What is it that she wants to "advance" in the final paragraph?
10. Though Wright's essay is a personal narrative, she in no way separates her own story from historical events. What role do historical events play in the shaping of her and her parents' lives?

The Way We Are Told

11. Wright uses descriptive language to give the reader of an image of her life growing up in the Nigerian village of Adikpo. How effective are these images? What impact do they have on you as a reader?
12. How does Wright use quotations throughout the text? At what points does she quote others directly and why?
13. Wright uses narrative to make a point about language, identity, and culture. How would you summarize her point?

Some Subjects for Writing

14. Write a narrative about the meaning and history of your own name. Does your name have a meaning that is significant to you? What language is your name derived from? Were you named after someone and, if so, how was this person significant to your parents?
15. Interview an older member of your family (a parent, grandparent, aunt, or uncle), focusing on the ways in which historical events shaped their lives and decisions, either here in the United States or in another country.

It may be a grand historical event—such as a revolution or civil war—or a seemingly smaller one—such as the closing of a factory in their hometown or a labor strike. Before interviewing them, research some of the events or eras you know they lived through. Using the answers from the interview, write a narrative in which you demonstrate how this event shaped his or her life.

Scents

Maria Laurino

In this essay, Maria Laurino begins by describing a scene in her high school gym class, a site of almost universal adolescent humiliation and embarrassment, and ends in an upscale perfumery in Paris. In between she takes the reader on a journey that describes the scents that are the emotional markers of her growing up. From her early adolescent efforts to distance herself from her Italian heritage to her efforts as an adult to reconnect to what she has lost, the sensuality of her culture plays an ever-present role.

Laurino, a New York journalist who wrote for the Village Voice *for many years, grew up in Short Hills, the suburban New Jersey town she describes here, and attended college at Georgetown University in Washington, DC. This essay is the opening chapter of her memoir* Were You Always an Italian? Ancestors, and Other Icons of Italian America *(2000), a national bestseller. The title of the book comes from a question posed to her by former New York governor Mario Cuomo, as she was interviewing him on his own Italian roots. At the time, she says, her honest answer was no. The book is an attempt to explore her memories and impressions of growing up Italian American, and perhaps an attempt to answer that question for herself.*

1 I can still remember the day when my ethnicity no longer felt like the tag line of my narrative, reluctantly affixed to my American self, but instead signified an inescapable me. I was a teenager standing in line before gym class, and we began to strut in sync, bare legs and barely covered bodies, to the gymnasium. Our uniforms were the baby blue of surgeons' gowns and prison uniforms. I felt both sick (or I feigned physical illness) and trapped (excuses about stomachaches rarely worked) during those fifty forced minutes of exercise.

2 Gym class, humiliating gym class, had provoked earlier difficult episodes. Once, in junior high—that particular place and time in which sameness is the prize, and a seed of adolescent difference could sprout into a field of skunk cabbage—a blond girl who had already developed curves that had captured the attention of a league of boys mentioned with a bored nonchalance how she needed to shave her legs. The blond girl's legs were as smooth and silky as a newly varnished oak floor, and I couldn't imagine why she'd put a razor to her skin. The hair on my legs, however, looked like a bed of wilted grass dipped in black ink.

3 "I need to shave too," I naïvely replied. To share the truth—that my mother thought I was too young to have a woman's legs—would have been mortifying, but I also lacked the instinct to distract her with a line like "You know, Cybill

Shepherd couldn't hold a candle to your thighs," and quickly change the topic. The look of horror on that girl's face when she peered down at my calves is as clear to me today as it was back then in 1973. I'm sure she had never encountered the hirsute beauty of the Italian-American body.

4   The girl, too young to be tactful, revealed her thoughts in wide-eyed disbelief. At about the same time, I received a more discreet reaction to my appearance from a motherly neighbor who casually mentioned that I should bleach my dark arm hair blond. For much of my childhood I stood out in homogenized suburbia (hard as I tried to mask the Italian side of my hyphen); I grew up in a neighborhood where, in every other home, Mazola poured from clear plastic bottles, while we lifted heavy golden-colored tins of olive oil. To a child who wished to imitate others with the precision of a forger's brush, that was a clumsy, humiliating distinction. While such incidents embarrassed me, none was as difficult as this conversation before gym class:

5   "You were shopping at Saks the other day?" the popular girl next to me asked.

6   "Uh-huh," I meekly replied. (She had never spoken to me before; in retrospect the visit to Saks probably provided a necessary credential.)

7   "Yeah, I told my mother, 'That's the smelly Italian girl who stands in front of me in gym class'."

8   I was stunned. I didn't move quickly enough in class even to perspire. But instead of challenging her, I just stood there. Silently. As she continued to chatter, I yearned to shed my smell, my self, that very instant. Standing in the powerless world of childhood, a world in which the words and actions of peers cast the parts that we play for years, I intuitively understood that I was bound to the sweat of my ancestors, peasants from southern Italy. Even the name of the region, the Mezzogiorno, or "midday," invokes an oppressive afternoon heat that parches the skin and then showers it with drops of sweat.

9   Yet despite my deep self-consciousness, the part of me that recognized the significance of a school social hierarchy was flattered: this pretty, popular girl was talking to me. Sloe-eyed with chocolate brown hair, she was Jewish; I could never be like the Waspy girls, but I could see myself as a darker, rawer version of her. We were both slightly above average height, but she was thin, shaved her legs, plucked her eyebrows, and dyed unwanted lip hairs blond with a jar of Jolene. I, on the other hand, was chubby, and had the leg hairs of a grizzly, a light mustache, and a bristly black feather of an eyebrow that rested proudly at the bottom of my forehead.

10   Comprising our basic similarities, I saw the potential for my own reform. So I decided that if she continued to befriend me, I would ignore the nasty comment. In the following weeks, I tried to ingratiate myself into her world and she began to accept me. But always she'd tell classmates about the incident that sparked our first conversation. "I saw her shopping at Saks," she would say with a high-pitched giggle, "and I told my mother, 'That's the smelly Italian girl who stands in front of me in gym class'."

11   She never talked about the smelly girl, or that smelly girl who is Italian, but rather that "smelly Italian girl"—in other words, I was smelly *because* I was Italian. She also acted surprised to have seen me at Saks; with a popular girl's unfailing instinct for the social ladder, perhaps she found it amusing that an Italian girl, who should have been on the bottom rung, would shop in the town's fanciest store.

12   Soon sympathetic friends pulled me aside to say that I never smelled and she must have confused me with someone else. I burned with embarrassment, but politely nodded as they defended me. Looking back on those days, I must have believed them, since I did not begin to shower three times a day to escape my odors. Instead, I continued the same bath regimen (although I can't say precisely if it was every day or every other) and sprayed myself with a fragrance called Love's Fresh Lemon, marketed for teens with a popular Donovan song about wearing your love like heaven. Did I smell like hell and rotten lemons? Probably not. Rather than believing that I smelled, I accepted the definition of being smelly. That is, if someone thought I had a body odor, there must be something unpleasant about me that needed to be changed.

13   Gym class wasn't the only time I heard the words "Italian" and "smelly" placed together, like a pungent clove of garlic sweating in a pan of warm olive oil. A few months later, I was sitting in the cafeteria with my new gym pal and a friend of hers, sharing gossip and news between bites of our sandwiches. The other girl mentioned that her father was planning a trip to Italy, and my friend and I swayed in delight at the idea of traveling to Europe.

14   "Are you going with him?" we asked in an enthusiastic chorus.

15   "Are you kidding?" she replied with a girlish laugh. "And be around all those smelly Italians?"

16   Suellen Hoy, the author of a book on cleanliness, tells this anecdote: In 1957, when she was a teenager and had recently begun to shave, she was lounging at a pool with several other bare-legged friends. There they saw an older woman in a beautiful bathing suit reveal her hairy legs and armpits. Hoy was "shocked and repulsed" to see this woman's unsightly hair in public, and her girlfriends decided that the woman must be "foreign" because European women didn't shave. The incident, Hoy explains, first taught her about America's obsession with being clean. Not much has changed—she also cites a "Dear Abby" column from 1985 in which a reader advises that if "'Rapunzel Legs' [is] too lazy to shave, she should move to Europe." Another woman wrote in that Europeans who don't shave also "think sweat and other natural body odors are sexy. Pee-ooey!"

17   It may be a peculiarly American habit to associate leg hair with dirt. Ultimately, however, looking dark and unkempt because of unwanted body hair is very different from being called smelly. I wonder if I earned that label because I seemed more foreign than the rest of the girls in my class. Not that we were recent Italian immigrants; I am third-generation, the youngest of my grandparents' youngest-born. Yet around the same time as the gym incident, a

teacher who called out my name for attendance on the first day of class asked if I spoke English.

18   The label "smelly Italian" was acceptable to many teenagers in my high school for another reason: body odor suggests that you are ill-bred, a member of the lower class. For centuries, the sweet scents of the upper class and the earthy smells of the lower class differentiated both groups in body and spirit. More than the clothes one wears or the language one speaks, the stink that fills the air of an unwashed person, the dirt and sweat that turn underarms and loins into a triangular estuary of odor, a repository of the unwanted emissions of our bodies, separates the classes. The "basement odor of the masses," as Flaubert once wrote, serves as one of the clearest demarcations between rich and poor.

19   The issue of smell and class plagued George Orwell for many years. In *The Road to Wigan Pier*, his treatise for a socialist state, Orwell wrote with characteristic bluntness that there are "four frightful words which people nowadays are chary of uttering," that is, "the lower classes smell." Orwell reasoned that class equality could never be achieved if the bourgeoisie continued to consider the lower classes "inherently dirty," making olfactory distinctions between *us* and *them*. Such a judgment can be impenetrable, he claimed, because a physical feeling of dislike is far more difficult to transcend than an intellectual one.

20   Orwell may have paid particular attention to odors because as a child he had his own fears that he smelled bad. Describing his experiences as a scholarship student in an elite public school, Orwell wrote in his essay "Such, Such Were the Joys . . .": "A child's belief in its own shortcomings is not much influenced by facts. I believed, for example, that I 'smelt' but this was based simply on general probability. It was notorious that disagreeable people smelt, and therefore presumably I did so too."

21   Orwell thought that he was "disagreeable" because his family was poorer than those of the other boys at his school, who came from the highest quarters of English society. The writer, with his flawless understanding of England's class system, famously described his family's economic status as "lower-upper-middle class." But because class distinction is relative and children want more than anything to be like their peers, Orwell must have imagined that a lower-class boy smelled—and that he took on this trait.

22   I may have accepted my classmates' assumptions because my family's economic position could be described as deep in the basement of upper-middle-class life, or, more accurately, we lived a middle-middle class life—in the strict American sense of annual income. (Orwell came from an established English family whose fortunes had dwindled.) The notion that I was called smelly because I was Italian seemed as logical a matter of cause and effect as that I was chubby because I ate brownies at lunch. Growing up in Short Hills, New Jersey, a suburb that produced debutantes just as Detroit manufactured steel, I learned as a child that the shrill whistle sounding every hour at the station signaled more than an approaching train: the town's dividing line was drawn at the railroad, and we were on the wrong side of the tracks. While many of my friends lived in

sprawling ranch houses with stone patios and outdoor pools, our little split-level house in a new development had a modest lawn that blended into the same-sized property of our neighbors, who were mostly small businessmen, middle managers, and teachers. As my neighborhood pal would remind me, we lived in "the ghetto of Short Hills."

23   Perhaps any child who is poor among the rich learns to kowtow to the needs of the wealthy, and in doing so carries a deep sense of shame over her own inadequacies. The child intuits the sense of privilege that the rich share, and knows she'll be rewarded by indulging them, commenting on how lovely their house is, oohing and aahing at the wall of mirrors in the bathroom, enthusiastically accepting the gracious invitation to swim in their pool. Her role is to be a constant reminder, like a grandfather clock that chimes reassuringly, of just how much they have.

24   But people pride themselves on degrees of wealth, so I never forgot that the real "ghetto" was in a section of Millburn, the neighboring town where my father had grown up, that housed an enclave of Italian-Americans. Because Short Hills was part of Millburn Township, the poor kids and young gents went to school together (the public school was so good that there was not the usual channeling of the elite to private schools). In both junior high and high school, there were mainly middle-, upper-middle-, and upper-class teens. Latinos and African-Americans were still excluded back then, so the only people of color in my high school were the children of the housekeeper at the local Catholic church. That left the largest dark ethnic group: the lower-middle-class Italians from Millburn, and the only kids labeled with an ethnic slur.

25   In high school, the Italian-American boys were known as the "Ginzo Gang"; they were greasers with beat-up cars that first chugged, then soared, thanks to their work at the local gas station (Palumbo's), owned by the father of one of them. Olive-skinned and muscular, they were sexy in their crudeness; and their faint gasoline scent and oiled-down hair defined the image of Italian-Americans in our school. The young women who hung out with them had little separate identity other than as the girlfriends of the Ginzos.

26   The Ginzos were my rearview mirror, a reflection of the near past that I wished to move beyond. They were an acknowledgment of my heritage, a recognition that the small sum of money my mother had inherited from her parents, used as the down payment on our house in a neighborhood a mile away, allowed me to escape from their world. But who was I fooling? My grandfather, who started a small construction company, earned his money by digging the earth; sweat and dirt were part of me, an oath of fealty to my family's peasant past. Yet I preferred to bury the memories of his labor, which provided us with some material comforts but not enough to rid me of the label of the "smelly Italian girl."

27   In the interval between the accusation of being smelly and an unspoken admission of my guilt, a denial of my ethic self emerged. Unprepared to confront my fears, I responded like a criminal who'd do anything to get the charges

dropped. If the cause of being called smelly were my Italian roots, then I would pretend not to be Italian.

28   At first I rejected the smells of my southern European heritage. Gone were the tastes and aromas of my youth: the sweet scent of tomato sauce simmering on the stove, soothing as a cup of tea on a rainy night; the paper-thin slices of prosciutto, salty and smooth on the tongue; and my own madeleine, oil-laden frying peppers, light green in color with long, curvaceous bodies that effortlessly glide down the throat and conjure up memories of summer day trips to Asbury Park, where we ate ham, Swiss, and fried pepper sandwiches prepared by my mother. Instead, I began to savor the old flavors of eastern Europe, new to my tongue: pickled herring and cured fish, sour and smoky, and the brisket I was served when I ate holiday meals with my new friend from gym class.

29   Decades later, when I told my Jewish husband that in high school I tried to assimilate by imitating his culture, he laughed. But in the uninformed world of the adolescent, narrow assumptions get made about the scheme of things. At the time, I didn't understand that the Jewish girls who zealously booked plastic surgery appointments with Howard Diamond, the Manhattan doctor famous for creating identical pug noses in Short Hills and Great Neck, Long Island, were undergoing a similar identity struggle.

30   Stripped of familiar smells, next I wanted to eliminate the extra baggage of vowels, those instant markers of ethnicity.

31   "Mom, why did you name me Maria?" went my familiar dinner-table question.

32   "Hun, why did we choose Maria?" she'd say, deferring to my father. He had wanted to name me Denise, after a Belgian child who greeted his troop during World War II and remained etched in his memory.

33   "Mama's name was Maria," my mom would add, interrupting her own question and recognizing that she was the keeper of tradition, the holder of the deciding vote. "Your father's mother was Maria, and I loved the actress Maria Montez."

34   Her last explanation was the consolation prize, the frayed ticket to the American scene that she had won and wished to hand to me. Naming me after a beautiful, vapid actress (Spanish, no less) would have revealed an unseen side of my mother, one that had rebelled against the expectation of having to show respect. A momentary fantasy, a chimera. I'm certain that I was named after my mother's mother.

35   But I would adopt the Montez interpretation. That both my grandmothers were named Maria bore little relevance at the time; a grade B movie actress, however, at least sounded glamorous.

36   "Why didn't you change your last name to Laurin?" I continued in my teenage whine. During these end-of-the-day efforts to sanitize myself, washing off an *o* seemed a clean, decisive stroke.

37   Only years later did I begin the precarious work of trying to replace the layers of ethnicity I had stripped away in order to dissociate myself from the smelly Italians. The alien surroundings of college fostered a nostalgia for familiar tastes

and allowed me to appreciate the foods I had grown up with, although not everyone shared my enthusiasm. Once my freshman roommate approached me, her face a picture of compassion and concern, as I entered our tiny dorm room. How was my weak stomach? she asked. Momentarily befuddled, I soon realized that she had confused the pungent aroma of the provolone I had recently eaten with that of vomit, and believed that I had thrown up in our room.

38   By my early twenties, I learned more about the girl at the cafeteria table who talked about the smelly Italians. According to the local grapevine, her parents were getting divorced because her father had been making seasonal trips to Italy to visit his secret mistress and their two children. Now I realize that she probably was never invited on her father's frequent sojourns, and the thoughtless remark was the defense of an insecure child, rejected by a man too busy sniffing the earthy scents of Italians to spend much time with her.

39   Today I have a new fear about smell; I fear that I lack a defining odor. I feel removed from my own sense of smell and the images it could conjure. I feel a languorous appreciation for everyday scents, like my pots of dried lavender, whose wildflower fragrance has faded to a docile sachet, as its deep purple buds grew pale with streaks of beige, a graceful bow to domesticity and old age. I refuse to linger by the coffeepot and sniff my carefully chosen beans, or inhale their smoky end, first ground, then muddied and scorched by a hot rain; instead, I quickly dump the grounds and wash the pot in soapy water, just as I will rush to lather the summer heat off my body. No smell, no mess. Life is measured, careful, far removed from the chaos of dirt and its primitive pleasures, and the smelly label of my youth.

40   Clean, but without texture; scrubbed of the salty drops that tell our singular stories. I fear that after years of trying to rid myself of the perceived stench of my ethnic group and its musty basement-class status, I sanitized my own voice, washed it away.

41   Certain incidents in life—like being told during gym class that you smell—become emotional markers, and around these events a series of reactions are set in motion: giving up pizza for pickled herring can take years to undo. I have recently come to notice how much time I spend scenting my body, covering it with colognes, milks, and creams, giving it a pleasant but artificial character, or voice, you could say. At first I was unaware that I had become perfume-obsessed, as people can often be unaware of their obsessions. But now I think I can link its beginnings to a time and a place.

42   Initially, I didn't realize the connection between a fragrance fixation and a freelance writing career, but neither did I fully understand that a spray of cologne can provide a narrative for your body in case your own story lacks luster. My aromatic addiction began when I decided not to return (after a brief stint in government) to the newspaper I had worked at for nearly a decade, which was as familiar as family. I was nervous about the decision to freelance, because it not only took away an important piece of identity but would force me

to choose my subjects, instead of writing about what others expected of me. And perhaps even worse, telling people that you are a full-time freelancer sounds more like a euphemism for unemployment than an adult career choice. So I acted a bit like the child who leaves home for the first time: one part wants to go while the other kicks and drags his way down the stairs, clutching the newel post. The final decision to step out the door and not return to my old work home coincided with a surprise birthday gift from my husband, a five-day trip to Paris. A perfect distraction, except that I found myself spending a good part of the time thinking about a particular French cologne.

43   I would like to chalk it up to coincidence rather than to Freud that I had occasionally been wearing a French cologne with a light lemon scent and Roman emperor's name Eau d'Hadrien, which seemed like an elegant version of the Love's Fresh Lemon of my youth. But maybe the alchemy of a new affection for Europe and my old need to hide Italian smells with lemons conjured an odd sensory experience—reluctance, relief!—when I first sniffed this cologne.

44   I went to a small Left Bank perfumery filled with fluted glass bottles capped in gold and bought my scent, one of my tasks in Paris, because it was cheaper there than back home. The saleswoman handed me the bag and then made an irresistible gesture: she sprayed my body, from my neck to my thighs, with cologne. Her hands flowed gently yet confidently around me, and the idea of being covered in fragrance, not frugally dabbed behind the ears, was so enticing that I went back to the store every day for a purchase and another spray. I had discovered a scented balm to soothe a shaky ego.

45   "Is this a gift for someone?" she asked upon my return.

46   "No it's for me," I happily responded, waiting for the soft mist to drape me like a gossamer veil.

47   After that trip, I became even more attached to the fragrance, or perhaps the idea of this fragrance. In department stores, I allowed myself one indulgent purchase: hand cream, body lotion, perfumed body cream (my favorite—it's as if I'm covered in lemons and cream), soaps, other colognes to mix with my fragrance to create a new, layered smell—the possibilities seemed endless. I no longer just sprayed behind the ears but covered myself completely in the scent, letting the perfume conquer the blandness of a scrubbed self, an elixir to enliven a diffident voice.

48   I used to think that my guilt-free desire for an expensive French cologne meant that I was at least coming to terms with the embarrassing bourgeois side of myself, which capitalized on the chic of a European heritage rather than my real-life peasant roots. But now I realize that, like the young girl who wanted to deny her heritage, again I was ducking for cover. I never quite unlearned the lesson from gym class long ago, when the voices of my family and my past were silenced as I altered the scents surrounding me. It's easier to shower away a smell, to censor yourself with a scent, than to accept your body's signature, the rawness of odor and sweat.

49   The smelly Italian girl no longer exists, if she ever did. In addition to my fragrance, my body is practically hairless, waxed from lip to toe by a Gallic woman who says "Voilà" after finishing each leg and who reminisces about her country, sharing with me that she knows the colorist who knows the colorist who mixes the blond hair dye for Catherine Deneuve (her six strands of separation from true glamour). During the months between waxings, I let my leg hair grow long and I run my fingers through it, still mystified by the abundance of those dark strands that I wish to find beautiful, but that I ultimately decide to remove once again.

50   I have tried to escape the class boundaries of my youth, but sometimes, in that lonely space between me and the bathwater, I wonder what has become of my own smell, and what it would be like to uncover a voice that could tell the stories of my past.

EXERCISES

Some of the Issues

1. After you have finished reading the essay, look again at the first sentence. What does Laurino mean when she states: "Ethnicity no longer felt like the tag line of my narrative, reluctantly affixed to my American self, but instead signified an inescapable me"?
2. What does Laurino see as some of the physical and sensory markers of her Italian identity? Does she describe these markers in a positive or negative light?
3. What does unmanaged hair symbolize in American culture, according to Laurino? What do people associate it with and how are these associations symbolic of social and economic status?
4. Ultimately, how does Laurino describe herself in terms of class (paragraph 22)? What do you feel Laurino is trying to say about class, particularly as it relates to American culture?
5. Why does Laurino refer to the Ginzos as her "rearview mirror" (paragraph 26)? What is she trying to move beyond?
6. Why does Laurino's husband laugh when she tells him that she tried to assimilate by imitating Jewish culture (paragraph 29)?
7. What is Laurino's "new fear about smell" (paragraph 39)?
8. What voices does Laurino want to uncover (paragraph 50)? How were they silenced? In your answer, use examples from throughout the essay.

The Way We Are Told

9. To what does Laurino compare the blue of the gym uniforms (paragraph 1)? What does the comparison imply?

10. Are there sections of Laurino's narrative that you find humorous? Which sections are they and why are they funny? How might humor help her set the tone of her essay?

11. At what points does Laurino use dialogue in her narrative? Is this effective?

12. As with many narratives, Laurino does not state her thesis directly. She does, however, want to convey specific messages about class, ethnic heritage, and identity. Summarize two or three of the claims you feel she is making.

13. Reflect on the title. Does the word "scents" usually carry negative or positive connotations? Why doesn't Laurino use the word "smells" as a title?

*14. From what perspective is Laurino writing: that of a teenager, an adult, or both? Where do you see indications of either of these perspectives? Compare her point of view to that of Gary Soto in "The Jacket."

Some Subjects for Writing

15. Of all the senses, smell has been thought to be the one that evokes our most vivid memories. Write a narrative about an incident, person, or place brought back to you by a certain smell. It might be the aroma of a specific food, a fragrance a person you knew wore, or a smell from a natural setting. Try to apply some of the same techniques Laurino uses such as dialogue, metaphor and simile, and detailed description to make your narrative vivid.

*16. How and why do certain attributes become markers of economic class? Using specific examples from "Scents" as well as from other essays in the book (for example, Gary Soto's "The Jacket") write an essay in which you examine the relationship between class and specific material markers (clothing, looks, or odors) in your own current environment or in the environment in which you grew up.

*17. How does food help reinforce and develop a sense of cultural, ethnic, and class identity? Using Laurino's essay, Harry Mark Petrakis's "Barba Nikos," and your own experience as examples, write an essay in which you explore some aspect of the relationship between food and identity.

Bikinis and Tiaras: Quinceañeras

Vendela Vida

In Girls on the Verge, *the collection of essays from which this selection is taken, Vendela Vida, a young writer who currently makes her home in New York, travels around the country documenting firsthand the initiation rites and rituals of contemporary American girls. In this essay she travels to Miami to interview girls and their families about their quinceañera, an event that marks a Latina girl's fifteenth birthday and also her symbolic transition into womanhood. Vida describes how some of these celebrations have become so elaborate and expensive that many families cannot afford the actual celebration, and instead opt simply for a photographic record of an event that never happened.*

Vida has been published in, among others, the Chicago Sun-Times, Jane, *and* Vogue. *She attended Middlebury College in Vermont and received her Masters of Fine Arts in writing from Columbia University.*

1   With a Giotto blue ceiling sprinkled with gold stars, gargoyles (the only ones I've seen both indoors and with wholly intact ears), and two fountain-sized cages in which colorful birds chirp along to Vivaldi's "Four Seasons" and pick at artfully prepared plates of lettuce and fresh fruit, the lobby of the Biltmore Hotel in Miami, Florida, has clearly been designed to scream "luxury." Three times a day—ten, noon, and two o'clock—use of the space is rented out for $175 to brides and *quinceañeras* who want to have a room—or rather, an opulent backdrop—of their own.

2   It's one of my first days in Miami and I've come to the Biltmore to observe the noon photo session because that's when fifteen-year-old Monica is scheduled to pose for her *quinceañera (Keen-se-*an-*yeh-ra)* photographs. The *quinceañera*, or *quince (keen-*say) as it's commonly referred to in America, is the coming-of-age ritual for Latin American girls that transforms them from *niñas* to *señoritas* when they're fifteen years old—*quince años*. In fact, many girls simply refer to the ritual as "having their fifteens." The reason I'm down in Miami, a hotbed of *quince* activity, is to learn more about the current state of the ritual in America.

3   Although the *quince* is often considered akin to the debutante ball, there are some substantial differences between the two fêtes: Unlike the debutante ball, in which upper-middle- to upper-class girls are presented to society, *quinceañeras*

can be of any class (tales of cars being sold and second mortgages taken out on homes to cover the cost of a *quince* are not uncommon), and while the debutante ball is usually held in honor of a group of girls, the *quince* party is typically thrown for one girl, who, as symbolized by her tiara, is queen for the day.

4   In addition to the requisite tiara, for her photo session today Monica is sporting a cotton-candy pink dress. The dress has six layers of organza ruffles that drape out around her like a multi-tiered cake. A heavyset woman who's wearing blue jeans and red high heels, Monica's mother issues stage directions to both Monica, her sister, and the photographer. "Have her stand over there," she commands. "Would you mind moving over there?" the sister says to hotel guests sitting in couches that could conceivably edge their way into a photograph's border. "*Gracias. Muchas gracias.*"

5   The *quinceañera* holds a rose in her gloved right hand and leans against a piano she doesn't know how to play. Next, she stands beside a gargoyle, her non-rose-holding hand resting on its head as though it's a child, or a dog. Some photos are meant to showcase the back of her dress, with its elaborate stitching and beading, and for these, Monica glances back at the camera over the puff of her leg-of-mutton sleeve.

6   All this is merely preparation for an even more impressive backdrop. For about half an hour Monica's mother has been eyeing the window that a large party of hotel guests has been congregated in front of, lounging and drinking. When they finally disperse, Monica's mother wobbles over to the window and stands there territorially, the way someone might save a parking space. Monica takes her position in front of a curtain held back with a wide sash and looks wistfully out a window she's never looked out before. The window affords her, and more important, the camera, a view of the hotel's manicured grounds—complete with fountains—and beyond, the upscale neighborhood of Coral Gables.

7   Like mannequin dressers in a department store, Monica's mother and sister tend to her. Her mother pushes back her shoulders to fix her posture and secures one of Monica's curling-ironed ringlets behind the tiara. Backing away, so as not to miss the spectacle for a moment, she smiles exaggeratedly at her daughter, the way mothers smile at babies whose pictures are being taken, hoping that this will encourage them to smile back.

8   The photographer glances at the mother and she nods and then holds her hands together, as though in prayer. "Smile," the photographer says to Monica. "You're not always going to be fifteen."

9   From the way Monica is dressed and the way her mother and sister are acting, I'm sure that she is headed off for the biggest party of her fifteen-year life. So when the photo session is over, I ask Monica where the *quince* festivities will be held.

10   Wearing perfume that smells like hibiscus, she smiles an equally sweet smile and says, "I decided not to have a party. Instead, my mom and I agreed that for my fifteens I would have my pictures."

11   This is it, she is telling me, and this, I think, is bizarre.

12   After a few more days in Miami I learn that increasingly, many Cuban girls who turn fifteen forego the ritual of the *quince* altogether and instead, like Monica, opt for what is known as "having your pictures." This isn't because the *quince* parties are any less popular than they used to be, but rather the opposite, because *quince* parties have become so important and elaborate and costly and competitive, many lower- to middle-class families in Miami today opt to devote all their time and effort to the end result: the photos.

13   No one knows the precise origins of the *quince*—some say it dates back to the Aztecs and Mayans. Michele Salcedo, author of *Quinceañera!: The Essential Guide to Planning the Perfect Sweet Fifteen Celebration*, writes that the Duchess of Alba, in eighteenth-century Spain, is credited with starting the custom.

> The duchess would invite girls on the cusp of womanhood to the palace and dress them up as adults for the first time. Similarly, although a century later, the Empress Carlota of Mexico invited the daughters of the members of her court to be presented as young ladies eligible for marriage. In both cases, there would be a party, with a feast and the dancing of intricate figures, as was the custom of the time, a custom that is carried over to the *quinceañera* celebration today.

14   Whatever its origins, in most Latin American cultures when a girl celebrates her *quince* she has a church ceremony, followed by a reception at which she has a court of fourteen couples, one representing each year of her life. Once the *quinceañera* has made her entrance in her simple white gown and her father has crowned her head with a tiara, removed her flat shoes, and fitted her feet with high heels, and she has waltzed with him, then boys her age, and finally with her escort, her *chambelán de honor*, it is finally understood that she is now an adult. What being an adult in *quince* terms means is that as of the day of the ritual, the young woman is allowed to start wearing makeup, high heels, and more revealing clothing; shaving her legs; going to parties; and dating men.

15   But much of this simplicity and tradition is a thing of the past.

16   "*Quinces* are all different now," says Angela Lopez, a fifty-year old Miami woman who went through her *quince* in Havana, Cuba, before her family moved to America. "It used to be the *experience* of the day of your *quince* that was important," she says. "My parents kept me at home all the time before I turned fifteen. My *quince* was a ritual that said I was allowed to start going out and be seen. I was allowed to start painting my lips and wear makeup in public."

17   "*Quince* parties today have turned into carnival theme shows with women in Marie Antoinette dresses pulling elaborate stunts," concurs Dulce Goldberg, a teacher at Miami High who went through her own *quince* in Cuba and is now regularly invited to her students' *quinces* in Miami. "I've been to *quinces* where the girls even make their entrance in a hot air balloon." She shakes her head. "Hot air balloons!"

18   These days the presentations compete to be more inventive and expensive than the *quince* the guests attended only the week before. This is especially the

case in Miami, where most of the young *quinceañera's* families are from Cuba. Salecedo, author of *Quinceañera!*, told me that in her research of *quince* parties across the country she found that Cubans in Miami often went to much greater, more elaborate and costly lengths for *quinces* than other Latinas celebrating their *quinces* in, say, San Antonio or Chicago.

19   "A lot of Cuban mothers who wanted to have *quinces* when they were young never got the chance to [because of the political situation]," Salecedo told me. "When they left Cuba, they left with nothing. When they came to America, however, a lot of them became successful, and their daughter's *quince* has become an important way of showing their friends and family that they've made it. While Mexican Americans in Texas might celebrate a *quince* with a rented dress and a five-dollar-per-person barbecue plate, Cubans in Miami buy the dress and even middle-class families can spend $100,000 a pop on the parties."

20   In Miami today, it's not uncommon for the *quinceañera* to make a formidable entrance to her party that entails, yes, a hot air balloon, a Cinderella-like horse-drawn carriage, a spinning carousel on which she sits side-saddle on a horse, or a large seashell that whirls around electronically and from which the *quinceañera* emerges like Botticelli's Venus. In fact, in some of the photos I've seen, the *quinceañera* is almost as scantily dressed as the Renaissance beauty: Posing in a bikini, her legs shaved, her lips red, she smiles seductively, as if to advertise her new status as a *señorita*/Lolita.

21   Of course, the extravagance of *quinces* exists all around the country, and so do its critics—many of whom are church officials and educators. Although, unlike the bat mitzvah, the *quince* doesn't have a particular religious significance, many families choose to have a private mass for their daughters on the day of the party so they can thank God for bringing them into the world. But many in the Catholic community feel that this is not enough, that the dress often becomes more important than God, and that the ritual—not to mention the photographs of bikini-clad poses—can emphasize a girl's sexuality. Addressing these concerns, in the past ten years many archdioceses, such as the archdioceses of Phoenix, Arizona, Los Angeles, California, and San Antonio, Texas, have begun issuing guidelines. The guidelines vary, but they can include advising that girls take five classes of Bible study, Hispanic history, *quince* history, and modern morals, and that the girls go on a church-sponsored retreat with their parents before the event.

22   After Father Antonio Sotelo, a vicar for Hispanic affairs and a pastor at Immaculate Heart in Phoenix, Arizona, circulated his guidelines around the diocese, several churches, including Immaculate Heart, started sponsoring *quince* classes and retreats. When I call Father Sotelo to ask what he thinks of *quinceañeras* who opt not to include a mass in their *quince* celebration, he bluntly tells me, "That's not a *quince*, that's just a party. The mass shows their special relationship to the Lord, to the community, to their parents."

23   "Do you think people should have to have masses as part of their *quinces?*" I ask.

24   "Well, it's a free country," he says. Despite his words, there's disapproval in his voice. Then his tone changes as he adds, "But all the girls who come here to Immaculate Heart are really committed to the *quince* mass. We have them write letters saying why they want to be a *quinceañera* and some of the letters are so personal you can hardly read them. In the letters they thank the Lord for their families and, if they've been fighting with their families they talk about how they want to start getting along, they talk about mistakes they've made, how they want to renew their baptismal vows, about how they miss their grandparents who have died.

25   "The girls are all so *sincere* in what they say," Father Sotelo continues. As his enthusiasm and praise for these young women increases, so does the speed with which he speaks. "People say the wild years are twelve, thirteen, fourteen years old. I think the wild years are eighteen and up. Some of the young brides who come to me to get married are spoiled brats. At least with the *quinceañeras* they mean what they say. I'd rather do ten *quinces* than one wedding. I could do *quinces* all day long."

26   One person in the Catholic Church who makes it her crusade, as she calls it, to educate and assist parents with their preparation of the *quince* is Sister Angela Erevia. Sister Angela, who has written a book about *quinces* entitled *Quince Años: Celebrating a Tradition*, travels around the country leading workshops that encourage parents of all religions and nationalities to plan at least one coming-of-age celebration for their daughters *and* their sons. In fact, she calls the *quinceañera*, the *quince años*, because she suggests young men go through a ritual at age fifteen as well.

27   When I ask Sister Angela what she thinks about the amount of money families put into their children's *quinces*, she says, "There's not a right way or a wrong way to celebrate. I don't tell people how much to spend on their weddings, so I don't tell them how much to spend on their child's *quince años*. But," she adds, "it doesn't have to cost a lot. In Dallas I helped the diocese organize a *quince años* for seventy-five teenagers and it only cost twenty dollars per family."

28   "Five hundred years ago in pre-Christian times in Mexico, kids went through ordeals to test their maturity and if they were successful they were considered mature members of their community," Sister Angela says to me during a phone conversation. Her voice was patient yet firm and I can't help but envision her as a Hispanic Julie Andrews in a modern adaptation of *The Sound of Music*. "Today we don't have to put our kids through ordeals. There is already so much pressure in the environment, with alcohol, divorce, suicide, premarital sex, teenage pregnancy, and there's nothing that affirms teenagers' presence."

29   In her workshops Sister Angela encourages parents to use the *quince años* to help their children understand who they are and where they come from. "It's an opportunity to develop their identity," she says.

30   Esther Nodarse who, with her husband, Aurelio, runs a successful party planning service in Miami called Pretty Party, says that she's seen a change in the *quince* in the twenty-five years since she started her company. It used to be

that girls born in the U.S. thought the *quince* was "a tacky, Cuban tradition, and they wanted to be more American than Cuban and celebrate their sweet sixteen." But today, she says, many of the girls encourage their parents to have *quinces,* and therefore in Miami it's becoming more popular than ever before. She estimates that nowadays about 90 percent of Cuban girls have some sort of celebration.

31   I spent some time at Miami High, talking to girls about the *quince* to find out what it meant to them. Miami High is an inner-city high school with a primarily Latino student body. It's not famous for much except that *Porky's* was filmed there. No one really knows for sure if the peephole still exists in the boys' locker room; many of the students haven't seen *Porky's,* they just know that an American movie was filmed at their school.

32   "I'm having my fifteens next month," says one sophomore in a pink halter top and denim miniskirt that exposes cheerleading-toned thighs. All the other girls in the room—those who have yet to have their fifteens, and especially those who have had their fifteens—ooh and ahh as though this weren't something they all went through.

33   But while these young women believe that getting their driver's license, or graduating high school, or even turning sixteen will all be significant transition points in their future lives, they don't pretend that turning fifteen is in and of itself transformative, because it doesn't give them any new sought-after independence.

34   So if it's not a big day in that it grants them license to wear makeup, or shave their legs, or date boys—most Miami High students have been doing all of the above for years—then why do they make such a big deal about their fifteens? One reason is that they have inherited their mothers' love for *quinces.* (This is where the oohing and ahhing comes from.) Their mothers are the ones with the memories and the stories of their *quinces* or the regret at not having one, and they are the ones with the dreams of their daughters' celebrations, and their daughters are born into these dreams. As one young woman with manicured red nails tells me, "I wasn't even born yet and my mother was already saying 'I can't wait for her to have her fifteens.'"

35   Just as they don't pretend that it means anything more to them than that they're fifteen, these young women don't pretend they go through their *quince* for the sake of tradition. As one young Cuban girl wearing a tight T-shirt with a Betty Boop decal says, "Your parents want it to be as important to you as it is to them, but it's not. Like, we want it because of the party, and they want it because of tradition so their friends will be 'Oh, wow.' To us, it's just a party."

36   "Yeah," says another, "Having my fifteens wasn't a turning point. It was just a way to celebrate."

37   A well-groomed young woman who has charm bracelets from both her *quince* and her sweet sixteen, explains why she wanted to have a party, even though her parents offered her a car or a cruise instead, simply to avoid the hassle: "I like to party, and I like being the center of attraction."

38   The prospect of being the center of attraction is one of the most appealing aspects of the *quince* for these girls. For a day, they get to have their photographs taken by professionals who specialize in child models. For a day they get to pose in bikinis as though for a fashion spread in *Seventeen* magazine. For a day, they get to wear ball gowns and tiaras and hold roses and when the camera snaps they look like they have just been crowned Miss America.

39   Even those who are at first reluctant usually enjoy their night in the spotlight. "I didn't want to have a *quince,* because I'm a liberal kind of girl," says Juanita, a sixteen-year-old of Columbian descent who lives in New Jersey. "I always thought that the *quince* was a way for people to say, 'Look at how pretty my daughter is. Look how much money I have. Don't you want to marry my daughter?' When I was fourteen, my mother asked me if I wanted to have one, and I told her 'Look, we're living comfortable, why waste the money?' and I thought she would leave it at that."

40   But Juanita's mother, Yolanda, who had four hundred people to her own *quince* in Columbia, did not leave it at that. For her daughter's sixteenth birthday, she threw her a combination surprise birthday party and *quince* because she wanted to keep up the tradition and also, she said, "It was more to have the pictures to send back home."

41   I went to the party, held at a banquet hall in Union City, New Jersey, complete with disco ball, a DJ who spun salsa, and figurines of Venus de Milo. There I saw an unsuspecting but happily surprised Juanita greeted with a chorus of "Surprise!" and colorful ribbons thrown in her direction before she was ushered off to the ladies' room to be changed by her mother into clothing fit for a *quinceañera*— a white gown, long white gloves, and slippers. (Yolanda took Juanita's measurements for the dress a few weeks earlier, under the guise of saying, "Juanita, you look like you've lost weight. Let me take your measurements so we can have a record.") When Juanita reentered the banquet hall, Yolanda stalled the start of the ceremony so she could load her camera with film (an oversight in all the excitement) and instructed the guests to make sure to give her their negatives so she could send the pictures to *her* mother, and then the ritual commenced.

42   Because Juanita's father left when she was three months old, his duties were fulfilled by a cousin who changed her slippers into size 8 white high heels (her mother tried them on Juanita, a heavy sleeper, in the middle of the night to make sure they fit) and crowned her curly-haired head with a tiara. All the while, Juanita held a rose in her gloved hand and sat upright in a wicker chair decorated with pink bows that had been placed in the middle of the banquet hall. "The chair is her temporary throne," her mother explained to me. "Tonight she is queen, but tomorrow she will be a regular person again."

43   After her shoes had been changed her mother made a toast: "I am toasting the birthday girl because I have been a mother and a father. Juanita, we are here to toast your future because you are starting a new future that's going to be harder." Then she danced the *quinceañera* waltz with her daughter—traditionally

reserved for the father—and there were tears in her eyes and tears in Juanita's eyes and tears in *my* eyes. At the end of the waltz, Juanita spun her mother around because even at that moment, she knew the ritual was more about her mother than her.

44   I spoke with Juanita the day after the party, and she said she now understood why the *quince* tradition was alive. While it made her want to celebrate her own daughter's sweet sixteen, however, she maintained that she won't incorporate elements of the *quince* into her daughter's party. "I think the *quince* is sort of a lost tradition among the second generation," she explained.

45   "For my fifteens I had my pictures," says a young Cuban woman named Rosa. When I ask her why she thinks young women are increasingly having their pictures taken in lieu of a party she says, "So we can have a memory. We could have a party but we can't, like, keep that to show our children. But if we have the pictures we can show our children, our grandchildren, and they can see, like, our favorite age."

46   Rosa is a nice girl but she hardly strikes me as having an easy time as a teenager. She complains that she's never been asked out by a boy and she suffers some standard teenage afflictions like being overweight, having a poor complexion, and wearing heavy glasses.

47   "Is fifteen *really* your favorite age?" I ask.

48   She gives me a winsome smile and answers, "You're only young once."

49   I am sitting in the courtyard of Miami High during a recess with Rosa and Melissa, a petite seventeen-year-old beauty with aqua eyes who also opted to just "have her pictures" for her fifteens. Unlike Rosa, Melissa has had an easy time making friends at Miami High, an easy time being a teenager. While Melissa's role model is Gloria Estefan, Rosa loves the Colorado Rockies, and she's wearing a jacket with their name across the back. The black jacket is much too hot for the Miami sun, but Rosa will do anything to show her loyalty to the team. Melissa's wearing a spaghetti-strapped sundress. What's striking is that both these girls—one thin, one fat, one popular, one with few friends—are prematurely nostalgic about the fifteenth year of their life that *quince* photographs capture.

50   "The day of your pictures is just the best," gushes Melissa. "It's the biggest rush and everything. Everyone's pampering you and everybody's helping you get dressed and the photographer's super nice and he's saying 'Look here' and 'Do this' and you feel like a model."

51   "Yeah," chimes in Rosa, "you feel like a model. For the one day you look beautiful—you're like, yeah, I know it, it's cool. You want to see some pictures?"

52   Before I respond Rosa pulls out a photo album from her backpack. The photo album says *"Mis Quince Años"* on the front and a gold-encircled peephole features her favorite picture. It's a little like looking through the peephole in *Porky's* because there is something prurient about the way Rosa has been made up. She's wearing a low-cut white dress and smiling seductively, leaning against a column that looks like it could be part of a costly mansion but isn't (it's just a

solitary column in Coral Gables that doesn't support anything; it is, however, a popular spot for many photo shoots of *quinceañeras*).

53   The first page of the album is designed for filling in the details of the party; it has spaces in which the names of all the fourteen couples who make up the *quinceañera's* court of honor are to be written. Since Rosa didn't have a party, this page is blank, as it is in the photo albums of all the other young Latinas who increasingly decide just to "have their pictures." In the back of her album are pictures of other girls' photo sessions. Students at Miami High exchange *quince* photos the way schoolgirls trade stickers. The other photos show the *quince-añeras* posing in front of fake backgrounds, blown-up photographs of waterfalls, white sand beaches, castles. Some even have magazine-like headings embossed on top: "Get attention"; "Looking good"; "Super body."

54   One of the photos in Rosa's album is of her sister with the president of a club she was trying to get into. "They took pictures and everything, but they didn't end up letting my sister in," Rosa says accusingly, as though they did something deceitful. "My father bought the pictures anyway."

55   There's something sad about this but not unexpected. This is, after all, a place and an environment where pictures mean more than the truth, where a day in a young woman's life is special because photographs are taken of her in various poses.

56   Of course, photographs from a young woman's fifteens aren't just collected in her album and wallet and those of her friends, they're sent to all the family's friends and relatives. Rosa sent some of the photographs to her grandmother and her parents' friends in Cuba. She says that she saw some of the photographs from girls' fifteens that were taken "over there" (Cuba) and that "the color was faded and the dress wasn't so pretty and the hotel where the pictures were taken was a cheap motel, a roach motel."

57   For Rosa and others who see the difference between *quince* pictures taken in Miami and their parents' homelands, that is really the issue—the difference in the quality of the photographs and the difference in their dresses. To these girls' parents, however, the difference is that between two worlds, and two social classes. Their parents send the photographs to all their friends in the countries they have left behind as though they were Hallmark cards. This is America—America!—these photographs say, and we have made it.

EXERCISES

Some of the Issues

1. How does Vida describe Monica and Monica's mother and sister in the opening section of the essay? What is your impression of them?
2. What did the author find "bizarre" about Monica's photo session (paragraph 11)? Did you also find it bizarre?

3. Why is "having your pictures" in lieu of an actual party becoming more common?
4. How are quinceañeras for Cuban Americans different now than they were in the past in Cuba?
5. In groups of three or four, describe and discuss other coming-of-age rituals that you have participated in or attended. Make a list of how are they similar to or different from the quinceañera.
6. Why are Cuban quinceañeras more elaborate than those of other Latino girls, according to Michele Salcedo (paragraph 19)?
7. Why is Father Antonio Sotelo critical of the elaborate quinceañeras and why is Sister Angela Erevia supportive of them? What is your response to their ideas and their reasoning?
8. Why is turning fifteen not a life-changing transformation for the girls Vida talks to at Miami High? Why do they still feel excited about it?
9. Whose words does Rosa echo in paragraph 48 when she says, "You're only young once"?
10. What do you feel is Vida's attitude toward the girls she interviews? Give specific examples to back up your point.
11. What is the significance of the quinceañera photographs for many Cuban families?

The Way We Are Told

12. How does Vida describe the lobby of the Biltmore Hotel? What impression do you have of it?
13. Why do you think Vida chooses to write in the first person at times? How does this affect what she says and how she says it?
14. How does Vida give the reader a sense of the personalities of the people she interviews? Give specific examples.

Some Subjects for Writing

15. Write a personal observation of a rite of passage or an event that marks a particular occasion. It might be a wedding, a funeral, a confirmation, a bar or bat mitzvah, or a quinceañera. Detail your impressions of the event. Through your description and tone, try to give the reader a feel for what it was like to be there.
16. Think of a rite of passage that is of particular interest to you. Using personal interviews with family members and acquaintances, as well as your own experience, investigate whether or not the rite has changed over time, or as the people who practice it move to different places. Write an essay in which you analyze the possible significance of those changes.

Incident

Countee Cullen

Countee Cullen (1903–46) gained recognition for his poetry while still in high school and published his first volume of poetry at the age of twenty-two. He attended New York University and Harvard and continued to publish poetry and fiction. "Incident" first appeared in Color *(1925).*

1   Once riding in old Baltimore
       Heart-filled head-filled with glee,
    I saw a Baltimorean
       Keep looking straight at me.

5   Now I was eight and very small,
       And he was no whit bigger,
    And so I smiled, but he poked out
       His tongue, and called me, "Nigger."

10   I saw the whole of Baltimore
       From May until December;
    Of all the things that happened there
       That's all that I remember.

EXERCISES

Some of the Issues

1. What are the author's feelings toward the Baltimorean at the beginning of the poem? Why are these feelings significant?
2. How old is the Baltimorean? How is age significant in the poem?
3. Why is the incident the only thing the author remembers?
4. Read the poem aloud several times. Does his insistent meter and rhyme remind you of poems that children may recite? How does the music of the poem contrast with its subject?

Some Subjects for Writing

5. Write about an incident in which someone called you a name. Describe the incident and your reaction.
6. There is a saying: "Sticks and stones will break my bones, but names will never hurt me." Is this statement true? Write an essay in which you examine whether or not words and names can be harmful.

PART **II**

EDUCATION

For most of us, school is one of our most formative experiences growing up. Our thoughts, opinions, and attitudes are shaped not only by what we learn in school, but also by our social interactions with our classmates and teachers. We carry with us fond memories of those teachers who fed our curiosity, inspiring us to learn more, and less fond memories of those who stifled it. There were probably some times when school felt like a broadening experience, and others when it felt simply like a test of both our intellectual and social skills. Sometimes it was simply a test of our patience.

One reason school is such a key reference point for most people is that it's an experience we all share. Education is one of the most equalizing forces in American society since, at least until a certain age, every child has access to schooling. But, as many of the writings in this chapter demonstrate, educational experiences can also prove to be a clear demonstration of our society's inequalities.

The writings in this chapter look at education from the perspective of both students and teachers. In "One Man's Kids" Daniel Meier writes about his choice to become a first grade teacher and describes his day in the classroom. Having chosen a profession that has generally been regarded as "female," Meier questions the degree to which we are confined by our definition of "traditional" male work.

Sherman Alexie, in his story "Indian Education," presents a series of vignettes demonstrating that much of what we learn in school, for better or worse, happens outside of the classroom. Maya Angelou, an African-American student in a segregated elementary school in Arkansas in the 1940s, recoils from the condescending attitude of the white speaker at her eighth-grade graduation.

Cheri Register writes of the insights she gained on an elementary school field trip to the Wilson & Co. packinghouse where her father, and the parents of many other students in her working-class town, spent their workdays. Mike Rose, with the help of a dedicated teacher, overcomes the limiting boundaries of working-class life and under-education.

In "Living in Two Worlds," Marcus Mabry, as a college junior, writes about the gap between his early and his present life. Returning home to his lower-class neighborhood in New Jersey from prestigious Stanford University in California, he finds himself with two identities that are hard to reconcile. In "No Kinda Sense," Lisa Delpit examines her conflicted response to her own daughter's use of African-American English and the role language plays in the development of children's identity and self-esteem.

By describing moments in the lives of friends and family that have touched upon her own life, Aurora Levins Morales, in "Class Poem," credits others with helping her define herself and demonstrates how much of our self-education comes from our encounters with others.

One Man's Kids

Daniel Meier

"One Man's Kids" originally appeared in the New York Times *"About Men" series in 1987, when Daniel Meier was teaching at a public elementary school in Boston. Meier begins this essay by describing part of his typical day as a first-grade teacher. He goes on to describe how, as a man who works with small children, his career choice sets him apart from other men he knows. Meier shows us that teaching can be a continual process of education for both teacher and student.*

Meier received a bachelor's degree in English from Wesleyan University and a master's degree in education from Harvard University. After this essay was written, Meier went on to earn a Ph.D. in education from the University of California, Berkeley. He is currently Associate Professor of Education at San Francisco State University. He is the author of three books, Learning in Small Moments: Life in an Urban Classroom *(1997),* Scribble Scrabble: Learning to Read and Write *(2000), and* The Young Child's Memory for Words *(2004).*

1   I teach first graders. I live in a world of skinned knees, double-knotted shoelaces, riddles that I've heard a dozen times, stale birthday cakes, hurt feelings, wandering stories and one lost shoe ("and if you don't find it my mother'll kill me"). My work is dominated by 6-year-olds.

2   It's 10:45, the middle of snack, and I'm helping Emily open her milk carton. She has already tried the other end without success, and now there's so much paint and ink on the carton from her fingers that I'm not sure she should drink it at all. But I open it. Then I turn to help Scott clean up some milk he has just spilled onto Rebecca's whale crossword puzzle.

3   While I wipe my milk- and paint-covered hands, Jenny wants to know if I've seen that funny book about penguins that I read in class. As I hunt for it in a messy pile of books, Jason wants to know if there is a new seating arrangement for lunch tables. I find the book, turn to answer Jason, then face Maya, who is fast approaching with a new knock-knock joke. After what seems like the 10th "Who's there?" I laugh and Maya is pleased.

4   Then Andrew wants to know how to spell "flukes" for his crossword. As I get to "u," I give a hand signal for Sarah to take away the snack. But just as Sarah is almost out the door, two children complain that "we haven't even had ours yet." I stop the snack mid-flight, complying with their request for graham crackers. I then return to Andrew, noticing that he has put "flu" for 9 Down, rather than 9 Across. It's now 10:50.

5   My work is not traditional male work. It's not a singular pursuit. There is not a large pile of paper to get through or one deal to transact. I don't have one area of expertise or knowledge. I don't have the singular power over language of a lawyer, the physical force of a construction worker, the command over fellow workers of a surgeon, the wheeling and dealing transactions of a businessman. My energy is not spent in pursuing, climbing, achieving, conquering or cornering some goal or object.

6   My energy is spent in encouraging, supporting, consoling and praising my children. In teaching, the inner rewards come from without. On any given day, quite apart from teaching reading and spelling, I bandage a cut, dry a tear, erase a frown, tape a torn doll and locate a long-lost boot. The day is really won through matters of the heart. As my students groan, laugh, shudder, cry, exult and wonder, I do too. I have to be soft around the edges.

7   A few years ago, when I was interviewing for an elementary-school teaching position, every principal told me with confidence that, as a male, I had an advantage over female applicants because of the lack of male teachers. But in the next breath, they asked with a hint of suspicion why I chose to work with young children. I told them that I wanted to observe and contribute to the intellectual growth of a maturing mind. What I really felt like saying, but didn't, was that I loved helping a child learn to write his name for the first time, finding someone a new friend, or sharing in the hilarity of reading about Winnie the Pooh getting so stuck in a hole that only his head and rear show.

8   I gave that answer to those principals, who were mostly male, because I thought they wanted a "male" response. This meant talking about intellectual matters. If I had taken a different course and talked about my interest in helping children in their emotional development, it would have been seen as closer to a "female" answer. I even altered my language, not once mentioning the word "love" to describe what I do indeed love about teaching. My answer worked; every principal nodded approvingly.

9   Some of the principals also asked what I saw myself doing later in my career. They wanted to know if I eventually wanted to go into educational administration. Becoming a dean of students or a principal has never been one of my goals, but they seemed to expect me, as a male, to want to climb higher on the career stepladder. So I mentioned that, at some point, I would be interested in working with teachers as a curriculum coordinator. Again, they nodded approvingly.

10   If those principals had been female instead of male, I wonder whether their questions, and my answers, would have been different. My guess is that they would have been.

11   At other times, when I'm at a party or a dinner and tell someone that I teach young children, I've found that men and women respond differently. Most men ask about the subjects I teach and the courses I took in my training. Then, unless they bring up an issue such as merit pay, the conversation stops.

Most women, on the other hand, begin the conversation on a more immediate and personal level. They say things like "those kids must love having a male teacher" or "that age is just wonderful, you must love it." Then, more often than not, they'll talk about their own kids or ask me specific questions about what I do. We're then off and talking shop.

12   Possibly, men would have more to say to me, and I to them, if my job had more of the trappings and benefits of more traditional male jobs. But my job has no bonuses or promotions. No complimentary box seats at the ball park. No cab fare home. No drinking buddies after work. No briefcase. No suit. (Ties get stuck in paint jars.) No power lunches. (I eat peanut butter and jelly, chips, milk and cookies with the kids.) No taking clients out for cocktails. The only place I take my kids is to the playground.

13   Although I could have pursued a career in law or business, as several of my friends did, I chose teaching instead. My job has benefits all its own. I'm able to bake cookies without getting them stuck together as they cool, buy cheap sewing materials, take out splinters, and search just the right trash cans for useful odds and ends. I'm sometimes called "Daddy" and even "Mommy" by my students, and if there's ever a lull in the conversation at a dinner party, I can always ask those assembled if they've heard the latest riddle about why the turkey crossed the road. (He thought he was a chicken.)

EXERCISES

Some of the Issues

1. Meier begins his essay by listing many specific things he does in his work as a first-grade teacher. What are they? In what way do they contribute to the children's lives?
2. How does Meier define "traditional male work" and how does he contrast it with his own work? Do you agree with his definition?
3. Meier tells us that he was not completely frank when he interviewed for his job. What reasons does he state for giving a "male" response to the principal's questions?
4. Meier claims that when he mentions his job to acquaintances, men and women respond differently. How does he characterize the different responses?
5. Do you think Meier's students are lucky to have a teacher like him? Why or why not?
6. Advertising and the media often reinforce, or call into question, gender stereotypes. Find two print advertisements, one focusing on male and one on female stereotypes. Working in groups of three to five, compare and discuss your advertisements with other students.

The Way We Are Told

7. Many writers believe that one can present an idea more effectively through description than through direct statements. Meier begins and ends his essay by describing specific activities, showing rather than telling about his daily routine. What does he gain by starting with specific details?

8. Much of Meier's analysis depends on his use of comparison and contrast. What does he compare and how does this technique strengthen his argument?

Some Subjects for Writing

9. In paragraph 6, Meier shows us what he feels a teacher should do beyond "teaching reading and spelling." Write an essay in which you develop your own philosophy of a teacher's role beyond reading, writing, and arithmetic. In other words, what can teachers teach us beyond academics?

10. As Meier implies, the majority of primary school teachers are female, while the majority of principals are male. Work in small groups or brainstorm with the entire class to determine other jobs that are typically held by either men or women. Choose one of these jobs to write about, either justifying the present situation or arguing for change.

11. Meier demonstrates how gender can impact our career choices. Clearly there are ways in which culture, education, and gender influence our career decisions, although those influences may be subtle at times. Consider the career choice of a family member or friend and write an essay in which you analyze the choice in relation to the person's gender, cultural background, or educational experience.

Indian Education

Sherman Alexie

Sherman Alexie was born in Washington State in 1966 and grew up on the Wellpinit Indian reservation, about 50 miles from Spokane. Alexie's mother is a Spokane Indian; his father is from the Coeur D'Alene tribe. Alexie was born hydroencephalic (with water on the brain) and underwent surgery as a small child. He was not expected to survive, and when he did, his doctors predicted he would be mentally retarded. Despite this prediction he learned to read at age three and soon became an avid reader, reading novels on his own by age five.

Like the narrator of his story, Alexie attended an Indian school for the primary grades but made a conscious decision as a teenager to attend high school off the reservation, where he thought he would get a better education. He graduated from Washington State University and has written prolifically since then, publishing more than a dozen books including poetry, novels, and short stories. He is also the author of the movie script for Smoke Signals, *which was released in 1998 and won several awards. Alexie also reads his work on the poetry slam circuit, and won the World Heavyweight Poetry competition in 1998. This selection is taken from his collection of short stories,* The Lone Ranger and Tonto Fistfight in Heaven *(1993).*

The history of Indian schools in America is a long, varied and complicated one. Over the course of its history from 1778 through 1871, the United States government entered into over 370 treaties with the various Indian nations it displaced. These treaties included agreements that the United States government would provide various services to Native American communities, including education.

The Indian schools were originally conceived as a way to assimilate young children and make them accept the white man's belief and value systems. Communities had little control over school curriculum and treatment of students was often harsh. Native languages and dress were forbidden, and there was little or no acknowledgment or understanding of native traditions.

In more recent years, beginning in the early 20th century, there have been movements to make Indian schools more sensitive to Native American cultures and to use teaching methods and curricula adapted to the unique characteristics and needs of Native communities. Indian schools in America, however, still remain often underfunded and ignored.

FIRST GRADE

1   My hair was too short and my U.S. Government glasses were horn-rimmed, ugly, and all that first winter in school, the other Indian boys chased me from one corner of the playground to the other. They pushed me down, buried me in the snow until I couldn't breathe, thought I'd never breathe again.

2   They stole my glasses and threw them over my head, around my outstretched hands, just beyond my reach, until someone tripped me and sent me falling again, facedown in the snow.

3   I was always falling down; my Indian name was Junior Falls Down. Sometimes it was Bloody Nose or Steal-His-Lunch. Once, it was Cries-Like-a-White-Boy, even though none of us had seen a white boy cry.

4   Then it was a Friday morning recess and Frenchy SiJohn threw snowballs at me while the rest of the Indian boys tortured some other *top-yogh-yaught* kid, another weakling. But Frenchy was confident enough to torment me all by himself, and most days I would have let him.

5   But the little warrior in me roared to life that day and knocked Frenchy to the ground, held his head against the snow, and punched him so hard that my knuckles and the snow made symmetrical bruises on his face. He almost looked like he was wearing war paint.

6   But he wasn't the warrior. I was. And I chanted *It's a good day to die, it's a good day to die*, all the way down to the principal's office.

SECOND GRADE

7   Betty Towle, missionary teacher, redheaded and so ugly that no one ever had a puppy crush on her, made me stay in for recess fourteen days straight.

8   "Tell me you're sorry," she said.

9   "Sorry for what?" I asked.

10   "Everything," she said and made me stand straight for fifteen minutes, eagle-armed with books in each hand. One was a math book; the other was English. But all I learned was that gravity can be painful.

11   For Halloween I drew a picture of her riding a broom with a scrawny cat on her back. She said that her God would never forgive me for that.

12   Once, she gave the class a spelling test but set me aside and gave me a test designed for junior high students. When I spelled all the words right, she crumpled up the paper and made me eat it.

13   "You'll learn respect," she said.

14   She sent a letter home with me that told my parents to either cut my braids or keep me home from class. My parents came in the next day and dragged their braids across Betty Towle's desk.

15   "Indians, indians, indians." She said it without capitalization. She called me "indian, indian, indian."

16   And I said, *Yes, I am. I am Indian. Indian, I am.*

THIRD GRADE

17   My traditional Native American art career began and ended with my very first portrait: *Stick Indian Taking a Piss in My Backyard.*

18   As I circulated the original print around the classroom, Mrs. Schluter intercepted and confiscated my art.

19   *Censorship,* I might cry now. *Freedom of expression,* I would write in editorials to the tribal newspaper.

20   In third grade, though, I stood alone in the corner, faced the wall, and waited for the punishment to end.

21   I'm still waiting.

FOURTH GRADE

22   "You should be a doctor when you grow up," Mr. Schluter told me, even though his wife, the third grade teacher, thought I was crazy beyond my years. My eyes always looked like I had just hit-and-run someone.

23   "Guilty," she said. "You always look guilty."

24   "Why should I be a doctor?" I asked Mr. Schluter.

25   "So you can come back and help the tribe. So you can heal people."

26   That was the year my father drank a gallon of vodka a day and the same year that my mother started two hundred different quilts but never finished any. They sat in separate, dark places in our HUD house and wept savagely.

27   I ran home after school, heard their Indian tears, and looked in the mirror. *Doctor Victor,* I called myself, invented an education, talked to my reflection. *Doctor Victor to the emergency room.*

FIFTH GRADE

28   I picked up a basketball for the first time and made my first shot. No. I missed my first shot, missed the basket completely, and the ball landed in the dirt and sawdust, sat there just like I had sat there only minutes before.

29   But it felt good, that ball in my hands, all those possibilities and angles. It was mathematics, geometry. It was beautiful.

30   At the same moment, my cousin Steven Ford sniffed rubber cement from a paper bag and leaned back on the merry-go-around. His ears rang, his mouth was dry, and everyone seemed so far away.

31   But it felt good, that buzz in his head, all the colors and noises. It was chemistry, biology. It was beautiful.

32   Oh, do you remember those sweet, almost innocent choices that the Indian boys were forced to make?

SIXTH GRADE

33   Randy, the new Indian kid from the white town of Springdale, got into a fight an hour after he first walked into the reservation school.

34   Stevie Flett called him out, called him a squawman, called him a pussy, and called him a punk.

35   Randy and Stevie, and the rest of the Indian boys, walked out into the playground.

36   "Throw the first punch," Stevie said as they squared off.

37   "No," Randy said.

38   "Throw the first punch," Stevie said again.

39   "No," Randy said again.

40   "Throw the first punch!" Stevie said for the third time, and Randy reared back and pitched a knuckle fastball that broke Stevie's nose.

41   We all stood there in silence, in awe.

42   That was Randy, my soon-to-be first and best friend, who taught me the most valuable lesson about living in the white world: *Always throw the first punch.*

SEVENTH GRADE

43   I leaned through the basement window of the HUD house and kissed the white girl who would later be raped by her foster-parent father, who was also white. They both lived on the reservation, though, and when the headlines and stories filled the papers later, not one word was made of their color.

44   *Just Indians being Indians,* someone must have said somewhere and they were wrong.

45   But on the day I leaned through the basement window of a HUD house and kissed the white girl, I felt the good-byes I was saying to my entire tribe. I held my lips tight against her lips, a dry, clumsy, and ultimately stupid kiss.

46   But I was saying good-bye to my tribe, to all the Indian girls and women I might have loved, to all the Indian men who might have called me cousin, even brother.

47   I kissed that white girl and when I opened my eyes, she was gone from the reservation, and when I opened my eyes, I was gone from the reservation, living in a farm town where a beautiful white girl asked my name.

48   "Junior Polatkin," I said, and she laughed.

49   After that, no one spoke to me for another five hundred years.

EIGHTH GRADE

50   At the farm town junior high, in the boys' bathroom, I could hear voices from the girls' bathroom, nervous whispers of anorexia and bulimia. I could hear the white girls' forced vomiting, a sound so familiar and natural to me after years of listening to my father's hangovers.

51   "Give me your lunch if you're just going to throw it up," I said to one of those girls once.

52   I sat back and watched them grow skinny from self-pity.

53   Back on the reservation, my mother stood in line to get us commodities. We carried them home, happy to have food, and opened the canned beef that even the dogs wouldn't eat.

54   But we ate it day after day and grew skinny from self-pity.

55   There is more than one way to starve.

NINTH GRADE

56   At the farm town high school dance, after a basketball game in an over-heated gym where I had scored twenty-seven points and pulled down thirteen rebounds, I passed out during a slow song.

57   As my white friends revived me and prepared to take me to the emergency room where doctors would later diagnose my diabetes, the Chicano teacher ran up to us.

58   "Hey," he said. "What's that boy been drinking? I know all about these Indian kids. They start drinking real young."

59   Sharing dark skin doesn't necessarily make two men brothers.

TENTH GRADE

60   I passed the written test easily and nearly flunked the driving, but still received my Washington State driver's license on the same day that Wally Jim killed himself by driving his car into a pine tree.

61   No traces of alcohol in his blood, good job, wife and two kids.

62   "Why'd he do it?" asked a white Washington State trooper.

63   All the Indians shrugged their shoulders, and looked down at the ground.

64   "Don't know," we all said, but when we look in the mirror, see the history of our tribe in our eyes, taste failure in the tap water, and shake with old tears, we understand completely.

65   Believe me, everything looks like a noose if you stare at it long enough.

ELEVENTH GRADE

66   Last night I missed two free throws which would have won the game against the best team in the state. The farm town high school I play for is nicknamed the "Indians," and I'm probably the only actual Indian ever to play for a team with such a mascot.

67   This morning I picked up the sport page and read the headline: INDIANS LOSE AGAIN.

68   Go ahead and tell me none of this is supposed to hurt me very much.

TWELFTH GRADE

69   I walk down the aisle, valedictorian of this farm town high school, and my cap doesn't fit because I've grown my hair longer than it's ever been. Later, I stand as the school board chairman recites my awards, accomplishments, and scholarships.

70   I try to remain stoic for the photographers as I look toward the future.

71   Back home on the reservation, my former classmates graduate: a few can't read, one or two are just given attendance diplomas, most look forward to the parties. The bright students are shaken, frightened, because they don't know what comes next.

72   They smile for the photographer as they look back toward tradition.

73   The tribal newspaper runs my photograph and the photograph of my former classmates side by side.

POSTSCRIPT: CLASS REUNION

74   Victor said, "Why should we organize a reservation high school reunion? My graduating class has a reunion every weekend at the Powwow Tavern."

EXERCISES

Some of the Issues

1. What is the significance of the narrator's glasses in the first-grade scenario?
2. What can you figure out about the narrator's elementary school? Who were his fellow classmates? His teachers?
3. What does the narrator mean when he tells us that his teacher said "indian" without capitalization (paragraph 15)? What is the significance of the narrator's response?
4. What does the narrator mean by the line "I'm still waiting" in paragraph 21?
5. What effect does kissing the white girl have on the narrator in seventh grade? Why does he say after that "no one spoke to me for another five hundred years"?
6. The narrator switches to a new school for junior high. What is different about the new school?
7. How do you interpret the line "There is more than one way to starve" (paragraph 55)?
8. What stereotypes do the teachers in the story hold about Native Americans?
9. Why does the narrator tell us that the teacher who assumed he was drunk in the eighth grade was Chicano? How did you respond to the narrator's assertion in paragraph 59?
10. What do you think the postscript means?

The Way We Are Told

11. Find examples of where Alexie uses humor. How would you characterize his sense of humor?
12. Why do you think Alexie chooses to write his story as a series of vignettes? How else might he have written it?
13. Consider the title. Is it meant to be ironic? Why or why not?
14. How does the author juxtapose optimistic scenes of possibility with bleaker ones? Give specific examples from the text. Why do you think he does this?
15. How would you characterize Alexie's tone? Is it appropriate to the story? Why or why not?

Some Subjects for Writing

16. Using Alexie's story as a model, retell the story of your own education from first through twelfth grade. Focus on specific incidents that taught you a lesson you could not have learned from a textbook.
17. With the help of your instructor, research the history of Native American schools in the United States. Write a paper in which you examine some aspect of the schools. You may choose to focus on such topics as changes in the schools over time; the level of student retention in reservation high schools, and the reasons why students stay or drop out; or innovative approaches to education in Native American schools.

Graduation

Maya Angelou

Maya Angelou was born Marguerite Johnson in St. Louis in 1928, and was raised by her grandmother in Stamps, Arkansas. She grew up in a rigidly segregated society. The Civil War had ended slavery but had not eliminated segregation. In fact, several decisions of the Supreme Court reaffirmed its legality. In the case of Plessy v. Ferguson *(1896) in particular, the Court gave its approval to segregation, declaring it to be constitutional as long as the affected facilities, such as public schools, were "separate but equal." Schools were separate after that in large parts of the country, but not equal, as Angelou's memory of the early 1940s demonstrates. In 1954 the Supreme Court reversed itself in* Brown v. Board of Education, *declaring that segregation was "inherently unequal" and, therefore, unconstitutional.*

Angelou—writer, teacher, actor, and civil rights activist—is the author of numerous books of poetry, which have been collected in The Complete Collected Poems *(1994).* I Know Why the Caged Bird Sings *(1970), from which this selection is taken, is the first in a series of autobiographical prose works that includes* Gather Together in My Name *(1975),* Singin' and Swingin' and Merry Like Christmas *(1976),* The Heart of a Woman *(1981), and* A Song Flung Up to Heaven *(2002).*

1   The children in Stamps trembled visibly with anticipation. Some adults were excited too, but to be certain the whole young population had come down with graduation epidemic. Large classes were graduating from both the grammar school and the high school. Even those who were years removed from their own day of glorious release were anxious to help with preparations as a kind of dry run. The junior students who were moving into the vacating classes' chairs were tradition-bound to show their talents for leadership and management. They strutted through the school and around the campus exerting pressure on the lower grades. Their authority was so new that occasionally if they pressed a little too hard it had to be overlooked. After all, next term was coming, and it never hurt a sixth grader to have a play sister in the eighth grade, or a tenth-year student to be able to call a twelfth grader Bubba. So all was endured in a spirit of shared understanding. But the graduating classes themselves were the nobility. Like travelers with exotic destinations on their minds, the graduates were remarkably forgetful. They came to school without their books, or tablets or even pencils. Volunteers fell over themselves to secure replacements for the missing equipment. When accepted, the willing workers might or might not be thanked, and it was of no importance to the pregraduation rites. Even teachers were respectful of the now quiet and aging seniors, and tended to speak to them,

if not as equals, as beings only slightly lower than themselves. After tests were returned and grades given, the student body, which acted like an extended family, knew who did well, who excelled, and what piteous ones had failed.

2   Unlike the white high school, Lafayette County Training School distinguished itself by having neither lawn, nor hedges, nor tennis court, nor climbing ivy. Its two buildings (main classrooms, the grade school and home economics) were set on a dirt hill with no fence to limit either its boundaries or those of bordering farms. There was a large expanse to the left of the school which was used alternately as a baseball diamond or a basketball court. Rusty hoops on the swaying poles represented the permanent recreational equipment, although bats and balls could be borrowed from the P.E. teacher if the borrower was qualified and if the diamond wasn't occupied.

3   Over this rocky area relieved by a few shady tall persimmon trees the graduating class walked. The girls often held hands and no longer bothered to speak to the lower students. There was a sadness about them, as if this old world was not their home and they were bound for higher ground. The boys, on the other hand, had become more friendly, more outgoing. A decided change from the closed attitude they projected while studying for finals. Now they seemed not ready to give up the old school, the familiar paths and classrooms. Only a small percentage would be continuing on to college—one of the South's A & M (agricultural and mechanical) schools, which trained Negro youths to be carpenters, farmers, handymen, masons, maids, cooks and baby nurses. Their future rode heavily on their shoulders, and blinded them to the collective joy that had pervaded the lives of the boys and girls in the grammar school graduating class.

4   Parents who could afford it had ordered new shoes and ready-made clothes for themselves from Sears and Roebuck or Montgomery Ward. They also engaged the best seamstresses to make the floating graduating dresses and to cut down secondhand pants which would be pressed to a military slickness for the important event.

5   Oh, it was important, all right. Whitefolks would attend the ceremony, and two or three would speak of God and home, and the Southern way of life, and Mrs. Parsons, the principal's wife, would play the graduation march while the lower-grade graduates paraded down the aisles and took their seats below the platform. The high school seniors would wait in empty classrooms to make their dramatic entrance.

6   In the Store I was the person of the moment. The birthday girl. The center. Bailey had graduated the year before, although to do so he had to forfeit all pleasures to make up for his time lost in Baton Rouge.

7   My class was wearing butter-yellow piqué dresses, and Momma launched out on mine. She smocked the yoke into tiny crisscrossing puckers, then shirred the rest of the bodice. Her dark fingers ducked in and out of the lemony cloth as she embroidered raised daisies around the hem. Before she considered herself finished she had added a crocheted cuff on the puff sleeves, and a pointy crocheted collar.

8   I was going to be lovely. A walking model of all the various styles of fine hand sewing and it didn't worry me that I was only twelve years old and merely graduating from the eighth grade. Besides, many teachers in Arkansas Negro schools had only that diploma and were licensed to impart wisdom.

9   The days had become longer and more noticeable. The faded beige of former times had been replaced with strong and sure colors. I began to see my classmates' clothes, their skin tones, and the dust that waved off pussy willows. Clouds that lazed across the sky were objects of great concern to me. Their shiftier shapes might have held a message that in my new happiness and with a little bit of time I'd soon decipher. During that period I looked at the arch of heaven so religiously my neck kept a steady ache. I had taken to smiling more often, and my jaws hurt from the unaccustomed activity. Between the two physical sore spots, I suppose I could have been uncomfortable, but that was not the case. As a member of the winning team (the graduating class of 1940) I had outdistanced unpleasant sensations by miles. I was headed for the freedom of open fields.

10   Youth and social approval allied themselves with me and we trammeled memories of slights and insults. The wind of our swift passage remodeled my features. Lost tears were pounded to mud and then to dust. Years of withdrawal were brushed aside and left behind, as hanging ropes of parasitic moss.

11   My work alone had awarded me a top place and I was going to be one of the first called in the graduating ceremonies. On the classroom blackboard, as well as on the bulletin board in the auditorium, there were blue stars and white stars and red stars. No absences, no tardinesses, and my academic work was among the best of the year. I could say the preamble to the Constitution even faster than Bailey. We timed ourselves often: "WethepeopleoftheUnitedStatesinordertoformamoreperfectunion . . ." I had memorized the Presidents of the United States from Washington to Roosevelt in chronological as well as alphabetical order.

12   My hair pleased me too. Gradually the black mass had lengthened and thickened, so that it kept at last to its braided pattern, and I didn't have to yank my scalp off when I tried to comb it.

13   Louise and I had rehearsed the exercises until we tired out ourselves. Henry Reed was class valedictorian. He was a small, very black boy with hooded eyes, a long, broad nose and an oddly shaped head. I had admired him for years because each term he and I vied for the best grades in our class. Most often he bested me, but instead of being disappointed I was pleased that we shared top places between us. Like many Southern Black children, he lived with his grandmother, who was as strict as Momma and as kind as she knew how to be. He was courteous, respectful and soft-spoken to elders, but on the playground he chose to play the roughest games. I admired him. Anyone, I reckoned, sufficiently afraid or sufficiently dull could be polite. But to be able to operate at a top level with both adults and children was admirable.

14   His valedictory speech was entitled "To Be or Not to Be." The rigid tenth-grade teacher had helped him write it. He'd been working on the dramatic stresses for months.

15   The weeks until graduation were filled with heady activities. A group of small children were to be presented in a play about buttercups and daisies and bunny rabbits. They could be heard throughout the building practicing their hops and their little songs that sounded like silver bells. The older girls (non-graduates, of course) were assigned the task of making refreshments for the night's festivities. A tangy scent of ginger, cinnamon, nutmeg and chocolate wafted around the home economics building as the budding cooks made samples for themselves and their teachers.

16   In every corner of the workshop, axes and saws split fresh timber as the woodshop boys made sets and stage scenery. Only the graduates were left out of the general bustle. We were free to sit in the library at the back of the building or look in quite detachedly, naturally, on the measures being taken for our event.

17   Even the minister preached on graduation the Sunday before. His subject was, "Let your light so shine that men will see your good works and praise your Father, Who is in Heaven." Although the sermon was purported to be addressed to us, he used the occasion to speak to backsliders, gamblers and general ne'er-do-wells. But since he had called our names at the beginning of the service we were mollified.

18   Among Negroes the tradition was to give presents to children going only from one grade to another. How much more important this was when the person was graduating at the top of the class. Uncle Willie and Momma had sent away for a Mickey Mouse watch like Bailey's. Louise gave me four embroidered handkerchiefs. (I gave her three crocheted doilies.) Mrs. Sneed, the minister's wife, made me an underskirt to wear for graduation, and nearly every customer gave me a nickel or maybe even a dime with the instruction "Keep on moving to higher ground," or some such encouragement.

19   Amazingly the great day finally dawned and I was out of bed before I knew it. I threw open the back door to see it more clearly, but Momma said, "Sister, come away from that door and put your robe on."

20   I hoped the memory of that morning would never leave me. Sunlight was itself still young, and the day had none of the insistence maturity would bring it in a few hours. In my robe and barefoot in the backyard, under cover of going to see about my new beans, I gave myself up to the gentle warmth and thanked God that no matter what evil I had done in my life He had allowed me to live to see this day. Somewhere in my fatalism I had expected to die, accidentally, and never have the chance to walk up the stairs in the auditorium and gracefully receive my hard-earned diploma. Out of God's merciful bosom I had won reprieve.

21   Bailey came out in his robe and gave me a box wrapped in Christmas paper. He said he had saved his money for months to pay for it. It felt like a box of

chocolates, but I knew Bailey wouldn't save money to buy candy when we had all we could want under our noses.

22   He was as proud of the gift as I. It was a soft-leather-bound copy of a collection of poems by Edgar Allan Poe, or, as Bailey and I called him, "Eap." I turned to "Annabel Lee" and we walked up and down the garden rows, the cool dirt between our toes, reciting the beautifully sad lines.

23   Momma made a Sunday breakfast although it was only Friday. After we finished the blessing, I opened my eyes to find the watch on my plate. It was a dream of a day. Everything went smoothly and to my credit. I didn't have to be reminded or scolded for anything. Near evening I was too jittery to attend to chores, so Bailey volunteered to do all before his bath.

24   Days before, we had made a sign for the Store, and as we turned out the lights Momma hung the cardboard over the doorknob. It read clearly: CLOSED, GRADUATION.

25   My dress fitted perfectly and everyone said that I looked like a sunbeam in it. On the hill, going toward the school, Bailey walked behind with Uncle Willie, who muttered, "Go on, Ju." We wanted him to walk ahead with us because it embarrassed him to have to walk so slowly. Bailey said he'd let the ladies walk together, and the men would bring up the rear. We all laughed, nicely.

26   Little children dashed by out of the dark like fireflies. Their crepe-paper dresses and butterfly wings were not made for running and we heard more than one rip, dryly, and the regretful "uh uh" that followed.

27   The school blazed without gaiety. The windows seemed cold and unfriendly from the lower hill. A sense of ill-fated timing crept over me, and if Momma hadn't reached for my hand I would have drifted back to Bailey and Uncle Willie, and possibly beyond. She made a few slow jokes about my feet getting cold, and tugged me along to the now-strange building.

28   Around the front steps, assurance came back. There were my fellow "greats," the graduating class. Hair brushed back, legs oiled, new dresses and pressed pleats, fresh pocket handkerchiefs and little handbags, all homesewn. Oh, we were up to snuff, all right. I joined my comrades and didn't even see my family go in to find seats in the crowded auditorium.

29   The school band struck up a march and all classes filed in as had been rehearsed. We stood in front of our seats, as assigned, and on a signal from the choir director, we sat. No sooner had this been accomplished than the band started to play the national anthem. We rose again and sang the song, after which we recited the pledge of allegiance. We remained standing for a brief minute before the choir director and the principal signaled to us, rather desperately I thought, to take our seats. The command was so unusual that our carefully rehearsed and smooth-running machine was thrown off. For a full minute we fumbled for our chairs and bumped into each other awkwardly. Habits change or solidify under pressure, so in our state of nervous tension we had been ready to follow our usual assembly pattern: the American national anthem,

then the pledge of allegiance, then the song every Black person I knew called the Negro National Anthem. All done in the same key, with the same passion and most often standing on the same foot.

30   Finding my seat at last, I was overcome with a presentiment of worse things to come. Something unrehearsed, unplanned, was going to happen, and we were going to be made to look bad. I distinctly remember being explicit in the choice of pronoun. It was "we," the graduating class, the unit, that concerned me then.

31   The principal welcomed "parents and friends" and asked the Baptist minister to lead us in prayer. His invocation was brief and punchy, and for a second I thought we were getting back on the high road to right action. When the principal came back to the dais, however, his voice had changed. Sounds always affected me profoundly and the principal's voice was one of my favorites. During assembly it melted and lowed weakly into the audience. It had not been in my plan to listen to him, but my curiosity was piqued and I straightened up to give him my attention.

32   He was talking about Booker T. Washington our "late great leader," who said we can be as close as the fingers on the hand, etc . . . Then he said a few vague things about friendship and the friendship of kindly people to those less fortunate than themselves. With that his voice nearly faded, thin, away. Like a river diminishing to a stream and then to a trickle. But he cleared his throat and said, "Our speaker tonight, who is also our friend, came from Texarkana to deliver the commencement address, but due to the irregularity of the train schedule, he's going to, as they say, 'speak and run.'" He said that we understood and wanted the man to know that we were most grateful for the time he was able to give us and then something about how we were willing always to adjust to another's program, and without more ado—"I give you Mr. Edward Donleavy."

33   Not one but two white men came through the door offstage. The shorter one walked to the speaker's platform, and the tall one moved over to the center seat and sat down. But that was our principal's seat, and already occupied. The dislodged gentleman bounced around for a long breath or two before the Baptist minister gave him his chair, then with more dignity than the situation deserved, the minister walked off the stage.

34   Donleavy looked at the audience once (on reflection, I'm sure that he wanted only to reassure himself that we were really there), adjusted his glasses and began to read from a sheaf of papers.

35   He was glad "to be here and to see the work going on just as it was in the other schools."

36   At the first "Amen" from the audience I willed the offender to immediate death by choking on the word. But Amens and Yes, sir's began to fall around the room like rain through a ragged umbrella.

37   He told us of the wonderful changes we children in Stamps had in store. The Central School (naturally the white school was Central) had already been

granted improvements that would be in use in the fall. A well-known artist was coming from Little Rock to teach art to them. They were going to have the newest microscopes and chemistry equipment for their laboratory. Mr. Donleavy didn't leave us long in the dark over who made these improvements available to Central High. Nor were we to be ignored in the general betterment scheme he had in mind.

38   He said that he had pointed out to people at a very high level that one of the first-line football tacklers at Arkansas Agricultural and Mechanical College had graduated from good old Lafayette County Training School. Here fewer Amens were heard. Those few that did break through lay dully in the air with the heaviness of habit.

39   He went on to praise us. He went on to say how he had bragged that "one of the best basketball players at Fisk sank his first ball right here at Lafayette County Training School."

40   The white kids were going to have a chance to become Galileos and Madame Curies and Edisons and Gauguins, and our boys (the girls weren't even in on it) would try to be Jesse Owenses and Joe Louises.

41   Owens and the Brown Bomber were great heroes in our world, but what school official in the white-goddom of Little Rock had the right to decide that those two men must be our only heroes? Who decided that for Henry Reed to become a scientist he had to work like George Washington Carver, as a bootblack, to buy a lousy microscope? Bailey was obviously always going to be too small to be an athlete, so which concrete angel glued to what county seat had decided that if my brother wanted to become a lawyer he had to first pay penance for his skin by picking cotton and hoeing corn and studying correspondence books at night for twenty years?

42   The man's dead words fell like bricks around the auditorium and too many settled in my belly. Constrained by hard-learned manners I couldn't look behind me, but to my left and right the proud graduating class of 1940 had dropped their heads. Every girl in my row had found something new to do with her handkerchief. Some folded the tiny squares into love knots, some into triangles, but most were wadding them, then pressing them flat on their yellow laps.

43   On the dais, the ancient tragedy was being replayed. Professor Parsons sat, a sculptor's reject, rigid. His large, heavy body seemed devoid of will or willingness, and his eyes said he was no longer with us. The other teachers examined the flag (which was draped stage right) or their notes, or the windows which opened on our now-famous playing diamond.

44   Graduation, the hush-hush magic time of frills and gifts and congratulations and diplomas, was finished for me before my name was called. The accomplishment was nothing. The meticulous maps, drawn in three colors of ink, learning and spelling decasyllabic words, memorizing the whole of *The Rape of Lucrece*—it was for nothing. Donleavy had exposed us.

45   We were maids and farmers, handymen and washerwomen, and anything higher that we aspired to was farcical and presumptuous.

46   Then I wished that Gabriel Prosser and Nat Turner had killed all white folks in their beds and that Abraham Lincoln had been assassinated before the signing of the Emancipation Proclamation, and that Harriet Tubman had been killed by that blow on her head and Christopher Columbus had drowned in the *Santa María.*

47   It was awful to be Negro and have no control over my life. It was brutal to be young and already trained to sit quietly and listen to charges brought against my color with no chance of defense. We should all be dead. I thought I should like to see us all dead, one on top of the other. A pyramid of flesh with the white folks on the bottom, as the broad base, then the Indians with their silly toma-hawks and teepees and wigwams and treaties, the Negroes with their mops and recipes and cotton sacks and spirituals sticking out of their mouths. The Dutch children should all stumble in their wooden shoes and break their necks. The French should choke to death on the Louisiana Purchase (1803) while silk-worms ate all the Chinese with their stupid pigtails. As a species, we were an abomination. All of us.

48   Donleavy was running for election, and assured our parents that if he won we could count on having the only colored paved playing field in that part of Arkansas. Also—he never looked up to acknowledge the grunts of acceptance— also, we were bound to get some new equipment for the home economics build-ing and the workshop.

49   He finished, and since there was no need to give any more than the most perfunctory thank-you's, he nodded to the men on the stage, and the tall white man who was never introduced joined him at the door. They left with the atti-tude that now they were off to something really important. (The graduation ceremonies at Lafayette County Training School had been a mere preliminary.)

50   The ugliness they left was palpable. An uninvited guest who wouldn't leave. The choir was summoned and sang a modern arrangement of "Onward, Christ-ian Soldiers," with new words pertaining to graduates seeking their place in the world. But it didn't work. Elouise, the daughter of the Baptist minister, recited "Invictus," and I could have cried at the impertinence of "I am the master of my fate, I am the captain of my soul."

51   My name had lost its ring of familiarity and I had to be nudged to go and receive my diploma. All my preparations had fled. I neither marched up to the stage like a conquering Amazon, nor did I look in the audience for Bailey's nod of approval. Marguerite Johnson, I heard the name again, my honors were read, there were noises in the audience of appreciation, and I took my place on the stage as rehearsed.

52   I thought about colors I hated: ecru, puce, lavender, beige and black.

53   There was shuffling and rustling around me, then Henry Reed was giving his valedictory address, "To Be or Not to Be." Hadn't he heard the white folks? We couldn't *be,* so the question was a waste of time. Henry's voice came out clear and strong. I feared to look at him. Hadn't he got the message? There was no "nobler in the mind" for Negroes because the world didn't think we had

minds, and they let us know it. "Outrageous fortune"? Now, that was a joke. When the ceremony was over I had to tell Henry Reed some things. That is, if I still cared. Not "rub," Henry, "erase." "Ah, there's the erase." Us.

54   Henry had been a good student in elocution. His voice rose on tides of promise and fell on waves of warnings. The English teacher had helped him to create a sermon winging through Hamlet's soliloquy. To be a man, a doer, a builder, a leader, or to be a tool, an unfunny joke, a crusher of funky toadstools. I marveled that Henry could go through with the speech as if we had a choice.

55   I had been listening and silently rebutting each sentence with my eyes closed; then there was a hush, which in an audience warns that something unplanned is happening. I looked up and saw Henry Reed, the conservative, the proper, the A student, turn his back to the audience and turn to us (the proud graduating class of 1940) and sing, nearly speaking,

> "Lift ev'ry voice and sing
> Till earth and heaven ring
> Ring with the harmonies of Liberty . . ."

It was the poem written by James Weldon Johnson. It was the music composed by J. Rosamond Johnson. It was the Negro national anthem. Out of habit we were singing it.

56   Our mothers and fathers stood in the dark hall and joined the hymn of encouragement. A kindergarten teacher led the small children onto the stage and the buttercups and daisies and bunny rabbits marked time and tried to follow:

> "Stony the road we trod
> Bitter the chastening rod
> Felt in the days when hope, unborn, had died.
> Yet with a steady beat
> Have not our weary feet
> Come to the place for which our fathers sighed?"

57   Every child I knew had learned that song with his ABC's and along with "Jesus Loves Me This I Know." But I personally had never heard it before. Never heard the words, despite the thousands of times I had sung them. Never thought they had anything to do with me.

58   On the other hand, the words of Patrick Henry had made such an impression on me that I had been able to stretch myself tall and trembling and say, "I know not what course others may take, but as for me, give me liberty or give me death."

59   And now I heard, really for the first time:

> "We have come over a way that with tears
> has been watered,
> We have come, treading our path through
> the blood of the slaughtered."

60   While echoes of the song shivered in the air, Henry Reed bowed his head, said "Thank you," and returned to his place in the line. The tears that slipped down many faces were not wiped away in shame.

61   We were on top again. As always, again. We survived. The depths had been icy and dark, but now a bright sun spoke to our souls. I was no longer simply a member of the proud graduating glass of 1940; I was a proud member of the wonderful, beautiful Negro race.

EXERCISES

Some of the Issues

1. How does Angelou establish the importance of the graduation? How does she build it stage by stage?
2. Why does Angelou distinguish between the high school graduates (paragraph 3) and the eighth-graders like herself? How do their attitudes differ? Why is she happier?
3. How does Angelou describe her rising expectations for "the great day" in paragraphs 15 through 28?
4. At what point in the narrative do we first get the idea that things may be going wrong with the "dream of a day"? What are later indications that something is wrong?
5. In paragraph 29 the children are confronted with a change in the usual order of things. Why does Angelou make this seem important? Why does the principal "rather desperately" signal for the children to sit down?
6. How do the first words Mr. Donleavy says indicate what his attitude is?
7. In paragraphs 50 through 59 Angelou describes her shifting thoughts and emotions. Explain them in your own words and relate them to the conclusion reached in paragraph 61.

The Way We Are Told

8. Paragraph 1 talks about the graduates and their schoolmates. Paragraphs 2 and 3 describe the school. Why does Angelou write in that order? What distinguishes paragraph 1 from 2 and 3 in addition to the content?
9. Explain the irony Angelou sees in Henry Reed's "To Be or Not to Be" speech.

Some Subjects for Writing

10. Have you ever experienced an event—a dance, a party, a trip—that you looked forward to and that turned out to be a disaster? Or have you ever dreaded an event, such as an interview or a blind date, that turned out better than you had expected? Tell it, trying to make the reader feel the anticipation

and the change through the specific, descriptive details you cite, rather than by direct statements. (You will find that the indirect way—making the reader feel or see the event—is more effective than simply saying, "I was bored" or "I found out it was a great evening after all.")

11. In his speech, Mr. Donleavy offers only sports figures like Jesse Owens and Joe Louis as cultural heroes for African-American students. Reflect on famous persons whom you have admired as role models. Write an essay in which you examine the importance of role models and cultural heroes in determining how we see ourselves.

12. Describe a ceremony you have witnessed or participated in. Do it in two separate essays. In the first, describe the event simply in a neutral way. In the second, tell it from the point of view of a witness or participant.

*13. Read Sherman Alexie's "Indian Education." Compare and contrast the kinds of discrimination Angelou's and Alexie's characters face. What are the sources of discrimination? From where and from whom do they come?

The Field Trip

Cheri Register

Cheri Register is a writer and teacher who grew up working class in Albert Lea, the Minnesota town she describes in this selection. Wilson & Co., the meatpacking plant where Register's father worked and where the field trip described in this essay takes place, was for many years the economic backbone of the town. In 1959, a violent strike at the plant divided the town and made national headlines, an event that Register describes in further detail in the book Packinghouse Daughter: A Memoir *(2000), from which "The Field Trip" is excerpted.*

Register left Albert Lea to attend the University of Chicago, where she earned her B.A., M.A., and Ph.D. degrees, all with honors. Register has written often of her working-class childhood and how it shaped her subsequent journey into academia. She has said of herself, "I find that I still experience the world as a working-class kid away from home. I walk the line between a feisty fidelity to the people of my childhood and a refined repugnance for the work they had to do. If I count up the meetings I attended, the protests I marched in, the feminist position papers I wrote, I have sound enough credentials to qualify as a Sixties activist, but I can't recall the politically charged days of my young adulthood without also remembering my ambivalence. When I look at the diploma on my bookcase, I still read 'Ph.D.' as 'Packinghouse Daughter.'"

Register's other books include "Are Those Kids Yours?": American Families with Children Adopted from Other Countries *(1991) and* The Chronic Illness Experience: Embracing the Imperfect Life *(1999). A former professor at the University of Idaho and the University of Minnesota, Register currently lives in Minneapolis and teaches writing at the Loft Literary Center.*

1   In a town without museums or amusement parks, which Albert Lea still was in the late 1950s, elementary school field trips tend to be excursions in industrial technology. Touring the sites where people do their daily work has to serve as both entertainment and education. My classmates and I clucked at baby chicks still wet and sticky and confused in the electric incubators at the hatchery, and watched a row of women at Kroger's Produce "candle" freshly laid eggs: lighting the eggs with a lamp from behind, they could see inside and check for embryos. We crowded around the printing press that clanked out the Albert Lea Evening Tribune, made our voices echo in the tall stairwell of a grain elevator, and stood entranced as bottles and cans moved along

conveyor belts to be automatically filled and sealed at the Morlea Dairy, the Coca-Cola bottling plant, and the National Cooperatives cannery. We never did visit the mysterious, brick-walled Olson Manufacturing Company on South Broadway, so we could still chime in with the local joke, "Why are there so many Olsons in Albert Lea? They make them here."

2   These field trips rarely bored us. I assumed my classmates were as fascinated as I was with the notion of work and its secret words and special skills. Mom taught me "dart" and "tuck" and "gusset" and showed me how to use a gauge and a tracing wheel. As I helped Dad with his house projects, I learned "dowel," "trowel," "sillcock," and "miter box." I looked forward to the day when I would master something and speak its language with confidence, but until then, I enjoyed peeking in on the work that grown-ups did, and seeing who did what, and where. For the parents of us Lincoln School kids, "where" was likely the Wilson & Co. packinghouse.

3   We knew that a visit to Wilson's required some degree of maturity, or at least the early signs of adolescence. A hodgepodge of brick buildings and tin and wooden sheds, Wilson's sat in a shallow depression between U.S. Highway 16, our Main Street, and the Chicago–Milwaukee–St. Paul and Pacific railroad line that ran along the weedy shore of Albert Lea Lake, also known as Lower Lake. "The plant," we called it, a name that marked it as the primary local industry. Security fences and a large employee parking lot made it look vast and impenetrable and even a little scary, yet it imposed itself on our lives in ways so familiar and habitual we rarely paid attention. The ceaseless industry of the packinghouse filled the air on the north side of town with a smoky, rancid odor, turned Albert Lea Lake slimy with effluents, alerted us to the passage of time with a steam whistle at noon, blared out livestock prices on our radios, and kept many of us fed and clothed and sheltered. "The Wilson label protects your table" was not only an advertising slogan, but the literal truth. We knew there would be no table to sit at if it weren't for Wilson's.

4   The closest I had come to the plant was the side gate where we picked Dad up from work on the days Mom needed the car. To reach this gate, we turned down a narrow gravel road that ran alongside another enterprise known as "the foundry" and dead-ended where the railroad tracks crossed the channel connecting Fountain and Albert Lea Lakes. Mom wrestled with the steering wheel of our hulking 1948 Pontiac to pull it over as close as possible to the scraggly willows that hung over the water. We sat silent in the shade, waiting and watching while one man, then a pair of men, and another, most of them swinging barn-shaped, black dinner pails, came streaming out under an arched sign that read Safety First. Some of the men exchanged good-byes with a guard who sat in a booth at the entryway. Finally, we would spot my dad, freshly washed and dressed in khaki pants and a checked shirt. He'd break into a grin as soon as he saw us, and I would climb over the seat into the back.

5   I had only a vague understanding of how Dad spent his days beyond the Safety First sign. I wasn't sure how to interpret the few clues he carried with

him at the end of the day. He might hand Mom a bottle of candy-sweet cough syrup that the nurse in the infirmary had given him, or a jar of drawing salve that pulled stubborn slivers out of your fingers overnight. Some days, he reached into his pocket and tossed me a heavy cylindrical magnet the size of his thumb that had been salvaged from a cow stomach. Farmers shoved these magnets down the animals' throats to catch nails and wires that might otherwise pierce their intestines. A magnet was already an object of mystery, and one that had been inside a cow's stomach was enhanced in value by its association with the grisly and the sacred. Our kitchen drawer at home was filled with butcher knives of thick, discolored metal that Dad bolted between matching hunks of wood in spare moments at work. He said he was a "millwright." For all I knew he made knives for a living.

6   When the phone rang at lunchtime each day, we knew it would be Dad, yelling above the roar and clatter of machinery, needing us to yell back. He talked loud when he first came home, too, until his ears had adjusted to the quiet. Starting out before dawn and working overtime most days left him tired and sore enough by late afternoon to stretch out on the living-room floor and fall asleep, regardless of what went on around him. We girls stepped over him to turn on TV or to read in the big chair in the corner where he worked his crossword puzzles in the evening.

7   Gradually I understood that animals were "slaughtered" at the plant, that the cattle and pigs hauled into town in semitrailers, their ears and snouts poking through red wooden cross-hatching, emerged from Wilson's as steaks and bacon. Dad seldom talked about how this transformation took place. Instead he told us stories about people with names like Booger and Buckshot and the tricks they played on one another. To celebrate Dad's birthday, they had carried him on their shoulders and sprayed him with the water hose. He didn't tell us how powerful the stream of water was or what the hose was normally used for. Once my sister asked him if he had a nickname at work. His face turned beet red and the grin stretched so tight he couldn't answer at all.

8   Many of Dad's funny stories had a dangerous edge, like the one about Buckshot falling into the condemned beef chute. There was a hole in the floor of the beef kill where anything that failed the federal inspector's test had to be tossed. One day Buckshot got too close to the hole, lost his balance, and fell three stories, headfirst, into a pile of contaminated beef. Dad saw him disappear and rushed down to find an inspector who could unlock the door to the chute. Buckshot's glasses had flown off and his face was covered with blood, "but it wasn't his own," Dad explained. He sat up, rolled his eyes, and muttered, "Where am I? Where am I?" "Well, Buck," Dad told him, "you're not in heaven."

9   Sheer good fortune put Lois Ann Kriesel in charge of our sixth-grade field trip to the packinghouse. A brand-new graduate from Mankato State Teacher's College, she seemed a species apart from the plump old-maid schoolteachers in their crinkly navy blue crepe, who shushed whispering girls and grabbed show-off

boys by the shirtcollar. At twenty-one, Miss Kriesel was young enough to be our sister, inquiring enough to understand our morbid curiosity, and wise enough to know that our illusions about hot dogs and the enticing freedoms of adult life could use a reality test.

10   Turning real-life events into teachable moments was Miss Kriesel's strong suit. When Billy Emstad threw a tennis ball through the open classroom window and hit Miss Kriesel on the shoulder, she arranged a trial with judge and jury, who acquitted him for lack of proof that he intended harm. When we grew tired of the school's meager record collection—Haydn's Surprise Symphony was no longer surprising, and we knew all too well what the *klo-kla-klo-kla-klo* of Ferde Grofé's Grand Canyon Suite was supposed to represent—Miss Kriesel invited us to bring our own music: Elvis Presley and Fats Domino and Albert Lea's own Eddie Cochran. We hummed chords and tapped out rhythms and never imagined we were learning anything. The 1956 presidential campaign was rife with educational possibility, and Miss Kriesel set up rival political conventions. To keep things even, some of the Democrats had to volunteer to be Republicans, a chasm I couldn't cross even for pretend. I beat David Peterson for the Democratic nomination, a serious blow to a boy who was already planning his strategy for the 1980 presidential election. To retaliate, he offered Tootsie Rolls to anyone who promised to vote for my Republican opponent, Kathy O'Neal. I voted for her, too, with no Tootsie Roll reward, because it would have been "conceited," as we labeled any display of confidence, to vote for myself. Kathy had no choice but to be Republican, as I understood it, because her dad was management. But she was a nice girl and a good friend, and she offered us her dad's job title as a tongue twister: "Pickled pigs' feet foreman, pickled pigs' feet foreman, fickle fig peet . . ."

11   A field trip to Wilson's required a good deal of preparation, for what we might experience there and for how we would need to behave. I knew already, from Dad's stories, that the federal inspectors were very finicky. They discarded whole slabs of meat just for one small dot of impurity. A child bumping up against a skinned carcass would require the sacrifice of potential spareribs, loins, chops, hocks, hams, sausage, bacon. It might also mean nightmares for the child. Meat, at this stage, was still, after all, dead animal. Miss Kriesel prepared us for both contingencies, reminding us to be cautious and follow directions, and warning us that some things we saw might not be pleasant. If we didn't think we could handle it, we could ask our parents to write a note excusing us from school that morning. Once inside, we were committed to finishing the tour. There would be no turning back.

12   Wilson's office was a brick building about the size of Lincoln School, and the other packinghouse buildings loomed over it much the way the high school next door dwarfed Lincoln. As we gathered out in front, Billy Emstad's dad walked by and greeted us. He was buttoning a white coat, like a doctor's, over his suit. The suit, of course, meant that he had an office job. Before we could go into the plant, we had to listen to headcounts and price figures that only a brain like David Peterson's would still contain by afternoon. There were moans of

disappointment from the boys when the guide announced that we would not be allowed to see the kill itself. I had heard my dad say that he spent the day working "up on the beef kill" or "up on the hog kill," and I imagined them up in a tower, like the Tower of London, where the kings of England had their enemies beheaded.

13　　In those days, before cholesterol scares, before pasta and veggies, bankruptcies and buyouts, Wilson's worked to full capacity. Semitrailers lined up outside the stockyards waiting to unload their mooing and grunting freight. Our tour started with that phase of the process, watching the animals get lured up the ramp by the Judas goat, who led them, as literally as we would ever see it, like lambs to slaughter.

14　　From there, we were ushered into the packaged meat division, where bacon was sliced and wrapped, and pork was ground and stuffed into casings or sealed in cellophane to be sold as wieners and bologna. There were women working in this area, a few familiar moms dressed in white coats and head coverings that looked like shower caps. Their hands moved quickly and they could look up only briefly to raise their eyebrows in greeting. It was strange, even a little shocking, to see them this way: hushed, restrained, their movements regulated by the rhythm of the machinery. It made their home behavior—the range of their voices, the rushing up and down basement stairs with baskets of wash— seem like random bursts of energy.

15　　With fresh memories of ham baking in the oven, I expected that walking into the smokeroom and inhaling deeply would be a pleasure. Up close, the aroma gave way to a stench. It was as if the odor that hovered in the air on the Northside and hit the rest of us with a shift in the wind had been bottled, left to stagnate, and then released with a quick twist of the lid. Kids made gagging noises, pinched their noses, and crowded around the door, ready to escape. The smokeroom employees went on working as if they had no sense of smell.

16　　So far, it was only raw and cured meat we saw, not much to remind us of the doomed creatures in the stockyard pens. Then, while we walked two abreast along a passageway, the line abruptly stopped and narrowed as the kids in front pressed their backs to the wall. "Those things are glaring at me," someone cried in a voice pitched so high with fright that it was unrecognizable. More shrieks, some laughter and jostling as we stared into pans piled with eyeballs, brains, hearts, and tongues. Tongues were a delicacy, the guide told us, and parts of the brain were used to make headcheese, a word that reminded me of toe jam, though I knew it was something that Danes ate in the Old Country, along with lard sandwiches. Stomach linings were cooked up and eaten as tripe, and the intestines were shipped down South, where Negroes ate them. Some internal organs were made into medicine to save us from deadly diseases. We might have taken the medicine without even realizing where it came from, the guide conjectured. Miss Kriesel slung her arms around the shoulders of the two rubber-legged kids standing nearest and reminded us of our promise to finish the tour.

17　　We were not in heaven, and there was no turning back. We climbed wooden staircases, wove in and out of large, high-windowed rooms, some filled with steam from vats of hot water, others damp and cold as the inside of a refrigerator, where men hacked at red flesh, ground blades against bone, stripped blue veins still leaking blood, and scraped pale yellow globs of fat from foul-smelling hides.

18   I kept an eye out for my dad the whole time. I knew from his stories that he was out and about a lot. By this time, I had learned that he spent his days fixing machines that had broken down. I watched for his khaki pants and the rust-and-green checked shirt he wore most often. He found my class before I spotted him. "Cheri! There's your dad!" someone called, and I turned and caught the gold-toothed grin on a man wearing jeans a little too large and a blue shirt gone limp in the moist air. I had never seen my dad in jeans. His legs looked even shorter and stubbier than I knew them to be. He looked frail, in spite of his stocky build, dwarfed by the proportions of the room and pale in the yellow-green light. But he was free, not moving to the pace of a machine or rooted to one square-foot of floor space. Years later I read in a book about the meat-packing industry that the millwrights are an elite among blue-collar workers, descendants of the skilled artisans who formed the guilds that preceded the labor union. But at that moment, against that backdrop, he just looked small.

19   Our tour indoors, we realized, was moving backward, from finish toward start, easing us into the reality of animal slaughter. As we climbed higher in the building, slabs of meat became carcasses, there were fewer women, and the men seemed to get larger and more muscular. A man I recognized as the father of a playground bully turned briefly to wink at us as he split one smooth, pink hog carcass after another in long, powerful, vertical strokes. Another man was cutting the necks at the spinal cord with a scissors larger and more threatening than a garden shears. Clip, clip, clip, the heads dropped loose so the next man could slice them off.

20   There was some hubbub in the group as we were routed into the space where newly killed hogs were hung to be drained of blood and then dropped into the dehairing tank. A couple of breathless boys claimed to have seen, through a briefly opened door, the killing itself, or at least the knock on the head that stunned the animal. Miss Kriesel pushed through the crowd to calm them, and we settled into reverential whispers before a sight that felt taboo, as though we were peering in on a secret ritual with the power to transform us. A conveyor mounted on the ceiling brought one huge, dead hog after another past us gawking children. The hog's expressions were not so different from ours— eyes fixed in fear, snouts and lower lips parted by gravity. Each body hung heavy from the chains that bound its legs, swinging slightly, ready to crack the ribs of anyone who got in the way. Blood was running in streams to the floor below. A younger man directed the blood toward the drain with a water hose, the kind they must have sprayed my dad with on his birthday. Still, blood splattered the shirts and soaked the workboots of the dads and uncles who would come home that afternoon deceptively clean.

21   One of the hogs was still half alive and squealing in agony. A man stabbed it quickly with a large knife and blood gushed from the wound in its throat. "Look

at that!" David Peterson burst out. "He got him right in the jugular!" What has preserved this moment in my memory, as much as the gruesome sight itself, is the word "jugular." I had never heard it before. I didn't know what it meant. It was mystery—jargon that belonged to the work we were witnessing. I wondered why David Peterson alone had been let in on the secret.

22   Back at school, we spent the rest of the day ridding ourselves of the horror by telling one another, over and over, what we had seen and what we only thought we saw. I don't remember Miss Kriesel ever spelling out the message she had planted deep inside us, where fear and desire lie waiting for the spark that welds them into will: *Start planning your escape. Everything you do from now on must help you out of here.*

EXERCISES

Some of the Issues

1. What sorts of field trips did Register take in elementary school and why? How does she use the idea of field trips to tell the reader about the town in which she grew up? Do the types of field trips she took differ from the ones you remember taking in elementary school?

2. What did Register and her classmates feel about these field trips (paragraph 2)?

3. Why was the advertising slogan "The Wilson label protects your table" also a "literal truth" (paragraph 3)?

4. What objects did Register's father sometimes bring out from the plant (paragraph 5)? How were these clues to the nature of his work there?

5. What kinds of stories did Register's father tell about work (paragraphs 7–8)? How did he use humor in his stories?

6. Based on her description of Lois Ann Kriesel, what is Register's view of her as a teacher?

7. What was "strange, even a little shocking" about seeing people's mothers working in the packaged meat division (paragraph 14)?

8. In what ways does the reality of the packinghouse differ from Register's expectations? Why are these differences significant?

9. How does Register's father look when she sees him at the plant (paragraph 18)? Why is this description significant?

10. What to you is the significance of Register's last line?

The Way We Are Told

11. How does Register describe the Wilson & Co. packinghouse (paragraph 3)? How do the physical aspects of the plant reflect the significance of the plant to the town and to Register herself?

12. Why does Register provide details like the full names of the other students? What impact does this have?

13. How would you describe Register's tone in this essay? At what points does she use humor and what impact does it have?
14. Why does Register write, "We were not in heaven, and there was no turning back" in paragraph 17?

Some Subjects for Writing

15. Write a narrative about a school field trip you took. Using Register's narrative as a model, include not only details about what you saw but also about the response of the students and the attitude of the teacher who organized the trip.
16. Write an essay analyzing your own and your friends' relationships to the work your parents do (or did, if they're retired) including the work of parenting and running a household. Interview several of your friends about their parents' work and whether or not they see themselves planning for a different kind of future. Beyond gathering facts about where and what kind of work their parents do, ask questions about how their parents seem to feel about their jobs. Would they enjoy doing the same type of work? Why or why not? Did their parents in any way influence their choice to go to college or their choice of career? In your essay, try to compare and contrast the different responses and come to some conclusions about what influences people's choices.

I Just Wanna Be Average

Mike Rose

Mike Rose was born in Chicago in 1938 and, when he was seven, moved with his parents to the south side of Los Angeles. His parents, who had immigrated from Italy and arrived at Ellis Island in the 1910s and 1920s, never escaped poverty; however, they managed to save enough money to send Rose to a parochial school. He was an average student but, after junior high, was misplaced in the vocational education track in high school, where he "drifted to the level of a really mediocre and unprepared student." His experience in "Voc. Ed." illustrates how students placed in the lower tracks live down to the expectations of their classrooms. Fortunately, Rose's biology teacher noticed his ability, looked at his academic record, and discovered that his grades had been switched with those of another student named Rose. Subsequently, he was reassigned to the college track. In his senior year, he encountered a nontraditional teacher who opened up the world of poetry, ideas, and language, and who helped Rose to get a scholarship to Loyola University in Los Angeles.

Rose became a teacher and worked with others on the margins of society: inner-city kids, Vietnam veterans, and underprepared adults. He is currently on the faculty of UCLA's Graduate School of Education and Information Studies.

In the following excerpt from his book Lives on the Boundary *(1989), he relates how poverty contributes to deep, lasting feelings of self-doubt, and how one caring person can make a fundamental difference in the lives of others. Rose is also the author of* Possible Lives: The Promise of Public Education in America *(1995) and* The Mind at Work: Valuing the Intelligence of the American Worker *(2004).*

1 The house was on a piece of land that rose about four feet up from heavily trafficked Vermont Avenue. The yard sloped down to the street, and three steps and a short walkway led up the middle of the grass to our front door. There was a similar house immediately to the south of us. Next to it was Carmen's Barber Shop. Carmen was a short, quiet Italian who, rumor had it, had committed his first wife to the crazy house to get her money. In the afternoons, Carmen could be found in the lot behind his shop playing solitary catch, flinging a tennis ball high into the air and running under it. One day the police arrested Carmen on charges of child molesting. He was released but became furtive and suspicious. I never saw him in the lot again. Next to Carmen's was a junk store where, one summer, I made a little money polishing brass and rewiring old lamps. Then came a dilapidated real estate office, a Mexican

restaurant, an empty lot, and an appliance store owned by the father of Keith Grateful, the streetwise, chubby boy who would become my best friend.

2   Right to the north of us was a record shop, a barber shop presided over by old Mr. Graff, Walt's Malts, a shoe repair shop with a big Cat's Paw decal in the window, a third barber shop, and a brake shop. It's as I write this that I realize for the first time that three gray men could have had a go at your hair before you left our street.

3   Behind our house was an unpaved alley that passed, just to the north, a power plant the length of a city block. Massive coils atop the building hissed and cracked through the day, but the doors never opened. I used to think it was abandoned—feeding itself on its own wild arcs—until one sweltering afternoon a man was electrocuted on the roof. The air was thick and still as two firemen—the only men present—brought down a charred and limp body without saying a word.

4   The north and south traffic on Vermont was separated by tracks for the old yellow trolley cars, long since defunct. Across the street was a huge garage, a tiny hot dog stand run by a myopic and reclusive man named Freddie, and my dreamland, the Vermont Bowl. Distant and distorted behind thick lenses, Freddie's eyes never met yours; he would look down when he took your order and give you your change with a mumble. Freddie slept on a cot in the back of his grill and died there one night, leaving tens of thousands of dollars stuffed in the mattress.

5   My father would buy me a chili dog at Freddie's, and then we would walk over to the bowling alley where Dad would sit at the lunch counter and drink coffee while I had a great time with pinball machines, electric shooting galleries, and an ill-kept dispenser of cheese corn. There was a small, dark bar abutting the lanes, and it called to me. I would devise reasons to walk through it: "'Scuse me, is the bathroom in here?" or "Anyone see my dad?" though I can never remember my father having a drink. It was dark and people were drinking and I figured all sorts of mysterious things were being whispered. Next to the Vermont Bowl was a large vacant lot overgrown with foxtails and dotted with car parts, bottles, and rotting cardboard. One day Keith heard that the police had found a human head in the brush. After that we explored the lot periodically, coming home with stickers all the way up to our waists. But we didn't find a thing. Not even a kneecap.

6   When I wasn't with Keith or in school, I would spend most of my day with my father or with the men who were renting the one-room apartments behind our house. Dad and I whiled away the hours in the bowling alley, watching TV, or planting a vegetable garden that never seemed to take. When he was still mobile, he would walk the four blocks down to St. Regina's Grammar School to take me home to my favorite lunch of boiled wieners and chocolate milk. There I'd sit, dunking my hot dog in a jar of mayonnaise and drinking my milk while Sheriff John tuned up the calliope music on his "Lunch Brigade." Though he never complained to me, I could sense that my father's health was failing, and I began devising child's ways to make him better. We had a box of rolled cotton

in the bathroom, and I would go in and peel off a long strip and tape it around my jaw. Then I'd rummage through the closet, find a sweater of my father's, put on one of his hats—and sneak around to the back door. I'd knock loudly and wait. It would take him a while to get there. Finally, he'd open the door, look down, and quietly say, "Yes, Michael?" I was disappointed. Every time. Somehow I thought I could fool him. And, I guess, if he had been fooled, I would have succeeded in redefining things: I would have been the old one, he much younger, more agile, with strength in his legs.

7   The men who lived in the back were either retired or didn't work that much, so one of them was usually around. They proved to be, over the years, an unusual set of companions for a young boy. Ed Gionotti was the youngest of the lot, a handsome man whose wife had run off and who spoke softly and never smiled. Bud Hall and Lee McGuire were two out-of-work plumbers who lived in adjacent units and who weekly drank themselves silly, proclaiming in front of God and everyone their undying friendship or their unequivocal hatred. Old Cheech was a lame Italian who used to hobble along grabbing his testicles and rolling his eyes while he talked about the women he claimed to have on a string. There was Lester, the toothless cabbie, who several times made overtures to me and who, when he moved, left behind a drawer full of syringes and burnt spoons. Mr. Smith was a rambunctious retiree who lost his nose to an untended skin cancer. And there was Mr. Berryman, a sweet and gentle man who eventually left for a retirement hotel only to be burned alive in an electrical fire.

8   Except for Keith, there were no children on my block and only one or two on the immediate side streets. Most of the people I saw day to day were over fifty. People in their twenties and thirties working in the shoe shop or tile garages didn't say a lot; their work and much of what they were working for drained their spirits. There were gang members who sauntered up from Hoover Avenue, three blocks to the east, and occasionally I would get shoved around, but they had little interest in me either as member or victim. I was a skinny, bespectacled kid and had neither the coloring nor the style of dress or carriage that marked me as a rival. On the whole, the days were quiet, lazy, lonely. The heat shimmering over the asphalt had no snap to it; time drifted by. I would lie on the couch at night and listen to the music from the record store or from Walt's Malts. It was new and quick paced, exciting, a little dangerous (the church had condemned Buddy Knox's "Party Doll"), and I heard in it a deep rhythmic need to be made whole with love, or marked as special, or released in some rebellious way. Even the songs about lost love—and there were plenty of them—lifted me right out of my socks with their melodious longing. In the midst of the heat and slow time the music brought the promise of its origins, a promise of deliverance, a promise that, if only for a moment, life could be stirring and dreamy.

9   But the anger and frustration of South Vermont could prove too strong for music's illusion; then it was violence that provided deliverance of a different order. One night I watched as a guy sprinted from Walt's to toss something on our lawn. The police were right behind, and a cop tackled him, smashing his face into the sidewalk. I ducked out to find the packet: a dozen glassine bags of heroin.

Another night, one August midnight, an argument outside the record store ended with a man being shot to death. And the occasional gang forays brought with them some fated kid who would fumble his moves and catch a knife.

10   It's popular these days to claim you grew up on the streets. Men tell violent tales and romanticize the lessons violence brings. But, though it was occasionally violent, it wasn't the violence in South L.A. that marked me, for sometimes you can shake that ugliness off. What finally affected me was subtler, but more pervasive: I cannot recall a young person who was crazy in love or lost in work or one old person who was passionate about a cause or an idea. I'm not talking about an absence of energy—the street toughs and, for that fact, old Cheech had energy. And I'm not talking about an absence of decency, for my father was a thoughtful man. The people I grew up with were retired from jobs that rub away the heart or were working hard at jobs to keep their lives from caving in or were anchorless and in between jobs and spouses or were diving headlong into a barren tomorrow: junkies, alcoholics, and mean kids walking along Vermont looking to throw a punch. I developed a picture of human existence that tendered it short and brutish or sad and aimless or long and quiet with rewards like afternoon naps, the evening newspaper, walks around the block, occasional letters from children in other states. When, years later, I was introduced to humanistic psychologists like Abraham Maslow and Carl Rogers, with their visions of self-actualization, or even Freud with his sober dictum about love and work, it all sounded like a glorious fairy tale, a magical account of a world full of possibility, full of hope and empowerment. Sindbad and Cinderella couldn't have been more fanciful.

11   Some people who manage to write their way out of the working class describe the classroom as an oasis of possibility. It became their intellectual playground, their competitive arena. Given the richness of my memories of this time, it's funny how scant are my recollections of school. I remember the red brick building of St. Regina's itself, and the topography of the playground: the swings and basketball courts and peeling benches. There are images of a few students: Erwin Petschaur, a muscular German boy with a strong accent; Dave Sanchez, who was good in math; and Sheila Wilkes, everyone's curly-haired heartthrob. And there are two nuns: Sister Monica, the third-grade teacher with beautiful hands for whom I carried a candle and who, to my dismay, had wedded herself to Christ; and Sister Beatrice, a woman truly crazed, who would sweep into class, eyes wide, to tell us about the Apocalypse.

12   All the hours in class tend to blend into one long, vague stretch of time. What I remember best, strangely enough, are the two things I couldn't understand and over the years grew to hate: grammar lessons and mathematics. I would sit there watching a teacher draw her long horizontal line and her short, oblique lines and break up sentences and put adjectives here and adverbs there and just not get it, couldn't see the reason for it, turned off to it. I would hide by slumping down in my seat and page through my reader, carried along by the flow of sentences in a story. She would test us, and I would dread that, for I

always got Cs and Ds. Mathematics was a bit different. For whatever reasons, I didn't learn early math very well, so when it came time for more complicated operations, I couldn't keep up and started day-dreaming to avoid my inadequacy. This was a strategy I would rely on as I grew older. I fell further and further behind. A memory: The teacher is faceless and seems very far away. The voice is faint and is discussing an equation written on the board. It is raining, and I am watching the streams of water form patterns on the windows.

13   I realize now how consistently I defended myself against the lessons I couldn't understand and the people and events of South L.A. that were too strange to view head-on. I got very good at watching a blackboard with minimum awareness. And I drifted more and more into a variety of protective fantasies. I was lucky in that although my parents didn't read or write very much and had no more than a few books around the house, they never debunked my pursuits. And when they could, they bought me what I needed to spin my web.

14   One early Christmas they got me a small chemistry set. My father brought home an old card table from the secondhand store, and on that table I spread out my test tubes, my beaker, my Erlenmeyer flask, and my gas-generating apparatus. The set came equipped with chemicals, minerals, and various treated papers— all in little square bottles. You could send away to someplace in Maryland for more, and I did, saving pennies and nickels to get the substances that were too exotic for my set, the Junior Chemcraft: Congo red paper, azurite, glycerine, chrome alum, cochineal—this from female insects!—tartaric acid, chameleon paper, logwood. I would sit before my laboratory and play for hours. My father rested on the purple couch in front of me watching wrestling or *Gunsmoke* while I measured powders or heated crystals or blew into solutions that my breath would turn red or pink. I was taken by the blends of names and by the colors that swirled through the beaker. My equations were visual and phonetic. I would hold a flask up to the hall light, imagining the veils of a million atoms dancing. Sulfur and alcohol hung in the air. I wanted to shake down the house.

15   One day my mother came home from Coffee Dan's with an awful story. The teenage brother of one of her waitress friends was in the hospital. He had been fooling around with explosives in his garage "where his mother couldn't see him," and something happened, and "he blew away part of his throat. For God's sake, be careful," my mother said. "Remember poor Ada's brother." Wow! I thought. How neat! Why couldn't my experiments be that dangerous? I really lost heart when I realized that you could probably eat the chemicals spread across my table.

16   I knew what I had to do. I saved my money for a week and then walked with firm resolve past Walt's Malts, past the brake shop, across Ninetieth Street, and into Palazolla's market. I bought a little bottle of Alka-Seltzer and ran home. I chipped up the wafers and mixed them into a jar of white crystals. When my mother came home, dog tired, and sat down on the edge of the couch to tell me and Dad about her day, I gravely poured my concoction into a beaker of water, cried something about the unexpected, and ran out from behind my table.

The beaker foamed ominously. My father swore in Italian. The second time I tried it, I got something milder—in English. And by my third near-miss with death, my parents were calling my behavior cute. Cute! Who wanted cute? I wanted to toy with the disaster that befell Ada Pendleton's brother. I wanted all those wonderful colors to collide in ways that could blow your voice box right off.

17   But I was limited by the real. The best I could do was create a toxic antacid. I loved my chemistry set—its glassware and its intriguing labels—but it wouldn't allow me to do the things I wanted to do. St. Regina's had an all-purpose room, one wall of which was lined with old books—and one of those shelves held a row of plastic-covered space novels. The sheen of their covers was gone, and their futuristic portraits were dotted with erasures and grease spots like a meteor shower of the everyday. I remember the rockets best. Long cylinders outfitted at the base with three slick fins, tapering at the other end to a perfect conical point, ready to pierce out of the stratosphere and into my imagination: X-fifteens and Mach 1, the dark side of the moon, the Red Planet, Jupiter's Great Red Spot, Saturn's rings—and beyond the solar system to swirling wisps of galaxies, to stardust.

18   Students will float to the mark you set. I and the others in the vocational classes were bobbing in pretty shallow water. Vocational education has aimed at increasing the economic opportunities of students who do not do well in our schools. Some serious programs succeed in doing that, and through exceptional teachers—like Mr. Gross in *Horace's Compromise*—students learn to develop hypotheses and troubleshoot, reason through a problem, and communicate effectively—the true job skills. The vocational track, however, is most often a place for those who are just not making it, a dumping ground for the disaffected. There were a few teachers who worked hard at education; young Brother Slattery, for example, combined a stern voice with weekly quizzes to try to pass along to us a skeletal outline of world history. But mostly the teachers had no idea of how to engage the imaginations of us kids who were scuttling along at the bottom of the pond.

19   And the teachers would have needed some inventiveness, for none of us was groomed for the classroom. It wasn't just that I didn't know things—didn't know how to simplify algebraic fractions, couldn't identify different kinds of clauses, bungled Spanish translations—but that I had developed various faulty and inadequate ways of doing algebra and making sense of Spanish. Worse yet, the years of defensive tuning out in elementary school had given me a way to escape quickly while seeming at least half alert. During my time in Voc. Ed., I developed further into a mediocre student and a somnambulant problem solver, and that affected the subjects I did have the wherewithal to handle: I detested Shakespeare; I got bored with history. My attention flitted here and there. I fooled around in class and read my books indifferently—the intellectual equivalent of playing with your food. I did what I had to do to get by, and I did it with half a mind.

20   But I did learn things about people and eventually came into my own socially. I liked the guys in Voc. Ed. Growing up where I did, I understood and admired physical prowess, and there was an abundance of muscle here. There was
Dave Snyder, a sprinter and halfback of true quality. Dave's ability and quick wit
gave him a natural appeal, and he was welcome in any clique, though he always
kept a little independent. He enjoyed acting the fool and could care less about
studies, but he possessed a certain maturity and never caused the faculty much
trouble. It was a testament to his independence that he included me among his
friends—I eventually went out for track, but I was no jock. Owing to the Latin
alphabet and a dearth of *R*s and *S*s, Snyder sat behind Rose, and we started exchanging one-liners and became friends.

21   There was Ted Richard, a much-touted Little League pitcher. He was
chunky and had a baby face and came to Our Lady of Mercy as a seasoned street
fighter. Ted was quick to laugh and he had a loud, jolly laugh, but when he got
angry he'd smile a little smile, the kind that simply raises the corner of the
mouth a quarter of an inch. For those who knew, it was an eerie signal. Those
who didn't found themselves in big trouble, for Ted was very quick. He loved to
carry on what we would come to call philosophical discussions: What is
courage? Does God exist? He also loved words, enjoyed picking up big ones like
salubrious and *equivocal* and using them in our conversation—laughing at himself
as the word hit a chuckhole rolling off his tongue. Ted didn't do all that well in
school—baseball and parties and testing the courage he'd speculated about took
up his time. His textbooks were *Argosy* and *Field and Stream*, whatever newspapers he'd find on the bus stop—from the *Daily Worker* to pornography—
conversations with uncles or hobos or businessmen he'd meet in a coffee shop,
The Old Man and the Sea. With hindsight, I can see that Ted was developing into
one of those rough-hewn intellectuals whose sources are a mix of the learned
and the apocryphal, whose discussions are both assured and sad.

22   And then there was Ken Harvey. Ken was good-looking in a puffy way and
had a full and oily ducktail and was a car enthusiast . . . a hodad. One day in religion class, he said the sentence that turned out to be one of the most memorable
of the hundreds of thousands I heard in those Voc. Ed. years. We were talking
about the parable of the talents, about achievement, working hard, doing the
best you can do, blah-blah-blah, when the teacher called on the restive Ken
Harvey for an opinion. Ken thought about it, but just for a second, and said
(with studied, minimal affect), "I just wanna be average." That woke me up. Average?! Who wants to be average? Then the athletes chimed in with the clichés
that make you want to laryngectomize them, and the exchange became a plati-
tudinous melee. At the time, I thought Ken's assertion was stupid, and I wrote
him off. But his sentence has stayed with me all these years, and I think I am finally coming to understand it.

23   Ken Harvey was gasping for air. School can be a tremendously disorienting
place. No matter how bad the school, you're going to encounter notions that
don't fit with the assumptions and beliefs that you grew up with—maybe you'll

hear these dissonant notions from teachers, maybe from the other students, and maybe you'll read them. You'll also be thrown in with all kinds of kids from all kinds of backgrounds, and that can be unsettling—this is especially true in places of rich ethnic and linguistic mix, like the L.A. basin. You'll see a handful of students far excel you in courses that sound exotic and that are only in the curriculum of the elite: French, physics, trigonometry. And all this is happening while you're trying to shape an identity, your body is changing, and your emotions are running wild. If you're a working-class kid in the vocational track, the options you'll have to deal with this will be constrained in certain ways: You're defined by your school as "slow"; you're placed in a curriculum that isn't designed to liberate you but to occupy you, or, if you're lucky, train you, though the training is for work the society does not esteem; other students are picking up the cues from your school and your curriculum and interacting with you in particular ways. If you're a kid like Ted Richard, you turn your back on all this and let your mind roam where it may. But youngsters like Ted are rare. What Ken and so many others do is protect themselves from such suffocating madness by taking on with a vengeance the identity implied in the vocational track. Reject the confusion and frustration by openly defining yourself as the Common Joe. Champion the average. Rely on your own good sense. Fuck this bullshit. Bullshit, of course, is everything you—and the others—fear is beyond you: books, essays, tests, academic scrambling, complexity, scientific reasoning, philosophical inquiry.

24   The tragedy is that you have to twist the knife in your own gray matter to make this defense work. You'll have to shut down, have to reject intellectual stimuli or diffuse them with sarcasm, have to cultivate stupidity, have to convert boredom from a malady into a way of confronting the world. Keep your vocabulary simple, act stoned when you're not or act more stoned than you are, flaunt ignorance, materialize your dreams. It is a powerful and effective defense—it neutralizes the insult and the frustration of being a vocational kid and, when perfected, it drives teachers up the wall, a delightful secondary effect. But like all strong magic, it exacts a price.

25   Jack MacFarland couldn't have come into my life at a better time. My father was dead, and I had logged up too many years of scholastic indifference. Mr. MacFarland had a master's degree from Columbia and decided, at twenty-six, to find a little school and teach his heart out. He never took any credentialing courses, couldn't bear to, he said, so he had to find employment in a private system. He ended up at Our Lady of Mercy teaching five sections of senior English. He was a beatnik who was born too late. His teeth were stained, he tucked his sorry tie in between the third and fourth buttons of his shirt, and his pants were chronically wrinkled. At first, we couldn't believe this guy, thought he slept in his car. But within no time, he had us so startled with work that we didn't much worry about where he slept or if he slept at all. We wrote three or four essays a month.

We read a book every two to three weeks, starting with the *Iliad* and ending up with Hemingway. He gave us a quiz on the reading every other day. He brought a prep school curriculum to Mercy High.

26   MacFarland's lectures were crafted, and as he delivered them he would pace the room jiggling a piece of chalk in his cupped hand, using it to scribble on the board the names of all the writers and philosophers and plays and novels he was weaving into his discussion. He asked questions often, raised everything from Zeno paradox to the repeated last line of Frost's "Stopping by Woods on a Snowy Evening." He slowly and carefully built up our knowledge of Western intellectual history—with facts, with connections, with speculations. We learned about Greek philosophy, about Dante, the Elizabethan world view, the Age of Reason, existentialism. He analyzed poems with us, had us reading sections from John Ciardi's *How Does a Poem Mean?*, making a potentially difficult book accessible with his own explanations. We gave oral reports on poems Ciardi didn't cover. We imitated the styles of Conrad, Hemingway, and *Time* magazine. We wrote and talked, wrote and talked. The man immersed us in language.

27   Even MacFarland's barbs were literary. If Jim Fitzsimmons, hung over and irritable, tried to smart-ass him, he'd rejoin with a flourish that would spark the indomitable Skip Madison—who'd lost his front teeth in a hapless tackle—to flick his tongue through the gap and opine, "good chop," drawing out the single "o" in stinging indictment. Jack MacFarland, this tobacco-stained intellectual, brandished linguistic weapons of a kind I hadn't encountered before. Here was this *egghead*, for God's sake, keeping some pretty difficult people in line. And from what I heard, Mike Dweetz and Steve Fusco and all the notorious Voc. Ed. crowd settled down as well when MacFarland took the podium. Though a lot of guys groused in the schoolyard, it just seemed that giving trouble to this particular teacher was a silly thing to do. Tomfoolery, not to mention assault, had no place in the world he was trying to create for us, and instinctively everyone knew that. If nothing else, we all recognized MacFarland's considerable intelligence and respected the hours he put into his work. It came to this: The troublemaker would look foolish rather than daring. Even Jim Fitzsimmons was reading *On the Road* and turning his incipient alcoholism to literary ends.

28   There were some lives that were already beyond Jack MacFarland's ministrations, but mine was not. I started reading again as I hadn't since elementary school. I would go into our gloomy little bedroom or sit at the dinner table while, on the television, Danny McShane was paralyzing Mr. Moto with the atomic drop, and work slowly back through *Heart of Darkness*, trying to catch the words in Conrad's sentences. I certainly was not MacFarland's best student; most of the other guys in College Prep, even my fellow slackers, had better backgrounds than I did. But I worked very hard, for MacFarland had hooked me. He tapped my old interest in reading and creating stories. He gave me a way to feel special by using my mind. And he provided a role model that wasn't

shaped on physical prowess alone, and something inside me that I wasn't quite aware of responded to that. Jack MacFarland established a literacy club, to borrow a phrase of Frank Smith's, and invited me—invited all of us—to join.

29   There's been a good deal of research and speculation suggesting that the acknowledgment of school performance with extrinsic rewards—smiling faces, stars, numbers, grades—diminishes the intrinsic satisfaction children experience by engaging in reading or writing or problem solving. While it's certainly true that we've created an educational system that encourages our best and brightest to become cynical grade collectors and, in general, have developed an obsession with evaluation and assessment, I must tell you that venal though it may have been, I loved getting good grades from MacFarland. I now know how subjective grades can be, but then they came tucked in the back of essays like bits of scientific data, some sort of spectroscopic readout that said, objectively and publicly, that I had made something of value. I suppose I'd been mediocre for too long and enjoyed a public redefinition. And I suppose the workings of my mind, such as they were, had been private for too long. My linguistic play moved into the world; like the intergalactic stories I told years before on Frank's berry-splattered truck bed, these papers with their circled, red B-pluses and A-minuses linked my mind to something outside it. I carried them around like a club emblem.

30   One day in the December of my senior year, Mr. MacFarland asked me where I was going to go to college. I hadn't thought much about it. Many of the students I teach today spent their last year in high school with a physics text in one hand and the Stanford catalog in the other, but I wasn't even aware of what "entrance requirements" were. My folks would say that they wanted me to go to college and be a doctor, but I don't know how seriously I ever took that; it seemed a sweet thing to say, a bit of supportive family chatter, like telling a gangly daughter she's graceful. The reality of higher education wasn't in my scheme of things: No one in the family had gone to college; only two of my uncles had completed high school. I figured I'd get a night job and go to the local junior college because I knew that Snyder and Company were going there to play ball. But I hadn't even prepared for that. When I finally said, "I don't know," MacFarland looked down at me—I was seated in his office—and said, "Listen, you can write."

31   My grades stank. I had As in biology and a handful of Bs in a few English and social science classes. All the rest were Cs—or worse. MacFarland said I would do well in his class and laid down the law about doing well in the others. Still, the record for my first three years wouldn't have been acceptable to any four-year school. To nobody's surprise, I was turned down flat by USC and UCLA. But Jack MacFarland was on the case. He had received his bachelor's degree from Loyola University, so he made calls to old professors and talked to somebody in admissions and wrote me a strong letter. Loyola finally accepted me as a probationary student. I would be on trial for the first year, and if I did okay, I would be granted regular status. MacFarland also intervened to get me a

loan, for I could never have afforded a private college without it. Four more years of religion classes and four more years of boys at one school, girls at another. But at least I was going to college. Amazing.

32   In my last semester of high school, I elected a special English course fashioned by Mr. MacFarland, and it was through this elective that there arose at Mercy a fledgling literati. Art Mitz, the editor of the school newspaper and a very smart guy, was the kingpin. He was joined by me and by Mark Dever, a quiet boy who wrote beautifully and who would die before he was forty. MacFarland occasionally invited us to his apartment, and those visits became the high point of our apprenticeship: We'd clamp on our training wheels and drive to his salon.

33   He lived in a cramped and cluttered place near the airport, tucked away in the kind of building that architectural critic Reyner Banham calls a *dingbat*. Books were all over: stacked, piled, tossed, and crated, underlined and dog eared, well worn and new. Cigarette ashes crusted with coffee in saucers or spilled over the sides of motel ashtrays. The little bedroom had, along two of its walls, bricks and boards loaded with notes, magazines, and oversized books. The kitchen joined the living room, and there was a stack of German newspapers under the sink. I had never seen anything like it: a great flophouse of language furnished by City Lights and Café le Metro. I read every title. I flipped through paperbacks and scanned jackets and memorized names: Gogol, *Finnegan's Wake*, Djuna Barnes, Jackson Pollock, *A Coney Island of the Mind*, F. O. Matthiessen's *American Renaissance*, all sorts of Freud, *Troubled Sleep*, Man Ray, *The Education of Henry Adams*, Richard Wright, *Film as Art*, William Butler Yeats, Marguerite Duras, *Redburn*, *A Season in Hell*, *Kapital*. On the cover of Alain-Fournier's *The Wanderer* was an Edward Gorey drawing of a young man on a road winding into dark trees. By the hotplate sat a strange Kafka novel called *Amerika*, in which an adolescent hero crosses the Atlantic to find the Nature Theater of Oklahoma. Art and Mark would be talking about a movie or the school newspaper, and I would be consuming my English teacher's library. It was heady stuff. I felt like a Pop Warner athlete on steroids.

34   Art, Mark, and I would buy stogies and triangulate from MacFarland's apartment to the Cinema, which now shows X-rated films but was then L.A.'s premiere art theater, and then to the musty Cherokee Bookstore in Hollywood to hobnob with beatnik homosexuals—smoking, drinking bourbon and coffee, and trying out awkward phrases we'd gleaned from our mentor's bookshelves. I was happy and precocious and a little scared as well, for Hollywood Boulevard was thick with a kind of decadence that was foreign to the South Side. After the Cherokee, we would head back to the security of MacFarland's apartment, slaphappy with hipness.

35   Let me be the first to admit that there was a good deal of adolescent passion in this embrace of the avant-garde: self-absorption, sexually charged pedantry, an elevation of the odd and abandoned. Still it was a time during which I absorbed an awful lot of information: long lists of titles, images from expressionist

paintings, new wave shibboleths, snippets of philosophy, and names that read like Steve Fusco's misspellings—Goethe, Nietzsche, Kierkegaard. Now this is hardly the stuff of deep understanding. But it was an introduction, a phrase book, a Baedeker to a vocabulary of ideas, and it felt good at the time to know all these words. With hindsight I realize how layered and important that knowledge was.

36   It enabled me to do things in the world. I could browse bohemian bookstores in far-off, mysterious Hollywood; I could go to the Cinema and see events through the lenses of European directors; and, most of all, I could share an evening, talk that talk, with Jack MacFarland, the man I most admired at the time. Knowledge was becoming a bonding agent. Within a year or two, the persona of the disaffected hipster would prove too cynical, too alienated to last. But for a time it was new and exciting: It provided a critical perspective on society, and it allowed me to act as though I were living beyond the limiting boundaries of South Vermont.

EXERCISES

Some of the Issues

1. Give a physical description of the neighborhood where Rose grew up.
2. How would you characterize the men who lived in the area (paragraph 7)?
3. Considering the view of life on Vermont Avenue, can you infer why Rose doesn't mention any women?
4. How do you think he felt about growing up in his neighborhood? What lines from the text support your idea?
5. The author says that his childhood days were quiet, lazy, and lonely. What kinds of neighborhood activities did attract his attention?
6. What defense mechanism did Rose develop to cope with school and the hopelessness of the neighborhood (paragraph 12)?
7. Rose spent hours with his chemistry set, yet he was disappointed that it didn't allow him "to do the things I wanted to do." Based on what you know about his life, what "things" do you suppose he had in mind?
8. According to Rose, what are the job skills that vocational education programs should teach (paragraphs 18–19)?
9. In paragraphs 22 through 24, how does Rose interpret Ken Harvey's sentence, "I just wanna be average"?
10. What kind of a person is Jack MacFarland? If you were a film director, which actor would you cast to play him?
11. What do you think was the key to MacFarland's success as a teacher?
12. The knowledge that Rose gained during his senior year enabled him "to do things in the world" and "to act as though I were living beyond the limiting boundaries of South Vermont." How does all this relate to his childhood dreams? Find lines from earlier portions of the text that support your idea.

The Way We Are Told

13. Reread Rose's description of his neighborhood (paragraphs 1–8). Which images best capture the feeling of place for you?

14. How would you characterize Rose's use of language in paragraph 18, "Students will float to the mark you set. I and the others in the vocational classes were bobbing in pretty shallow water." Can you find similar phrases in paragraphs 18 through 24 that continue the comparison?

Some Subjects for Writing

15. Rose describes several of his classmates in Voc. Ed. who attempted to cope with the "disorienting" atmosphere of their high school (paragraphs 20–24). Did you or any of your high school classmates develop special ways of coping with the system or with the teachers? Recount this experience.

16. In paragraphs 18 through 24, Rose sharply criticizes traditional vocational education programs. What kinds of programs do you think are appropriate for students who do not plan to go to college or who want to enter the job market immediately after high school?

17. Write a letter to your high school principal (you do not need to send it) explaining the ways in which the school was successful or unsuccessful in meeting your needs and those of students like you. If it seems relevant, make realistic suggestions for change.

18. Many high schools, perhaps including the one you attended, use "tracking" to place students in separate classes according to their presumed ability for academic success. Rose, as well as other educators, questions this system. Write an essay detailing the advantages or disadvantages of such a system for schools and their students. Consider the question of how and whether one can determine ahead of time if a student has the ability to succeed academically.

Living in Two Worlds

Marcus Mabry

Marcus Mabry was a junior at Stanford University when he wrote this essay for the April 1988 issue of Newsweek on Campus, *a supplement to the popular newsmagazine distributed on college campuses. As he himself tells it, he comes from a poor family in New Jersey whose lives seem far removed from the life at Stanford, one of the most affluent universities in the United States. It is this wide gap between home—African-American, poor— and college—white, mainstream, and affluent—that Mabry discusses. His double identity attests to both the mobility in American society and the tensions that it may create.*

Mabry has been bureau chief for Newsweek *in Johannesburg, and before that was their Paris correspondent. He is currently chief of correspondents, and a senior editor at* Newsweek. *He is the author of* White Bucks and Black-Eyed Peas: Coming of Age Black in White America *(1995).*

1   A round, green cardboard sign hangs from a string proclaiming, "We built a proud new feeling," the slogan of a local supermarket. It is a souvenir from one of my brother's last jobs. In addition to being a bagger, he's worked at a fast-food restaurant, a gas station, a garage and a textile factory. Now, in the icy clutches of the Northeastern winter, he is unemployed. He will soon be a father. He is 19 years old.

2   In mid-December I was at Stanford, among the palm trees and weighty chores of academe. And all I wanted to do was get out. I joined the rest of the undergrads in a chorus of excitement, singing the praises of Christmas break. No classes, no midterms, no finals. . .and no freshmen! (I'm a resident assistant.) Awesome! I was looking forward to escaping. I never gave a thought to what I was escaping to.

3   Once I got home to New Jersey, reality returned. My dreaded freshmen had been replaced by unemployed relatives; badgering professors had been replaced by hard-working single mothers, and cold classrooms by dilapidated bedrooms and kitchens. The room in which the "proud new feeling" sign hung contained the belongings of myself, my mom and my brother. But for these two weeks it was mine. They slept downstairs on couches.

4   Most students who travel between the universes of poverty and affluence during breaks experience similar conditions, as well as the guilt, the helplessness and, sometimes, the embarrassment associated with them. Our friends are willing to listen, but most of them are unable to imagine the pain of the impoverished lives that we see every six months. Each time I return home I feel further away from the realities of poverty in America and more ashamed that they are

allowed to persist. What frightens me most is not that the American socioeconomic system permits poverty to continue, but that by participating in that system I share some of the blame.

5   Last year I lived in an on-campus apartment, with a (relatively) modern bathroom, kitchen and two bedrooms. Using summer earnings, I added some expensive prints, a potted palm and some other plants, making the place look like the more-than-humble abode of a New York City Yuppie. I gave dinner parties, even a *soirée française.*

6   For my roommate, a doctor's son, this kind of life was nothing extraordinary. But my mom was struggling to provide a life for herself and my brother. In addition to working 24-hour-a-day cases as a practical nurse, she was trying to ensure that my brother would graduate from high school and have a decent life. She knew that she had to compete for his attention with drugs and other potentially dangerous things that can look attractive to a young man when he sees no better future.

7   Living in my grandmother's house this Christmas break restored all the forgotten, and the never acknowledged, guilt. I had gone to boarding school on a full scholarship since the ninth grade, so being away from poverty was not new. But my own growing affluence has increased my distance. My friends say that I should not feel guilty: what could I do substantially for my family at this age, they ask. Even though I know that education is the right thing to do, I can't help but feel, sometimes, that I have it too good. There is no reason that I deserve security and warmth, while my brother has to cope with potential unemployment and prejudice. I, too, encounter prejudice, but it is softened by my status as a student in an affluent and intellectual community.

8   More than my sense of guilt, my sense of helplessness increases each time I return home. As my success leads me further away for longer periods of time, poverty becomes harder to conceptualize and feels that much more oppressive when I visit with it. The first night of break, I lay in our bedroom, on a couch that let out into a bed that took up the whole room, except for a space heater. It was a little hard to sleep because the springs from the couch stuck through at inconvenient spots. But it would have been impossible to sleep anyway because of the groans coming from my grandmother's room next door. Only in her early 60s, she suffers from many chronic diseases and couldn't help but moan, then pray aloud, then moan, then pray aloud.

9   This wrenching of my heart was interrupted by the 3 A.M. entry of a relative who had been allowed to stay at the house despite rowdy behavior and threats toward the family in the past. As he came into the house, he slammed the door, and his heavy steps shook the second floor as he stomped into my grandmother's room to take his place, at the foot of her bed. There he slept, without blankets on a bare mattress. This was the first night. Later in the vacation, a Christmas turkey and a Christmas ham were stolen from my aunt's refrigerator on Christmas Eve. We think the thief was a relative. My mom and I decided not to exchange gifts that year because it just didn't seem festive.

10   A few days after New Year's I returned to California. The Northeast was soon hit by a blizzard. They were there, and I was here. That was the way it had to be, for now. I haven't forgotten; the ache of knowing their suffering is always there. It has to be kept deep down, or I can't find the logic in studying and partying while people, my people, are being killed by poverty. Ironically, success drives me away from those I most want to help by getting an education.

11   Somewhere in the midst of all that misery, my family has built, within me, "a proud feeling." As I travel between the two worlds it becomes harder to remember just how proud I should be—not just because of where I have come from and where I am going, but because of where they are. The fact that they survive in the world in which they live is something to be very proud of, indeed. It inspires within me a sense of tenacity and accomplishment that I hope every college graduate will someday possess.

EXERCISES

Some of the Issues

1. Describe the two worlds Mabry lives in.
2. Mabry looks forward to "escaping" from school (paragraph 2), not an unusual sentiment at the end of a semester. What is he escaping to? Considering the rest of what he tells the reader, what is the real direction of escape?
3. "Once I got home to New Jersey, reality returned" (paragraph 3). Why does Mabry refer to life in New Jersey as "reality"? Is life at Stanford not real?
4. In paragraph 8, Mabry says "More than my sense of guilt, my sense of helplessness increases each time I return home." What events does he describe that contribute to this feeling?
5. Why does Mabry say in paragraph 11 that his family built "a proud feeling" within him?

The Way We Are Told

6. Consider the order of the first two paragraphs. Why does Mabry start with his brother rather than himself?
7. In the opening and concluding paragraphs and again in paragraph 3, Mabry refers to the supermarket sign about a "proud new feeling." How does the reference change each time he uses it? How does the repetition of the phrase help him to unify the essay? Try to define the kind of pride he is talking about.
8. Account for Mabry's use of expressions like "weighty chores of academe," "awesome!" "more-than-humble abode," and "*soirée française*." From which of Mabry's two worlds do these phrases come? What does he gain by including them?

Some Subjects for Writing

9. Many people have had the experience of living in two different worlds, though perhaps not the same two as Mabry's. If you have had such an experience—in family life, as a result of a job, a vacation, or some other cause—discuss your worlds and your relation to them.

10. Most students experience some change when they go to college that distances them from their family or alters their family role. Describe a change that you have either gone through or that you see yourself going through in the future.

11. Interview three students at your college who come from different ethnic or socioeconomic backgrounds. How have their college experiences varied? Write an essay in which you draw conclusions about how students' backgrounds may affect their experiences at and their adjustments to college life and academics.

No Kinda Sense

Lisa Delpit

Lisa Delpit is executive director of the Center for Urban Education and Innovation at Florida International University in Miami. Delpit writes frequently on issues of education and is the author of the bestselling book Other People's Children: Cultural Conflict in the Classroom *(1995), which addressed the question of finding culturally relevant ways and means to educate urban students, particularly students of color.*

The book stirred a substantial amount of debate in the education community, much of it centering around Ebonics, and the question of how and whether "non-standard" English should be used in a classroom setting. Delpit was actively involved in this debate, eventually co-editing the book The Real Ebonics Debate: Power, Language and the Education of African-American Children *(1998).*

A graduate of Antioch College and Harvard University, Delpit is the recipient of the award for outstanding contribution to education from the Harvard Graduate School of Education, which hailed her as a "visionary scholar and woman of courage." She received a MacArthur "genius grant" in 1990.

The following piece is an excerpt from The Skin That We Speak: Thoughts on Language and Culture in the Classroom *(2002), which Delpit co-edited with Joanne Kilgour Dowdy. In it, Delpit reflects on the question of what happens when an educational theorist sends her own daughter, Maya, to school. Delpit examines her conflicted response to Maya's use of African-American English, and the role language can play in the development of a child's identity and self-esteem.*

1 "She be all like, 'What ch'all talkin' 'bout?' like she ain't had no kinda sense."

2 When I heard these words spoken by my eleven-year-old daughter it seemed as though a hundred conflicting scripts raced through my mind all at the same time.

3 My mother to her ten-year-old daughter: "Lisa, would you please speak correctly? Don't sound so ignorant!"

4 Me to a group of teachers a few decades later: "All people have the right to their own language. We cannot constantly correct children and expect them to continue to want to talk like us."

5 Me, arguing a point with my sister, the English teacher: "Okay, the bottom line is, if you had to choose, which would you rather your children be able to say, 'I be rich' or 'I am poor'"?

6 My sister's response, with no hesitation: "I am poor!"

7   I find myself back to the present saying, "Maya, would you please speak to me in a language I can understand!" She responds, grimacing, "Aw, mom!" And, pulling her mouth into a primly taut circle, she goes through what she said to me again, this time enunciating with exaggerated, overly precise diction, "She said, 'What are you people speaking about,' as if she didn't have any sense."

8   I've carried that interchange, and others like it, around with me daily as I work in schools and other educational settings. What was my response about?

9   There was at once a horror at the words emanating from my daughter's mouth, and a sense of immense shame at feeling that horror. What was it about her language that evoked such a strong response?

10   Maya is a middle-class, African American child whose mother is a university professor. Her first language, her mother tongue, is standard American English. This is the language she learned at home and the language she used in the predominantly White schools she attended until fifth grade. Certainly she was exposed to, and used, casual forms of what has been referred to as Black English or Ebonics, which is typical in "M-m-m g-i-r-r-r-l, that sweet potato pie is smokin'! I don't know how you do it, but that pie is callin' my name!"

11   When Maya was in the middle of the fifth grade, I became concerned with her emotional state in a small, predominantly White private school. Although the instruction was excellent, she seemed to be sinking into some sort of emotional abyss. Although her class had several African American boys, she was the only African American girl. She was often excluded by the other girls. She began to say things like, "Maybe if I were prettier I'd have more friends." When she approached me one day and requested that she be allowed to get plastic surgery because her lips were "too big," I knew I had to act. She transferred midyear to a new start-up public charter school with a population of about 98 percent African American children.

12   As she developed new friends, her self-esteem soared and once more she became the funny, creative, self-assured kid I recognized. But she also acquired new speech codes. And while my head looked on in awe at how my child could so magically acquire a second language form, at how brilliant her mind was to be able to adapt so readily to new circumstances, my heart lurched at some unexamined fear because she had done so.

13   As I sought to examine my reaction, I realized there were two questions lurking in my consciousness. The first, why did I react with such heart-pounding emotion to my daughter's words? The second, if it was that easy for my child to "pick up" at school a new language clearly not her home language, then what was preventing the millions of African American children whose home language was different from the school's from acquiring the dialect of Standard English? In attempting to answer the first, I gained insight into the second.

14   Initially, I wondered if I had been infected by that collective shame we African Americans have internalized about our very beings. Having come of age in a racist society, we double-think every aspect of our beings—are we good enough to be accepted by the white world? If it feels right, then it must be

wrong. We have to change our natural selves to just be adequate. I used to think that our biggest communal shame was our hair. We have spent millions of hours and tens of millions of dollars to acquire the "swing hair" that white American society says is beautiful. I remember when I returned home from my first year of college with an Afro and discovered that my mother, who remained publicly stalwart through most of the tragedies of her life, was overcome by tears in restaurants, gas stations, and drug stores over what her daughter "had done to herself." From discussions with friends, that story is in no way unique in our collective history. When the Oakland School Board gave birth to the "Ebonics debate" in 1996, I realized that language might be an even greater source of collective disgrace.

15   Although the purpose of the now infamous Oakland Policy was to allow teachers to gain enough knowledge about the home language of children to respect it and learn to use it to build knowledge of "standard English," African Americans in all walks of life were incensed. How dare anyone suggest that that ignorant-sounding trash was "our language," that we couldn't learn to speak properly? Do they think we're all stupid? From Kweisi Mfume, head of the NAACP, to Rev. Jesse Jackson to Maya Angelou, all expressed to sensation-crazed reporters—with no knowledge of the real policy—that what Oakland was doing was a terrible, grievous mistake. Maya Angelou spoke with quiet intensity, "I am incensed. The very idea that African American language is a language separate and apart can be very threatening because it can encourage young men and women not to learn standard English." Jesse Jackson fired out with his customary passionate oratory, "You don't have to go to school to learn to talk garbage."*

16   As the media created a mounting furor, never were African American linguistic experts consulted. For that matter, neither were the teachers who were implementing the program. Aileen Moffitt, a white teacher trained in the Standard English Proficiency Program (on which the Oakland policy was based), posted an open letter on the Internet in 1997 [members.tripod.com] in which she praised the effect of the program on her students' achievement and on her own teaching. Never was this kind of information brought to the general public. The black radio stations had a field day. One parodied the televised advertisements for a mail order reading program by presenting fictional endorsements by several characters, including a white cab driver, "Hooked on Ebonics worked for me! Since I got dat stuff, I ain't had nobody stealin' mah money no more!" And another from a professional basketball player: "Hooked on Ebonics worked for me! Ah plays basketball and ah makes millions of dollars. If you gets Hooked on Ebonics, you can be a millionaire, too, jes' like me!" One group, "Atlanta's Black Professionals," managed to get a full-page

*Year in Review, 1996, cnn.com.

ad in the *New York Times* (October 9, 1998), without paying a penny. The ad depicts a black man in an overcoat with his back facing the reader, but clearly intended to resemble Dr. Martin Luther King. The headline, "I HAS A DREAM" is written over the image. Below the picture are two paragraphs of small print, with the words, "SPEAK OUT AGAINST EBONICS" printed in large type at the end. In apparent support of the message portrayed by the ad, the Newspaper Association of America awarded it the prestigious Annual Athena Award for 1998 (www.naa.org/display/athena98/grandprize.html).*

17   Behind the humor and outrage was the shame that some group of black folks had dared to air our dirty little secret—that a lot of us didn't know how to "talk right," and some didn't much care what other folk thought about it. The even deeper secret was that even those of us who had acquired the "standard dialect" still loved and used aspects of Ebonics all the time. From the call and response rhyming speeches of Reverend Jackson, to the perfectly rendered voices of Alice Walker's, Toni Morrison's, and Zora Neale Hurston's heart-touching characters, to the jivin' d.j.'s on all the Black radio stations, to all of our mothers, brothers, and ourselves, our language has always been a part of our very souls. When we are with our own, we revel in the rhythms and cadences of connection, in the "sho nuf"s, and "what go roun' come roun' "s, and in the "ain' nothin' like the real thing"s. So what was the problem?

18   The real issue was our concern about what others would think. We worried how, after years and years of trying to prove ourselves good enough, we might again be dismissed as ignorant and unworthy by those in power, by "the white folks." We worried that our children would be viewed, and subsequently treated, as "less than"—in schools now, and in the workplace later. Consequently, those of us who reach for or attempt to maintain middle-class acceptability work hard to stamp out the public expression of the language with which we enjoy such a love/hate relationship.

19   Our fears are not unfounded. When I searched the Internet during the Ebonics debate, I found some of the most horrendous racist comments I could have imagined. Although I cannot find the exact quote, I believe I paraphrase pretty accurately what one man wrote: "Well, the niggers have finally admitted what we all knew all along. They are just too stupid to learn to speak English like the rest of us." Other comments echoed the same sentiments—if in slightly more polite words—that the language spoken by many African Americans was merely further evidence of their cognitive deficiency.

20   Recently, a friend who is a speech pathologist told me about one of her current clients. A major national consulting firm contacted my friend and asked if

---

*I was included in a group of linguists and scholars from all over the country who attempted unsuccessfully to get the *New York Times* to offer equal space for a rebuttal of the ad. The editors refused to publish either the ad or a letter to the editor.

she could work with one of their employees on language improvement. Apparently, the employee was absolutely brilliant in computer technology, but problems arose each time she was sent out on a job. The hiring company invariably called the consulting firm and requested they send someone more knowledgeable. Even after the consulting firm assured the company representatives that this woman was absolutely the best in the country for what they wanted, they still balked. The consultant in question is an African American woman whose speech patterns reflect her Southern, rural roots. None of the companies that hired her could move past her language to appreciate her expertise. Indeed, just before the consulting firm contacted the speech pathologist, one company had sent the firm a long, insulting letter listing every word the consultant had "mispronounced" and every grammatical "mistake" she had made. The consulting firm desperately wanted her expertise, but needed it to be packaged in a form that was acceptable to its clients. Perhaps we have in our country's development reached a stage in which some of the American populace is willing to see beyond skin color to access intellectual competence, but there are as yet few pockets which can "listen beyond" language form.

21   So, when my child's language reflects that of some of her peers, I feel the eyes of "the other" negatively assessing her intelligence, her competence, her potential, and yes, even her moral fiber. So, I forgive myself for my perhaps overly emotional reaction, my painful ambivalence, for I know that it is less a rejection of the language form created by my people, and more a mother's protective instinct to insure that her child's camouflage is in order when she must encounter potential enemy forces.

22   But my child has other thoughts on the matter. I ask her if she knows why I critique her language, if she understands that there will be people who judge her on the basis of the words that she speaks. She answers, without hesitation, "Well, that's their problem!" And I hear my own words spoken back to me: "It doesn't matter what other people think about you, you have to be who you are. It's their problem if they can't appreciate how wonderful you are." I try another tack. "You're right, it is their problem. But suppose they are in charge of whether you get the job you want or the college you want to attend?" "Mom," she grins back at me, "you don't have to worry about me." "And just why is that?" She answers with a cheery nonchalance, "'Cause I know how to code switch!" "Code switch," I repeat in astonishment. "Where did you hear that term?" The eleven year-old who has accompanied me to conferences and speaking engagements since she was an infant answered, "You know, I do listen to you sometimes!" as she bolts out of the door to ride her new scooter.

23   This code-switching business pushes my thinking. She is, of course, absolutely right. She and many of her friends do know how to code switch. Indeed, after further questioning, I learn that they even have names for the various codes they easily switch to and from, two of my favorites being "ghetto" and "chetto" (pronounced "ketto"). The first is probably self-explanatory, the second, they tell

me—being Southern children, after all—is "a combination of 'country' and 'ghetto'."

24   This metalinguistic facility is amazing, and brings me to my second question. How is it that we spend upwards of twelve years trying to get the standard English dialect into the heads of African American children, when my daughter, and many more like her (including some middle-class White children who go to school with African American children) acquire additional dialects almost as quickly and easily as they change sneaker brand allegiances. Clearly it is not due to a high number of "contact hours" with the new dialect. The only contact is really in school and most of school time is devoted to listening to teachers talk. No, there must be another explanation. I have come to realize that acquiring an additional code comes from identifying with the people who speak it, from connecting the language form with all that is self-affirming and esteem-building, inviting and fun. When we're relaxed and enjoying ourselves on a long-awaited vacation, many of us tend to take on aspects of the lilt of the Irish or the rhythm of Caribbean speech patterns. We do it subconsciously because we associate the language with good times.

25   Through his study of second-language acquisition, Stephen Krashen distinguishes the processes of conscious learning (rule-based instruction) from unconscious acquisition ("picking up" a language in a social setting). Krashen found unconscious acquisition to be much more effective. In further studies, however, he found that in some cases people did not easily acquire the new language form. This led him to suggest what he called an *affective filter*. The filter operates "when affective conditions are not optimal, when the student is not motivated, does not identify with the speakers of the second language, or is overanxious about his performance, . . . [creating] a mental block . . . [which] will prevent the input from reaching those parts of the brain responsible for language acquisition."* In other words, the less stress and the more fun connected to the process, the more easily it is accomplished. When she left her previous school, Maya's self-esteem was low. She considered herself an outcast, once even referring to herself as among the "dregs" of the school. When she arrived at her new school, she was embraced by the children there. She was invited into the group, appreciated for what she brought, and she found that her interests were a vital part of these children's culture. In Krashen's words, her affective filter was lowered and she subconsciously embraced the language of her new friends, as she felt embraced by them.

26   How does this differ from schools' attempts to produce standard English speakers? First of all, students rarely get to talk in classrooms. The percentage of talk by the teacher far outweighs that by all the students put together. When

---

*Stephen D. Krashen, *Principles and Practices in Second Language Acquisition* (New York: Pergamon, 1982).

students do get a chance to speak, if anyone uses what the teacher considers to be "bad English," the transgressor is told that he or she is speaking incorrectly and must "fix" the language in order to gain a response: "Say it right or don't say it at all," or an even harsher equivalent. Secondly, the standard dialect is embedded in instruction that has little connection to children's cultural lives and personal interests. Children are taught through worksheets or textbooks that make no reference to their lived experiences. Teachers seldom know much about the children's lives and communities outside of the classroom and either don't know how to or aren't willing to connect instruction to issues that matter to students, their families, and their community. Nowhere is the student's very personhood acknowledged or celebrated. Thirdly, the children whose language is considered defective are themselves viewed as defective. Spoken language has been shown to be one of the key means that teachers, like the corporate world, use to assess the intellect of individuals (Ray Rist). There are doubts in the school adults' minds about some children's cognitive competence since they don't "sound" intelligent.

27   Finally, there is little in the curriculum that apprises the students of their intellectual legacy—of the fact that people who look like them created much of the knowledge base of today's world. When instruction is stripped of children's cultural legacies, then they are forced to believe that the world and all the good things in it were created by others. This leaves students further alienated from the school and its instructional goals, and more likely to view themselves as inadequate. In short, it would appear that every feature of Krashen's affective filter is in place in the school's attempt to "teach" the standard dialect. The students don't identify with the teachers who question their intelligence or with a curriculum that ignores their existence. They have little opportunity to speak, and become overanxious about being corrected when they do. Subsequently, even when given teacher-sanctioned speaking opportunities, they opt not to. And they are not motivated to learn the new dialect because nothing presented within it connects to their own interests.

28   I, however, don't believe this need be the case. Watching Maya and her friends skillfully and easily acquire a second code, I am compelled to look for ways that their accomplishment might be replicated in a classroom context. One of the first measures that must be addressed is connected to the Ebonics debate and the Oakland policy which precipitated it. The Oakland School Board realized that as long as teachers viewed children who spoke a particular language form as deficient, then no amount of instructional modification would make much difference. Therefore, they sought to help teachers understand that no language form was better than another from a linguistic or cognitive standpoint. Further, they wanted teachers to understand that Ebonics was rule-based, just like the standard dialect, and that those rules had an historic basis in West African languages. Once teachers really internalize these facts, then it is much more difficult for them to judge their students' abilities solely on the basis of their language form. If the students feel the linguistic equivalent of Maya's feeling

the need to be prettier in order to have friends, or having to have lip reduction plastic surgery in order to be acceptable, then they will eventually reject those who make them feel inferior and unacceptable. Just as Maya's new friends made her feel beautiful, brilliant, and "part of the club," teachers have to create similar conditions for their students. If students are to acquire a second language form in school, teachers must not only see their students as nondeficient, they must understand their brilliance, and the brilliance of their home language. To quote Aileen Moffitt, the White teacher in Oakland who published the open letter on the Internet during the Ebonics mania: "[As a result of studying Ebonics through the Oakland Standard English Proficiency Project] I have also developed an appreciation of the language. Ebonics has a richness that goes beyond the obvious features (of grammar, syntax, phonology, phonetics, morphology, and semantics). There are also characteristics of the non-verbal, the gestural, the rhythmic, and the emotional quality of the speech. I may be fluent in the grammatical rules of Ebonics, but I am definitely NOT proficient in these other qualities. Yet I can appreciate and admire them for the richness of expression that they provide. Poetry in Ebonics (including Maya Angelou's) can be music to my ears".*

29   Secondly, if we are to invite children into the language of school, we must make school inviting to them. In almost every school I have visited, private conversations with children will elicit the same response: Almost no one in the school ever listens to them. There is no more certain a way to insure that people do not listen to you as to not listen to them. Furthermore, by not listening, teachers cannot know what students are concerned about, what interests them, or what is happening in their lives. Without that knowledge it is difficult to connect the curriculum to anything students find meaningful. And just how do we do that, even if we want to connect children's lives to the curriculum? After all, isn't school about what kids need to know, not what interests them? There are many possible examples, but I will proffer only a few.

30   I have spent a great deal of time in schools, most recently in one middle school that is 98 percent African American. I was often at the school during its weekly assembly, and at every assembly the teachers spent a good chunk of time berating the students for engaging in grooming during school or class time. "You don't comb your hair at school. You comb it in the morning and you leave it alone. You are not here for a beauty pageant, you are here to learn." Etc., etc., etc. I knew the kids were pretty much ignoring the lectures because even I was tired of hearing it. Furthermore, I had seen little or no change in their behavior— the hair combing continued. Of course anyone who has been anywhere near a middle school knows that there are few things of more interest to eighth-grade girls (and nowadays boys) than hair. Indeed, many African American girls will tell you that they want to be hairdressers. Although it had not apparently

*January 26, 1997, http://members.tripod.com~cdorsett/aileen.htm.

dawned on the teachers, it was clear that nothing they said was going to change the students' behavior. I had been thinking about all this for a few days when I woke up in the middle of one night with the thought, "Okay, if those kids want to do hair, we're going to do hair!"

31   A staple in most twelve-year-old African American girls' book-bag is a bottle of "Luster's Pink Oil Lotion Moisturizer." The first step was to give a bottle of this to the science teacher. His job was to develop a unit on the chemical content of the hair dressing (and other popular hair and makeup products). Students could learn the names and properties of the chemicals and what other purposes they served. They would also learn the effects of these chemicals on human beings. The teacher could further have students explore the processes for testing the products by contacting the pertinent companies. Next was a trip to the Internet, where I found the work of Dr. Gloria Gilmer. Dr. Gilmer is an ethnomathematician (one who looks at mathematics through a cultural lens), and founding President of the International Study Group on Ethnomathematics.* Dr. Gilmer created a unit on patterns and tesselations (filling up a two-dimensional space by congruent copies of a figure that do not overlap) by studying African braiding. She interviewed braiders, along with students and teachers, and then developed several classroom activities as a result of the interviews, including 1) Draw a tesselation using an octagon and square connected along a side as a fundamental shape, and 2) Have a hairstyle show featuring different tesselations. As I read Dr. Gilmer's ideas, I thought of other ideas that would use braiding as a basis for academic studies:

> Have students interview braiders as to the cultural significance of the patterns.
> Study symmetry and asymmetry in corn rows.
> Since most braiders are from Africa, interview the braiders as to what is going on in their home countries and why they decided to leave.
> Create a linguistic map of Africa based on the interviews.

I also found a Web site that traced hairstyles through history (www.queensnewyork.com/history/hair.html) and found wonderful tidbits about a subject that has apparently interested humankind since the dawn of history. For instance, Sumerian noblewomen dressed their hair in a heavy, netted chignon, rolls and plaits, powdered it with gold dust or scented yellow starch, and adorned it with gold hairpins and other ornaments; Babylonian and Assyrian men dyed their long hair and square beards black, and crimped and curled them with curling irons; and in classical Greece the upper classes used curling irons, and some women dyed their hair red (or in Athens, even blue, dusted with gold, white, or red powder). The site referred to the hairstyles of many other cultures

*www.math.buffalo.edu/mad/special/gilmer-gloria_HAIRSTYLES.html.

and time periods, and could provide the perfect entrée into the study of history for the girls in question.

32   Since so many of these girls say that they want to be hairdressers when they grow up, I decided to look into what is entailed in being a successful cosmetologist. I found that it was ideal to have a working knowledge of bookkeeping/record keeping; marketing; small business operation and entrepreneurship; chemistry; anatomy; physiology; basic psychology; public speaking; interpersonal communication; and computer operations. Furthermore, they would have to use math to formulate chemicals for different hair types; study angles so as to achieve the right amount of layers or volume; study biology, anatomy, and chemistry to obtain the knowledge to give proper facial treatments for a particular skin type or structure and to maintain proper hygiene. Finally, in order to use the various kinds of electrical apparatus needed in their trade, cosmetologists need to understand galvanic and faradic currents.

33   With some attention and thought, any teacher should be able to create a curriculum for many school-based subjects from that spectrum of topics. The object is not to lower standards or just teach what is interesting to the students, but to find the students' interests and build an academic program around them. Learning a new language form is not just a matter of teaching language. It is teaching, period. How we do it affects how children choose to talk. When students' interests are addressed in school, they are more likely to connect with the school, with the teacher, with the academic knowledge, and with the school's language form. Just as Maya found her interests reflected by her new schoolmates and subsequently adopted their language form, so students who find their interests reflected in their school would likely do the same.

34   The final aspect of my thinking on how schools can change their modus operandi to better enable students to reduce their affective filter and gain access to the standard dialect also stems from Maya's example. Just as she felt inadequate—"less than," one of the "dregs"—before leaving her former school, so many African American children feel upon entering any school. We have not fully realized the extent to which the media and general American belief systems have permeated the consciousness of African American children. Many have internalized the beliefs of the larger society that they and people who look like them are less than the intellectual norm. From media portrayals of African American criminals, to news broadcasts which ignore the positive models of African American maleness, to a focus in schools on slavery rather than on the brilliance of the African intellectual legacy, children come to believe that there is nothing in their heritage to connect to schooling and academic success.

35   Recently, a young student teacher confessed to me that she did not know what to say when an African American middle-school boy said to her, "So, Ms. Summers, they made us the slaves because we're dumb, huh?" I have spoken often of the young teenager who wondered why I was trying to teach her multiplication because "Black people don't multiply, they just add and subtract. White people multiply!" And then there was the young man whose teacher

asked him to look in a mirror and tell her what he saw. His response, "I don't see nothin'." Those of us who teach must first make our students recognize their potential brilliance. When we know the real history of Africa—the Egyptian wonders of technology and mathematics, the astronomical genius of the Mali Dogon, the libraries of Timbuktu—then we can teach our children that if they do not feel they are brilliant, then it is only because they do not know whence they came. Their not achieving is not the way things should be, but a serious break in the history of the world.

36   What happens when we do so, when we convince them that they come from brilliance, when we encourage them to understand their amazing potential? When they recognize that we believe in them, then they come to trust us, to accept us, to identify with us, and to emulate us. They will come, as Maya came, to adopt aspects of who we are, including our language. If we were to put all of these classroom techniques to work, we would create schools in which children would more readily learn the standard dialect. Moreover, we would create settings in which children would learn all that we wish to teach them. Language form, after all, is merely one small part of a desired curriculum.

37   So, how do my two initial questions intersect? What is the connection between my emotional response to Maya's new-found language and the fact that schools fare so dismally in teaching the standard dialect? I propose that the negative responses to the children's home language on the part of the adults around them insures that they will reject the school's language and everything else the school has to offer. What can it mean to a child who encounters an adult whose goal is to "Speak Out Against Ebonics"? It can only represent the desire to speak out against those who are speakers of Ebonics—to stamp out not only the child, but those from whom the child first received nurturance, from whom she first felt love, for whom she first smiled. There is a reason our first language is called our mother tongue. To speak out against the language that children bring to school means that we are speaking out against their mothers, that their mothers are not good enough to be a part of the school world. And in the African American community, talking about someone's mother is the worst form of insult!

38   Ironically, the more determined we are to rid the school of children's home language, the more determined they must become to preserve it. Since language is one of the most intimate expressions of identity, indeed, "the skin that we speak," then to reject a person's language can only feel as if we are rejecting him. But what if we really do want what is good for the African American children in our care? What if we only want to protect them from the deprecating opinions of the larger society? What if we only want to provide them with the tools needed for success in the mainstream? Despite any good intentions, if we cannot understand and even celebrate the wonders of the language these children bring with them to the school—the language forged on African soil, tempered by two hundred years of love, laughter, and survival in the harshest of

conditions—then we have little hope of convincing them that we hold their best interests at heart. If we are truly to add another language form to the repertoire of African American children, we must embrace the children, their interests, their mothers, and their language. We must treat all with love, care, and respect. We must make them feel welcomed and invited by allowing their interests, culture, and history into the classroom. We must reconnect them to their own brilliance and gain their trust so that they will learn from us. We must respect them, so that they feel connected to us. Then, and only then, might they be willing to adopt our language form as one to be added to their own.

EXERCISES

Some of the Issues

1. Summarize the "conflicting scripts" (paragraph 2) that run through Delpit's head when she hears her daughter. What roles does Delpit herself play in those scripts? What do the scripts represent?

2. Why does Delpit decide to switch Maya to a different school (paragraph 11)? What does Maya's situation at her first school tell us about the relationship between education and personal identity?

3. How does Delpit use the terms "new language" and "home language" in paragraph 13? Why are her two questions significant?

4. From what do you think the "collective" shames of hair and language stem (paragraph 14)?

5. According to Delpit, what was a common response to the Oakland policy (paragraph 15)? Why does she feel this response was misguided?

6. Why are African American's fears about Ebonics "not unfounded" (paragraph 19)?

7. How do Delpit and her daughter see the issue of language differently from one another (paragraphs 21–23)? You may want to use the Internet to look up the term "code-switching" if you're not already familiar with it.

8. Why does Delpit conclude that it's easier for students who speak standard American English to learn non-standard dialects than vice versa?

9. In paragraph 25, Delpit cites linguist Stephen Krashen, who concludes that not only is "unconscious acquisition" much more effective but that we also have an "affective filter" when it comes to learning. What does Krashen mean by this? Reflecting on your own experience, do you agree with him?

10. What, according to Delpit, are the various factors that cause student's "affective filters" to kick in (paragraphs 26–27)? What are your views on Delpit's critique?

11. How does Maya's story come to be an important case for Delpit? How does it relate to the Ebonics debate (paragraph 28)?

12. What do you think of the science assignment that Delpit asked the science teacher to develop (paragraphs 31–32) and the principles behind it? Reflecting on your own educational background, do you think the assignment is a useful one?
13. What does Delpit conclude schools and educators need to do, and how should they do it?
14. In what ways did reading Delpit's essay influence your own views about the use of non-standard English in the classroom?

The Way We Are Told

15. Delpit begins the essay with a quote. Why does she begin her essay this way? What effect do her daughter's words have?
16. Carefully examine Delpit's use of pronouns, such as her use of "our" and "we" at points where she might have used "their" or "they." Why is her choice of pronouns significant? How does her use of pronouns reflect Delpit's own sense of responsibility?

Some Subjects for Writing

17. Write a personal narrative or short story that explores your own use of language. You might focus on your own attempts to learn a second language, on a time when you felt out of place because of your own language dialect, or a time when you became conscious of the fact that you were code-switching.
18. Delpit states that "language is one of the most intimate expressions of identity." Using examples from your own experience or the experiences of those you know, and drawing from readings you have done in this class and elsewhere, write an essay exploring this idea. In what ways is language an expression of our identity? How does language influence our interactions with others and the connections, or disconnections, we might feel?
19. With the help of your instructor, conduct further research on the Ebonics debate and the Oakland policy. Using Delpit's essay and the information you gather from newspaper and magazine articles, write an essay in which you analyze the key issues and motivations underlying the debate.

Class Poem

Aurora Levins Morales

Aurora Levins Morales was born in 1954 in Indiera Baja, Puerto Rico, the daughter of an American Jewish father and a Puerto Rican mother, both Communists. She came to the United States at the age of thirteen. Much of her work focuses on the many strands that, woven together, make up her identity. This poem originally appeared in Getting Home Alive *(1986), a book of poetry she coauthored with her mother, Rosario Morales. Her latest book is* Remedies: Stories of Earth and Iron from the History of Puertoriqueñas *(1998). Her poem "Shema," about the events of September 11th, was widely shared on the Internet and has been read at rallies and religious services across the country and aired repeatedly on Pacifica Radio.*

The author currently lives in the San Francisco Bay Area where she works as a teacher, writer, and performer.

This is my poem in celebration of my middle class privilege
This is my poem to say out loud
I'm glad I had food, and shelter, and shoes,
glad I had books and travel, glad there was air and light
5   and room for poetry.

This poem is for Tita, my best friend
who played in the dirt with me
and married at eighteen (which was late) and who was a scientist
but instead she bore six children and four of them died
10   Who wanted to know the exact location of color
in the hibiscus petal, and patiently peeled away the thinnest,
most translucent layers to find it
and who works in a douche bag factory in Maricao.

This poem is for the hunger of my mother
15   discovering books at thirteen in the New York Public Library
who taught me to read when I was five
and when we lived on a coffee farm
subscribed to a mail-order library,
who read the Blackwell's catalogue
20   like a menu of delights
and when we moved from Puerto Rico to the States
we packed 100 boxes of books and 40 of everything else.

This poem is for my father's immigrant Jewish family.
For my great-grandfather Abe Sackman
25   who worked in Bridgeport making nurse's uniforms
and came home only on weekends, for years, and who painted
on bits of old wooden crates, with housepaint,
birds and flowers for his great-grandchildren
and scenes of his old-country childhood.

30   This poem celebrates my father the scientist
who left the microscope within reach,
with whom I discovered the pomegranate eye of the fruitfly,
and yes, the exact location of color in a leaf.

This poem celebrates my brother the artist
35   who began to draw when he was two,
and so my parents bought him reams of paper
and when he used them up, bought him more,
and today it's a silkscreen workshop
and posters that travel around the world,
40   and I'm glad for him and for Pop with his housepaints
and Tita staining the cement with crushed flowers
searching for color
and my mother shutting out the cries of her first-born
ten minutes at a time
45   to sketch the roofs and elevated tracks
in red-brown pastels.

This is for Norma
who died of parasites in her stomach when she was four
I remember because her mother wailed her name
50   screaming and sobbing
one whole afternoon in the road in front of our school
and for Angélica
who caught on fire while stealing kerosene for her family
and died in pain
55   because the hospital she was finally taken to
knew she was poor
and would not give her the oxygen she needed to live
but wrapped her in greased sheets
so that she suffocated.

60   This is a poem against the wrapped sheets,
against guilt.

This is a poem to say:
my choosing to suffer gives nothing
to Tita and Norma and Angélica
65   and that not to use the tongue, the self-confidence, the training
my privilege bought me
is to die again for people who are already dead
and who wanted to live.

And in case anyone here confuses the paraphernalia
70   with the thing itself
let me add that I lived with rats and termites
no carpet   no stereo   no TV
that the bath came in buckets and was heated on the stove
that I read by kerosene lamp and had Sears mail-order clothes
75   and that that has nothing to do
with the fact of my privilege.

Understand, I know exactly what I got: protection and choice
and I am through apologizing.
I am going to strip apology from my voice
80   my posture
my apartment
my clothing
my dreams
because the voice that says the only true puertorican
85   is a dead or dying puertorican
is the enemy's voice—
the voice that says
"How can you let yourself shine when Tita, when millions
are daily suffocating in those greased sheets . . ."
90   I refuse to join them there.
I will not suffocate.
I will not hold back.
Yes, I had books and food and shelter and medicine
and I intend to survive.

EXERCISES

Some of the Issues

1. Morales begins her poem by saying that she will be grateful "out loud" for her middle-class privilege. Why do you think it may have been difficult in the past for her to say some of the things she now says publicly?

2. In her poem, Morales celebrates several persons who have contributed to her life by deed or by example. How and why are they important to her?
3. In line 61 Morales mentions guilt. Why would anyone expect her to feel guilty? In Morales's view, or in your own, is there anything to be gained from feeling guilt?
4. What does Morales mean when she writes "in case anyone here confuses the paraphernalia with the thing itself" (lines 69–70)?
5. What is the "enemy's" voice in the last stanza of the poem? Why does she refuse to listen to it?
6. What are the possible meanings of the title? How many different meanings can you think of for the word *class?*

Some Subjects for Writing

7. Write an essay (or a poem) in which you celebrate some aspect of your identity. You can even begin with the line "This essay is in celebration of . . ."
8. Who has influenced you in determining the values you now hold? Write about one or more persons whose ideas or actions have played an important role in your life. Be sure to cite specific actions or to quote things people have said.
9. Morales talks about a turning point in the way she views her experience— she is through apologizing. Was there a moment in your life when you changed the way you viewed things? What was the change? How did it change you?

PART III

FAMILIES

The American family once considered the norm in the postwar generation of the 1940s and 1950s is now the minority. The traditional family in which children grow up in the same household with two biological parents who are married to each other is being replaced by an array of differently formed families. The selections in Part III call into question assumptions about what makes a "normal" family, and ask whether indeed such a thing has ever existed.

Dan Savage, a gay man raising a son, confronts his own assumptions about gender and sexual orientation as he muses on what kinds of toys and clothes his son should have. In "Where Are the Good Old Days," Stephanie Coontz challenges the notion that there ever was such a thing as a "traditional" family. Ginia Bellafante, in "Courtship Ideas of South Asians Get a U.S. Touch," examines how traditions of marriage and family change as immigrants and their children encounter American customs.

Alfred Kazin recounts the story of his eastern European immigrant family living in the tenements of New York City early in the twentieth century in "The Kitchen." His family is held together by the ceaseless work and worry of his mother. Amy Harmon traces her roots back even further and explores the impact DNA testing can have on notions of family, heritage, and identity. Finally, in a short poem by Theodore Roethke, we get a brief glimpse of a child's memory of his father, a memory filled with mixed emotions.

Role Reversal

Dan Savage

*Dan Savage is best known as the author of "Savage Love," a weekly syndi-
cated sex advice column that appears in alternative newspapers across the
country. Savage, who is openly gay, began dispensing advice in 1991 in*
The Stranger, *a Seattle alternative weekly where he remains an editor. Savage's column is known for its caustic wit combined with practical common
sense. Many of his columns have been collected into a book,* Savage Love:
Straight Answers from America's Most Popular Sex Columnist *(1997).*

*In 1998, Dan and his partner Terry adopted a son, DJ, through open
adoption, a process in which an adoptive family often maintains contact with
birth parents throughout the life of the child. Savage describes the experience of adopting DJ in his book* The Kid: What Happened After My
Boyfriend and I Decided To Go Get Pregnant: An Adoption Story
(1999). This selection, originally published in the New York Times,
*describes in a humorous way the struggles parents go through in addressing
the complex issue of gender roles in a child's upbringing. Savage is also the
author of* Skipping Towards Gomorrah: The Seven Deadly Sins and the
Pursuit of Happiness in America *(2002) and* The Commitment: Love,
Sex, Marriage and My Family *(2005).*

1   She was homeless by choice and seven months pregnant by accident when she
selected my boyfriend and me from our adoption agency's pool of pre-
screened parent wannabes. Six weeks later, the three of us sat in a recovery room
at the hospital taking turns holding our son, DJ. Some adoptive parents abuse
pronouns ("*our* son," "*my* child") to establish possession; it's as if they're saying,
"Our child now, not her child anymore." But doing an open adoption means
embracing the "most plural" definition of every plural pronoun, at least where
your child is concerned. When I say "our" son, his mother is included. We may
be DJ's full-time parents, but she is his parent, too, and stealth-hostile pronouns
can't change that.

2   But one parent was missing that day in the hospital.

3   When DJ's mom was a 19-year-old street kid, she had hooked up with Bacchus, our son's biological father, for a few weeks one summer. By the time she
realized she was pregnant, the god of wine was gone. When we adopted DJ,
Bacchus didn't know he was a father—or that his son had been adopted by a gay
couple. We were tense when Bacchus surfaced in New Orleans, appropriately
enough, shortly before DJ's first birthday, but in the end Bacchus wanted only
what we had agreed to give his mother: pictures a few times a year and the occasional visit. DJ met his biological father, whose real name is Jacob, in a hotel off

Bourbon Street a few weeks later. When Jacob's own dad, a truck driver living in Texas, called to thank us for taking "good care of my grandson," we started sending him pictures too. The gay thing didn't appear to be an issue with Jacob or his father. It never came up.

4   Since the day we brought DJ home from the hospital, people have been asking us if we're going to bring DJ up gay. The idea that two gay men, of all people, would even think it possible for a parent to select their child's sexual orientation is absurd. Didn't our own parents try that on us? Didn't it fail? Yet the question is put to us by the most unlikely people; relatives present at our long-ago coming-out dramas; friends we assumed to be more sophisticated. And as a result of hearing it so many times, my boyfriend and I have come to feel . . . scrutinized.

5   So watching my son tear into an unexpected late bonus round of Christmas gifts, I couldn't help wondering if the gay thing was coming up. Last month, Jacob's father and his father's new wife sent an enormous package filled with a toy workbench, a battery-powered toy drill, a battery-powered toy saw, a hammer and two screwdrivers. It looked to my slightly paranoid eyes like a grow-up-straight care package from some concerned grandparents. (Of course, as my boyfriend points out, there's a good chance DJ's biograndparents bought him tools because DJ's a boy.)

6   Most hip, modern, urban parents have a sense of humor about sex roles. Not us. I had given the sons of straight friends little pink dresses as baby gifts for years. "Don't assume anything," I wanted each pink dress to say. Almost all of my friends put their sons in their pink dresses once and took a picture before exchanging them. A few payback pink dresses arrived in the first weeks we had DJ, but we didn't have a single pink-dress photo-op. If we put him in a dress, my God, people might think we were trying to make him gay.

7   Walking home with DJ the day his preschool teacher painted DJ's fingernails red, I wanted to scream, "I didn't do it!" Then there was the neighbor who started calling our sons, who play together, "cute little boyfriends," much to her husband's consternation—and mine. A friend threatened to give DJ a "Future Hooters Girl" T-shirt on his birthday until I told him it would wind up at Goodwill faster than a crate of eight-track tapes.

8   So if DJ's Texan grandparents sent tools because they worry his gay dads are buying him nothing but Barbie dolls, well, their fears are misplaced. All we buy DJ are trucks and planes and cars and trains and blocks—which, as it turns out, is all DJ wants. He's a standard-issue boy, not a sissy like I was. Of course, I would love him just as much if he were into dolls, even if I have to admit it's a relief that he isn't.

9   But if he wanted dolls I would give him dolls; if he wanted to paint his nails red and wear a "Future Hooters Girl" T-shirt to school, I would let him. But I would still worry that people might think that my boyfriend and I were, as a relative put it, "pushing DJ in *that* direction." So I guess we're lucky DJ loves—adores—his new tools. He could still grow up gay; I know plenty of

adult gay men who played with toolboxes when they were boys. I never did, but I'm playing with them now. Being DJ's dad has forced me to take a belated interest in all the boy stuff I wouldn't touch when I was a kid. I spend an awful lot of time on the floor with my son these days playing with cars and trucks, blocks and Legos, hammers and saws. DJ is the kind of boy I never was, and now, thanks to my son, so am I.

EXERCISES

Some of the Issues

1. Why does Savage emphasize the pronoun "our" in paragraph 1? Why does he feel that adoptive parents often abuse the pronoun? What does he imply about the significance of language?
2. Why does Savage recount the responses of DJ's father and grandfather to their adoption?
3. What questions do people keep asking Savage and his boyfriend (paragraph 4)? Why does Savage find this question "absurd"? What does he imply when he writes: "Didn't our own parents try that on us?"
4. What kinds of conflicts does Savage feel about the kinds of gifts he and other people buy for his son? Why does he buy his friends' boys pink dresses, but then refuse to dress his son in one for a "photo-op"?
5. How does choice fit into Savage's decisions about what kinds of toys DJ plays with and the kinds of clothes he wears? Does Savage think that the toys and clothes a child is exposed to have no impact on their understanding of gender roles?
6. What does Savage's last paragraph tell us about his own interests as a child? How does this fit in with the ideas presented in the rest of the essay?
7. What does Savage appear to value in parenting? What, in the end, has the most influence on a child?

The Way We Are Told

8. Why do you think Savage tells us DJ's father's nickname is Bacchus (the Greek god of wine), before he tells us his real name, Jacob?
9. What is the tone of the essay? How does the tone affect your interpretation?
10. Savage's thesis is implied rather than stated directly. If you had to come up with a thesis for the essay, what would it be?

Some Subjects for Writing

11. Visit a local toy store or a toy section of a department store. Determine which products are marketed to girls and which ones are marketed to boys. Write an essay in which you analyze the assumptions about gender that lie

behind the marketing. You should consider not only the product itself (including what it does and what it looks like), but also the design of and the text written on the packaging of the product.

12. Interview several of your peers about the kinds of toys they played with when they were children and how they feel it affected their lives. If they have children or expect to have children, include questions about what kinds of toys they will and won't buy for them. Using specific examples from your interviews with them, write an essay in which you analyze their responses.

Where Are the Good Old Days?

Stephanie Coontz

Born in 1944, Stephanie Coontz is a writer and college professor whose work often addresses the myths and realities of the American family. In this essay, she investigates how families were structured at various points in history, and concludes that our nostalgia for the "good old days" of family life (as embodied in the 1950s ideal of two parents, married to each other, supporting their children comfortably on one income) is nostalgia based on an imagined reality, not an actual one. Coontz points out that the 1950s were perhaps the most atypical decade in terms of family structure, and that throughout American history, families have existed in an infinite variety of configurations. If we look at the big picture of the American family, we find an enormous variety of experiences, and to presume the prevalence of one kind of "ideal" family is to long for "good old days" that indeed never were.

Coontz is the author of several books, including The Way We Never Were: American Families and the Nostalgia Trap *(1992),* The Way We Really Are: Coming to Terms with America's Changing Families *(1997), and* Marriage: A History *(2005), all of which address in greater detail some of the ideas in this essay. Coontz teaches history and family studies at Evergreen State College in Olympia, Washington.*

1   The American family is under siege. To listen to the rhetoric of recent months, we have all fallen down on the job. We're selfish; too preoccupied with our own gratification to raise our children properly. We are ungrateful; we want a handout, not a hand.

2   If only we'd buckle down, stay on the straight and narrow, keep our feet on the ground, our shoulder to the wheel, our eye on the ball, our nose to the grindstone. Then everything would be all right, just as it was in the family-friendly '50s, when we could settle down in front of the television after an honest day's work and see our lives reflected in shows like Ozzie and Harriet and Father Knows Best.

3   But American families have been under siege more often than not during the past 300 years. Moreover, they have always been diverse, both in structure and ethnicity. No family type has been able to protect its members from the roller-coaster rides of economic setbacks or social change. Changes that improved the lives and fortunes of one family type or individual often resulted in losses for another.

4   A man employed in the auto industry, for example, would have been better off financially in the 1950s than now, but his retired parents would be better off today. If he had a strong taste for power, he might prefer Colonial times, when a man was the undisputed monarch of the household and any disobedience by wife, child, or servant was punishable by whipping. But woe betide that man if he wasn't born to property. In those days, men without estates could be told what to wear, where to live, and whom to associate with.

5   His wife, on the other hand, might have been happier in the 1850s, when she might have afforded two or three servants. We can be pretty sure, though, that the black or Irish servants of that day would not have found the times so agreeable. And today's children, even those scarred by divorce, might well want to stay put rather than live in the late 19th century, when nearly half of them died before they reached their late teens.

A HISTORY OF TRADEOFFS

6   These kinds of tradeoffs have characterized American family life from the beginning. Several distinctly different types of families already coexisted in Colonial times: On the East Coast, the Iroquois lived in longhouses with large extended families. Small families were more common among the nomadic Indian groups, where marital separation, though frequent, caused no social stigma or loss of access to group resources. African-American slaves, whose nuclear families had been torn apart, built extended family networks through ritual coparenting, the adoption of orphans, and complex naming patterns designed to preserve links among families across space and time.

7   White Colonial families were also diverse: High death rates meant that a majority spent some time in a stepfamily. Even in intact families, membership ebbed and flowed; many children left their parents' home well before puberty to work as servants or apprentices to other households. Colonial family values didn't sentimentalize childhood. Mothers were far less involved in caring for their children than modern working women, typically delegating the task to servants or older siblings. Children living away from home usually wrote to their fathers, sometimes adding a postscript asking him to "give my regards to my mother, your wife."

A REVOLUTION OF SORTS

8   Patriarchal authority started to collapse at the beginning of the Revolutionary War: The rate of premarital conception soared and children began to marry out of birth order. Small family farms and shops flourished and, as in Colonial days, a wife's work was valued as highly as her husband's. The revolutionary ferment also produced the first stirrings of feminism and civil rights. A popular 1773

Massachusetts almanac declared: "Then equal Laws let custom find, and neither Sex oppress: More Freedom give to Womankind or to Mankind give less." New Jersey women had the right to vote after the Revolution. In several states slaves won their freedom when they sued, citing the Declaration of Independence.

9   But commercial progress undermined these movements. The spread of international trade networks and the invention of the cotton gin in 1793 increased slavery's profits. Ironically, when revolutionary commitment to basic human equality went head-to-head with economic dependence on slavery, the result was an increase in racism: Apologists now justified slavery on the grounds that blacks were less than human. This attitude spilled over to free blacks, who gradually lost both their foothold in the artisan trades and the legal rights they'd enjoyed in early Colonial times. The subsequent deterioration in their status worked to the advantage of Irish immigrants, previously considered nonwhite and an immoral underclass.

10   Feminist ideals also faded as industrialization and wage labor took work away from the small family farms and businesses, excluding middle-class wives from their former economic partnerships. For the first time, men became known as breadwinners. By the post-Civil War era of 1870 through 1890, the participation of married women in the labor force was at an all-time low; social commentators labeled those wives who took part in political or economic life sexual degenerates or "semi-hermaphrodites."

WOMEN LOSE; CHILDREN LOSE MORE

11 As women left the workforce children entered it by the thousands, often laboring in abysmal conditions up to ten hours a day. In the North, they worked in factories or tenement workshops. As late as 1900, 120,000 children worked in Pennsylvania's mines and factories. In the South, states passed "apprentice" laws binding black children out as unpaid laborers, often under the pretext that their parents neglected them. Plantation owners (whose wives and daughters encased themselves in corsets and grew their fingernails long) accused their former female slaves of "loaferism" when they resisted field labor in order to stay closer to home with their children.

12   So for every 19th-century middle-class family that was able to nurture its women and children comfortably inside the family circle, there was an Irish or German girl scrubbing floors, a Welsh boy mining coal, a black girl doing laundry, a black mother and child picking cotton, and a Jewish or Italian daughter making dresses, cigars, or artificial flowers in a sweatshop.

13   Meanwhile, self-styled "child-saver" charity workers, whose definition of an unfit parent had more to do with religion, ethnicity, or poverty than behavior, removed other children from their families. They sent these "orphans" to live with Western farmers who needed extra hands—or merely dumped them in a farm town with a dollar and an earnest lecture about escaping the evils of city life.

THE OUTER FAMILY CIRCLE

14   Even in the comfortable middle-class households of the late 19th century, norms and values were far different from those we ascribe to "traditional" families. Many households took in boarders, lodgers, or unmarried relatives. The nuclear family wasn't the primary focus of emotional life. The Victorian insistence on separate spheres for men and women made male–female relations extremely stilted, so women commonly turned to other women for their most intimate relationships. A woman's diary would rhapsodize for pages about a female friend, explaining how they carved their initials on a tree, and then remark, "Accepted the marriage proposal of Mr. R. last night" without further comment. Romantic friendships were also common among young middle-class men, who often recorded that they missed sleeping with a college roommate and laying an arm across his bosom. No one considered such relationships a sign of homosexuality; indeed, the term wasn't even invented until the late 19th century.

15   Not that 19th-century Americans were asexual: By midcentury New York City had one prostitute for every 64 men; the mayor of Savannah estimated his city had one for every 39. Perhaps prostitution's spread was inevitable at a time when the middle class referred to the "white meat" and "dark meat" of chicken to spare ladies the embarrassment of hearing the terms "breast" or "thigh."

THE ADVENT OF THE COUPLE

16   The early 20th century brought more changes. Now the emotional focus shifted to the husband and wife. World War I combined with a resurgence of feminism to hasten the collapse of Victorian values, but we can't underestimate the role the emergence of a mass consumer market played: Advertisers quickly found that romance and sexual titillation worked wonders for the bottom line.

17   Marriage experts and the clergy, concerned that longer lifespans would put a strain on marriages, denounced same-sex friendships as competitors to love; people were expected to direct all their emotional, altruistic and sensual impulses into marriage. While this brought new intimacy and sexual satisfaction to married life, it also introduced two trends that disturbed observers. One was an increased dissatisfaction with what used to be considered adequate relationships. Great expectations, social historian Elaine Tyler May points out in her book of the same name, could generate great disappointments. It's no surprise that the U. S. has had both the highest consumption of romance novels and the highest divorce rates in the world since the early part of the 20th century.

18   The second consequence of this new cult of married bliss was the emergence of an independent and increasingly sexualized youth culture. In the late 19th century, middle-class courtship revolved around the institution of "calling." A boy was invited to call by the girl or her parents. It was as inappropriate

then for a boy to hint he'd like to be asked over as it was in the 1950s for a girl to hint she'd like to be asked out. By the mid-1920s, calling had been almost totally replaced by dating, which took young people away from parental control but made a girl far more dependent on the boy's initiative. Parents especially worried about the moral dangers the automobile posed—and with reason: A middle-class boy was increasingly likely to have his first sexual encounter with a girlfriend rather than a prostitute.

19   The early part of the century brought a different set of changes to America's working class. In the 1920s, for the first time, a majority of children were born to male-breadwinner, female-homemaker families. Child labor laws and the spread of mass education allowed more parents to keep their children out of the workforce. Numerous immigrant families, however, continued to pull their offspring out of school so they could help support the family, often arousing intense generational conflicts. African-American families kept their children in school longer than other families in those groups, but their wives were much more likely to work outside the home.

THERE GOES THE FAMILY

20   In all sectors of society, these changes created a sense of foreboding. Is Marriage on the Skids? asked one magazine article of the times; What Is the Family Still Good For? fretted another. Popular commentators harkened back to the "good old days," bemoaning the sexual revolution, the fragility of nuclear-family ties, the cult of youthful romance, and the threat of the "emancipated woman."

21   The stock market crash, the Great Depression, and the advent of World War II moved such fears to the back burner. During the '30s and '40s, family trends fluctuated from one extreme to another. Depression hardship—contrary to its television portrayal on The Waltons—usually failed to make family and community life stronger. Divorce rates fell, but desertion and domestic violence rose sharply; economic stress often translated into punitive parenting that left children with emotional scars still apparent to social researchers decades later. Murder rates in the '30s were as high as in the 1980s; rates of marriages and births plummeted.

22   WWII started a marriage boom, but by 1946 the number of divorces was double that in 1941. This time the social commentators blamed working women, interfering in-laws and, above all, inadequate mothers. In 1946, psychiatrist Edward Strecker published *Their Mothers' Sons: The Psychiatrist Examines an American Problem*, which argued that women who were old-fashioned "moms" instead of modern "mothers" were emasculating American boys.

23   Moms, he said disapprovingly, were immature and unstable and sought emotional recompense for the disappointments of their own lives. They took care of aging parents and tried to exert too much control over their children. Mothers, on the other hand, put their parents in nursing homes and derived all

their satisfaction from the nuclear family while cheerfully urging independence on their children. Without motherhood, said the experts, a woman's life meant nothing. Too much mothering, though, would destroy her own marriage and her son's life. These new values put women in an emotional doublebind, and it's hardly surprising that tranquilizers, which came on the scene in the '50s, were marketed and prescribed almost exclusively to housewives.

THE '50S: PARADISE LOST?

24   Such were the economic and cultural ups and downs that created the 1950s. If that single decade had actually represented the "tradition" it would be reasonable to argue that the family has indeed collapsed. By the mid 1950s, the age of marriage and parenthood had dropped dramatically, divorce rates bottomed out and the birthrate, one sociologist has recently noted, "approached that of India." The proportion of children in Ozzie-and-Harriet type families reached an all-time high of 60 percent.

25   Today, in contrast, a majority of mothers, including those with preschool children, work outside the home. Fifty percent of children live with both biological parents, almost one quarter live with single parents and more than 21 percent are in stepfamilies. Three quarters of today's 18–24-year-olds have never been married, while almost 50 percent of all first marriages—and 60 percent of remarriages—will end in divorce. Married couples wait longer to bear children and have fewer of them. For the first time there are more married couples without children than with them. Less than one quarter of contemporary marriages are supported by one wage earner.

26   Taking the 1950s as the traditional norm, however, overstates both the novelty of modern family life and the continuity of tradition. The 1950s was the most atypical decade in the entire history of American marriage and family life. In some ways, today's families are closer to older patterns than were '50s families. The median age at first marriage today is about the same as it was at the beginning of the century, while the proportion of never-married people is actually lower. The number of women who are coproviders and the proportion of children living in stepfamilies are both closer to that of Colonial days than the 1950s. Even the ethnic diversity among modern families is closer to the patterns of the early part of this century than to the demographics of the 1950s. And the time a modern working mother devotes to childcare is higher than in Colonial or Revolutionary days.

27   The 1950s family, in other words, was not at all traditional; nor was it always idyllic. Though many people found satisfactions in family life during that period, we now know the experiences of many groups and individuals were denied. Problems such as alcoholism, battering, and incest were swept under the rug. So was discrimination against ethnic groups, political dissidents, women, elders, gays, lesbians, religious minorities and the handicapped. Rates of divorce

and unwed motherhood were low, but that did not prevent 30 percent of American children from living in poverty, a higher figure than at present.

IT'S ALL RELATIVE

28   Why then, do many people remember the 1950s as so much easier than today? One reason is that after the hardships of the Depression and WWII, things were improving on many fronts. Though poverty rates were higher than today, they were falling. Economic inequality was also decreasing. The teenage birthrate was almost twice as high in 1957 as today, but most young men could afford to marry. Violence against African-Americans was appallingly widespread, yet many blacks got jobs in the expanding manufacturing industries and for the first time found an alternative to Southern agriculture's peonage.

29   What we forget when politicians tell us we should revive the 1950s family is that the social stability of that period was due less to its distinctive family forms than to its unique socioeconomic and political climate. High rates of unionization, heavy corporate investment in manufacturing, and generous government assistance in the form of public-works projects, veterans' benefits, student loans and housing subsidies gave young families a tremendous jump start, created predictable paths out of poverty, and led to unprecedented increases in real wages. By the time the "traditional male breadwinner" reached age 30, in both the 1950s and '60s, he could pay the principal and interest on a median-priced home on only 15–18 percent of his income. Social Security promised a much-needed safety net for the elderly, formerly the poorest segment of the population. These economic carrots combined with the sticks of McCarthyism and segregation to keep social dissent on the back burner.

THE NEW TRENDS

30   Because the '60s were a time of social protest, many people forget that families still made economic gains throughout the decade. Older workers and homeowners continued to build security for their retirement years. The postwar boom and government subsidies cut child poverty in half from 1949 to 1959. It was halved again, to its lowest levels ever, from 1959 to 1969. The high point of health and nutrition for poor children came in 1970, a period that coincided with the peak years of the Great Society, not the high point of the '50s family.

31   Since 1973, however, a new phase has emerged. Some things have continued to improve: High school graduation rates are at an all-time high; minority test scores rose steadily from 1970 to 1990; poverty rates among the elderly have continued to fall while life expectancy has risen.

32   Other trends show mixed results: The easy availability of divorce has freed individuals from oppressive or even abusive marriages, but many divorces have caused emotional and economic suffering for both children and adults. Women

have found new satisfaction at work, and there's considerable evidence that children can benefit from having a working mother, but the failure of businesses—and some husbands—to adjust to working mothers' needs has caused much family stress and discord.

33   In still other areas, the news is quite bleak. Children have now replaced seniors as the poorest segment of the population; the depth and concentration of child poverty has increased over the past 20 years so it's now at 1965 levels. Many of the gains ethnic groups made in the 1960s and '70s have been eroded.

34   History suggests that most of these setbacks originate in social and economic forces rather than in the collapse of some largely mythical traditional family. Perhaps the most powerful of these sources is the breakdown of America's implicit postwar wage bargain with the working class, where corporations ensured labor stability by increasing employment, rewarding increased productivity with higher wages, and investing in jobs and community infrastructure. At the same time, the federal government subsidized home ownership and higher education.

35   Since 1973, however, real wages have fallen for most families. It increasingly requires the work of two earners to achieve the modest upward mobility one could provide in the 1950s and '60s. Unemployment rates have risen steadily as corporations have abandoned the communities that grew up around them, seeking cheap labor overseas or in nonunionized sectors of the South. Involuntary part-time work has soared. As *Time* magazine noted in 1993, the predictable job ladders of the '50s and '60s have been sawed off: "Companies are portable, workers are throwaway." A different article in the same issue found, "Long-term commitments . . . are anathema to the modern corporation."

36   During the 1980s the gap between the rich and middle-class widened in 46 states, and each year since 1986 has set a new postwar record for the gap between rich and poor. In 1980 a CEO earned 30 to 40 times as much as the average worker, by 1994 he earned 187 times as much. Meanwhile, the real wages of a young male high school graduate are lower today than those earned by his 1963 counterpart.

37   These economic changes are not driven by the rise in divorce and unwed motherhood. Decaying wage and job structures—not changing family structures—have caused the overwhelming bulk of income redistribution. And contrary to what has been called a new bipartisan consensus, marriage is not the solution to poverty. According to sociologist Donald J. Hernandez, Ph.D., formerly with the U. S. Census Bureau, even if every child in America were reunited with both biological parents, two thirds of those who are poor today would still be poor.

OUR UNCERTAIN FUTURE

38   History's lessons are both positive and negative. We can take comfort from the fact that American families have always been in flux and that a wide variety of family forms and values have worked well for different groups at different times.

There's no reason to assume that recent changes are entirely destructive. Families have always been vulnerable to rapid economic change and have always needed economic and emotional support from beyond their own small boundaries. Our challenge is to grapple with the sweeping transformations we're currently undergoing. History demonstrates it's not as simple as returning to one or another family form from the past. Though there are many precedents for successfully reorganizing family life, there are no clear answers to the issues facing us as we enter the 21st century.

EXERCISES

Some of the Issues

1. Does Coontz believe most of what she writes in the first two paragraphs? If not, who does she assume does believe it?
2. What does Coontz mean by the word "rhetoric" in the first paragraph? Where does the issue of rhetoric come up again in other parts of the essay?
3. According to Coontz, what decade do people think of when they think of the ideal family? Do you think this is still true for your generation?
4. What does Coontz mean by the statement, "No family type has been able to protect its members from the roller-coaster rides of economic setbacks and social change" (paragraph 3)? What does the statement indicate about what Coontz believes to be the relationship between social forces and the more intimate lives of families?
5. According to Coontz, what impact did the American Revolution have on the American family? How and why did the ideals of the revolution fade?
6. When and why did men become known as breadwinners (paragraph 10)?
7. What group replaced women in the workforce in the late 1800s? What kinds of work did they do?
8. How does Coontz characterize the Victorian family and intimate relationships during Victorian times (paragraph 14)? When did Victorian values start to change and why?
9. What effect did the consumer market have on marriage and romantic relationships in the twentieth century?
10. Why is it ironic that the family of the 1950s is considered to be the norm?
11. What does Coontz feel is our challenge today? How does this challenge relate to her thesis?
12. How would you characterize the "ideal" family if such a thing exists? Did the Coontz essay in any way change your perception of the family? If so, how?
13. What similarities do you see between today's family and Coontz's descriptions of the family in earlier periods? Give specific examples to back up your answer.

14. In several parts of this essay, Coontz points to the fact that depictions of the "ideal" of the American family leave out large segments of the actual population. Who is left out at various times? Are there groups that seem to be always left out?

15. Find articles, photos, and advertisements that describe or show families and bring your examples to class. In groups of three or four, compare your examples and consider the messages they convey and underlying assumptions they make about the contemporary family. Present your conclusions to the rest of the class.

The Way We Are Told

16. How does Coontz set up her thesis statement? What is she arguing against?

17. Coontz deliberately employs several clichés in paragraph 2. What purpose does this device serve?

18. Coontz often uses two techniques, compare and contrast and cause and effect, to back up her thesis. Find examples of both.

19. Consider the title of the essay. Why do you think Coontz chose this as a title?

Some Subjects for Writing

20. Interview friends and relatives, including at least one person from a generation other than your own, about the specifics of family life during their childhood. Does their experience—and your own—correspond with Coontz's depiction of family life? Using specific examples, write an essay in which you present and analyze your findings.

21. Coontz's analysis of the history of the American family covers a large amount of ground in a relatively short essay, providing only what she sees as the relevant facts about specific eras in order to back up her points. With the help of your instructor, write a research paper that explores the family during one era in more depth. Develop your thesis based on what you determine to be the key factors that influenced the family at that time.

Courtship Ideas of South Asians Get a U.S. Touch

Ginia Bellafante

Ginia Bellafante is a staff writer for the New York Times, *where this article originally appeared on August 23, 2005. In it, Bellafante describes ways in which South Asian families in the United States have adapted the ritual of finding a mate—something that was once determined and arranged almost entirely by a prospective couple's parents—to the changing technology and mores of American society.*

Though the author of this essay focuses on South Asian families, some form of arranged marriage still remains the norm among many religious, cultural, and ethnic groups, especially those that place a high value on maintaining cultural and religious traditions that might easily be lost as they move from tightly knit communities in their homelands to more liberal, foreign, and dispersed environments.

1   At 10 A.M. one Saturday in July, a few weeks after he finished his medical residency at Brown University, Ronak Shah married Kunal Patel, another doctor, in a union that embraced every ritual of the Hindu nuptial script.

2   Dr. Shah arrived at the Hanover Marriott in Whippany, N.J., by horse and carriage. He wore a traditional sherwani. And he greeted, before all others, his bride's mother, in a gesture that signified the importance of parental engineering in Indian marriage.

3   But for Dr. Shah and Dr. Patel, both 28, and thousands of young Indians raised in the United States, that engineering is undergoing a change. The venerable South Asian tradition of arranged marriages has taken on an American reinvention. Dr. Patel's mother and father had a hand in their daughter's selection. They were in touch with friends, cousins and cousins of cousins for suggestions about whom she should marry. But Dr. Patel was free to reject them all.

4   Only over dinner with Dr. Shah—her ninth suitor—did she finally begin a courtship that was fueled as much by chemical attraction as by familial interest. Her marriage, as some young Indians refer to it, was "love-cum-arranged."

5   Less than a decade ago, the decision about whom a South Asian woman here might marry was still often left to her parents, the prospective bride's individual preference for tall dentists or contemplative artists notwithstanding. But recently, purely arranged marriage has evolved into a new culture of what might be called "assisted" marriage, in which parents are free to arrange all

they like—allowing their sons and daughters choice among nominees screened for caste, lineage and geography, among other measures—and giving the children veto power.

6   These young people may have come of age in an America of "Moonstruck" and "Dawson's Creek," but in many cases they have not completely accepted the Western model of romantic attachment. Indeed, some of the impetus for assisted marriage is coming from young people themselves—men and women who have delayed marriage into their late 20's and early 30's, said Ayesha Hakki, the editor of Bibi, a South Asian bridal and fashion magazine based in New Jersey.

7   "That has been the most remarkable trend," Ms. Hakki said, citing the example of a male acquaintance, who, after dating on his own, turned to his parents for guidance.

8   As Madhulika Khandelwal, a historian who has studied Indians here, said, "Young people don't want to make individual decisions alone."

9   The Patel–Shah union was instigated by the chance encounter two years ago of Dr. Shah's mother and Dr. Patel's at Famous Pizza, a restaurant in Queens that is favored by Indian immigrants. Friends from the town of Nadiad in India, the two had not seen each other in 30 years. Their conversation moved to the subject of their still-single children.

10   In large part, Ms. Khandelwal said, the transition from formally arranged marriage reflects social changes in India itself, where assisted marriage is now common among the educated, urban middle class. That is because, she said, there are fewer extended-family living arrangements and more women pursuing higher education.

11   The purpose of assisted marriage here is not simply to preserve Indian cultural identity, but more pointedly to maintain class, religious and regional identities in a place where they might easily be diffused, those who have studied the Indian diaspora say. When Mona Mahajan, a recent graduate of Harvard Business School from New Jersey, married an Indian she met on her own, she was the first in five generations of her family not to have wed a Punjabi.

12   Arranged and assisted marriage have left Indians with the lowest rate of intermarriage of any major immigrant group in the United States. Among South Asian men and women here in their 20's and 30's, the vast majority of whom are foreign born, fewer than 10 percent marry outside their ethnic group, according to an analysis of the Census Bureau's 2003 American Community Survey conducted for this article. "In the beginning I was pretty against all of this," Dr. Patel said of this newer approach. "Growing up here, you feel that you're supposed to fall in love, but once you figure out that everyone goes on blind dates it doesn't feel quite as strange."

13   Among Indian parents here who are traditionally inclined, many begin to seek husbands when their daughters are 22 or 23, but the search may be forestalled if the woman is pursuing a graduate degree, Indian women report. Men begin looking for wives with their families' help at about age 26; within more liberal households, children often marry those they meet on their own.

14   Preceding any planned meeting is the exchange of the all important "bio-data" between families, the term used for a portfolio with the potential bride or groom's profile.

15   The embrace of more traditional habits is apparent in other ways. Weddings are often elaborate and last three or four days. Families of the betrothed often still consult a Hindu astrologer who schedules wedding ceremonies according to the stars. When Anamika Tavathia, 24, was engaged to a young Indian she met in college, his family visited hers to propose on his behalf and the priest determined they should marry on June 26 of this year between 10:30 and 11 A.M.

16   This fall is expected to be an unusually busy wedding season in Indian communities, because many couples postponed weddings last year when many days were deemed inauspicious.

17   Royal Albert Palace, a five-year-old catering facility in Woodbridge, N.J., with a 21-foot statue of a former deputy prime minister of India out front, has become the locus for Indian weddings, and it was there, at a wedding last month, that two young women discussed assisted marriage.

18   "My dad's parents didn't even see each other until the day they were married," said Kesha Patel, 25, who came to the United States as a child and is looking for someone, with her family's help. "So when I think about that, I'm grateful for the system we have."

19   Kesha Patel has taken trips to India to meet prospective partners, and her family has arranged for her to meet men here, as well.

20   "Sometimes you'll get the bio-data and it will be great, and then when you meet the person, you're disappointed," she said. "My parents won't understand, they'll say, 'But he's from a good family, he's a doctor, he's a doctor.' And I'll say, 'But he's short.'"

21   Alienating one's parents is anathema to Indian culture, and most young people wish to avoid doing so through marriage. Four years ago, Preet Singh, a 28-year-old teacher in Chicago, fell in love with a woman seven years his senior and not a Sikh. He hoped to marry her and live with her in his parents' home.

22   "My mother might have accepted the marriage but she would not have lived with us," he said. "It was one of the nastiest breakups of all because that person helped me mature into a man." Not long ago, Mr. Singh's sisters posted his profile on an Indian matrimonial Web site, and he will marry this fall.

23   Part of his parents' displeasure with the previous relationship was the fact that he was dating at all. Though a Bibi magazine survey conducted three years ago revealed that the majority of married men and women questioned had had sex before marriage, dating, as Mr. Singh put it, "does not exist in our culture." This view leaves parents encouraging children to resolve the marriage question quickly.

24   The parents of Leena Singh waited until she was older than 25 and had earned a master's degree in mathematics and an M.B.A. to find a husband. Ms. Singh's father eventually found someone to her liking, Sanjeev Tavathia, a young man studying engineering in Iowa. They met in the company of relatives,

then went out alone. Back in San Diego, where she was living with her parents, she called Mr. Tavathia and told him she was ready for marriage. He said he was 90 percent certain. They married several months later.

25   "From the beginning, I felt there was a physical chemistry," Ms. Singh said, "but it took years to develop a mature bond, and I guess you could call that love."

26   Despite its groundings in pragmatism, assisted marriage is spoken about among some young Indians in highly romanticized terms—implicit in it is the cinematic idea that immediate attraction should result in an eternity spent together.

27   Kesha Patel's sister married a man to whom she was introduced through her aunts. She decided to marry him the day after they met. "A lot of my friends," Kesha Patel said, her eyes gleaming, "tell me you know in an instant."

EXERCISES

Some of the Issues

1. How does Bellafante describe the changes in the tradition of arranged marriages among South Asians? What makes them "love-cum-arranged" marriages?
2. According to Bellafante, what are some of the factors that have spurred these changes (paragraphs 6–8)?
3. Why are the changes in attitude in India primarily affecting the educated, urban middle class (paragraph 10)?
4. Are the changes in the United States happening for the same reasons as they are in India?
5. How does Kesha Patel's attitude differ from that of her parents?
6. Why does Bellafante refer to the attitude toward arranged marriage among young Indians as both romantic and pragmatic (paragraph 26)? Do you agree with her definitions of pragmatism and romanticism?

The Way We Are Told

7. This piece was written for a daily newspaper, the *New York Times*. What about its style indicates that it is a piece of journalism rather than an academic text or a magazine piece?
8. What kinds of sources does Bellafante use in her article? Do you find the article and the evidence convincing?

Some Subjects for Writing

9. What was your initial reaction to his piece? Taking into consideration your own view of marriage, and those of your friends and family, analyze both the benefits and the drawbacks of arranged marriages.

10. Most likely, some or many of your attitudes toward social customs differ from those of your parents or your grandparents. These may include attitudes toward marriage, education, dress, or religion. Choose one area in which your own attitude is different from those of your parents and write an essay in which you analyze those differences. Consider what factors, beyond age difference, may have influenced these differences.

*11. Read Stephanie Coontz's piece "Where Are the Good Old Days." Taking into consideration both Coontz's cultural history of family and Bellafante's account of the changing trends in arranged marriages, write an essay in which you analyze the cultural purpose of marriage. Use specific examples from both the text and from your own experiences to back up your points.

The Kitchen

Alfred Kazin

Alfred Kazin (1915–98) was born in Brooklyn, New York, to eastern European parents. He was a scholar, critic, and cultural historian who taught at several universities, last at the City University of New York. He held several distinguished fellowships and was a member of the American Academy of Arts and Sciences. His books include On Native Grounds *(1942),* The Inmost Leaf *(1955),* Starting Out in the Thirties *(1965),* New York Jew *(1978), and* An American Procession *(1984). Selections from Kazin's journals were published as* A Lifetime Burning in Every Moment: From the Journals of Alfred Kazin *(1996).*

In this selection from A Walker in the City *(1957), Kazin describes the setting in which he grew up. It was not unusual for its time and place: a tenement district in a large American city, peopled with immigrants from eastern Europe, working hard, struggling for a life for themselves and, more importantly, for their children.*

The large-scale immigration that brought as many as one million new inhabitants annually from Europe to America lasted from the 1880s to the First World War. The majority of the immigrants in those years came from eastern, southern, and central Europe. They included large numbers of Jewish families like Kazin's, escaping not only the stifling poverty of their regions but also the outright persecution to which they were subjected in Czarist Russia.

1 In Brownsville tenements the kitchen is always the largest room and the center of the household. As a child I felt we lived in a kitchen to which four other rooms were annexed. My mother, a "home" dressmaker, had her workshop in the kitchen. She told me once that she had begun dressmaking in Poland at thirteen; as far back as I can remember, she was always making dresses for the local women. She had an innate sense of design, a quick eye for all the subtleties in the latest fashions, even when she despised them, and great boldness. For three or four dollars she would study the fashion magazines with a customer, go with the customer to the remnants store on Belmont Avenue to pick out the material, argue the owner down—all remnants stores, for some reason, were supposed to be shady, as if the owners dealt in stolen goods—and then for days would patiently fit and baste and sew and fit again. Our apartment was always full of women in their housedresses sitting around the kitchen table waiting for a fitting. My little bedroom next to the kitchen was the fitting room. The sewing machine, an old nut-brown Singer with golden scrolls painted along the black arm and engraved along the two tiers of little drawers massed with needles and

thread on each side of the treadle, stood next to the window and the great coal-black stove which up to my last year in college was our main source of heat. By December the two outer bedrooms were closed off, and used to chill bottles of milk and cream, cold borscht and jellied calves' feet.

2   The kitchen held our lives together. My mother worked in it all day long, we ate in it almost all meals except the Passover *seder*, I did my homework and first writing at the kitchen table, and in winter I often had a bed made up for me on three kitchen chairs near the stove. On the wall just over the table hung a long horizontal mirror that sloped to a ship's prow at each end and was lined in cherry wood. It took up the whole wall, and drew every object in the kitchen to itself. The walls were a fiercely stippled whitewash, so often rewhitened by my father in slack seasons that the paint looked as if it had been squeezed and cracked into the walls. A large electric bulb hung down the center of the kitchen at the end of a chain that had been hooked into the ceiling; the old gas ring and key still jutted out of the wall like antlers. In the corner next to the toilet was the sink at which we washed, and the square tub in which my mother did our clothes. Above it, tacked to the shelf on which were pleasantly ranged square, blue bordered white sugar and spice jars, hung calendars from the Public National Bank on Pitkin Avenue and the Minsker Progressive Branch of the Workman's Circle; receipts for the payment of insurance premiums, and household bills on a spindle; two little boxes engraved with Hebrew letters. One of these was for the poor, the other to buy back the Land of Israel. Each spring a bearded little man would suddenly appear in our kitchen, salute us with a hurried Hebrew blessing, empty the boxes (sometimes with a sidelong look of disdain if they were not full), hurriedly bless us again for remembering our less fortunate Jewish brothers and sisters, and so take his departure until the next spring, after vainly trying to persuade my mother to take still another box. We did occasionally remember to drop coins in the boxes, but this was usually only on the dreaded morning of "mid-terms" and final examinations, because my mother thought it would bring me luck. She was extremely superstitious, but embarrassed about it, and always laughed at herself whenever, on the morning of an examination, she counseled me to leave the house on my right foot. "I know it's silly," her smile seemed to say, "but what harm can it do? It may calm God down."

3   The kitchen gave a special character to our lives; my mother's character. All my memories of that kitchen are dominated by the nearness of my mother sitting all day long at her sewing machine, by the clacking of the treadle against the linoleum floor, by the patient twist of her right shoulder as she automatically pushed at the wheel with one hand or lifted the foot to free the needle where it had got stuck in a thick piece of material. The kitchen was her life. Year by year, as I began to take in her fantastic capacity for labor and her anxious zeal, I realized it was ourselves she kept stitched together. I can never remember a time when she was not working. She worked because the law of her life was work, work and anxiety; she worked because she would have found life meaningless without work. She read almost no English; she could read the Yiddish

paper, but never felt she had time to. We were always talking of a time when I would teach her how to read, but somehow there was never time. When I awoke in the morning she was already at her machine, or in the great morning crowd of housewives at the grocery getting fresh rolls for breakfast. When I returned from school she was at her machine, or conferring over *McCall's* with some neighborhood woman who had come in pointing hopefully to an illustration— "Mrs. Kazin! Mrs. Kazin! Make me a dress like it shows here in the picture!" When my father came home from work she had somehow mysteriously interrupted herself to make supper for us, and the dishes cleared and washed, was back at her machine. When I went to bed at night, often she was still there, pounding away at the treadle, hunched over the wheel, her hands steering a piece of gauze under the needle with a finesse that always contrasted sharply with her swollen hands and broken nails. Her left hand had been pierced through when as a girl she had worked in the infamous Triangle Shirtwaist Factory on the East Side. A needle had gone straight through the palm, severing a large vein. They had sewn it up for her so clumsily that a tuft of flesh always lay folded over the palm.

4   The kitchen was the great machine that set our lives running; it whirred down a little only on Saturdays and holy days. From my mother's kitchen I gained my first picture of life as a white, overheated, starkly lit workshop redolent with Jewish cooking, crowded with women in housedresses, strewn with fashion magazines, patterns, dress material, spools of thread—and at whose center, so lashed to her machine that bolts of energy seemed to dance out of her hands and feet as she worked, my mother stamped the treadle hard against the floor, hard, hard, and silently, grimly at war, beat out the first rhythm of the world for me.

EXERCISES

Some of the Issues

1. Kazin writes about the kitchen in his childhood home. Is he writing from the point of view of a child or an adult? What indications do you have of one or the other?
2. In speaking of his mother, Kazin says, "The law of her life was work, work and anxiety." In an age in which many people's goal is self-fulfillment, this does not seem to be a happy life. Can you find any evidence as to whether Mrs. Kazin was happy or unhappy? What pleasures did she have?
3. What is the meaning of the first sentence in paragraph 4? Why does Kazin call the kitchen "the great machine"?

The Way We Are Told

4. The same two words are repeated in the first sentence of each paragraph. What purpose does that repetition serve?

5. Compare the first two paragraphs. How do they differ from each other in content and in the way they are written?
6. Kazin talks about the kitchen of his childhood home but does not describe it until the second paragraph. What might be the effect if he had started with that description?
7. Reread the second paragraph. What details does Kazin give? How are they arranged—in which kind of order? Could an artist draw a picture on the basis of Kazin's description? Could an architect draw a plan from it?
8. Kazin describes several items in detail—the sewing machine, aspects of the kitchen itself, and his mother's work. Find some adjectives that stand out because they are unusual or that add precision or feeling to his descriptions.

Some Subjects for Writing

9. Write a paragraph about a place of significance for you, using Kazin's second paragraph as your model. Try to show its significance by the way you describe it.
10. Consider the role of work in the life of Kazin's mother. If you know someone whose life seems completely tied up with some specific activity, describe that person through his or her activity.

Love You, K2a2a, Whoever You Are

Amy Harmon

In "Love You, K2a2a, Whoever You Are," Amy Harmon explores the rapid rise in the availability and popularity of genealogical DNA testing, and what its potential results may, or may not, be able to tell us about our own identities. In recent years, as DNA testing has become cheaper and more widely available, many Americans have used it to try to find clues about ancestors further back in time than conventional genealogical records might be able to document. Particularly for African Americans descended from slaves, who until now had virtually no way to trace their ancestry back to Africa, genealogical DNA has shed new light on histories that were formerly lost. In 2005, the scholar Henry Louis Gates, Jr. hosted a popular television show on PBS in which several prominent African Americans, including Oprah Winfrey, Whoopi Goldberg, and Mae Jemison, submitted their DNA for analysis, with sometimes surprising results.

Amy Harmon is a feature writer for the New York Times, *covering a range of subjects including health and technology. She joined the* Times *in 1997 as a technology correspondent, and before that, served for seven years as a reporter for the* Los Angeles Times. *She has written extensively about the emerging role of technology in business and culture. She was also a contributor to the* New York Times' *series on race relations, which won a Pulitzer Prize in 2001.*

Harmon received a B.A. degree in American Culture from the University of Michigan in 1990 and began her career in journalism as the opinion page editor of that school's student newspaper, the Michigan Daily.

1   There are a lot of things I may never know about K2a2a, one of four founding mothers of a large chunk of today's Ashkenazi Jewish population and the one from whom—I learned last week—I am directly descended.

2   I may never know whether she lived 1,000 years ago or 3,000. I may never know if she was born in the Judea, as the scientists who identified her through mitochondrial DNA say they suspect. I will certainly never know her name.

3   I do know that I carry her distinctive genetic signature. My mother carried it, my mother's mother carried it, my daughter now carries it, too.

4   And the thrill of that knowledge—for the price of the $100 cheek swab test of my own DNA—may be all I can handle.

5   The popular embrace of DNA genealogy speaks to the rising power of genetics to shape our sense of self. By conjuring a biologically based history, the tests forge a visceral connection to our ancestors that seems to allow us to transcend our own lives.

6   But will our genetic identity undermine our cultural identity? The tests can add depth to what we have long believed, but they can also challenge our conception of who we are. The trauma some experience when their tests conflict with what they have always believed to be true has prompted some researchers to call for counseling to accompany the results.

7   Just how informative the tests are is also a matter of considerable debate.

8   Because the Y chromosome, which determines maleness, is passed unchanged from father to son, scientists can use it to determine whether two men share a common ancestor. When rare mutations do occur, they are unique to a single man and his male descendants, and scientists can often pinpoint when and where this founding father lived.

9   Mitochondrial DNA, which is passed on largely intact from mothers to their children, can be used similarly to trace maternal ancestry.

10   But each test can trace only one lineage back to a single ancestor. K2a2a was my mother's mother's mother's . . . mother, for instance, and my father has taken the test so we can learn about his father's father's father's . . . father.

11   But these kinds of tests can't teach me anything about any of the thousands of other ancestors of mine who were living 1,000 or 2,000 years ago.

12   A different kind of test, which promises to parse the percentage of a customer's genome that came from different geographical regions, can be misled by the reproductive shuffling of each generation.

13   Some anthropologists worry that what they call the "geneticization of identity" could lead to a dangerous view of race and ethnicity as biologically based. But many who have taken the tests say that the details of their DNA can underscore that we are all genetic cousins.

14   Why the genetic claiming of an ancient grandmother holds such emotional sway I am not quite sure. I mean, I've never even been to Ellis Island. And I have spent too many Christmases ordering in Chinese for it to come as a surprise that I am more likely to share mitochondrial DNA with Ashkenazi Jews than other groups.

15   But to judge by the growing throngs of other newly minted DNA genealogists, I'm not the only one to find appeal in the idea that the key to our past is lodged in our own genes.

16   On the "DNA-Genealogy" e-mail group last week, the buzz about the Jewish founding mothers was quickly supplanted by the news that scientists had traced a widely distributed genetic signature among people of Irish descent to a legendary Irish king.

17   "I've never felt more Irish," e-mailed Larry Slavens, a computer programmer in Des Moines whose family had immigrated from Ireland in 1740 but hadn't known of ties to Niall of the Nine Hostages, a high king of the fifth century, until

last week. "I tell ya, my next tattoo is going to incorporate the Red Hand of Ulster in honor of my O'Neill kin."

18   Others were less impressed by the connection. "My understanding was that he was one of the nine hostages, not that he took nine hostages," wrote a disdainful John O'Connor, whose DNA links him to a different genealogical pretender to the ancient Irish throne.

19   Once used almost exclusively by research scientists, the tests used to cost thousands of dollars apiece. Now, thanks largely to the Human Genome Project, they are relatively cheap, and a cottage industry of commercial test companies has sprung up to take advantage of it.

20   By some estimates, 200,000 Americans have explored their ancestry through such ventures, which include a collaboration between the National Geographic Society, I.B.M. and Family Tree DNA of Houston whose goal is to build a database of 100,000 DNA samples from ethnic groups around the world to detail the history of human migrations. The project charges the public $99.95 to send in their DNA and find out where they fit on the resulting map.

21   Genetic genealogy may simply be the most recent way of fulfilling an age-old need to tell stories about our origins, anthropologists say. But because Americans put so much faith in science, our DNA results can seem more meaningful than the more standard family lore, or even years of painstaking archival research.

22   "DNA don't lie," said Ed Martin, 61, a retired telecommunications engineer in Orange Park, Fla., whose test put his paternal ancestors in Central Asia.

23   Mr. Martin had already traced his paternal line through the 1500's to a town in Germany using family records. The DNA test results, however, have persuaded him that he is descended from the Huns, who invaded an area of Germany where he still has living relatives—an area, he wrote in an e-mail message, "known as the HUNSruck."

24   "I spend time now visualizing what their lives may have been like, moving and attacking and conquering," he said with obvious relish. "All these groups were trying to kill the other one off. They were just brutal."

25   The adoption of new ancestral identities does not come so easy to everyone.

26   Given her previous research, Lisa B. Lee, a black systems administrator in Oakland, Calif., was sure she would find a link to Africa when she submitted her father's DNA for testing. Family lore had it that his people were from Madagascar. But after tests at three companies, the results stubbornly reported that he shared genetic ancestry with Native Americans, Chinese and Sardinians. No Africa.

27   "What does this mean; who am I then?" said Ms. Lee, who was active in the Black Power movement of the 1960's. "For me to have a whole half of my identity to come back and say, 'Sorry, no African here.' It doesn't even matter what the other half says. It just negates it all."

28   "Am I Sardinian?" she said. "Am I Chinese? Well that doesn't mean anything to me. It doesn't fit, it doesn't feel right."

29   DNA skeptics worry that there is a threatening side to the rise of DNA genealogy. Historically, associating human difference with genetic characteristics has had disastrous social consequences. These tests, marketed as tools to connect to a familial past, DNA skeptics say, often rely on the ability to differentiate people by the parts of our genetic makeup that correlate with racial identity.

30   DNA Print Genomics in Sarasota, Fla., for instance, produces reports stating that an individual is, say, 15 percent Native American, 50 percent Western European, 10 percent African, 5 percent South Asian and 20 percent Middle Eastern.

31   Sandra Soo-Jin Lee, senior research scholar at the Stanford Center for Biomedical Ethics, said that history teaches the dangers of trying to define racial groups with science. "If we're going to relinquish control of our identities to science, we need to realize that we're embarking on that trajectory," she said.

32   When I called Dr. Karl Skorecki, one of the scientists in Israel who had tracked down K2a2a, to ask him what more he could tell me about her, he acknowledged that he finds the potential social implications of his work troubling.

33   "I like to confine it to what it tells us about history, and to insights about disease patterns," said Dr. Skorecki, a professor of medicine at Technion and Rambam Medical Center in Haifa. "That's different than identity. Identity is metaphysical, not physical."

34   So why had K2a2a's line thrived, I had wanted to know, while others had died out?

35   "It is rather remarkable, after having gone through plague and wars left and right, still having left a number of descendants," Dr. Skorecki said, tantalizingly. "But I think it's random."

36   Still, at Family Tree DNA's Web site, I paid $75 to get another test, a higher-resolution scan of my mitochondrial DNA.

EXERCISES

Some of the Issues

1. What does Harmon know about K2a2a? What doesn't she know? How does what the author knows and doesn't know about her ancestor shape the points she goes on to make later in her essay?

2. Harmon states that the "popular embrace of DNA genealogy speaks to the rising power of genetics to shape our own sense of self" (paragraph 5). What does she mean by this statement? Do you agree?

3. Why do some people experience trauma after learning the results of their DNA tests? What examples does the author give of people who have experienced such trauma?

4. Based on Harmon's article, as well as your own thoughts about cultural identity and DNA testing, why do you think so many people are intrigued

by the possibilities offered by DNA testing? Do you find the idea appealing, unappealing, or a bit of both?

5. In paragraph 29 Harmon writes that "[h]istorically, associating human difference with genetic characteristics has had disastrous consequences." To what does she seem to be referring?

The Way We Are Told

6. Harmon uses her own experience with DNA testing to introduce a discussion about the process as a whole. Do you think the author's use of her own experience is effective in this case? Why or why not?

7. Though Harmon tells us aspects of her own story with DNA testing, she never states directly where she stands on the issue. Based on evidence from the article, how would you define Harmon's position on the issue of DNA testing?

Some Subjects for Writing

8. Write an essay in which you analyze the factors that determine your own sense of cultural identity. What do you know about your own ancestry and to what extent does that shape your sense of identity? Do you feel that your sense of identity is based more on parenting and your cultural environment growing up, or on your biological ancestry?

9. In your opinion, what might be the benefits or dangers of widespread DNA testing? Using specific examples write an essay in which you explore the pros and cons.

*10. DNA testing could, and possibly has, influenced how we think about various issues relating to family—adoption, marriage, family lineage. Choose one issue and analyze how DNA testing might impact societal attitudes toward that issue. Depending on the issue you choose, you might look at other readings in this section, such as Dan Savage's "Role Reversal" or Stephanie Coontz's "Where Are the Good Old Days?"

My Papa's Waltz

Theodore Roethke

Theodore Roethke (1908–63), a widely published and much honored American poet, received a Pulitzer Prize in 1953 and a Bollingen Prize in 1958, among other awards. Two of his collections of poems, Words for the Wind *(1958) and* The Far Field *(1964), received National Book Awards. His Collected Poems appeared in 1966. He taught at several universities, last as Poet in Residence at the University of Washington.*

This brief poem is like a snapshot—a recollection of a moment that sums up the relationship of father and son.

The whiskey on your breath
Could make a small boy dizzy;
But I hung on like death:
Such waltzing was not easy.

5 We romped until the pans
Slid from the kitchen shelf;
My mother's countenance
Could not unfrown itself.

10 The hand that held my wrist
Was battered on one knuckle;
At every step you missed
My right ear scraped a buckle.

15 You beat time on my head
With a palm caked hard by dirt,
Then waltzed me off to bed
Still clinging to your shirt.

EXERCISES

Some of the Issues

1. Read the poem aloud several times. The poem describes a waltz—a turning dance that is usually thought of as sedate and graceful but can be dizzyingly fast. How does the rhythm of the poem suggest the dance?

2. The poem is like a snapshot—a recollection of a moment that sums up the relationship of father and son. What indications are there that the relationship was a close one, despite difficulties?

Some Subjects for Writing

3. Describe an incident from your early childhood that you remember well. In your description, try to make the reader understand how you felt about the event.

PART IV

WORKING AND SPENDING

We are, some would say, a nation of workers and consumers. By most accounts, Americans, on average, work and spend significantly more than people in most other countries. And many Americans define themselves by what they do and what they own. But our emphasis on working and spending raises many questions: Do we work too much at the expense of leisure and family? Do we spend too much at the expense of the environment? Do we consume and dispose of more than our share of the world's resources? Are workers in the United States receiving fair treatment and fair wages for the work they do? And are we able to consume as much as we do because of our reliance on cheap labor from other countries?

The pieces in this section explore the way we work and the way we spend in the United States. In "'Proud to Work for the University'," Kristin Kovacic tells the story of her father's experience working for many years as an electrician for Carnegie Mellon University in Pittsburgh. Kovacic's essay describes both the pride her father felt in being affiliated with the university, and the hopes he placed in the prospect of his children's future education there. Sadly, he eventually finds that in the end the university is much less committed to him than he is to the university. Barbara Brandt, in "Less Is More: A Call for Shorter Work Hours," analyzes the American impulse toward overwork, and advocates a change to a thirty-hour workweek. According to Brandt, "Americans often assume that overwork is an inevitable fact of life," and we too easily accept this assumption without considering the sacrifices we make in terms of the time we devote to our families, communities, and personal leisure.

The next two essays look at different facets of the way Americans consume and discard things, one from a personal perspective and the other from a more general viewpoint. Lars Eighner's description of scavenging in "On Dumpster Diving" provides a commentary on both homelessness and wastefulness in American society. Through this vivid and meticulous description of his daily dives into the Dumpster, Eighner delivers a poignant commentary on consumer society and the irony of homelessness in a country of abundance. In "High-Tech Wasteland," Elizabeth Grossman examines the complex and often disturbing world of technological waste, and argues for a more environmentally conscious and humane approach to recycling our seemingly endless stream of computers, iPods, cell phones, and other electronic gadgets

Clive Thompson's article "Meet the Life Hackers" examines technology from the perspective of the office worker coping with the numerous modes of communication that continually compete for our attention. Thompson explores the field of "interruption science," which helps us better understand how we cope with a workplace that has become increasingly full of potential distractions.

In the poem that closes this chapter, Martín Espada looks back on his days as a worker in a factory that makes legal pads. Now a law student, he realizes that he knows something about paper, and labor, that other law students may not know.

"Proud to Work for the University"

Kristin Kovacic

Kristin Kovacic is a writer of poetry, fiction, and essays whose work has appeared in many periodicals, including Brain, Child Magazine, *and the* Pittsburgh Post-Gazette. *She is also co-editor of the anthology* Birth: A Literary Companion (2002). *She teaches writing at Chatham College and the Pittsburgh High School for the Creative and Performing Arts, and received a fellowship in poetry from the Pennsylvania Council on the Arts. Kovacic holds degrees in writing from the University of Pittsburgh and Carnegie Mellon University, where her father, the subject of this essay, worked loyally as an electrician for more than twenty years.*

"'Proud to Work for the University'" was originally published in Women's Studies Quarterly *in 1995.*

1   In June 1958 Bogdan Kovacic, my father, emigrated from Zagreb, Yugoslavia, to Pittsburgh, Pennsylvania. As he likes to tell the story, he had a quarter in his pocket as the train rolled into Penn Station, and he used that to buy some crackers, hedging his bets against his next meal. He was twenty-six years old and spoke little English. He had left behind family, all of his good friends, his teammates from the professional handball team he played for. He was alone, he figured, and about to see the world.

2   This is part of the myth of my family, a story familiar to many Pittsburghers with immigrant roots. I am, I'm afraid, about to tell you a very old story.

3   Jobs, in 1958, were plentiful in Pittsburgh. Cousin Francie got him in at the plate factory. He hauled plates, dropping them now and then and making a big crash. He went to English classes at night, penciled neat meaningless sentences in a grammar book I have here—"Only a few friends are bidden to come," and, with emphasis, "You are never too old to learn." He signed his new American name, Andrew, over and over in the margins. He learned the questions he'd soon have to answer: "Are you a Bolshevik, anarchist, communist, or polygamist?" "What does Thanksgiving Day mean?" He met my mother, practiced his new words.

4   Trained as an electrician in Zagreb, he looked for work in his field. A friend told him he could get him in at the mill, and he went to have a look: the heat, the smoke, the filth over everything. He said no thanks; he'd have to work in

hell soon enough. He found a job as an electrician at West Penn Hospital, good, clean work. He was promoted to foreman. He bought a Chevy, sky blue.

5   Then we were born: my brother Andy, my sister Lara, and I. This, apparently, changed everything. He started night school again, and, with an electrical degree from Allegheny Technical Institute, he landed a job at Carnegie Mellon University in 1969—two years before Richard Cyert assumed the presidency of the university. I remember the day Dad started, the new uniform my mother pressed off, and the first time the promise was made to us: you will get an education there. At that time, all Carnegie Mellon University employees were promised full undergraduate tuition for their children who were accepted there. That day, too, was the first time the challenge was set down: you will have to do well enough in school to be accepted. I was six, my brother seven, my sister was learning to crawl. It was a challenge we took very seriously; it was, we figured, our shot at seeing the world.

6   In those days we were required, on the first day of school, to say our names and what our fathers did for a living. One by one the kids would recite their names and then, simply, "J&L" or "Homestead" or "Duquesne Works." I would wait my turn, and then somewhat haughtily announce, "My dad is an electrician at Carnegie Mellon University. I'm going to college there, free." I told people even when they didn't ask me.

7   Carnegie Mellon became our identity, the greatest part of our family myth. While the men in the mills, our neighbors, were making much more money than Dad, locked into contracts in the glory days of steel, he, at least, had *invested*, had guaranteed our futures. We got Carnegie Mellon sweatshirts, T-shirts, and notebooks for our birthdays. We cheered the buggys at carnival. When Dad worked weekends, we'd sometimes visit him on campus and ride in his little electric car, surveying what we knew would someday be ours—our library, our gymnasium, our student union. At night, passing by, we saw the beacon light in Hamerschlag Hall which Dad had installed. "That's my light," he'd say, and there it was, beckoning.

8   We also participated, through him, in Carnegie Mellon's road to academic glory. My dad didn't work at a factory, he worked for the university—among artists, engineers, and scientists. I didn't, for most of my early lifetime, see any fundamental difference between what my father and a professor of electrical engineering did for a living. They both worked for the university.

9   My father worked on experiments with monkeys and with robots. He helped harness energy from still water, bringing the physicists home for dinner after their hard day's work. Dad's work allowed Kathleen Mulcahy, the glass artist, to safely power her magnificent kiln. When he brought home the beautiful vase she made for him, my mother set it on the television set in the living room, eventually decorating the whole room around it—such colors we had never thought of bringing together. If my father was never going to see the world, Carnegie Mellon brought it closer to him and, by consequence, to us.

10   He was there when the computers arrived; the machines that would launch Carnegie Mellon's international star. I remember sitting at the dinner table while Dad told us about the computers, how, when we got to college, there would be a computer for every student; how we'd find a book in the library just by pushing a button; how there might not *be* any more books in the library, the computer taking over every aspect of our education. I remember being somewhat skeptical—this was long before *computer* was a household word, much less a household item. But, finally, I believed. Dad had the plans; he knew what was coming. He was the man who powered those glorious machines, who would later coordinate the installation of the "Andrew" computer network.

11   In 1981 I arrived and began my Carnegie Mellon education. On my first day of my first class—a core curriculum sociology course—we read about the concept of class in American society. We learned how to identify the working class from the middle class; there were just a few simple rules. The working class, my textbook said, works with its hands or, in the case of women, does clerical work like typing or filing. I did a little figuring. My mother is a secretary. My father is an electrician. His hands can get very dirty when he works, and he is scrupulous about washing them. He always carries Band-Aids in his wallet, ready for the daily cuts he gets at work, usually on his hands.

12   You can identify the working class, my textbook said, by the arrangement of their homes. The working class keeps its television set in the living room, for example, while the middle class keeps it in another place, like a den. I thought about our living room, Kathleen Mulcahy's vase crowning the television like a jewel. I thought, for the very first time, that I was working class. It was a genuine surprise.

13   I'm told that Andrew Carnegie founded Carnegie Institute of Technology for the education of the working classes of Pittsburgh. Long before I arrived, that mission had been abandoned as unprestigious and, more to the point, unprofitable. My classmates were from out of town, the daughters and sons of doctors, entrepreneurs, foreign financiers. Many of them rarely saw their parents, much less ran into them in Baker Hall, fixing a switch box. I learned the difference between an electrician and an electrical engineer. None of that bothered me; it surprised me, opening my picture of the world, and where I fit into it, much wider. Likewise, much about my life surprised my friends, whom I would bring home with me on holidays and weekends, introducing them to a genuine working-class home, television set and all. During my years in school my parents responded generously to Carnegie Mellon's requests for giving from parents, believing, in a way that other parents could not, that the money was going to the university's collective pot, whose assets were essentially our own. They also, I think, enjoyed the letters that came to the house afterward: "Dear Mr. and Mrs. Kovacic, thank you for your generous gift."

14   In May 1985 I graduated, valedictorian of my college. I was selected to deliver the student commencement address, and on that day, under the big tent, a

number of our family dreams came together. My father was sitting, suit and tie, in the audience. My sister, who had just been accepted for admission in the fall, sat next to him, checking out *her* campus. My brother, who, after receiving his associates' degree in forestry from Penn State University, was hired by Carnegie Mellon as a gardener—following my father's path—stood on the edge of the tent in his uniform. His boss had given him special permission to attend; normally the gardeners have to stay in their shop during the ceremonies. I dedicated the speech to my father, and I used my remarks to remind my classmates about the wonder, the absolute fortune, that we were going to do our work in life with questions, theories, problems, and poems—not with our backs, not with our bleeding hands. "Very well done," President Cyert said, shaking my hand on the dais. He told the audience that he was pleased to see the daughter of a staff member be so successful at the university.

15   When I think about that day now, the memory is very sweet, but I am also reminded that certain dread wheels were already in motion. The university, at the time of my graduation, was about to divide the workers' union (SEIU Local 29), selling off the janitors to a management firm (ABM) and cutting them off from Carnegie Mellon benefits, including tuition benefits. Those people, many of whom were Dad's friends, no longer worked for the university. Shortly after my graduation the administration dropped *university* from its official name, suggesting that it was more like a corporation than an institution of higher education, more like a factory than a school.

16   Contract battles for Dad's union became increasingly difficult to win. The administration, which for years claimed that its pay scale could never compete with the steel industry's, took advantage of the labor climate in the wake of steel's collapse to demand concessions. The administration hired outside firms to "consult" on the efficiency of the physical plant. There were layoffs. One of those firms became the manager of Carnegie Mellon's building and maintenance operations, introducing suspicion among the physical plant workers—in spite of the administration's written assurances—that there would be further layoffs and that what had happened to the janitors might eventually happen to them.

17   In May 1990 my sister graduated with high honors, and we gathered again under the tent, to celebrate again the fulfillment of Dad's promise. President Cyert, saying his last farewells, recalled the achievements of his twenty-one years in office, the remarkable rise of Pittsburgh's Carnegie Tech to the global institution called Carnegie Mellon. My father, in the audience, could look back on those very same years, knowing that he had had a hand in all of it and that he had, in spite of all of the hard, physical work, made a very good investment in a growing institution. A steel mill might close, rust, and be razed to a clear toxic field, like the J&L South Side works he passed every day on his way to Oakland. But the university would always be there.

18   My sister and I were on our way. My brother was doing well in his job. Dad had three years until he could retire, and he was already planning. He would

play more tennis (he is still, at sixty, a remarkable athlete). He and my mother would travel, back to Yugoslavia, where his family still lives, and to the other parts of the world they hadn't gotten around to seeing.

19   In June, after the tent had come down and the campus emptied out, the faculty and students returning to the cities that they come from, Dad reported to work, punched his clock. He was told not to work but to go directly through a door that closed behind him and seventeen other people, including two-thirds of all of the university's electricians, who were about to lose their jobs. They were told, for the first time, that there was a budget crisis that would require layoffs. They were told to turn in their keys and to be off the campus grounds by 10:00 a.m. They saw university police as they emerged, dazed by the blindsided blow. "Like criminals," my mother told me, through tears, over the phone. She didn't think about the cost, the financial straits this would place them in. She thought about betrayal. "They treated him like a criminal, after all those years."

20   My father harbored no illusions about Carnegie Mellon's benevolence. He had seen, over the years, the university's antagonism toward its union. But in 1969 he had signed what he thought was a lifetime contract—he would give them a lifetime of hard labor; they would educate his children and allow him to retire, not comfortably, but in peace. It was not an extravagant plan.

21   Unfortunately for him, the Carnegie Mellon that let him go was not the university that had hired him, or perhaps, sadly, it was. How could he have known that the master plan of the global university, like that of a global corporation, included the abandonment of its responsibility to the blue-collar workers in its community, not to mention its utter disregard for their intelligence and pride? At the same moment that my father and sixteen other skilled construction and maintenance workers were shown, by an armed guard, the door, the administration announced the acceptance of a five-million-dollar gift from Paul Mellon toward new campus construction. Who, these men and women were forced to wonder, would be doing it? Who would design, construct, wire, and maintain the growth for which, as Dr. Cyert so elegantly phrased it for the reporters, "Carnegie Mellon's appetite continues to grow the larger [it] gets"? The arithmetic is tragically easy to do, even without a Carnegie Mellon education—why support loyal, lifetime employees when you can buy contract work for less? At the same moment that my father faced the prospect of finding, at sixty, a new job, President Cyert eased into his retirement. The administration, as reported by the *Pittsburgh Post-Gazette*, was then finalizing plans to purchase a $1.9 million Sewickley estate for its new president, his wife, and their six horses.

22   "The emerging global company is divorced from where it produces its goods," Robert B. Reich, lecturer in public policy at the Harvard University Kennedy School of Government told the *New York Times*. "It has no heart, and it has no soul. It is a financial enterprise designed to maximize profits. Many of the people who inhabit it may be fine, upstanding human beings, but the organization has its own merciless logic."

23   It was just this merciless logic, I have to believe, that caused my father to lose his job. Carnegie Mellon is a thriving, growing institution. It is not facing a budgetary crisis; it is facing a moral one—whether to cultivate the community of a university or the elite positioning of a corporation. My family felt, with great pride, a part of an educational community, until, without ceremony, Carnegie Mellon abandoned its role in it. Now, like too many other working-class families in Pittsburgh, we're left with the caution that it was foolish to have believed.

24   So now my father, writing in the workbook he received at his "transition" seminar, dutifully answers their questions. What do you feel is your greatest accomplishment? "My greatest accomplishment," he writes in the clipped, impossible language he has never learned to love, "is my family." What was most satisfying about your previous employment? "I was very proud," he says, carefully calling up the past tense, "to work for the university."

EXERCISES

Some of the Issues

1. Why does Kovacic describe her father's story as a "myth" (paragraph 2)? What are the different meanings of the word *myth?*
2. Why would Kovacic's father had to answer the questions: "Are you a Bolshevik, anarchist, communist, or polygamist?" and "What does Thanksgiving Day mean" (paragraph 3)?
3. How and why did Carnegie Mellon become Kovacic's family identity (paragraph 7)? How does this idea foreshadow later events in Kovacic's narrative?
4. What changes were occurring at the point that Kovacic graduated (paragraphs 15–16)? How would these changes influence how people in her father's position would think of themselves in the future?
5. Why did Kovacic's father lose his job at the university? How did this loss affect him and his family, both emotionally and materially?
6. In small groups, discuss your own attitude toward "the university" by the end of the essay.

The Way We Are Told

7. What is the significance of the title of the piece?
8. Kovacic uses a mix of short and long sentences. How does she use sentence length to emphasize a certain point? Is this effective?
9. What is Kovacic's tone when she describes what her sociology textbook says about class (paragraphs 11–12)?

10. How does Kovacic portray the university at the beginning of her essay? How did this influence your attitude toward the university at the end of the piece?

Some Subjects for Writing

11. Consider the workers at your university who do jobs like Kovacic's father's. Do students, professors, and administrators see or recognize the work they do? In what ways do they make the university function? Write an essay in which you describe one aspect of the invisible labor that makes your university function day to day.

*12. Read Cheri Register's "The Field Trip." How is her attitude toward her father's work both similar and different to Kovacic's? Write an essay that analyzes their differences and similarities.

13. With the help of your instructor, research the management structure of the staff at your own university. Is it staffed by a private company or are workers hired directly by the university? You might investigate who manages the custodial staff or the food service staff, or you might look into other agreements that your campus has with private companies (for example, fast food chains or a bottling company that supplies beverages in your school's stores and cafeterias). Write a paper in which you describe the nature of these agreements and their history. When were they formed? Under what circumstances? Who benefits from them and how?

Less Is More: A Call for Shorter Work Hours

Barbara Brandt

Barbara Brandt is a community organizer and social change activist who lives in the Boston area and focuses her work on issues of gender, community, economics, and environment. She is the author of Whole Life Economics: Revaluing Daily Life *(1995). This essay was written in conjunction with a collective called the "Shorter Work Time Group," of which Brandt was a member, and appeared in the* Utne Reader *as part of a section on work.*

Brandt argues that increases in technology such as computers and fax machines, while they initially seem to offer us more convenience, save us time, and decrease our workload, have actually increased the pace of our lives and raised our standards of productivity. Brandt makes the case that, while the typical American work week—eight hours a day, forty hours a week—seems to most Americans like "the natural rhythm of the universe," we could all benefit from a conception of work that included more free time to care for families, explore hobbies and interests, and develop community.

1   America is suffering from overwork. Too many of us are too busy, trying to squeeze more into each day while having less to show for it. Although our growing time crunch is often portrayed as a personal dilemma, it is in fact a major social problem that has reached crisis proportions over the past 20 years.

2   The simple fact is that Americans today—both women and men—are spending too much time at work, to the detriment of their homes, their families, their personal lives, and their communities. The American Dream promised that our individual hard work paired with the advances of modern technology would bring about the good life for all. Glorious visions of the leisure society were touted throughout the '50s and '60s. But now most people are working more than ever before, while still struggling to meet their economic commitments. Ironically, the many advances in technology, such as computers and fax machines, rather than reducing our workload, seem to have speeded up our lives at work. At the same time, technology has equipped us with "conveniences" like microwave ovens and frozen dinners that merely enable us to adopt a similar frantic pace in our home lives so we can cope with more hours at paid work.

3   A recent spate of articles in the mainstream media has focused on the new problems of overwork and lack of time. Unfortunately, overwork is often

portrayed as a special problem of yuppies and professionals on the fast track. In reality, the unequal distribution of work and time in America today reflects the decline in both standard of living and quality of life for most Americans. Families whose members never see each other, women who work a double shift (first on the job, then at home), workers who need more flexible work schedules, and unemployed and underemployed people who need more work are all casualties of the crisis of overwork.

4   Americans often assume that overwork is an inevitable fact of life—like death and taxes. Yet a closer look at other times and other nations offers some startling surprises.

5   Anthropologists have observed that in pre-industrial (particularly hunting and gathering) societies, people generally spend 3 to 4 hours a day, 15 to 20 hours a week, doing the work necessary to maintain life. The rest of the time is spent in socializing, partying, playing, storytelling, and artistic or religious activities. The ancient Romans celebrated 175 public festivals a year in which everyone participated, and people in the Middle Ages had at least 115.

6   In our era, almost every other industrialized nation (except Japan) has fewer annual working hours and longer vacations than the United States. This includes all of Western Europe, where many nations enjoy thriving economies and standards of living equal to or higher than ours. Jeremy Brecher and Tim Costello, writing in *Z Magazine* (Oct. 1990), note that "European unions during the 1980s made a powerful and largely successful push to cut working hours. In 1987 German metalworkers struck and won a 37.5-hour week; many are now winning a 35-hour week. In 1990, hundreds of thousands of British workers have won a 37-hour week."

7   In an article about work-time in the *Boston Globe*, Suzanne Gordon notes that workers in other industrialized countries "enjoy—as a statutory right—longer vacations [than in the U.S.] from the moment they enter the work force. In Canada, workers are legally entitled to two weeks off their first year on the job. . . . After two or three years of employment, most get three weeks of vacation. After 10 years, it's up to four, and by 20 years, Canadian workers are off for five weeks. In Germany, statutes guarantee 18 days minimum for everyone, but most workers get five or six weeks. The same is true in Scandinavian countries, and in France."

8   In contrast to the extreme American emphasis on productivity and commitment, which results in many workers, especially in professional-level jobs, not taking the vacations coming to them, Gordon notes that "In countries that are America's most successful competitors in the global marketplace, all working people, whether lawyers or teachers, CEOs or janitors, take the vacations to which they are entitled by law. 'No one in West Germany,' a West German embassy's officer explains, 'no matter how high up they are, would ever say they couldn't afford to take a vacation. Everyone takes their vacation.'"

9   And in Japan, where dedication to the job is legendary, Gordon notes that the Japanese themselves are beginning to consider their national workaholism a

serious social problem leading to stress-related illnesses and even death. As a result, the Japanese government recently established a commission whose goal is to promote shorter working hours and more leisure time.

10   Most other industrialized nations also have better family-leave policies than the United States, and in a number of other countries workers benefit from innovative time-scheduling opportunities such as sabbaticals.

11   While the idea of a shorter workweek and longer vacations sounds appealing to most people, any movement to enact shorter work-time as a public policy will encounter surprising pockets of resistance, not just from business leaders but even from some workers. Perhaps the most formidable barrier to more free time for Americans is the widespread mind-set that the 40-hour workweek, 8 hours a day, 5 days a week, 50 weeks a year, is a natural rhythm of the universe. This view is reinforced by the media's complete silence regarding the shorter work-time and more favorable vacation and family-leave policies of other countries. This lack of information, and our leaders' reluctance to suggest that the United States can learn from any other nation (except workaholic Japan) is one reason why more Americans don't identify overwork as a major problem or clamor for fewer hours and more vacation. Monika Bauerlein, a journalist originally from Germany now living in Minneapolis, exclaims, "I can't believe that people here aren't rioting in the streets over having only two weeks of vacation a year."

12   A second obstacle to launching a powerful shorter work-time movement is America's deeply ingrained work ethic, or its modern incarnation, the workaholic syndrome. The work ethic fosters the widely held belief that people's work is their most important activity and that people who do not work long and hard are lazy, unproductive, and worthless.

13   For many Americans today, paid work is not just a way to make money but is a crucial source of their self-worth. Many of us identify ourselves almost entirely by the kind of work we do. Work still has a powerful psychological and spiritual hold over our lives—and talk of shorter work-time may seem somehow morally suspicious.

14   Because we are so deeply a work-oriented society, leisure-time activities—such as play, relaxation, engaging in cultural and artistic pursuits, or just quiet contemplation and "doing nothing"—are not looked on as essential and worthwhile components of life. Of course, for the majority of working women who must work a second shift at home, much of the time spent outside of paid work is not leisure anyway. Also much of our non-work time is spent not just in personal renewal, but in building and maintaining essential social ties—with family, friends, and the larger community.

15   Today, as mothers and fathers spend more and more time on the job, we are beginning to recognize the deleterious effects—especially on our young people—of the breakdown of social ties and community in American life. But unfortunately, our nation reacts to these problems by calling for more paid professionals—more police, more psychiatrists, more experts—without recognizing the possibility that shorter work hours and more free time could enable

us to do much of the necessary rebuilding and healing, with much more gratifying and longer-lasting results.

16   Of course, the stiffest opposition to cutting work hours comes not from citizens but from business. Employers are reluctant to alter the 8-hour day, 40-hour workweek, 50 weeks a year because it seems easier and more profitable for employers to hire fewer employees for longer hours rather than more employees—each of whom would also require health insurance and other benefits—with flexible schedules and work arrangements.

17   Harvard University economist Juliet B. Schor, who has been studying issues of work and leisure in America, reminds us that we cannot ignore the larger relationship between unemployment and overwork: While many of us work too much, others are unable to find paid work at all. Schor points out that "workers who work longer hours lose more income when they lose their jobs. The threat of job loss is an important determinant of management's power on the shop floor." A system that offers only two options—long work hours or unemployment—serves as both a carrot and a stick. Those lucky enough to get full-time jobs are bribed into docile compliance with the boss, while the spectre of unemployment always looms as the ultimate punishment for the unruly.

18   Some observers suggest that keeping people divided into "the employed" and "the unemployed" creates feelings of resentment and inferiority/superiority between the two groups, thus focusing their discontent and blame on each other rather than on the corporations and political figures who actually dictate our nation's economic policies.

19   Our role as consumers contributes to keeping the average work week from falling. In an economic system in which addictive buying is the basis of corporate profits, working a full 40 hours or more each week for 50 weeks a year gives us just enough time to stumble home and dazedly—almost automatically—shop; but not enough time to think about deeper issues or to work effectively for social change. From the point of view of corporations and policymakers, shorter work time may be bad for the economy, because people with enhanced free time may begin to find other things to do with it besides mindlessly buying products. It takes more free time to grow vegetables, cook meals from scratch, sew clothes, or repair broken items than it does to just buy these things at the mall.

20   Any serious proposal to give employed Americans a break by cutting into the eight-hour work day is certain to be met with anguished cries about international competitiveness. The United States seems gripped by the fear that our nation has lost its economic dominance, and pundits, policymakers, and business leaders tell us that no sacrifice is too great if it puts America on top again.

21   As arguments like this are put forward (and we can expect them to increase in the years to come), we need to remember two things. First, even if America maintained its dominance (whatever that means) and the economy were booming again, this would be no guarantee that the gains—be they in wages, in employment opportunities, or in leisure—would be distributed equitably between

upper management and everyone else. Second, the entire issue of competitiveness is suspect when it pits poorly treated workers in one country against poorly treated workers in another; and when the vast majority of economic power, anyway, is in the control of enormous multinational corporations that have no loyalty to the people of any land.

EXERCISES

Some of the Issues

1. What was your immediate reaction to Brandt's first paragraph? Do you agree or disagree? Why or why not?
2. What does Brandt see as the irony of modern technology (paragraph 2)? How, in your opinion, has technology changed our commitments to work, family, and community?
3. According to Brandt, who in America suffers from overwork (paragraph 3)?
4. In paragraphs 4 through 10 Brandt contrasts the work habits of preindustrial and other industrialized nations with those of the United States. Why does she make these comparisons?
5. In paragraphs 11 through 15, Brandt discusses two reasons why individuals resist a shorter workweek. What are they? Do you agree with her comments on the "work ethic"?
6. Why are employers reluctant to alter the eight-hour day (paragraph 16)?
7. According to Brandt and Juliet B. Schor, how does overwork divide us (paragraphs 16–19) and which groups are pitted against each other (paragraph 21)? What are the consequences of this division?
8. According to Brandt, what role do corporations play in encouraging consumption and keeping the workweek long (paragraph 19)? Do you agree with her analysis?

The Way We Are Told

9. Brandt makes certain points in her argument by first stating a common assumption and then presenting evidence against that assumption. Find places in the essay where she does this. Does it make her argument more effective?
10. How does Brandt use comparison and contrast to provide evidence for her argument?

Some Subjects for Writing

11. In a journal, document your own work habits for three or four days. Take note of how much time you devote to your work, school, leisure, family,

and community. Using examples and descriptions from your journal, write an essay in which you define and examine your own work habits.

12. Interview three or four people from different social or cultural backgrounds about their work habits. Make sure to prepare a list of questions beforehand and ask follow-up questions during the interview. Write an essay in which you compare and contrast their attitudes toward both work and leisure.

13. Do you agree with Brandt that Americans overvalue the "work ethic" and undervalue leisure-time activities? Write an essay explaining your views.

14. In a section of the article not reprinted here, Brandt makes specific proposals for shortening the workweek to thirty hours. Write a persuasive essay in which you argue for or against a shorter workweek. Make sure to back up your claims with specific evidence, and to qualify your argument by showing that you understand the other side.

On Dumpster Diving

Lars Eighner

Lars Eighner was born in 1948 in Corpus Christi, Texas. "On Dumpster Div-
ing" is excerpted from Travels with Lizbeth *(1993), a chronicle of Eighner's*
three years as a homeless person. Lizbeth is the author's dog and traveling
companion. Typed on equipment found in the garbage, Travels with Lizbeth
began as a series of letters to friends describing the events that took Eighner
from a job in a mental institution to life as a homeless person. The book is
written as a series of vignettes because, as the author says, "A homeless life
has no story line."

In a sober tone punctuated with sharp detail, Eighner describes, ana-
lyzes, and philosophizes about the things we as a society discard. Often
these are things Eighner finds perfectly usable. Although the author doesn't
directly draw conclusions for the reader, his careful descriptions of what we
consider "garbage" make a statement about our "disposable" society and
about what we value, whether we are homeless or not.

Eighner received much acclaim for Travels with Lizbeth *and its unique*
point of view. He is no longer homeless and lives in Austin, Texas. He has
written several books of gay erotic fiction, and his most recent book is a novel,
Pawn to Queen Four *(1994). He writes a blog at www.larseighner.com*

1   Long before I began Dumpster diving I was impressed with Dumpsters, enough so that I wrote the Merriam-Webster research service to discover what I could about the word *Dumpster.* I learned from them that it is a propri-etary word belonging to the Dempster Dumpster company. Since then I have dutifully capitalized the word, although it was lowercased in almost all the cita-tions Merriam-Webster photocopied for me. Dempster's word is too apt. I have never heard these things called anything but Dumpsters. I do not know anyone who knows the generic name for these objects. From time to time I have heard a wino or hobo give some corrupted credit to the original and call them Dipsy Dumpsters.

2   I began Dumpster diving about a year before I became homeless.

3   I prefer the word *scavenging* and use the word *scrounging* when I mean to be obscure. I have heard people, evidently meaning to be polite, use the word *foraging,* but I prefer to reserve that word for gathering nuts and berries and such, which I do also according to the season and the opportunity. *Dumpster div-ing* seems to me to be a little too cute and, in my case, inaccurate because I lack the athletic ability to lower myself into the Dumpsters as the true divers do, much to their increased profit.

4   I like the frankness of the word *scavenging*, which I can hardly think of without picturing a big black snail on an aquarium wall. I live from the refuse of others. I am a scavenger. I think it a sound and honorable niche, although if I could I would naturally prefer to live the comfortable consumer life, perhaps—and only perhaps—as a slightly less wasteful consumer, owing to what I have learned as a scavenger.

5   While Lizbeth and I were still living in the shack on Avenue B as my savings ran out, I put almost all my sporadic income into rent. The necessities of daily life I began to extract from Dumpsters. Yes, we ate from them. Except for jeans, all my clothes came from Dumpsters. Boom boxes, candles, bedding, toilet paper, a virgin male love doll, medicine, books, a typewriter, dishes, furnishings, and change, sometimes amounting to many dollars—I acquired many things from the Dumpsters.

6   I have learned much as a scavenger. I mean to put some of what I have learned down here, beginning with the practical art of Dumpster diving and proceeding to the abstract.

7   What is safe to eat?

8   After all, the finding of objects is becoming something of an urban art. Even respectable employed people will sometimes find something tempting sticking out of a Dumpster or standing beside one. Quite a number of people, not all of them of the bohemian type, are willing to brag that they found this or that piece in the trash. But eating from Dumpsters is what separates the dilettanti from the professionals. Eating safely from the Dumpsters involves three principles: using the senses and common sense to evaluate the condition of the found materials, knowing the Dumpsters of a given area and checking them regularly, and seeking always to answer the question "Why was this discarded?"

9   Perhaps everyone who has a kitchen and a regular supply of groceries has, at one time or another, made a sandwich and eaten half of it before discovering mold on the bread or got a mouthful of milk before realizing the milk had turned. Nothing of the sort is likely to happen to a Dumpster diver because he is constantly reminded that most food is discarded for a reason. Yet a lot of perfectly good food can be found in Dumpsters.

10   Canned goods, for example, turn up fairly often in the Dumpsters I frequent. All except the most phobic people would be willing to eat from a can, even if it came from a Dumpster. Canned goods are among the safest of foods to be found in Dumpsters but are not utterly foolproof.

11   Although very rare with modern canning methods, botulism is a possibility. Most other forms of food poisoning seldom do lasting harm to a healthy person, but botulism is almost certainly fatal and often the first symptom is death. Except for carbonated beverages, all canned goods should contain a slight vacuum and suck air when first punctured. Bulging, rusty, and dented cans and cans that spew when punctured should be avoided, especially when the contents are not very acidic or syrupy.

12   Heat can break down the botulin, but this requires much more cooking than most people do to canned goods. To the extent that botulism occurs at all, of course, it can occur in cans on pantry shelves as well as in cans from Dumpsters. Need I say that home-canned goods are simply too risky to be recommended.

13   From time to time one of my companions, aware of the source of my provisions, will ask, "Do you think these crackers are really safe to eat?" For some reason it is most often the crackers they ask about.

14   This question has always made me angry. Of course I would not offer my companion anything I had doubts about. But more than that, I wonder why he cannot evaluate the condition of the crackers for himself. I have no special knowledge and I have been wrong before. Since he knows where the food comes from, it seems to me he ought to assume some of the responsibility for deciding what he will put in his mouth. For myself I have few qualms about dry foods such as crackers, cookies, cereal, chips, and pasta if they are free of visible contaminates and still dry and crisp. Most often such things are found in the original packaging, which is not so much a positive sign as it is the absence of a negative one.

15   Raw fruits and vegetables with intact skins seem perfectly safe to me, excluding of course the obviously rotten. Many are discarded for minor imperfections that can be pared away. Leafy vegetables, grapes, cauliflower, broccoli, and similar things may be contaminated by liquids and may be impractical to wash.

16   Candy, especially hard candy, is usually safe if it has not drawn ants. Chocolate is often discarded only because it has become discolored as the cocoa butter de-emulsified. Candying, after all, is one method of food preservation because pathogens do not like very sugary substances.

17   All of these foods might be found in any Dumpster and can be evaluated with some confidence largely on the basis of appearance. Beyond these are foods that cannot be correctly evaluated without additional information.

18   I began scavenging by pulling pizzas out of the Dumpster behind a pizza delivery shop. In general, prepared food requires caution, but in this case I knew when the shop closed and went to the Dumpster as soon as the last of the help left.

19   Such shops often get prank orders; both the orders and the products made to fill them are called *bogus*. Because help seldom stays long at these places, pizzas are often made with the wrong topping, refused on delivery for being cold, or baked incorrectly. The products to be discarded are boxed up because inventory is kept by counting boxes: A boxed pizza can be written off; an unboxed pizza does not exist.

20   I never placed a bogus order to increase the supply of pizzas and I believe no one else was scavenging in this Dumpster. But the people in the shop became suspicious and began to retain their garbage in the shop overnight. While it lasted I had a steady supply of fresh, sometimes warm pizza. Because I knew the

Dumpster I knew the source of the pizza, and because I visited the Dumpster regularly I knew what was fresh and what was yesterday's.

21   The area I frequent is inhabited by many affluent college students. I am not here by chance; the Dumpsters in this area are very rich. Students throw out many good things, including food. In particular they tend to throw everything out when they move at the end of a semester, before and after breaks, and around midterm, when many of them despair of college. So I find it advantageous to keep an eye on the academic calendar.

22   Students throw food away around breaks because they do not know whether it has spoiled or will spoil before they return. A typical discard is a half jar of peanut butter. In fact, nonorganic peanut butter does not require refrigeration and is unlikely to spoil in any reasonable time. The student does not know that, and since it is Daddy's money, the student decides not to take a chance. Opened containers require caution and some attention to the question, "Why was this discarded?" But in the case of discards from student apartments, the answer may be that the item was thrown out through carelessness, ignorance, or wastefulness. This can sometimes be deduced when the item is found with many others, including some that are obviously perfectly good.

23   Some students, and others, approach defrosting a freezer by chucking out the whole lot. Not only do the circumstances of such a find tell the story, but also the mass of frozen goods stays cold for a long time and items may be found still frozen or freshly thawed.

24   Yogurt, cheese, and sour cream are items that are often thrown out while they are still good. Occasionally I find a cheese with a spot of mold, which of course I just pare off, and because it is obvious why such a cheese was discarded, I treat it with less suspicion than an apparently perfect cheese found in similar circumstances. Yogurt is often discarded, still sealed, only because the expiration date on the carton had passed. This is one of my favorite finds because yogurt will keep for several days, even in warm weather.

25   Students throw out canned goods and staples at the end of semesters and when they give up college at midterm. Drugs, pornography, spirits, and the like are often discarded when parents are expected—Dad's Day, for example. And spirits also turn up after big party weekends, presumably discarded by the newly reformed. Wine and spirits, of course, keep perfectly well even once opened, but the same cannot be said of beer.

26   My test for carbonated soft drinks is whether they still fizz vigorously. Many juices or other beverages are too acidic or too syrupy to cause much concern, provided they are not visibly contaminated. I have discovered nasty molds in vegetable juices, even when the product was found under its original seal; I recommend that such products be decanted slowly into a clear glass. Liquids always require some care. One hot day I found a large jug of Pat O'Brien's Hurricane mix. The jug had been opened but was still ice cold. I drank three large glasses before it became apparent to me that someone had added the rum to the

mix, and not a little rum. I never tasted the rum, and by the time I began to feel the effects I had already ingested a very large quantity of the beverage. Some divers would have considered this a boon, but being suddenly intoxicated in a public place in the early afternoon is not my idea of a good time.

27   I have heard of people maliciously contaminating discarded food and even handouts, but mostly I have heard of this from people with vivid imaginations who have had no experience with the Dumpsters themselves. Just before the pizza shop stopped discarding its garbage at night, jalapeños began showing up on most of the thrown-out pizzas. If indeed this was meant to discourage me, it was a wasted effort because I am a native Texan.

28   For myself, I avoid game, poultry, pork, and egg-based foods, whether I find them raw or cooked. I seldom have the means to cook what I find, but when I do I avail myself of plentiful supplies of beef, which is often in very good condition. I suppose fish becomes disagreeable before it becomes dangerous. Lizbeth is happy to have any such thing that is past its prime and, in fact, does not recognize fish as food until it is quite strong.

29   Home leftovers, as opposed to surpluses from restaurants, are very often bad. Evidently, especially among students, there is a common type of personality that carefully wraps up even the smallest leftover and shoves it into the back of the refrigerator for six months or so before discarding it. Characteristic of this type are the reused jars and margarine tubs to which the remains are committed. I avoid ethnic foods I am unfamiliar with. If I do not know what it is supposed to look like when it is good, I cannot be certain I will be able to tell if it is bad.

30   No matter how careful I am I still get dysentery at least once a month, oftener in warm weather. I do not want to paint too romantic a picture. Dumpster diving has serious drawbacks as a way of life.

31   I learned to scavenge gradually, on my own. Since then I have initiated several companions into the trade. I have learned that there is a predictable series of stages a person goes through in learning to scavenge.

32   At first the new scavenger is filled with disgust and self-loathing. He is ashamed of being seen and may lurk around, trying to duck behind things, or he may try to dive at night. (In fact, most people instinctively look away from a scavenger. By skulking around, the novice calls attention to himself and arouses suspicion. Diving at night is ineffective and needlessly messy.)

33   Every grain of rice seems to be a maggot. Everything seems to stink. He can wipe the egg yolk off the found can, but he cannot erase from his mind the stigma of eating garbage.

34   That stage passes with experience. The scavenger finds a pair of running shoes that fit and look and smell brand-new. He finds a pocket calculator in perfect working order. He finds pristine ice cream, still frozen, more than he can eat or keep. He begins to understand: People throw away perfectly good stuff, a lot of perfectly good stuff.

35   At this stage, Dumpster shyness begins to dissipate. The diver, after all, has the last laugh. He is finding all manner of good things that are his for the taking. Those who disparage his profession are the fools, not he.

36   He may begin to hang on to some perfectly good things for which he has neither a use nor a market. Then he begins to take note of the things that are not perfectly good but are nearly so. He mates a Walkman with broken earphones and one that is missing a battery cover. He picks up things that he can repair.

37   At this stage he may become lost and never recover. Dumpsters are full of things of some potential value to someone and also of things that never have much intrinsic value but are interesting. All the Dumpster divers I have known come to the point of trying to acquire everything they touch. Why not take it, they reason, since it is all free? This is, of course, hopeless. Most divers come to realize that they must restrict themselves to items of relatively immediate utility. But in some cases the diver simply cannot control himself. I have met several of these pack-rat types. Their ideas of the values of various pieces of junk verge on the psychotic. Every bit of glass may be a diamond, they think, and all that glisters, gold.

38   I tend to gain weight when I am scavenging. Partly this is because I always find far more pizza and doughnuts than water-packed tuna, nonfat yogurt, and fresh vegetables. Also I have not developed much faith in the reliability of Dumpsters as a food source, although it has been proven to me many times. I tend to eat as if I have no idea where my next meal is coming from. But mostly I just hate to see food go to waste and so I eat much more than I should. Something like this drives the obsession to collect junk.

39   As for collecting objects, I usually restrict myself to collecting one kind of small object at a time, such as pocket calculators, sunglasses, or campaign buttons. To live on the street I must anticipate my needs to a certain extent: I must pick up and save warm bedding I find in August because it will not be found in Dumpsters in November. As I have no access to health care, I often hoard essential drugs, such as antibiotics and antihistamines. (This course can be recommended only to those with some grounding in pharmacology. Antibiotics, for example, even when indicated are worse than useless if taken in insufficient amounts.) But even if I had a home with extensive storage space, I could not save everything that might be valuable in some contingency.

40   I have proprietary feelings about my Dumpsters. As I have mentioned, it is no accident that I scavenge from ones where good finds are common. But my limited experience with Dumpsters in other areas suggests to me that even in poorer areas, Dumpsters, if attended with sufficient diligence, can be made to yield a livelihood. The rich students discard perfectly good kiwifruit; poorer people discard perfectly good apples. Slacks and Polo shirts are found in the one place; jeans and T-shirts in the other. The population of competitors rather than the affluence of the dumpers most affects the feasibility of survival

by scavenging. The large number of competitors is what puts me off the idea of trying to scavenge in places like Los Angeles.

41   Curiously, I do not mind my direct competition, other scavengers, so much as I hate the can scroungers.

42   People scrounge cans because they have to have a little cash. I have tried scrounging cans with an able-bodied companion. Afoot a can scrounger simply cannot make more than a few dollars a day. One can extract the necessities of life from the Dumpsters directly with far less effort than would be required to accumulate the equivalent value in cans. (These observations may not hold in places with container redemption laws.)

43   Can scroungers, then, are people who must have small amounts of cash. These are drug addicts and winos, mostly the latter because the amounts of cash are so small. Spirits and drugs do, like all other commodities, turn up in Dumpsters and the scavenger will from time to time have a half bottle of a rather good wine with his dinner. But the wino cannot survive on these occasional finds; he must have his daily dose to stave off the DTs. All the cans he can carry will buy about three bottles of Wild Irish Rose.

44   I do not begrudge them the cans, but can scroungers tend to tear up the Dumpsters, mixing the contents and littering the area. They become so specialized that they can see only cans. They earn my contempt by passing up change, canned goods, and readily hockable items.

45   There are precious few courtesies among scavengers. But it is common practice to set aside surplus items: pairs of shoes, clothing, canned goods, and such. A true scavenger hates to see good stuff go to waste, and what he cannot use he leaves in good condition in plain sight.

46   Can scroungers lay waste to everything in their path and will stir one of a pair of good shoes to the bottom of a Dumpster, to be lost or ruined in the muck. Can scroungers will even go through individual garbage cans, something I have never seen a scavenger do.

47   Individual garbage cans are set out on the public easement only on garbage days. On other days going through them requires trespassing close to a dwelling. Going through individual garbage cans without scattering litter is almost impossible. Litter is likely to reduce the public's tolerance of scavenging. Individual cans are simply not as productive as Dumpsters; people in houses and duplexes do not move so often and for some reason do not tend to discard as much useful material. Moreover, the time required to go through one garbage can that serves one household is not much less than the time required to go through a Dumpster that contains the refuse of twenty apartments.

48   But my strongest reservation about going through individual garbage cans is that this seems to me a very personal kind of invasion to which I would object if I were a householder. Although many things in Dumpsters are obviously meant never to come to light, a Dumpster is somehow less personal.

49   I avoid trying to draw conclusions about the people who dump in the Dumpsters I frequent. I think it would be unethical to do so, although I know many people will find the idea of scavenger ethics too funny for words.

50   Dumpsters contain bank statements, correspondence, and other documents, just as anyone might expect. But there are also less obvious sources of information. Pill bottles, for example. The labels bear the name of the patient, the name of the doctor, and the name of the drug. AIDS drugs and antipsychotic medicines, to name but two groups, are specific and are seldom prescribed for any other disorders. The plastic compacts for birth-control pills usually have complete label information.

51   Despite all of this sensitive information, I have had only one apartment resident object to my going through the Dumpster. In that case it turned out the resident was a university athlete who was taking bets and who was afraid I would turn up his wager slips.

52   Occasionally a find tells a story. I once found a small paper bag containing some unused condoms, several partial tubes of flavored sexual lubricants, a partially used compact of birth-control pills, and the torn pieces of a picture of a young man. Clearly she was through with him and planning to give up sex altogether.

53   Dumpster things are often sad—abandoned teddy bears, shredded wedding books, despaired-of sales kits. I find many pets lying in state in Dumpsters. Although I hope to get off the streets so that Lizbeth can have a long and comfortable old age, I know this hope is not very realistic. So I suppose when her time comes she too will go into a Dumpster. I will have no better place for her. And after all, it is fitting, since for most of her life her livelihood has come from the Dumpster. When she finds something I think is safe that has been spilled from a Dumpster, I let her have it. She already knows the route around the best ones. I like to think that if she survives me she will have a chance of evading the dog catcher and of finding her sustenance on the route.

54   Silly vanities also come to rest in the Dumpsters. I am a rather accomplished needleworker. I get a lot of material from the Dumpsters. Evidently sorority girls, hoping to impress someone, perhaps themselves, with their mastery of a womanly art, buy a lot of embroider-by-number kits, work a few stitches horribly, and eventually discard the whole mess. I pull out their stitches, turn the canvas over, and work an original design. Do not think I refrain from chuckling as I make gifts from these kits.

55   I find diaries and journals. I have often thought of compiling a book of literary found objects. And perhaps I will one day. But what I find is hopelessly commonplace and bad without being, even unconsciously, camp. College students also discard their papers. I am horrified to discover the kind of paper that now merits an A in an undergraduate course. I am grateful, however, for the number of good books and magazines the students throw out.

56   In the area I know best I have never discovered vermin in the Dumpsters, but there are two kinds of kitty surprise. One is alley cats whom I meet as they leap, claws first, out of Dumpsters. This is especially thrilling when I

have Lizbeth in tow. The other kind of kitty surprise is a plastic garbage bag filled with some ponderous, amorphous mass. This always proves to be used cat litter.

57   City bees harvest doughnut glaze and this makes the Dumpster at the doughnut shop more interesting. My faith in the instinctive wisdom of animals is always shaken when ever I see Lizbeth attempt to catch a bee in her mouth, which she does whenever bees are present. Evidently some birds find Dumpsters profitable, for birdie surprise is almost as common as kitty surprise of the first kind. In hunting season all kinds of small game turn up in Dumpsters, some of it, sadly, not entirely dead. Curiously, summer and winter, maggots are uncommon.

58   The worse of the living and near-living hazards of the Dumpsters are the fire ants. The food they claim is not much of a loss, but they are vicious and aggressive. It is very easy to brush against some surface of the Dumpster and pick up half a dozen or more fire ants, usually in some sensitive area such as the underarm. One advantage of bringing Lizbeth along as I make Dumpster rounds is that, for obvious reasons, she is very alert to ground-based fire ants. When Lizbeth recognizes a fire-ant infestation around our feet, she does the Dance of the Zillion Fire Ants. I have learned not to ignore this warning from Lizbeth, whether I perceive the tiny ants or not, but to remove ourselves at Lizbeth's first pas de bourée. All the more so because the ants are the worst in the summer months when I wear flip-flops if I have them. (Perhaps someone will misunderstand this. Lizbeth does the Dance of the Zillion Fire Ants when she recognizes more fire ants than she cares to eat, not when she is being bitten. Since I have learned to react promptly, she does not get bitten at all. It is the isolated patrol of fire ants that falls in Lizbeth's range that deserves pity. She finds them quite tasty.)

59   By far the best way to go through a Dumpster is to lower yourself into it. Most of the good stuff tends to settle at the bottom because it is usually weightier than the rubbish. My more athletic companions have often demonstrated to me that they can extract much good material from a Dumpster I have already been over.

60   To those psychologically or physically unprepared to enter a Dumpster, I recommend a stout stick, preferably with some barb or hook at one end. The hook can be used to grab plastic garbage bags. When I find canned goods or other objects loose at the bottom of a Dumpster, I lower a bag into it, roll the desired object into the bag, and then hoist the bag out—a procedure more easily described than executed. Much Dumpster diving is a matter of experience for which nothing will do except practice.

61   Dumpster diving is outdoor work, often surprisingly pleasant. It is not entirely predictable; things of interest turn up every day and some days there are finds of great value. I am always very pleased when I can turn up exactly the thing I most wanted to find. Yet in spite of the element of chance, scavenging more than most other pursuits tends to yield returns in some proportion to the

effort and intelligence brought to bear. It is very sweet to turn up a few dollars in change from a Dumpster that has just been gone over by a wino.

62   The land is now covered with cities. The cities are full of Dumpsters. If a member of the canine race is ever able to know what it is doing, then Lizbeth knows that when we go around to the Dumpsters, we are hunting. I think of scavenging as a modern form of self-reliance. In any event, after having survived nearly ten years of government service, where everything is geared to the lowest common denominator, I find it refreshing to have work that rewards initiative and effort. Certainly I would be happy to have a sinecure again, but I am no longer heartbroken that I left one.

63   I find from the experience of scavenging two rather deep lessons. The first is to take what you can use and let the rest go by. I have come to think that there is no value in the abstract. A thing I cannot use or make useful, perhaps by trading, has no value however rare or fine it may be. I mean useful in a broad sense—some art I would find useful and some otherwise.

64   I was shocked to realize that some things are not worth acquiring, but now I think it is so. Some material things are white elephants that eat up the possessor's substance. The second lesson is the transience of material being. This has not quite converted me to a dualist, but it has made some headway in that direction. I do not suppose that ideas are immortal, but certainly mental things are longer lived than other material things.

65   Once I was the sort of person who invests objects with sentimental value. Now I no longer have those objects, but I have the sentiments yet.

66   Many times in our travels I have lost everything but the clothes I was wearing and Lizbeth. The things I find in Dumpsters, the love letters and rag dolls of so many lives, remind me of this lesson. Now I hardly pick up a thing without envisioning the time I will cast it aside. This I think is a healthy state of mind. Almost everything I have now has already been cast out at least once, proving that what I own is valueless to someone.

67   Anyway, I find my desire to grab for the gaudy bauble has been largely sated. I think this is an attitude I share with the very wealthy—we both know there is plenty more where what we have came from. Between us are the rat-race millions who nightly scavenge the cable channels looking for they know not what.

68   I am sorry for them.

EXERCISES

Some of the Issues

1. Why might Eighner begin his essay by defining words and terms?
2. In paragraphs 7 through 30, Eighner describes how to select safe food from Dumpsters. What information do you recall from his descriptions?

How does Eighner establish his authority on the issue of Dumpster diving? What indications does he give that his judgment is not infallible?

3. What is Eighner's attitude toward the students in the neighborhood where he scavenges (paragraphs 21–25)? How did you, as a student, react to his comments?

4. What does Eighner say are the stages people go through as scavengers (paragraphs 31–37)?

5. Who are the scavengers Eighner disapproves of and why? Do you feel he is too judgmental?

6. What reasons does Eighner give for not scavenging in individual garbage cans? Can you think of a similar way in which you set boundaries for respecting the privacy of others?

7. What does Eighner feel he shares with the wealthy (paragraph 67)? How does he describe the "rat-race millions" and why does he feel sorry for them?

8. Eighner tells us in paragraph 4 that, as a scavenger, he has learned how wasteful consumers can be. Having finished his essay, summarize what he has learned about wastefulness, citing examples from throughout the text.

9. What are some of the ethical issues Eighner raises in this essay? What do you think of Eighner's sense of ethics?

10. What were your responses to this essay? Did it change your perceptions of the homeless in any way?

The Way We Are Told

11. "On Dumpster Diving" could be classified as a "process" essay, a type of writing that describes how to do something. How does Eighner use this form to tell us more than simply "how to" scavenge?

12. What is the tone of the essay? Does it vary?

13. Eighner gives detailed descriptions throughout the essay. What is their effect?

Some Subjects for Writing

14. Describe how to do something that you do well. Begin in a way that establishes your authority on the issue. If possible, choose something that is important to you, but whose value to others may not be obvious.

15. What provisions should be made for the homeless? Should they be allowed to share public buildings such as libraries, or sleep in sheltered areas of buildings, train, subway, or bus stations? Should churches open space for

them? Write an essay explaining your views using specific examples to back up your claims.

16. Do you feel there is too much wastefulness in American society? Give evidence based on personal experience and observations. For example, you may want to observe the habits of students in your school cafeteria, patrons in a local restaurant, or employees in your workplace.

High-Tech Wasteland

Elizabeth Grossman

Have you ever wondered how to get rid of an old, obsolete computer? A broken cell phone? Americans currently own more than two billion pieces of high-tech electronics, and discard five to seven million tons of them each year. In this essay, environmental journalist Elizabeth Grossman issues a wake-up call to the rapidly increasing problem of high-tech trash—the mostly unseen and often toxic waste that is a byproduct of our culture's appetite for and easy access to cheap, disposable consumer electronics.

A native of New York City, Grossman now makes her home in Portland, Oregon. She holds a B.A. in literature from Yale University. Grossman is a widely published freelance writer as well as the author of the books Watershed: The Undamming of America *(2002),* Adventuring Along the Lewis and Clark Trail *(2003), and most recently* High-Tech Trash: Digital Devices, Hidden Toxins, and Human Health *(2006), which expands further on the issues she explores here.*

This article originally appeared in 2004 in Orion, *an environmental literary quarterly magazine.*

1   The scenario is familiar. The day arrives when the computer that was going to be your personal bridge to the twenty-first century has become a dinosaur. The salesperson who touted that machine's efficiency now explains in tones of pity and derision just how far from the cutting edge of technology you are. The only solution is a new computer. And so, in early 2001, when it became clear that my old laptop could not handle most websites and could not be upgraded, it had to go. I tried to find someone who wanted a Macintosh 5300c, but no one was interested in a computer that couldn't surf the web without crashing.

2   Thanks to our appetite for gadgets, convenience, and innovation (and the current system of world commerce that makes them relatively affordable), Americans now own some two billion pieces of consumer electronics. For over two decades, rapid technological advances have doubled the computing capacity of semiconductor chips almost every eighteen months, bringing us faster computers, smaller cell phones, more efficient machinery and appliances, and an increasing demand for new products. With some five million to seven million tons of this stuff becoming obsolete in the U.S. each year, high-tech electronics are now the fastest growing part of the municipal waste stream. For the most part we have been so bedazzled by figuring out how to use the new PC, PDA, TV, DVD player, or cell phone, that until recently we haven't given this waste much thought.

3   From my desk in Portland, the tap of a few keys on my laptop sends a message to Hong Kong, retrieves articles filed in Brussels, displays pictures of my nieces in New York, and plays the song of a wood stork recorded in Florida. Traveling with my laptop and cell phone, I have access to a whole world of information and personal communication—a world that, as electricity grids, phone towers, and wireless networks proliferate, exists with diminishing regard for geography. This universe of instant information, conversation, and entertainment is so powerful and absorbing—and its currency so physically ephemeral—that it's hard to remember that the technology that makes it possible has anything to do with the natural world.

4   But this digital wizardry relies on a complex array of materials—metals, elements, plastics, and chemical compounds. Each tidy piece of equipment has a story that begins in mines, refineries, factories, rivers, and aquifers, and ends on pallets and in dumpsters, smelters, and landfills all around the world.

5   Where the garbage goes, where a plume of smoke travels, where waste flows and settles when it is washed downstream, how human communities, wildlife, and the landscape respond to the waste—these are costs that are traditionally left off the industrial balance sheet, and which industry is now just beginning to figure into the cost of doing business. As Jim Puckett, director of Basel Action Network (BAN), a nonprofit environmental advocacy group that tracks the global travels of hazardous waste, has said, "Humans have this funny idea that when you get rid of something, it's gone." The high-tech industry is no exception.

6   According to the Environmental Protection Agency (EPA), more than two million tons of high-tech electronics are dumped in U.S. landfills each year, and only about 10 percent of discarded personal computers are recycled. The EPA expects at least 200 million televisions to be discarded between 2003 and 2010, 250 million computers to become obsolete in the next five years, and 65,000 tons of used and broken cell phones to accumulate by 2005. And these numbers are for the U.S. alone.

7   What makes this waste so problematic is that compared to the items we're used to recycling, high-tech electronics are a particularly complex kind of trash. Soda cans, bottles, and newspapers are made of one or no more than a few materials. High-tech electronics contain dozens of tightly packed substances, which complicates separation and recycling. Many of the substances are harmful to human and environmental health.

8   The cathode ray tubes (CRTs) in computer and television monitors contain lead, a well-documented neurotoxin, as do printed circuit boards. Mercury, another neurotoxin, is used to light flat-panel display screens. Some batteries and circuit boards contain cadmium, a recognized carcinogen. Polyvinyl chloride, a plastic used to insulate wires, generates dioxins and furans—both persistent organic pollutants—when burned. Brominated flame retardants, some of which have been documented to disrupt thyroid hormone function and act as neurotoxins in animals, are used in plastics that house electronics. Some of these

flame retardants have been found in the breast milk of women across the U.S., and in marine mammals around the globe. Copper, beryllium, barium, zinc, chromium, silver, and nickel are among the other toxic and hazardous substances used in high-tech electronics. These materials do not pose hazards while the equipment is intact, but when it is trashed they become a huge problem.

9   Scientists are just beginning to quantify precisely how the toxic ingredients of high-tech electronics may be leaching into the environment via landfills, unregulated dumping, and crude recycling that can involve open burning of plastics and other materials. But it's clear from studies undertaken around the world that these substances are present in groundwater, accumulating in the marine food web, and traveling as airborne particles. A 2001 EPA report estimated that discarded electronics, or e-waste, account for approximately 70 percent of the heavy metals and 40 percent of the lead now found in U.S. landfills.

10   So where does the e-waste go? Where should it go? Despite electronics' toxic contents, the U.S.—unlike a half-dozen or more other countries—has no national legislation regulating e-waste disposal and no national system for electronics recycling. The EPA considers discarded electronics hazardous waste. But unless your state or local government bans specific electronic components (such as CRTs) or the materials they contain—and unless you're dumping over 220 pounds of e-waste a month (a federal violation)—it's perfectly legal to toss it with the rest of your trash. Curbside recycling bins are given the once-over before being pitched into the truck, but no one picks through your trash on its way to the dump. Consumer education and conscience are often the only safeguards against putting small quantities of hazardous waste into the bin.

11   If I'd dumped my old laptop in the trash, it would have been eventually trucked out to a landfill in eastern Oregon. If I took an old Macintosh out of my closet today and shipped it to the manufacturer's designated recycler, it would end up in a shredder in California. But first it would be dismantled, assuming the equipment cannot be reused or refurbished as is. The recycler separates certain components—batteries, CRTs, mercury elements, and some plastics—for special handling and hazardous materials recovery. The remainder, including circuit boards, is shredded, and later melted and smelted to extract the valuable metals, primarily copper and gold, for resale and reuse.

12   However, the way electronics are designed makes their disassembly and materials recycling cumbersome and expensive. This is especially true of older, obsolete equipment now making its way into the waste stream. So despite laws intended to prevent the export of hazardous waste, there's a good chance that had I deposited my computer in a used electronics collection facility, it might have been loaded onto a ship bound for China, following what Jim Puckett of the Basel Action Network calls "the economic path of least resistance."

13   A woman squats over an open flame in a backyard workshop. In the pan she holds over the fire, a plastic and metal circuit board begins to melt into a smoky, noxious stew. With bare hands she plucks out the chips. Another woman wields

a hammer and cracks the back of an old monitor to remove the copper yoke. The lead-laden glass is tossed onto a riverside pile. Nearby, a man wearing no protective clothing sluices a pan of acid over a pile of computer chips, releasing a puff of steam. When the chemical vapor clears, a small fleck of gold will emerge. Another worker crouches over a pile of broken ink cartridges, brushing the carbon black out by hand. A child stands on a pile of smashed electronics, eating an apple. At night, thick black dioxin-laden smoke rises from a mountain of burning wires, whose plastic insulation melts to expose the valuable copper within.

14   These images of Guiyu, a southern Chinese city, are from a film called *Exporting Harm*, produced by BAN and the Silicon Valley Toxics Coalition, a group that's been watchdogging the computer industry for more than twenty years. Released in 2002, the film shows the city filled with enormous mounds of trashed electronics piled in open heaps: computer parts of all sorts, monitors, keyboards, wires, printers, cartridges, fax machines, and circuit boards—all imported from throughout the developed world for inexpensive, labor-intensive recycling. The city's water has been rendered undrinkable, the soil poisoned, and its river polluted with heavy concentrations of dioxins, as well as lead, barium, chromium, and other heavy metals.

15   Jim Puckett calls this e-waste the "effluent of the affluent." According to *Exporting Harm's* estimates for early 2002, some 50 to 80 percent of the electronics collected for recycling in the western half of the United States were being exported for cheap dismantling overseas, predominantly in China and Southeast Asia. The film's footage, which includes pictures of equipment I.D. tags reading "Property of the City of Los Angeles" and "State of California Medical Facility," startled officials from states around the country.

16   No one wants to see their state's name on equipment handled by workers who might earn two dollars a day toiling under hazardous conditions, or to risk the liabilities of improper toxic-waste disposal. Consequently, the past few years have seen a flurry of state e-waste regulation bills. In 2003 alone, more than fifty bills were introduced in more than two dozen states. Meanwhile, in the absence of national legislation, a group of electronics manufacturers, government agencies, and nongovernmental organizations is negotiating the National Product Stewardship Initiative, which would create a nationwide policy for dealing with used and obsolete electronics.

17   For now, a patchwork of different programs addresses e-waste. Some states have banned CRTs from landfills. Others will bar specific hazardous substances from products sold in the state. Some have initiated recycling programs—both ongoing and one-day collection events. Others have created task forces to recommend further action. Meanwhile, electronics manufacturers are carrying on with existing voluntary take-back schemes and developing new ones.

18   Under California's recently passed electronics recycling bill, collections will begin with a fee based on screen size. Iowa began its electronics recycling program with one-day collection events that charged five dollars per item.

Over 275 Massachusetts cities and towns now collect electronics for recycling —many at curbside. And community websites often announce upcoming collection events. But that nifty new PC or PDA does not yet come with end-of-life instructions.

19   Large-scale purchasers—corporations, governments, schools, hospitals— are now returning most used equipment to manufacturers. But none of the take-back programs up and running has the capacity to capture the vast amount of e-waste generated by households and small businesses, over 90 percent of which is currently not recycled.

20   Electronic waste—indeed, all trash and recycling in the U.S.—is regulated and financed by local governments and taxpayers. But e-waste is expensive to handle and piling up fast. According to research by a coalition of U.S. nonprofit groups, the cost of collecting and processing this waste from 2006 to 2015—not counting cleanup of contamination from improperly managed e-waste—will exceed ten billion dollars.

21   Because of these costs, consumer groups, environmental advocates, and local governments have begun to question a basic assumption about handling the waste. "All the parts of a product's lifecycle that involve making money, being profitable, are considered the realm of the private sector," says Sego Jackson, solid-waste planner for Snohomish County, Washington. "But as soon as that product has lost its value, it crosses some magic line where it becomes the government's responsibility. Clearly we need a different kind of system."

22   In the U.S., that need has spawned the Computer Take Back Campaign, an effort to further involve manufacturers in the recycling of electronics. Launched in 2001 by a coalition of nonprofits that includes the GrassRoots Recycling Network and Silicon Valley Toxics Coalition, the campaign is helping communities craft legislation to control the hazards of e-waste, and is working with manufacturers and retailers on collection events. "Our biggest allies in this campaign are local governments," says David Wood, executive director of the GrassRoots Recycling Network.

23   High-tech electronics are resource-intensive to produce, lose value quickly, and are expensive to dispose of—a "dysfunctional" cycle, according to Sego Jackson. He has his own test for what would be functional: "It should be as easy to recycle a computer as it is to buy one." But reaching that goal will require "a fundamental paradigm shift," says Jim Puckett. At the heart of this shift is the idea that end-of-product-life costs and responsibilities—traditionally borne by consumers, taxpayers, government, and the environment—should be shouldered by the manufacturer.

24   This concept, known as Extended Producer Responsibility, is new to Americans but in use across Europe, where it will soon be applied to electronics. The European Union recently passed legislation requiring electronics manufacturers to take back and facilitate the recycling of used products, in a system financed by "advanced recovery" fees attached to the price of new equipment. If revenues from the fees fail to cover the recycling costs, producers have to absorb the difference.

The system provides an incentive to design products for easier, cheaper recycling. A companion piece of legislation will require manufacturers to eliminate some hazardous substances from new equipment.

25   Because Europe is a significant market for consumer electronics, U.S. companies, including Dell, HP, and IBM, will be making products to meet EU requirements. And given the industry's global manufacturing and distribution efficiencies, those products will be sold worldwide.

26   To meet the EU regulations, engineers are rushing to find alternatives to lead solder now used in computers, and to eliminate certain flame retardants. And as companies fall under growing pressure to conserve resources and reduce toxics, they are moving away from piecemeal elimination of undesirables and toward redesign. Mercury, for example, is highly toxic and expensive to dispose of. As HP environmental product steward Nathan Moin explains, the company could rework the current design of flat panel display screens to make it easier to remove the mercury lamp now used. But it will be more efficient to design a new lighting device that eliminates mercury altogether. This is an example of what architect William McDonough, coauthor of *Cradle to Cradle: Remaking the Way We Make Things*, describes as going beyond the "less bad approach" of reducing and eliminating individual toxics, to addressing the problem holistically.

27   Imagine what it would be like if upgrading software meant not having to buy a whole new computer, but simply snapping in a new processor. Or if printers and other accessories were universally compatible. Imagine if the price of a new laptop or mobile phone covered the cost of a convenient system to collect old equipment for reuse or recycling. Imagine if that price guaranteed a living wage in safe conditions to those engaged in every step of electronics disassembly, materials recovery, and manufacturing. Imagine if there were no such thing as garbage.

28   The high-tech industry is one of the first that is being pushed to internalize its costs, a move that will have fundamental implications for other industries as well. These changes will not mean that the economy or high-tech innovation will come to a screeching halt. There will still be commerce, education, entertainment, electronic love letters, and wireless calls to far-flung friends and family, but it won't be business as usual.

29   Meanwhile, my old printer, laptop, cell phone, and Zip drive are still in the closet, even though I now know where they should go. As for my old Macintosh 5300C, I believe it ended its useful life in an apartment on the Upper West Side of Manhattan, a neighborhood where I once recycled an old TV by taking it down to the street, where it was immediately carted off by a passer-by who said, "Hey, can I have that?"

EXERCISES

Some of the Issues

1. What is the problem Grossman presents us with at the end of paragraph 2? How does she lead up to it?
2. According to Grossman, why is it hard to remember that technology is connected to the natural world (paragraph 3)? In what ways is this connection made?
3. What costs are "traditionally left off the industrial balance sheet" (paragraph 4)? How does Grossman document these costs?
4. What distinguishes high-tech waste from other kinds of trash (paragraph 7)?
5. What regulations does the United States have for discarding electronic waste, and how easy is it to do so (paragraphs 10–12)? What do you know about how to discard technological waste in your own community?
6. According to Grossman and the film *Exporting Harm*, how is much of our e-waste disposed of? How have state legislatures in the United States responded?
7. To what extent, according to Grossman, can these regulations address the problem of e-waste? What is needed to fully address the problem?
8. What is the "paradigm shift" that Jim Puckett refers to? How does it differ from the way we currently think of electronic manufacturing and waste in the United States?
9. As Grossman points out, it is not longer common to repair technology such as televisions and VCRs. We are more likely to discard them and purchase new ones. How likely are you to try to get technological materials repaired? Would you know where to go to do this if you chose to do so? If possible, ask your parents or grandparents what kinds of electronic items they owned, and whether they were more likely to repair them if they broke.

The Way We Are Told

10. Grossman opens her article by speaking directly to the reader. Why does she do this? Is it effective?
11. Grossman describes specific scenes in great detail. Where does she use descriptive detail in the text and what effect does it have on you as a reader?

Some Subjects for Writing

12. Write an essay in which you analyze your own relationship to technology. You might start by documenting all of the technology you have purchased over the past one or two years. Then consider various questions about your use of this technology: Why did you buy it? Do you use it regularly, or as

much as you thought you would? Did it last as long as you expected? If you've gotten rid of a piece of technology (e.g., a computer, a television, or an iPod), why did you do so? Does Grossman's article make you reconsider any of the choices you've made? Why or why not?

*13. Though Grossman focuses on how we dispose of technology, she also implies that our thirst for new technology has serious environmental consequences. Write an essay in which you examine how or why people often seem to seek out the latest technology or gadget. What drives this search? Are there other consequences besides the environmental hazards? Do we, as a society, simply consume and throw away too much? You might also read Lars Eighner's "On Dumpster Diving" and consider his views about consumerism and wastefulness.

14. With the help of your instructor, research two or three means of discarding technological waste (batteries, computers, televisions, etc.) in your community. Write an essay in which you describe and, to the best of your ability, evaluate the programs and their impact. When were these programs started and under whose impetus? How effective are they?

Meet the Life Hackers

Clive Thompson

In "Meet the Life Hackers," journalist Clive Thompson introduces us to the field of "interruption science," a byproduct of an age in which more and more of us spend large portions of our lives stationed in front of a computer screen, and many more and varied modes of communication compete for our time and attention

As one of Thompson's sources points out, twenty years ago, an office worker had only two types of communication technology: telephones, which were relatively quick, and postal mail, which was relatively slow. In contrast, the office worker of the twenty-first century has a whole slew of communication possibilities between these poles, all competing for his or her attention at once. As a result, researchers have begun to study the science of interruption, trying to figure out ways to allow us to work (and, inevitably, to be interrupted) more efficiently. Thompson also introduces us to a loosely affiliated group of techies calling themselves "life hackers" who have developed ways to radically simplify their lives in order to rise above the chaos of modern communication.

Clive Thompson often writes about science and technology for the Washington Post, Wired, Details, *and many other publications. His is a frequent commentator for NPR, CNN, and the Canadian Broadcasting Corporation. He is also a contributing writer for* The New York Times Magazine, *where this article originally appeared in 2005.*

1   In 2000, Gloria Mark was hired as a professor at the University of California at Irvine. Until then, she was working as a researcher, living a life of comparative peace. She would spend her days in her lab, enjoying the sense of serene focus that comes from immersing yourself for hours at a time in a single project. But when her faculty job began, that all ended. Mark would arrive at her desk in the morning, full of energy and ready to tackle her to-do list—only to suffer an endless stream of interruptions. No sooner had she started one task than a colleague would e-mail her with an urgent request; when she went to work on that, the phone would ring. At the end of the day, she had been so constantly distracted that she would have accomplished only a fraction of what she set out to do. "Madness," she thought. "I'm trying to do 30 things at once."

2   Lots of people complain that office multitasking drives them nuts. But Mark is a scientist of "human-computer interactions" who studies how high-tech devices affect our behavior, so she was able to do more than complain: she set out to measure precisely how nuts we've all become. Beginning in 2004, she persuaded two West Coast high-tech firms to let her study their cubicle

dwellers as they surfed the chaos of modern office life. One of her grad students, Victor Gonzalez, sat looking over the shoulder of various employees all day long, for a total of more than 1,000 hours. He noted how many times the employees were interrupted and how long each employee was able to work on any individual task.

3   When Mark crunched the data, a picture of 21st-century office work emerged that was, she says, "far worse than I could ever have imagined." Each employee spent only 11 minutes on any given project before being interrupted and whisked off to do something else. What's more, each 11-minute project was itself fragmented into even shorter three-minute tasks, like answering e-mail messages, reading a Web page or working on a spreadsheet. And each time a worker was distracted from a task, it would take, on average, 25 minutes to return to that task. To perform an office job today, it seems, your attention must skip like a stone across water all day long, touching down only periodically.

4   Yet while interruptions are annoying, Mark's study also revealed their flip side: they are often crucial to office work. Sure, the high-tech workers grumbled and moaned about disruptions, and they all claimed that they preferred to work in long, luxurious stretches. But they grudgingly admitted that many of their daily distractions were essential to their jobs. When someone forwards you an urgent e-mail message, it's often something you really do need to see; if a cellphone call breaks through while you're desperately trying to solve a problem, it might be the call that saves your hide. In the language of computer sociology, our jobs today are "interrupt driven." Distractions are not just a plague on our work—sometimes they are our work. To be cut off from other workers is to be cut off from everything.

5   For a small cadre of computer engineers and academics, this realization has begun to raise an enticing possibility: perhaps we can find an ideal middle ground. If high-tech work distractions are inevitable, then maybe we can re-engineer them so we receive all of their benefits but few of their downsides. Is there such a thing as a perfect interruption?

6   Mary Czerwinski first confronted this question while working, oddly enough, in outer space. She is one of the world's leading experts in interruption science, and she was hired in 1989 by Lockheed to help NASA design the information systems for the International Space Station. NASA had a problem: how do you deliver an interruption to a busy astronaut? On the space station, astronauts must attend to dozens of experiments while also monitoring the station's warning systems for potentially fatal mechanical errors. NASA wanted to ensure that its warnings were perfectly tuned to the human attention span: if a warning was too distracting, it could throw off the astronauts and cause them to mess up million-dollar experiments. But if the warnings were too subtle and unobtrusive, they might go unnoticed, which would be even worse. The NASA engineers needed something that would split the difference.

7   Czerwinski noticed that all the information the astronauts received came to them as plain text and numbers. She began experimenting with different types

of interruptions and found that it was the style of delivery that was crucial. Hit an astronaut with a textual interruption, and he was likely to ignore it, because it would simply fade into the text-filled screens he was already staring at. Blast a horn and he would definitely notice it—but at the cost of jangling his nerves. Czerwinski proposed a third way: a visual graphic, like a pentagram whose sides changed color based on the type of problem at hand, a solution different enough from the screens of text to break through the clutter.

8   The science of interruptions began more than 100 years ago, with the emergence of telegraph operators—the first high-stress, time-sensitive information-technology jobs. Psychologists discovered that if someone spoke to a telegraph operator while he was keying a message, the operator was more likely to make errors; his cognition was scrambled by mentally "switching channels." Later, psychologists determined that whenever workers needed to focus on a job that required the monitoring of data, presentation was all-important. Using this knowledge, cockpits for fighter pilots were meticulously planned so that each dial and meter could be read at a glance.

9   Still, such issues seemed remote from the lives of everyday workers—even information workers—simply because everyday work did not require parsing screenfuls of information. In the 90's, this began to change, and change quickly. As they became ubiquitous in the workplace, computers, which had until then been little more than glorified word-processors and calculators, began to experience a rapid increase in speed and power. "Multitasking" was born; instead of simply working on one program for hours at a time, a computer user could work on several different ones simultaneously. Corporations seized on this as a way to squeeze more productivity out of each worker, and technology companies like Microsoft obliged them by transforming the computer into a hub for every conceivable office task, and laying on the available information with a trowel. The Internet accelerated this trend even further, since it turned the computer from a sealed box into our primary tool for communication. As a result, office denizens now stare at computer screens of mind-boggling complexity, as they juggle messages, text documents, PowerPoint presentations, spreadsheets and Web browsers all at once. In the modern office we are all fighter pilots.

10   Information is no longer a scarce resource—attention is. David Rose, a Cambridge, Mass.-based expert on computer interfaces, likes to point out that 20 years ago, an office worker had only two types of communication technology: a phone, which required an instant answer, and postal mail, which took days. "Now we have dozens of possibilities between those poles," Rose says. How fast are you supposed to reply to an e-mail message? Or an instant message? Computer-based interruptions fall into a sort of Heisenbergian uncertainty trap: it is difficult to know whether an e-mail message is worth interrupting your work for unless you open and read it—at which point you have, of course, interrupted yourself. Our software tools were essentially designed to compete with one another for our attention, like needy toddlers.

11   The upshot is something that Linda Stone, a software executive who has worked for both Apple and Microsoft, calls "continuous partial attention": we

are so busy keeping tabs on everything that we never focus on anything. This can actually be a positive feeling, inasmuch as the constant pinging makes us feel needed and desired. The reason many interruptions seem impossible to ignore is that they are about relationships—someone, or something, is calling out to us. It is why we have such complex emotions about the chaos of the modern office, feeling alternately drained by its demands and exhilarated when we successfully surf the flood.

12   "It makes us feel alive," Stone says. "It's what makes us feel important. We just want to connect, connect, connect. But what happens when you take that to the extreme? You get overconnected." Sanity lies on the path down the center —if only there was some way to find it.

13   It is this middle path that Czerwinski and her generation of computer scientists are now trying to divine. When I first met her in the corridors of Microsoft, she struck me as a strange person to be studying the art of focusing, because she seemed almost attention-deficit disordered herself: a 44-year-old with a pageboy haircut and the electric body language of a teenager. "I'm such a spaz," she said, as we went bounding down the hallways to the cafeteria for a "bio-break." When she ushered me into her office, it was a perfect Exhibit A of the go-go computer-driven life: she had not one but three enormous computer screens, festooned with perhaps 30 open windows—a bunch of e-mail messages, several instant messages and dozens of Web pages. Czerwinski says she regards 20 solid minutes of uninterrupted work as a major triumph; often she'll stay in her office for hours after work, crunching data, since that's the only time her outside distractions wane.

14   In 1997, Microsoft recruited Czerwinski to join Microsoft Research Labs, a special division of the firm where she and other eggheads would be allowed to conduct basic research into how computers affect human behavior. Czerwinski discovered that the computer industry was still strangely ignorant of how people really used their computers. Microsoft had sold tens of millions of copies of its software but had never closely studied its users' rhythms of work and interruption. How long did they linger on a single document? What interrupted them while they were working, and why?

15   To figure this out, she took a handful of volunteers and installed software on their computers that would virtually shadow them all day long, recording every mouse click. She discovered that computer users were as restless as hummingbirds. On average, they juggled eight different windows at the same time —a few e-mail messages, maybe a Web page or two and a PowerPoint document. More astonishing, they would spend barely 20 seconds looking at one window before flipping to another.

16   Why the constant shifting? In part it was because of the basic way that today's computers are laid out. A computer screen offers very little visual real estate. It is like working at a desk so small that you can look at only a single sheet of paper at a time. A Microsoft Word document can cover almost an entire screen. Once you begin multitasking, a computer desktop very quickly becomes buried in detritus.

17   This is part of the reason that, when someone is interrupted, it takes 25 minutes to cycle back to the original task. Once their work becomes buried beneath a screenful of interruptions, office workers appear to literally forget what task they were originally pursuing. We do not like to think we are this flighty: we might expect that if we are, say, busily filling out some forms and are suddenly distracted by a phone call, we would quickly return to finish the job. But we don't. Researchers find that 40 percent of the time, workers wander off in a new direction when an interruption ends, distracted by the technological equivalent of shiny objects. The central danger of interruptions, Czerwinski realized, is not really the interruption at all. It is the havoc they wreak with our short-term memory: What the heck was I just doing?

18   When Gloria Mark and Mary Czerwinski, working separately, looked at the desks of the people they were studying, they each noticed the same thing: Post-it notes. Workers would scrawl hieroglyphic reminders of the tasks they were supposed to be working on ("Test PB patch DAN's PC—Waiting for AL," was one that Mark found). Then they would place them directly in their fields of vision, often in a halo around the edge of their computer screens. The Post-it notes were, in essence, a jury-rigged memory device, intended to rescue users from those moments of mental wandering.

19   For Mark and Czerwinski, these piecemeal efforts at coping pointed to ways that our high-tech tools could be engineered to be less distracting. When Czerwinski walked around the Microsoft campus, she noticed that many people had attached two or three monitors to their computers. They placed their applications on different screens—the e-mail far off on the right side, a Web browser on the left and their main work project right in the middle—so that each application was "glanceable." When the ding on their e-mail program went off, they could quickly peek over at their in-boxes to see what had arrived.

20   The workers swore that this arrangement made them feel calmer. But did more screen area actually help with cognition? To find out, Czerwinski's team conducted another experiment. The researchers took 15 volunteers, sat each one in front of a regular-size 15-inch monitor and had them complete a variety of tasks designed to challenge their powers of concentration—like a Web search, some cutting and pasting and memorizing a seven-digit phone number. Then the volunteers repeated these same tasks, this time using a computer with a massive 42-inch screen, as big as a plasma TV.

21   The results? On the bigger screen, people completed the tasks at least 10 percent more quickly—and some as much as 44 percent more quickly. They were also more likely to remember the seven-digit number, which showed that the multitasking was clearly less taxing on their brains. Some of the volunteers were so enthralled with the huge screen that they begged to take it home. In two decades of research, Czerwinski had never seen a single tweak to a computer system so significantly improve a user's productivity. The clearer your screen, she found, the calmer your mind. So her group began devising tools that maximized screen space by grouping documents and programs together—making it

possible to easily spy them out of the corner of your eye, ensuring that you would never forget them in the fog of your interruptions. Another experiment created a tiny round window that floats on one side of the screen; moving dots represent information you need to monitor, like the size of your in-box or an approaching meeting. It looks precisely like the radar screen in a military cockpit.

22   In late 2003, the technology writer Danny O'Brien decided he was fed up with not getting enough done at work. So he sat down and made a list of 70 of the most "sickeningly overprolific" people he knew, most of whom were software engineers of one kind or another. O'Brien wrote a questionnaire asking them to explain how, precisely, they managed such awesome output. Over the next few weeks they e-mailed their replies, and one night O'Brien sat down at his dining-room table to look for clues. He was hoping that the self-described geeks all shared some common tricks.

23   He was correct. But their suggestions were surprisingly low-tech. None of them used complex technology to manage their to-do lists: no Palm Pilots, no day-planner software. Instead, they all preferred to find one extremely simple application and shove their entire lives into it. Some of O'Brien's correspondents said they opened up a single document in a word-processing program and used it as an extra brain, dumping in everything they needed to remember—addresses, to-do lists, birthdays—and then just searched through that file when they needed a piece of information. Others used e-mail—mailing themselves a reminder of every task, reasoning that their in-boxes were the one thing they were certain to look at all day long.

24   In essence, the geeks were approaching their frazzled high-tech lives as engineering problems—and they were not waiting for solutions to emerge from on high, from Microsoft or computer firms. Instead they ginned up a multitude of small-bore fixes to reduce the complexities of life, one at a time, in a rather Martha Stewart-esque fashion.

25   Many of O'Brien's correspondents, it turned out, were also devotees of "Getting Things Done," a system developed by David Allen, a personal-productivity guru who consults with Fortune 500 corporations and whose seminars fill Silicon Valley auditoriums with anxious worker bees. At the core of Allen's system is the very concept of memory that Mark and Czerwinski hit upon: unless the task you're doing is visible right in front of you, you will half-forget about it when you get distracted, and it will nag at you from your subconscious. Thus, as soon as you are interrupted, Allen says, you need either to quickly deal with the interruption or—if it's going to take longer than two minutes—to faithfully add the new task to your constantly updated to-do list. Once the interruption is over, you immediately check your to-do list and go back to whatever is at the top.

26   "David Allen essentially offers a program that you can run like software in your head and follow automatically," O'Brien explains. "If this happens, then do this. You behave like a robot, which of course really appeals to geeks."

27   O'Brien summed up his research in a speech called "Life Hacks," which he delivered in February 2004 at the O'Reilly Emerging Technology Conference. Five hundred conference-goers tried to cram into his session, desperate for tips on managing info chaos. When O'Brien repeated the talk the next year, it was mobbed again. By the summer of 2005, the "life hacks" meme had turned into a full-fledged grass-roots movement. Dozens of "life hacking" Web sites now exist, where followers of the movement trade suggestions on how to reduce chaos. The ideas are often quite clever: O'Brien wrote for himself a program that, whenever he's surfing the Web, pops up a message every 10 minutes demanding to know whether he's procrastinating. It turns out that a certain amount of life-hacking is simply cultivating a monklike ability to say no.

28   "In fairness, I think we bring some of this on ourselves," says Merlin Mann, the founder of the popular life-hacking site 43folders.com. "We'd rather die than be bored for a few minutes, so we just surround ourselves with distractions. We've got 20,000 digital photos instead of 10 we treasure. We have more TV Tivo'd than we'll ever see." In the last year, Mann has embarked on a 12-step-like triage: he canceled his Netflix account, trimmed his instant-messaging "buddy list" so only close friends can contact him and set his e-mail program to bother him only once an hour. ("Unless you're working in a Korean missile silo, you don't need to check e-mail every two minutes," he argues.)

29   Mann's most famous hack emerged when he decided to ditch his Palm Pilot and embrace a much simpler organizing style. He bought a deck of 3-by-5-inch index cards, clipped them together with a binder clip and dubbed it "The Hipster P.D.A."—an ultra-low-fi organizer, running on the oldest memory technology around: paper.

30   In the 1920's, the Russian scientist Bluma Zeigarnik performed an experiment that illustrated an intriguing aspect of interruptions. She had several test subjects work on jigsaw puzzles, then interrupted them at various points. She found that the ones least likely to complete the task were those who had been disrupted at the beginning. Because they hadn't had time to become mentally invested in the task, they had trouble recovering from the distraction. In contrast, those who were interrupted toward the end of the task were more likely to stay on track.

31   Gloria Mark compares this to the way that people work when they are "co-located"—sitting next to each other in cubicles—versus how they work when they are "distributed," each working from different locations and interacting online. She discovered that people in open-cubicle offices suffer more interruptions than those who work remotely. But they have better interruptions, because their co-workers have a social sense of what they are doing. When you work next to other people, they can sense whether you're deeply immersed, panicking or relatively free and ready to talk—and they interrupt you accordingly.

32   So why don't computers work this way? Instead of pinging us with e-mail and instant messages the second they arrive, our machines could store them

up—to be delivered only at an optimum moment, when our brains are mostly relaxed.

33   One afternoon I drove across the Microsoft campus to visit a man who is trying to achieve precisely that: a computer that can read your mind. His name is Eric Horvitz, and he is one of Czerwinski's closest colleagues in the lab. For the last eight years, he has been building networks equipped with artificial intelligence (A.I.) that carefully observes a computer user's behavior and then tries to predict that sweet spot—the moment when the user will be mentally free and ready to be interrupted.

34   Horvitz booted the system up to show me how it works. He pointed to a series of bubbles on his screen, each representing one way the machine observes Horvitz's behavior. For example, it measures how long he's been typing or reading e-mail messages; it notices how long he spends in one program before shifting to another. Even more creepily, Horvitz told me, the A.I. program will—a little like HAL from "2001: A Space Odyssey"—eavesdrop on him with a microphone and spy on him using a Webcam, to try and determine how busy he is, and whether he has company in his office. Sure enough, at one point I peeked into the corner of Horvitz's computer screen and there was a little red indicator glowing.

35   "It's listening to us," Horvitz said with a grin. "The microphone's on."

36   It is no simple matter for a computer to recognize a user's "busy state," as it turns out, because everyone is busy in his own way. One programmer who works for Horvitz is busiest when he's silent and typing for extended periods, since that means he's furiously coding. But for a manager or executive, sitting quietly might actually be an indication of time being wasted; managers are more likely to be busy when they are talking or if PowerPoint is running.

37   In the early days of training Horvitz's A.I., you must clarify when you're most and least interruptible, so the machine can begin to pick up your personal patterns. But after a few days, the fun begins—because the machine takes over and, using what you've taught it, tries to predict your future behavior. Horvitz clicked an onscreen icon for "Paul," an employee working on a laptop in a meeting room down the hall. A little chart popped up. Paul, the A.I. program reported, was currently in between tasks—but it predicted that he would begin checking his e-mail within five minutes. Thus, Horvitz explained, right now would be a great time to e-mail him; you'd be likely to get a quick reply. If you wanted to pay him a visit, the program also predicted that—based on his previous patterns—Paul would be back in his office in 30 minutes.

38   With these sorts of artificial smarts, computer designers could re-engineer our e-mail programs, our messaging and even our phones so that each tool would work like a personal butler—tiptoeing around us when things are hectic and barging in only when our crises have passed. Horvitz's early prototypes offer an impressive glimpse of what's possible. An e-mail program he produced seven years ago, code-named Priorities, analyzes the content of your incoming

e-mail messages and ranks them based on the urgency of the message and your relationship with the sender, then weighs that against how busy you are. Super-urgent mail is delivered right away; everything else waits in a queue until you're no longer busy. When Czerwinski first tried the program, it gave her as much as three hours of solid work time before nagging her with a message. The soft-ware also determined, to the surprise of at least one Microsoft employee, that e-mail missives from Bill Gates were not necessarily urgent, since Gates tends to write long, discursive notes for employees to meditate on.

39   This raises a possibility both amusing and disturbing: perhaps if we gave arti-ficial brains more control over our schedules, interruptions would actually decline —because A.I. doesn't panic. We humans are Pavlovian; even though we know we're just pumping ourselves full of stress, we can't help frantically checking our e-mail the instant the bell goes ding. But a machine can resist that temptation, be-cause it thinks in statistics. It knows that only an extremely rare message is so im-portant that we must read it right now.

40   So will Microsoft bring these calming technologies to our real-world com-puters? "Could Microsoft do it?" asks David Gelernter, a Yale professor and longtime critic of today's computers. "Yeah. But I don't know if they're motivated by the lust for simplicity that you'd need. They're more interested in piling more and more toys on you."

41   The near-term answer to the question will come when Vista, Microsoft's new operating system, is released in the fall of 2006. Though Czerwinski and Horvitz are reluctant to speculate on which of their innovations will be included in the new system, Horvitz said that the system will "likely" incorporate some way of detecting how busy you are. But he admitted that "a bunch of features may not be shipping with Vista." He says he believes that Microsoft will eventu-ally tame the interruption-driven workplace, even if it takes a while. "I have viewed the task as a 'moon mission' that I believe that Microsoft can pull off," he says.

42   By a sizable margin, life hackers are devotees not of Microsoft but of Apple, the company's only real rival in the creation of operating systems—and a com-pany that has often seemed to intuit the need for software that reduces the com-plexity of the desktop. When Apple launched its latest operating system, Tiger, earlier this year, it introduced a feature called Dashboard—a collection of glanceable programs, each of which performs one simple function, like display-ing the weather. Tiger also includes a single-key tool that zooms all open win-dows into a bingo-card-like grid, uncovering any "lost" ones. A superpowered search application speeds up the laborious task of hunting down a missing file. Microsoft is now playing catch-up; Vista promises many of the same tweaks, al-though it will most likely add a few new ones as well, including, possibly, a 3-D mode for seeing all the windows you have open.

43   Apple's computers have long been designed specifically to soothe the con-fusions of the technologically ignorant. For years, that meant producing com-puter systems that seemed simpler than the ones Microsoft produced, but were

less powerful. When computers moved relatively slowly and the Internet was little used, raw productivity—shoving the most data at the user—mattered most, and Microsoft triumphed in the marketplace. But for many users, simplicity now trumps power. Linda Stone, the software executive who has worked alongside the C.E.O.'s of both Microsoft and Apple, argues that we have shifted eras in computing. Now that multitasking is driving us crazy, we treasure technologies that protect us. We love Google not because it brings us the entire Web but because it filters it out, bringing us the one page we really need. In our new age of overload, the winner is the technology that can hold the world at bay.

44   Yet the truth is that even Apple might not be up to the task of building the ultimately serene computer. After all, even the geekiest life hackers find they need to trick out their Apples with duct-tape-like solutions; and even that sometimes isn't enough. Some experts argue that the basic design of the computer needs to change: so long as computers deliver information primarily through a monitor, they have an inherent bottleneck—forcing us to squeeze the ocean of our lives through a thin straw. David Rose, the Cambridge designer, suspects that computers need to break away from the screen, delivering information through glanceable sources in the world around us, the way wall clocks tell us the time in an instant. For computers to become truly less interruptive, they might have to cease looking like computers. Until then, those Post-it notes on our monitors are probably here to stay.

EXERCISES

Some of the Issues

1. Did Glora Mark's situation at her new job (paragraph 1) seem familiar to you in any way? How and why?
2. What did Mark find in her study of work interruptions (paragraphs 3–4)? Were you surprised by her data?
3. What was Mary Czerwinski's primary concern when she worked for Lockheed (paragraph 6)? What were some of the ways she addressed the problem?
4. When did the science of interruptions first appear and why?
5. How did the office workplace begin to change in the 1990s?
6. What, according to Linda Stone, is "continuous partial attention"? Do you agree with her explanation of why we are drawn to this type of multitasking?
7. What did Microsoft hire Czerwinski to figure out, how did she set up her study, and what did she find? What were some of the solutions she and Gloria Mark came up with through their work?
8. What common tricks do the "self-described geeks" that Danny O'Brien surveyed share (paragraphs 22–27)?

9. What is "life hacking"? Why do you suppose O'Brian uses that term?
10. What does Gloria Mark conclude about the differences between those workers who are co-located and those who work remotely (paragraph 31)? Why are her findings significant?
11. What kinds of behavior does Eric Horvitz's computer, equipped with artificial intelligence, detect (paragraphs 33–38)? Do you feel you could benefit from this kind of technology? Why or why not?
12. Why, according to Thompson, might artificial detections of how prepared we are for interruptions be better than human judgment (paragraph 39)?
13. What is your response to Thompson's statement: "In our new age of overload, the winner is the technology that can hold the world at bay" (paragraph 43)?
14. How many different forms of communication do you use in one day? What is your primary means of communication and why? Do you feel that you are able to make smart choices about how you communicate with others? Why or why not?

The Way We Are Told

15. Examine Thompson's use of description throughout the article. What kinds of details does he give? Are they effective?
16. To what extent were you familiar with the concept of life hacking before reading this article? To what extent was Thompson able to engage you with the topic and how did he do it? Use specific examples from the article to back up your points.
17. Though Thompson's piece can be classified as a magazine article, he also uses more literary techniques, such as metaphor and simile. Find at least two examples of these techniques and explain why you do or do not find them effective.
18. Who do you see as the audience for Thompson's piece? On what evidence do you base your answer?

Some Subjects for Writing

*19. Thompson looks at the ways in which technological developments have made life both easier and more complicated. Barbara Brandt raises similar issues in "Less Is More: The Call for Shorter Work Hours." Using both Thompson's and Brandt's articles, along with examples from your own experience or other readings, write an essay analyzing the degree to which technology has both complicated and simplified our lives.
20. Develop and write out your own life hacking plan, or write out a plan for friend or relative whom you feel needs it. You should write the plan in a way that's detailed, but also clear and easy to follow. Include an introduction to the plan, stating your rationale for it and highlighting the plan's primary goals. You might check out a life hacking site such as 43folders.com to help you develop your ideas.

Who Burns for the Perfection of Paper

Martín Espada

Born in Brooklyn, New York, to a Puerto Rican father and a Jewish-Jehovah's Witness mother, poet and essayist Martín Espada was raised in the working-class housing projects of East New York. Espada's own life experiences provide the subject matter for much of his creative work, which focuses heavily on issues of class, ethnicity, and social justice. His sense of social justice is deeply rooted in his family and upbringing. In his essay "Zapata's Disciple and Perfect Brie," Espada traces the influence of his father's activism and Puerto Rican identity on the development of his own social conscience, saying "My father's social class was defined by the opportunities denied him because of racism, and the opportunities he created for himself in spite of racism."

Espada's work history is interesting and varied. He has worked as a night desk clerk at a transient hotel, telephone solicitor, gas station attendant, bouncer, bartender, and tenants' rights attorney, among other jobs. He is currently a professor of English at the University of Massachusetts at Amherst. This poem is informed both by his experience as a factory worker at a company that made yellow legal pads and by his time as a law student. It is reprinted from his poetry collection entitled City of Coughing and Dead Radiators *(1993).*

At sixteen, I worked after high school hours
at a printing plant
that manufactured legal pads:
Yellow paper
5   stacked seven feet high
and leaning
as I slipped cardboard
between the pages,
then brushed red glue
10   up and down the stack.
No gloves: fingertips required
for the perfection of paper,
smoothing the exact rectangle.
Sluggish by 9 PM, the hands
15   would slide along suddenly sharp paper,
and gather slits thinner than the crevices

of the skin, hidden.
Then the glue would sting,
hands oozing
20   till both palms burned
at the punchclock.

Ten years later, in law school,
I knew that every legal pad
was glued with the sting of hidden cuts,
25   that every open lawbook
was a pair of hands
upturned and burning.

EXERCISES

Some of the Issues

1. Why does Espada emphasize the idea of perfection? What does he say is required in order for the paper to achieve perfection?
2. The making of legal pads may seem like an odd topic for a poem. Why does Espada think it's important?
3. Where does Espada use alliteration? How does this help the flow of the poem?
4. In the middle of the poem, Espada moves from the first person to the third person. Why do you suppose he does this? What effect does it have on the reader?
5. How do you interpret the last stanza of the poem? What images does Espada evoke? How does it follow from the rest of the poem?

Some Subjects for Writing

6. Do you think many of Espada's law school classmates shared his experience of working in a factory? Describe a situation where you had an insight into an experience that you felt others around you might not share. Describe how you gained that experience, and how it affected your feelings about, or your approach to, that situation.

PART V

DEFINING
OURSELVES

Each of us carries a number of identities. We are identified as sons or daughters, as parents, as students, as members of clubs or teams, professions or unions, religious denominations, or social classes. In some cases our particular identities will not only associate us with specific groups of people, but also type us. In American society, as multiethnic and multiracial as it is, this attribution of identity is particularly complex and often carries with it, rightly or wrongly, certain notions about the members of a group. Often, when we define ourselves, it is in reaction to these notions.

Recently, the issues of multiracial or multiethnic identity has been an important part of American conversation, though it's hardly a new phenomenon. For the first time in the 2000 census, Americans were able to identify themselves as a member of more than one racial or ethnic group. The decision to make this change in the census was a reflection of the fact that increasing numbers of Americans do not identify with only one group.

In "An Ethnic Trump," Gish Jen, a Chinese American, and her husband, of Irish descent, consider whether to send their four-year-old son to Chinese day school. The debate centers around the question of whether some identities are immutable and others are matters of choice. Robin D.G. Kelley begins his essay "The People in Me" with the question, "So, what are you?" and concludes that this is not a simple question, nor one that he feels he can answer without a more detailed history of his family background. He implies that there are many people whose answer to this question would be equally complex. Roxanne Farmanfarmaian, born of an Iranian father and a Utah Mormon mother, compares the interwoven strands of her identity with the DNA strands of the double helix, and concludes that one can't be separated from the other.

For Nicolette Toussaint, partially deaf since childhood, deafness is a part of her identity. She must decide whether to declare her disability to others to whom it may not be immediately apparent. If she does not, she risks being misunderstood; if she does, she risks being set aside as "other."

Sometimes, other people's perceptions of us are clouded by myths and popular images. In "The Myth of the Latin Woman: I Just Met a Girl Named María," Judith Ortiz Cofer writes about the stereotypical, often demeaning images of Latinas generated by popular culture. A writer and professor raised alternately in Puerto Rico and in the United States, she has always balanced two identities, but to the outside world she is often taken to be the "María" of *West Side Story* or the "Evita" of the musical. Malcolm X describes how as a young boy in 1914 he sought to be more like the white majority by straightening his hair. Later in life he realizes how degrading the process was and decides to take pride in his African-American identity. In "The College Dropout Boom," David Leonhardt analyzes some of the reasons working-class students drop out of college at a higher rate than their classmates from more privileged backgrounds. The chapter concludes with Pennie Holmes-Brinson's poem "Time Stood Still Again," which explores identities seen and unseen.

An Ethnic Trump

Gish Jen

Born in 1956, Gish Jen grew up Chinese American in predominantly Jewish suburbs of New York City. She graduated from Harvard College and received her master's degree in creative writing from the University of Iowa Writer's Workshop.

Jen is the author of a collection of short stories entitled Who's Irish *(1999), and three novels,* Typical American *(1991),* Mona in the Promised Land *(1996) and* The Love Wife *(2004), all of which deal with issues of family and ethnic identity.*

In this essay, Jen raises the question of why certain ethnicities "trump" others—why her son, for example, whose heritage is both Irish and Chinese, attends a Chinese culture school and not an Irish one. Jen concludes that one of the reasons might be "the relative distance of certain cultures from mainstream America." Most Irish Americans today are descended from ancestors who came to the United States during the great wave of Irish immigration in the mid-1800s. Though Irish immigrants were seen as outsiders by mainstream American culture at the time, they have since become more accepted and assimilated. Though there have been Chinese immigrants to the United States since the Gold Rush of 1847 and earlier, most Chinese Americans trace their arrival to this country to much more recent times.

1   That my son, Luke, age 4, goes to Chinese-culture school seems inevitable to most people, even though his father is of Irish descent. For certain ethnicities trump others; Chinese, for example, trumps Irish. This has something to do with the relative distance of certain cultures from mainstream American culture, but it also has to do with race. For as we all know, it is not only certain ethnicities that trump others but certain colors: black trumps white, for example, always and forever; a mulatto is not a kind of white person, but a kind of black person.

2   And so it is, too, that my son is considered a kind of Asian person whose manifest destiny is to embrace Asian things. The Chinese language. Chinese food. Chinese New Year. No one cares whether he speaks Gaelic or wears green on St. Patrick's Day. For though Luke's skin is fair, and his features mixed, people see his straight black hair and "know" who he is.

3   But is this how we should define ourselves, by other people's perceptions? My husband, Dave, and I had originally hoped for Luke to grow up embracing his whole complex ethnic heritage. We had hoped to pass on to him values and habits of mind that had actually survived in both of us.

4   Then one day, Luke combed his black hair and said he was turning it yellow. Another day, a fellow mother reported that her son had invited all blond-haired children like himself to his birthday party. And yet another day, Luke was happily scooting around the Cambridge Common playground when a pair of older boys, apparently brothers, blocked his way. "You're Chinese!" they shouted, leaning on the hood of Luke's scooter car. "You are! You're Chinese!" So brazen were these kids, that even when I, an adult, intervened, they continued to shout. Luke answered, "No, I'm not!"—to no avail; it was not clear if the boys even heard him. Then the boys' mother called to them from some distance away, outside the fence, and though her voice was no louder than Luke's, they left obediently.

5   Behind them opened a great, rippling quiet, like the wash of a battleship.

6   Luke and I immediately went over things he could say if anything like that ever happened again. I told him that he was 100 percent American, even though I knew from my own childhood in Yonkers that these words would be met only with derision. It was a sorry chore. Since then I have not asked him about the incident, hoping that he has forgotten about it, and wishing that I could, too. For I wish I could forget the sight of those kids' fingers on the hood of Luke's little car. I wish I could forget their loud attack, but also Luke's soft defense: *No, I'm not.*

7   Chinese-culture school. After dozens of phone calls, I was elated to discover the Greater Boston Chinese Cultural Association nearby in West Newton. The school takes children at 3, has a wonderful sense of community and is housed in a center paid for, in part, by great karaoke fund-raising events. (Never mind what the Japanese meant to the Chinese in the old world. In this world, people donate at least $200 each for a chance at the mike, and the singing goes on all night.) There are even vendors who bring home-style Chinese food to sell after class—stuff you can't get in a restaurant. Dave and I couldn't wait for the second class, and a chance to buy more *bao* for our freezer.

8   But in the car on the way to the second class, Luke announced that he didn't want to go to Chinese school anymore. He said that the teacher talked mostly about ducks and bears and that he wasn't interested in ducks and bears. And I knew this was true. I knew that Luke was interested only in whales and ships. And what's more, I knew we wouldn't push him to take swimming lessons if he didn't want to, or music. Chinese school was a wonderful thing, but there was a way in which we were accepting it as somehow non-optional. Was that right? Hadn't we always said that we didn't want our son to see himself as more essentially Chinese than Irish?

9   Yet we didn't want him to deny his Chinese heritage, either. And if there were going to be incidents on the playground, we wanted him to at least know what Chinese meant. So when Luke said again that he didn't want to go to Chinese school, I said, "Oh, really?" Later on we could try to teach him to define himself irrespective of race. For now, though, he was going to Chinese school. I exchanged glances with Dave. And then together, in a most carefully casual manner, we squinted at the road and kept going.

EXERCISES

Some of the Issues

1. What does the author mean when she says that certain ethnicities trump others? Do you agree with this statement?
2. What incidents does the author describe in paragraph 4? Why are they significant and how do they relate to each other?
3. In the end, does the author come to see Chinese school as optional for her son?
4. What are both the literal and figurative meanings of the last line?
5. What are some of the issues Jen brings up concerning families with parents of different ethnic, religious, or racial groups? What are your feelings on this issue?

The Way We Are Told

6. What is the tone of the essay? Why might Jen have chosen this tone?
7. How does Jen use humor in paragraphs 7 and 8?
8. Throughout the essay, Jen uses direct quotations to emphasize certain points or ideas. Where does she use them, and are they effective?

Some Subjects for Writing

9. Jen concludes that, at least for now, Chinese school is not optional for Luke in the same way swimming and music lessons are. Were certain schools, events, or programs not optional for you as a child because they were highly significant to your family? Write a narrative in which you describe this experience. From your perspective as an adult, analyze its importance in your life.
10. Consider what it means to be multiracial or multiethnic. Is it important that people choose to identify more strongly with one aspect of their ethnic identity, or is it possible for people to see themselves as comprised of many identities, histories, and backgrounds?

The People in Me

Robin D.G. Kelley

Robin D.G. Kelley spent the earliest years of his life in New York's Harlem and later moved with his family to Seattle before settling in Pasadena, California. He attended college at California State University in Long Beach, where he chose four different majors before settling on history, and still managed to earn his degree in three years. Within four years of graduating college he had earned both a masters and a doctorate in history from UCLA.

Kelley is a social historian whose work focuses on how black people, particularly in America, have defined the notion of liberation and the strategies they've developed to achieve it. He has a keen interest in grass-roots movements and on how culture, especially popular culture like hip-hop music and graffiti, expresses people's desire for liberation.

Kelley is currently Professor of Cultural and Historical studies at Columbia University, but much of his writing has been published outside of academic circles. He has written for the Nation, Monthly Review, The New York Times Magazine, *and the* Voice Literary Supplement, *among others. He is the author of several books about history and popular culture, most recently* Yo' Mama's DisFunktional! Fighting the Culture Wars in Urban America *(1997) and* Freedom Dreams: The Black Radical Imagination *(2002). This selection was originally published in* ColorLines, *a magazine about race and culture.*

1   "So, what are you?" I don't know how many times people have asked me that. "Are you Puerto Rican? Dominican? Indian or something? You must be mixed." My stock answer has rarely changed: "My mom is from Jamaica but grew up in New York, and my father was from North Carolina but grew up in Boston. Both black."

2   My family has lived with "the question" for as long as I can remember. We're "exotics," all cursed with "good hair" and strange accents—we don't sound like we from da Souf or the Norwth, and don't have that West Coast-by-way-of-Texas Calabama thang going on. The only one with the real West Indian singsong vibe is my grandmother, who looks even more East Indian than my sisters. Whatever Jamaican patois my mom possessed was pummeled out of her by cruel preteens who never had sensitivity seminars in diversity. The result for us was a nondescript way of talking, walking, and being that made us not black enough, not white enough—just a bunch of not-quite-nappy-headed enigmas.

3   My mother never fit the "black momma" media image. A beautiful, demure, light brown woman, she didn't drink, smoke, curse, or say things like "Lawd Jesus"

210

or "hallelujah," nor did she cook chitlins or gumbo. A vegetarian, she played the harmonium (a foot-pumped miniature organ), spoke softly with textbook diction, meditated, followed the teachings of Paramahansa Yogananda, and had wild hair like Chaka Khan. She burned incense in our tiny Harlem apartment, sometimes walked the streets barefoot, and, when she could afford it, cooked foods from the East.

4   To this day, my big sister gets misidentified for Pakistani or Bengali or Ethiopian. (Of course, changing her name from Sheral Anne Kelley to Makani Themba has not helped.) Not long ago, an Oakland cab driver, apparently a Sikh who had immigrated from India, treated my sister like dirt until he discovered that she was not a "scoundrel from Sri Lanka," but a common black American. Talk about ironic: How often are black women spared indignities *because* they are African American?

5   "What are you?" dogged my little brother more than any of us. He came out looking just like his father, who was white. In the black communities of Los Angeles and Pasadena, my baby bro' had to fight his way into blackness, usually winning only when he invited his friends to the house. When he got tired of this, he became what people thought he was—a cool white boy. Today he lives in Tokyo, speaks fluent Japanese, and is happily married to a Japanese woman (who is actually Korean passing as Japanese!). He stands as the perfect example of our mulattoness: a black boy trapped in a white body who speaks English with a slight Japanese accent and has a son who will spend his life confronting "the question."

6   Although folk had trouble naming us, we were never blanks or aliens in a "black world." We were and are "polycultural," and I'm talking about all peoples in the Western world. It is not skin, hair, walk, or talk that renders black people so diverse. Rather, it is the fact that most of them are products of different "cultures"—living cultures, not dead ones. These cultures live in and through us every day, with almost no self-consciousness about hierarchy or meaning. "Polycultural" works better than "multicultural," which implies that cultures are fixed, discrete entities that exist side by side—a kind of zoological approach to culture. Such a view obscures power relations, but often reifies race and gender differences.

7   Black people were polycultural from the get-go. Most of our ancestors came to these shores not as Africans, but as Ibo, Yoruba, Hausa, Kongo, Bambara, Mende, Mandingo, and so on. Some of our ancestors came as Spanish, Portuguese, French, Dutch, Irish, English, Italian. And more than a few of us, in North America as well as in the Caribbean and Latin America, have Asian and Native American roots.

8   Our lines of biological descent are about as pure as O.J.'s blood sample, and our cultural lines of descent are about as mixed up as a pot of gumbo. What we know as "black culture" has always been fluid and hybrid. In Harlem in the late 1960s and 1970s, Nehru suits were as popular—and as "black"—as dashikis, and martial arts films placed Bruce Lee among a pantheon of black heroes that

included Walt Frazier of the New York Knicks and Richard Roundtree, who played John Shaft in blaxploitation cinema. How do we understand the zoot suit—or the conk—without the pachuco culture of Mexican American youth, or low riders in black communities without Chicanos? How can we discuss black visual artists in the interwar years without reference to the Mexican muralists, or the radical graphics tradition dating back to the late 19th century, or the Latin American artists influenced by surrealism?

9   Vague notions of "Eastern" religion and philosophy, as well as a variety of Orientalist assumptions, were far more important to the formation of the Lost-Found Nation of Islam than anything coming out of Africa. And Rastafarians drew many of their ideas from South Asians, from vegetarianism to marijuana, which was introduced into Jamaica by Indians. Major black movements like Garveyism and the African Blood Brotherhood are also the products of global developments. We won't understand these movements until we see them as part of a dialogue with Irish nationalists from the Easter Rebellion, Russian and Jewish émigrés from the 1905 and 1917 revolutions, and Asian socialists like India's M.N. Roy and Japan's Sen Katayama.

10   Indeed, I'm not sure we can even limit ourselves to Earth. How do we make sense of musicians Sun Ra, George Clinton, and Lee "Scratch" Perry or, for that matter, the Nation of Islam, when we consider the fact that space travel and notions of intergalactic exchange constitute a key source of their ideas?

11   So-called "mixed race" children are not the only ones with a claim to multiple heritages. All of us are inheritors of European, African, Native American, and Asian pasts, even if we can't exactly trace our bloodlines to these continents.

12   To some people that's a dangerous concept. Too many Europeans don't want to acknowledge that Africans helped create so-called Western civilization, that they are both indebted to and descendants of those they enslaved. They don't want to see the world as One—a tiny little globe where people and cultures are always on the move, where nothing stays still no matter how many times we name it. To acknowledge our polycultural heritage and cultural dynamism is not to give up our black identity. It does mean expanding our definition of blackness, taking our history more seriously, and looking at the rich diversity within us with new eyes.

13   So next time you see me, don't ask where I'm from or what I am, unless you're ready to sit through a long-ass lecture. As singer/songwriter Abbey Lincoln once put it, "I've got some people in me."

EXERCISES

Some of the Issues

1. In paragraph 2, Kelley describes his family as "not-quite-nappy-headed enigmas." What does he mean by this? What details does he use to back up his claim?

2. How does Kelley describe his mother in paragraph 3? What is significant about her interests?
3. Why does Kelley see irony in the way his sister is treated by the Sikh cab driver (paragraph 4)?
4. Kelley uses the term "polycultural" (paragraph 6). What does he mean by this term? Why does he feel it works better than the word "multicultural"?
5. How does Kelley go on to complicate the issue of culture? What does he mean by the term "rich diversity" (paragraph 12)?
6. Have you ever been asked "the question"? Describe the time(s) you have been asked it, and analyze the situation. Who asked you and under what circumstances? What do you think was the person's reason for asking it?
7. Another question people often ask to type strangers is, "What do you do?" Do you see ways in which this is similar to the "What are you?" question?

The Way We Are Told

8. Kelley begins his essay with what he later refers to as "the question": "So what are you?" Why do you think he does this? To whom is he speaking?
9. Why does the author put quotation marks around the words "exotics" and "good hair" in paragraph 2, and "black momma" in paragraph 3?
10. What would you say Kelley's attitude is toward "the question"? What is it about the tone of the essay that indicates this? Use specific examples from the reading to back up your claim.
11. Kelley does not state his thesis directly. If you were to come up with a one- or two-sentence thesis for this essay, what would it be?

Some Subjects for Writing

12. Write about your response to a frequently asked question that is, at least in some ways, similar to the question, "What are you?" Some examples might be, "What do you do?" "How old are you?" "Where are you from?" Do you ever feel like people want to know more than just the factual answer when they ask it? If yes, what do you think they really want to know?
*13. Multiracial and multiethnic identity has become an important topic of late, particularly with the change in the 2000 census that allowed respondents to identify themselves as a member of more than one ethnic/racial group. Read Gish Jen's "An Ethnic Trump" and Roxane Farmanfarmaian's "The Double Helix." How do their perspectives on the issue differ? In what ways do the authors agree or disagree? Focus on the language and the terms they use, and cite specific examples from each reading.

The Double Helix

Roxane Farmanfarmaian

Half Iranian and half American Mormon, Roxane Farmanfarmaian was raised in Holland and went to college in the United States. Her father Manucher Farmanfarmaian, who she describes in this essay as having had a harem, was born in Iran in 1917 to an aristocratic family. He eventually rose to a high position in the Iranian government and was influential in the creation of OPEC, the alliance of oil-producing nations. Like many Iranians with means, he fled the country in 1979 when the Ayatollah Khomeini came to power in a fundamentalist revolution. Together, Roxane and her father co-authored an account of his experiences in Iran entitled Blood and Oil: Inside the Shah's Iran *(1998).*

Farmanfarmaian is currently a journalist and has written for many publications, including the New York Times, Interview, Time, *and* USA Today. *She also co-founded and wrote for* The Iranian, *an independent news magazine in Iran before the revolution. This essay is taken from* Half and Half *(1998), an anthology of essays by authors who grew up binational, biracial, or bicultural. In it, Farmanfarmaian describes her experience growing up between her American and Iranian worlds, never quite feeling at home in either, though acknowledging that in spite of their enormous differences, they also have some unexpected similarities.*

1   Call me the foreigner. Though I was born a child of deep, strong roots, I have no sense of cultural belonging. I grew up in Europe, in a country that was not my own. In my parents' homelands, on the other hand, I felt no sense of self-recognition. Their worlds were thousands of miles apart, and both extreme. "What home is this?" I would wonder, seeing nothing of myself in them. And yet, like haunting background music that I could barely hear, the symmetries between my parents' worlds, repeated with uncanny consistency, implied a unity I could not grasp. Was there a purpose to their patterns, I wondered, seeing nothing beyond the haphazard coincidence of nature. Or was it simply that one always searches for parallels, trying to find the familiar in the unknown?

2   As a child, I was oblivious to the contradictions between my ancestral worlds. But as I grew older, I felt increasingly lost among the people who were supposed to be my countrymen, and at sea in the cities that held my heritage.

3   My mother was born a Mormon, my father a Muslim. This almost always is cause for amazement in those just brought into the know. I respond like a spitting snake, pointing out that the religions share not only their initial *M*s, but that their women wear special garments, that they both eschew certain foods, and, of course, that they both believe in the practice of polygamy.

214

4   Polygamy was, in fact, one of the elements that brought my parents together when they met in New York back in the fifties. My father, an outspoken
critic of Iran's regime at the time, was cooling his heels as an exile, living in a
small apartment on the Upper East Side of Manhattan. My mother, fresh from
Salt Lake City, was attending Columbia University's Teachers College while
making ends meet as a governess. They met at a production of T.S. Eliot's
Murder in the Cathedral being staged in the university's chapel. A few weeks
later, he invited her to his apartment for tea. There, in the powder room, she
saw a watercolor of Brigham Young sitting in the middle of a wide bed, a line
of wives stretching out on either side of him. Stunned to see the father of the
Latter-day Saints so prominently displayed in the home of a Muslim, she let
out a cry.

5   "It reminds me of my father," he explained. "He had a harem—with nine
wives."

6   The parallels between the worlds of my parents did not end with Brigham
Young. Once, while I was still in college, I flew from Tehran directly to Salt
Lake City. It was not something I'd really planned to do. I'd spent the summer
in Iran, and flew into New York intending to go straight on to university. But
somehow I'd miscalculated my dates and, upon arrival, realized that classes did
not start for another week. I called my mother from Kennedy Airport. As mothers will, she told me to come right out. Sixteen hours after stepping onto an Iran
Air flight out of Tehran—and because of the time change, only a few hours later
in the afternoon—I stepped off an America West flight in Salt Lake City.

7   I could have been disembarking at the same place I had boarded from. The
mountains, rising into the twilight, were twins of the ones I'd just left. The
ranges were both snowcapped, with the cities' lights running down their slopes
like molten lava into the dusty plain. The air was the same dry air, tinged with
the taste of salt from the wind off the saline lakes that lay embedded in their
deserts. Iran's brackish lake lay farther off than Salt Lake City's, and dried up
and cracked in the summer. But still, it gave off the same acrid smell.

8   It always struck me as one of those ironies that I, so tenuously American,
should be from Utah, such a totally American place and yet, in all the United
States, there is no more foreign a place, either. My mother's family are apiarists,
and it is the honeycomb that is the emblem of Utah. It is also home to the Rain-
bow Arch, which graces so many of the posters hanging in travel agencies
around the world. Yet it is the Mormon religion that is the true hallmark of
Utah. And Mormons make other Americans feel slightly uncomfortable. Maybe
it's the fact that the Book of Mormon is drawn from golden tablets which were
miraculously unearthed by the teenaged Joseph Smith in the forests of New
York, and which then as miraculously disappeared again before anyone else could
see them. Or perhaps it is because Mormons don't drink coffee because they're
not supposed to consume caffeine, but have been allowed to drink Coca-Cola
ever since the church bought a goodly number of the company's shares. Or, most
onerous of all, is it because, in the midst of a perfectly normal conversation, the

Mormon missionary zeal will suddenly spring out like an attacking pit bull, forcing the victim to wriggle away as best he or she can?

9   To be fair, both faiths are deceptive in order to get around their rigid doctrines. Is it any more self-serving on the part of the Mormon religion to ban the consumption of alcohol and yet allow private clubs to serve liquor to anyone who joins for a day, a week, or a month, than for the Muslim religion to ban prostitution but allow the purchase of a wife for a day, a week, or a month?

10   Not surprisingly, for a person born into two of the most fanatic religions in the world, I turned out rather religiously bland. To be honest, neither of my parents is particularly devout. I am glad of it. But it did weaken my footing in trying to find my place in their cultures. In Utah, strong religious conviction is imperative: you are either of the faith or not, and if not, and you've chosen to leave the faith behind, you even have a name—you are a "Jack Mormon." Feeling freed from the manacles of religion—especially such a controlling one—I considered myself above my Salt Lake relatives. Without realizing it, I replaced my need to belong with preemptive disdain—an attitude that ensured that I could not be rejected because I'd already done the rejecting. This was dangerously self-serving, but since I lived abroad, I did not need to reckon with this false sense of superiority for many years. Instead, as an expat based in Holland, I hopped blithely from one nation to another, simultaneously from nowhere and everywhere like so many others of my ilk: the army brats, the Eurotrash, the diplomatic crowd, and all the rest who were the human equivalents of the Eurodollar. In The Hague, midway between my parent's homelands, I attended an American school and thought of myself as American. Yet, when my friends said they were from Ohio or Texas, I did not say I was from Utah. No, I was just generally American.

11   Culture shock, with a capital *C*, came when I moved to the States for college. The realization that I was not American, no matter how general, was blistering. I didn't understand the Whopper jokes; I didn't know who Topper was; I'd never seen a Corvair. When Easter came around, and everyone gathered to watch *The Wizard of Oz* on TV, I retired alone to my room, unable to relate to a movie whose characters bore no resemblance to the way I'd imagined them since childhood, and alienated by a culture that had fostered a tradition around a film I'd never seen.

12   That first year of college was one of the loneliest of my life.

13   After living through it, however, I was more American than I'd ever been. At the same time, I made an important discovery: that I was rather happy I wasn't as American as I'd previously thought I wanted to be. The America that had held such an aura for me was the one defined by Tootsie Rolls, and Ked sneakers, and even *Bonanza*—none of which could easily be obtained, or viewed, abroad. Once I was in America, however, these became commonplace, along with the avalanche of other products that filled the supermarkets and the time on TV. I soon felt saturated with the consumerism and the waste, and tired of

the constant advertisements, and the claims to be the biggest and the best in the world. Perhaps one has to be a foreigner to clearly see a culture. For me, the emphasis on "things" ran through American life like too much fat in an overrich meal. It was a constant irritant, and I recoiled, hankering for the more family-oriented, simpler life I'd grown up with. I was different from most other Americans, I realized, in some ways I did not want to change.

14   When it came to feeling Persian, on the other hand, I thought I had no illusions. I was, to my own mind, clearly an outsider. I did not speak the language; I had no Iranian friends; I did not pretend to know the culture. This was before the revolution and the hostage crisis. It was not politically incorrect yet to be from Iran. Still, there were pitfalls. Deep inside, unnamed, unrecognized, I had a sense of entitlement. Because my father's family was large and powerful, because it had been instrumental in Persia's modern history, and could track its ancestors back as far as the 800s, I felt the country was stamped upon my bones. Like brown hair or a flair for languages, I believed I had somehow genetically inherited an innate Persian sensibility. Though outwardly I was a foreigner, I subconsciously presumed that once I returned to my fatherland, I would quickly feel I belonged.

15   I was mistaken. This was made crystal clear the summer I spent in Tehran before I flew on to Salt Lake City. It was the first time I'd gone alone, the first time I'd gone without my father there. And I was lost. My savvy as a world traveler forsook me. I was more estranged in Iran than anywhere I'd ever been.

16   My roommate from college came through to visit for a couple weeks. It was an opportunity to explore Iran, and, acting the knowledgeable host, I suggested we travel to Yazd, the capital of the Zoroastrians, a midsize town located somewhere in the middle of the central plain. Upon our arrival, we drove to the one hotel I'd been told existed there, only to find it shut. Thank God I'd thought to get the name of a friend of a friend before leaving Tehran, and he kindly put us up for the night in his office. To this day, I don't know where regular tourists stay when visiting Yazd's Zoroastrian fire monuments and its houses with their unusual wind towers.

17   Our first night, we went to the local bazaar, a dark cavernous place, and bought dried figs for dinner. We slept on cots set up in the office hallway. The next night, we did the same. Two nights were enough. The following morning, we decided to decamp to Isfahan, where I knew there were sumptuous mosques, a glittering bazaar, and a four-star hotel called the Shah Abbas in an old, stately caravansary.

18   The friend of a friend said he'd drive us. In fact, it was his chauffeur at the wheel, while he sat in the front seat and talked at us for six hours as we drove across the bleached stones of the desert.

19   "I went to the University of Nebraska," he said. "I lived for four years at the Holiday Inn. I never had to make my bed. And I ate french fries and ice cream every night for dinner."

20   I looked out the window, mortified, as though he epitomized all Persians and his words reflected directly on me. My roommate, on the other hand, thought him a fool—if a kindly one—and simply ignored him.

21   Going to Isfahan was a good choice. Though neither of us could understand the words, we listened to a storyteller in the hotel courtyard that evening, his singsong voice punctuated by the hubbly-bubbly pipes being smoked by many of the other listeners. The air was languid, the stars close, and we could always tell when we'd reached a good part in the story because the smokers would suddenly start inhaling quickly and the pipes would gurgle loudly in unison.

22   The next day, however, my sense of equilibrium vanished at the airport. Expecting to get a routine confirmation of our ticket change through Isfahan, I was met with a typical Middle Eastern scene: a mobbed departure desk, no one in line, everyone shouting at the harried clerk, who paid no mind to who was first or second but only to whoever shoved their tickets most insistently into his face. Instantly, I knew I'd gone about the tickets all wrong. I should have had them confirmed earlier by someone in the hotel, paid a little bakshish, and avoided this scene altogether. Instead, I now had to claw my way through this melee. I felt I had let my roommate down—acting as though I knew my way around when in fact I was just an impostor, as ill at ease as she—if not more so— among my countrymen.

23   It was not until three years later, caught amid revolution and religious revival, my Persian family fleeing and my American countrymen taken hostage, that I came to understand my roots as an Iranian. I'd moved there just in time to catch the turmoil. Thank God I did, for it was the last chance I had to get to know the country. I stayed for two years. As Iran lurched toward political Islam, I developed a circle of friends, published a liberal English-language magazine, and traveled to hot spots around the country. Despite the guns in the streets, I grew used to driving around in the back alleyways, and came to understand the women in their tentlike chadors. Once, on a visit to the holy city of Qom, I even wore one myself, which caught the wind in its folds and elicited catcalls from some youths lurking nearby.

24   The revolution caught me once again in a personal conflict of national identity: Iran rejecting America—or was it the other way around? I was as much at risk of being arrested in the streets of Tehran for being an American as for being a member of the Persian elite. I felt shame for both my countries. But at last, I felt love for one.

25   That stay in Iran was a watershed for me. Although the country was lurching in a direction I could not condone, I felt a common identity with the passions and sentiments of the people. I loved the Persian wit, the street jokes about Ayatollah Khomeini and his wife and all the other mullahs who were so seriously taking over the country. I loved the ancient architecture, the food, and the strange third-world contrasts that would serve up a camel train caught in a

traffic jam on the Tehran beltway. As more and more of my family fled the revolution, while I stayed, I felt less and less the impostor. In the past, everyone had seemed so much more "Persian" than I was. Now, I felt I knew something about Iran that only an Iranian could know—which gave me a sense of credibility. I no longer felt embarrassed that others spoke the language better than I did, or had memories of childhood summers on the Caspian, or had gone on camel trips across the desert. They had left, while I stayed on to experience the turmoil— and the baring of the country's soul. I knew what the villagers were saying about the demonstrations, how people reacted to the postrevolution drivel on TV, and where the last place was in town to get a glass of wine with dinner. I no longer needed to pretend that I belonged.

26   And yet, in my heart of hearts, I knew that it was more than that. Such intimate details I knew about Utah, too, and still I did not feel the same sense of belonging there. One summer in particular I had tapped its inner sanctum, selling encyclopedias door to door in hundred-degree heat. I saw inside the houses of hundreds of people, spoke to them about their families and their hopes, and asked them for money. They were good people, generous people, who gave me water and cake, and lived with too many children and too little time. But I did not feel they were my people.

27   Was it the sense of history that permeated all aspects of Iran that I related to so well? Was it the excitement of revolution that gave me a sense of real involvement? Or was it the fact that I had to lose Iran, and that I would have felt the same about Utah if it instead had been the one I had had to leave? I do not know. But when the Iranian revolution ejected me, and most of my Persian family, I left with a heavy heart, knowing that I was at last leaving a homeland behind me.

28   Today, I still cannot go back to Iran. The political situation makes me at once an outcast and a wanted woman. Finally, however, I understand the symmetry that, like a double helix, seems to turn my mother's country back into my father's, and back again. I have come to grips with my need for reflected identity. Though Utah never has drawn me the way Iran did, it now offers me the legacy of both. Now every time I fly into Salt Lake City and disembark from the plane, I look up at the mountains, and at the city cascading down their slopes, and for one fleeting moment I taste the salt air and feel I'm stepping onto the dusty plain of Tehran.

EXERCISES

Some of the Issues

1. How does Farmanfarmaian define the question of home in paragraph 1?
2. What kinds of parallels does Farmanfarmaian see between her parents' worlds?

3. Why does Farmanfarmaian say that Utah is at once "such a totally American place, and yet, in all the United States there is no more foreign a place, either" (paragraph 8)?
4. In paragraph 10, Farmanfarmaian describes herself as "just generally American." How does this differ from the way other students at the American school in The Hague describe themselves? Why in paragraph 11 does she say that she changed her mind about being American?
5. For Farmanfarmaian, what role does popular culture play in the formation of people's identity (paragraphs 11–13)?
6. How does Farmanfarmaian describe her first visit alone to Iran? What does she learn from it?
7. What does Farmanfarmaian mean when she writes, "But at last I felt love for one" in paragraph 24? What makes that feeling complex? What does Farmanfarmaian say she loves about Iran and what circumstances lead her to this realization?
8. In paragraph 1, Farmanfarmaian makes a distinction between "roots" and a sense of "cultural belonging." The essay is, in many ways, an elaboration on this specific claim. Using specific examples from the reading, show how she distinguishes between the two.
9. What does the title refer to? Do you think it's an appropriate title?

The Way We Are Told

10. Farmanfarmaian's opening sentence speaks directly to the reader. What is she asking us to do? What is the effect?
11. Look carefully at the paragraphs where Farmanfarmaian's writing is particularly descriptive (for example, paragraph 7). What techniques does she use? Do the images work for you? Why or why not?
12. Farmanfarmaian often uses short sentences to punctuate her ideas. Find instances where she does this. How do they help her make her point?

Some Subjects for Writing

13. To what extent is identity tied to a specific place? Write an essay in which you explore the extent to which your own identity developed out of the place or places you grew up.
*14. In paragraph 10, Farmanfarmaian describes herself as "simultaneously from nowhere and everywhere." Read Pico Iyer's "Home Is Everyplace." How are her views and experiences similar to those of Iyer? What might account for the differences? Explain your answer using specific examples from the texts.

Hearing the Sweetest Songs

Nicolette Toussaint

Nicolette Toussaint is a writer, painter, and political activist who lives in San Francisco. This essay originally appeared in a 1994 issue of Newsweek.

Toussaint, who is hearing impaired, describes her experience of having a disability that "doesn't announce itself." Toussaint examines the advantages and disadvantages of choosing whether to "pass" as a nondisabled person or to announce her disability openly. In doing so she calls into question society's reactions to and acceptance of disability. As Toussaint concludes, "We're all just temporarily abled, and every one of us, if we live long enough, will become disabled in some way."

1   Every year when I was a child, a man brought a big, black, squeaking machine to school. When he discovered I couldn't hear all his peeps and squeaks, he would get very excited. The nurse would draw a chart with a deep canyon in it. Then I would listen to the squeaks two or three times, while the adults—who were all acting very, very nice—would watch me raise my hand. Sometimes I couldn't tell whether I heard the squeaks or just imagined them, but I liked being the center of attention.

2   My parents said I lost my hearing to pneumonia as a baby; but I knew I hadn't *lost* anything. None of my parts had dropped off. Nothing had changed: if I wanted to listen to Beethoven, I could put my head between the speakers and turn the dial up to 7, I could hear jets at the airport a block away. I could hear my mom when she was in the same room—if I wanted to. I could even hear my cat purr if I put my good ear right on top of him.

3   I wasn't aware of *not* hearing until I began to wear a hearing aid at the age of 30. It shattered my peace: shoes creaking, papers crackling, pencils tapping, phones ringing, refrigerators humming, people cracking knuckles, clearing throats and blowing noses! Cars, bikes, dogs, cats, kids all seemed to appear from nowhere and fly right at me.

4   I was constantly startled, unnerved, agitated—exhausted. I felt as though inquisitorial Nazis in an old World War II film were burning the side of my head with a merciless white spotlight. Under that onslaught, I had to break down and confess: I couldn't hear. Suddenly, I began to discover many things I couldn't do.

5   I couldn't identify sounds. One afternoon, while lying on my side watching a football game on TV, I kept hearing a noise that sounded like my cat playing with a flexible-spring doorstop. I checked, but the cat was asleep. Finally, I happened to lift my head as the noise occurred. Heard through my good ear, the metallic buzz turned out to be the referee's whistle.

6   I couldn't tell where sounds came from. I couldn't find my phone under the blizzard of papers on my desk. The more it rang, the deeper I dug, I shoveled mounds of paper onto the floor and finally had to track it down by following the cord from the wall.

7   When I lived alone, I felt helpless because I couldn't hear alarm clocks, vulnerable because I couldn't hear the front door open and frightened because I wouldn't hear a burglar until it was too late.

8   Then one day I missed a job interview because of the phone. I had gotten off the subway 20 minutes early, eager and dressed to the nines. But the address I had written down didn't exist! I must have misheard it: I searched the street, becoming overheated, late and frantic, knowing that if I confessed that I couldn't hear on the phone, I would make my odds of getting hired even worse.

9   For the first time, I felt unequal, disadvantaged and disabled. Now that I had something to compare, I knew that I *had* lost something; not just my hearing, but my independence and my sense of wholeness. I had always hated to be seen as inferior, so I never mentioned my lack of hearing. Unlike a wheelchair or a white cane, my disability doesn't announce itself. For most of my life, I chose to pass as abled, and I thought I did it quite well.

10   But after I got the hearing aid, a business friend said, "You know, Nicolette, you think you get away with not hearing, but you don't. Sometimes in meetings you answer the wrong question. People don't know you can't hear, so they think you're daydreaming, eccentric, stupid—or just plain rude. It would be better to just tell them."

11   I wondered about that then, and I still do. If I tell, I risk being seen as *un*able rather than *dis*abled. Sometimes, when I say I can't hear, the waiter will turn to my companion and say, "What does she want?" as though I have lost my power of speech.

12   If I tell, people may see *only* my disability. Once someone is labeled "deaf," "crippled," "mute" or "aged," that's too often all they are. I'm a writer, a painter, a slapdash housekeeper, a gardener who grows wondrous roses; my hearing is just part of the whole. It's a tender part, and you should handle it with care. But like most people with a disability, I don't mind if you ask about it.

13   In fact, you should ask, because it's an important part of me, something my friends see as part of my character. My friend Anne always rests a hand on my elbow in parking lots, since several times, drivers who assume that I hear them have nearly run me over. When I hold my head at a certain angle, my husband, Mason, will say, "It's a plane" or "It's a siren." And my mother loves to laugh about the things I *thought* I heard: last week I was told that "the Minotaurs in

the garden are getting out of hand." I imagined capering bullmen and I was disappointed to learn that all we had in the garden were overgrown "baby tears."

14   Not hearing can be funny, or frustrating. And once in a while, it can be the cause of something truly transcendent. One morning at the shore I was listening to the ocean when Mason said, "Hear the bird?" What bird? I listened hard until I heard a faint, unbirdlike, croaking sound. If he hadn't mentioned it, I would never have noticed it. As I listened, slowly I began to hear—or perhaps imagine—a distant song. Did I *really* hear it? Or just hear in my heart when he shared with me? I don't care. Songs imagined are as sweet as songs heard, and songs shared are sweeter still.

15   That sharing is what I want for all of us. We're all just temporarily abled, and everyone of us, if we live long enough, will become disabled in some way. Those of us who have gotten there first can tell you how to cope with phones and alarm clocks. About ways of holding a book, opening a door and leaning on a crutch all at the same time. And what it's like to give up in despair on Thursday, then begin all over again on Friday, because there's no other choice—and because the roses are beginning to bud in the garden.

16   These are conversations we all should have, and it's not that hard to begin. Just let me see your lips when you speak. Stay in the same room. Don't shout. And ask what you want to know.

EXERCISES

Some of the Issues

1. In paragraphs 1 and 2 Toussaint talks about her childhood attitudes toward her loss of hearing. How did her attitudes differ from those of the adults around her?
2. In paragraphs 3 through 9 Toussaint tells what happened when she began wearing a hearing aid at age thirty. How did things change? How did she feel about the changes?
3. Why does Toussaint question whether she should tell people about her disability when they may not immediately notice it (paragraphs 11 and 12)? Having read the rest of the essay, what do you think her solution was?
4. In paragraph 14, Toussaint describes an important moment in her life—a bird's song that she may or may not have actually heard—and says "Songs imagined are as sweet as songs heard, and songs shared are sweeter still." What does she mean? Do you agree?
5. What, according to Toussaint, do all of us share (paragraph 15)?
6. Throughout the essay Toussaint mentions both positive and negative aspects of her disability. What are they?
7. Did Toussaint's essay influence how you consider and talk about either your own or others' disabilities? In what way? How are disabilities that are easily seen different from those that aren't?

The Way We Are Told

8. What do you think Toussaint gains by beginning her essay with a description of her childhood?

9. Many good writers use sensual details, describing what they see, hear, smell, or touch to add vividness to their writing. More often than not, the details writers provide are mostly visual. Give several examples of the sensual details Toussaint uses.

10. Toussaint gives several examples of sounds that she interprets differently than a person with normal hearing might. What does she gain by telling you of her "mistakes"?

Some Subjects for Writing

11. Toussaint is keenly aware of the sounds around her. Many of us with normal hearing block out some of the sounds around us. Increase your own awareness of sound by finding a place where you can close your eyes and listen for several minutes at a time. Concentrate on the sounds around you. Write a description of the place focusing on details of sound.

12. Toussaint tells how her hearing loss has had both positive and negative consequences. Many of us have experienced some physical challenge, whether genetic or caused by illness or injury. Some of these challenges, like poor eyesight, can be temporarily or permanently corrected; some cannot. Also, as Toussaint reminds us, we are all "temporarily abled" since our abilities will diminish with age. Write about how you, or someone you know, has coped with a loss of ability.

13. Research what your school or community does to provide for people with serious disabilities. If possible, interview people who are disabled or get information from groups that represent the disabled. Evaluate the effectiveness of current provisions.

The Myth of the Latin Woman: I Just Met a Girl Named María

Judith Ortiz Cofer

Judith Ortiz Cofer was born in 1952 in Hormigueros, Puerto Rico, and emigrated with her family to the United States in 1956 when her father joined the U.S. Navy and was assigned to a ship in Brooklyn Yard. Cofer's family returned frequently to Puerto Rico to stay with relatives while her father was away at sea.

Cofer has published several volumes of poetry and has said of her poems, "The 'infinite variety' and power of language interest me. I never cease to experiment with it. As a native Puerto Rican, my first language was Spanish. It was a challenge, not only to learn English, but to master it enough to teach it and—the ultimate goal—to write poetry in it."

Cofer is the author of numerous books of poetry, memoir, and fiction. This essay is taken from The Latin Deli: Telling the Lives of Barrio Women *(1993), a collection of stories, poems, and essays that describe the cultural duality of growing up both Puerto Rican and American. She is currently Professor of English at the University of Georgia.*

The song referred to in the title of this essay is from West Side Story, *a popular Broadway musical and film about two teenagers who fall in love despite their different ethnic backgrounds and allegiances to rival gangs.*

1   On a bus trip to London from Oxford University where I was earning some graduate credits one summer, a young man, obviously fresh from a pub, spotted me and as if struck by inspiration went down on his knees in the aisle. With both hands over his heart he broke into an Irish tenor's rendition of "María" from *West Side Story*. My politely amused fellow passengers gave his lovely voice the round of gentle applause it deserved. Though I was not quite as amused, I managed my version of an English smile: no show of teeth, no extreme contortions of the facial muscles—I was at this time of my life practicing reserve and cool. Oh, that British control, how I coveted it. But María had followed me to London, reminding me of a prime fact of my life: you can leave the Island, master the English language, and travel as far as you can, but if you are a

Latina, especially one like me who so obviously belongs to Rita Moreno's gene pool, the Island travels with you.

2   This is sometimes a very good thing—it may win you that extra minute of someone's attention. But with some people, the same things can make *you* an island—not so much a tropical paradise as an Alcatraz, a place nobody wants to visit. As a Puerto Rican girl growing up in the United States and wanting like most children to "belong," I resented the stereotype that my Hispanic appearance called forth from many people I met.

3   Our family lived in a large urban center in New Jersey during the sixties, where life was designed as a microcosm of my parents' casas on the island. We spoke in Spanish, we ate Puerto Rican food bought at the bodega, and we practiced strict Catholicism complete with Saturday confession and Sunday mass at a church where our parents were accommodated into a one-hour Spanish mass slot, performed by a Chinese priest trained as a missionary for Latin America.

4   As a girl I was kept under strict surveillance, since virtue and modesty were, by cultural equation, the same as family honor. As a teenager I was instructed on how to behave as a proper señorita. But it was a conflicting message girls got, since the Puerto Rican mothers also encouraged their daughters to look and act like women and to dress in clothes our Anglo friends and their mothers found too "mature" for our age. It was, and is, cultural, yet I often felt humiliated when I appeared at an American friend's party wearing a dress more suitable to a semiformal than to a playroom birthday celebration. At Puerto Rican festivities, neither the music nor the colors we wore could be too loud. I still experience a vague sense of letdown when I'm invited to a "party" and it turns out to be a marathon conversation in hushed tones rather than a fiesta with salsa, laughter, and dancing—the kind of celebration I remember from my childhood.

5   I remember Career Day in our high school, when teachers told us to come dressed as if for a job interview. It quickly became obvious that to the barrio girls, "dressing up" sometimes meant wearing ornate jewelry and clothing that would be more appropriate (by mainstream standards) for the company Christmas party than as daily office attire. That morning I had agonized in front of my closet, trying to figure out what a "career girl" would wear because, essentially, except for Marlo Thomas on TV, I had no models on which to base my decision. I knew how to dress for school: at the Catholic school I attended we all wore uniforms; I knew how to dress for Sunday mass, and I knew what dresses to wear for parties at my relatives' homes. Though I do not recall the precise details of my Career Day outfit, it must have been a composite of the above choices. But I remember a comment my friend (an Italian-American) made in later years that coalesced my impressions of that day. She said that at the business school she was attending the Puerto Rican girls always stood out for wearing "everything at once." She meant, of course, too much jewelry, too many accessories. On that day at school, we were simply made the negative models by the nuns who were themselves not credible fashion experts to any of us. But it was painfully obvious to me that to the others, in their tailored skirts

and silk blouses, we must have seemed "hopeless" and "vulgar." Though I now know that most adolescents feel out of step much of the time, I also know that for the Puerto Rican girls of my generation that sense was intensified. The way our teachers and classmates looked at us that day in school was just a taste of the culture clash that awaited us in the real world, where prospective employers and men on the street would often misinterpret our tight skirts and jingling bracelets as a come-on.

6   Mixed cultural signals have perpetuated certain stereotypes—for example, that of the Hispanic woman as the "Hot Tamale" or sexual firebrand. It is a one-dimensional view that the media have found easy to promote. In their special vocabulary, advertisers have designated "sizzling" and "smoldering" as the adjectives of choice for describing not only the foods but also the women of Latin America. From conversations in my house I recall hearing about the harassment that Puerto Rican women endured in factories where the "boss men" talked to them as if sexual innuendo was all they understood and, worse, often gave them the choice of submitting to advances or being fired.

7   It is custom, however, not chromosomes, that leads us to choose scarlet over pale pink. As young girls, we were influenced in our decisions about clothes and colors by the women—older sisters and mothers who had grown up on a tropical island where the natural environment was a riot of primary colors, where showing your skin was one way to keep cool as well as to look sexy. Most important of all, on the island, women perhaps felt freer to dress and move more provocatively, since, in most cases, they were protected by the traditions, mores, and laws of a Spanish/Catholic system of morality and machismo whose main rule was: *You may look at my sister, but if you touch her I will kill you.* The extended family and church structure could provide a young woman with a circle of safety in her small pueblo on the island; if a man "wronged" a girl, everyone would close in to save her family honor.

8   This is what I have gleaned from my discussions as an adult with older Puerto Rican women. They have told me about dressing in their best party clothes on Saturday nights and going to the town's plaza to promenade with their girlfriends in front of the boys they liked. The males were thus given an opportunity to admire the women and to express their admiration in the form of *piropos:* erotically charged street poems they composed on the spot. I have been subjected to a few piropos while visiting the Island, and they can be outrageous, although custom dictates that they must never cross into obscenity. This ritual, as I understand it, also entails a show of studied indifference on the woman's part; if she is "decent," she must not acknowledge the man's impassioned words. So I do understand how things can be lost in translation. When a Puerto Rican girl dressed in her idea of what is attractive meets a man from the mainstream culture who has been trained to react to certain types of clothing as a sexual signal, a clash is likely to take place. The line I first heard based on this aspect of the myth happened when the boy who took me to my first formal dance leaned over to plant a sloppy overeager kiss painfully on my mouth, and

when I didn't respond with sufficient passion said in a resentful tone: "I thought you Latin girls were supposed to mature early"—my first instance of being thought of as a fruit or vegetable—I was supposed to *ripen*, not just grow into womanhood like other girls.

9   It is surprising to some of my professional friends that some people, including those who should know better, still put others "in their place." Though rarer, these incidents are still commonplace in my life. It happened to me most recently during a stay at a very classy metropolitan hotel favored by young professional couples for their weddings. Late one evening after the theater, as I walked toward my room with my new colleague (a woman with whom I was coordinating an arts program), a middle-aged man in a tuxedo, a young girl in satin and lace on his arm, stepped directly into our path. With his champagne glass extended toward me, he exclaimed, "Evita!"

10   Our way blocked, my companion and I listened as the man half-recited, half-bellowed "Don't Cry for Me, Argentina." When he finished, the young girl said: "How about a round of applause for my daddy?" We complied, hoping this would bring the silly spectacle to a close. I was becoming aware that our little group was attracting the attention of the other guests. "Daddy" must have perceived this too, and he once more barred the way as we tried to walk past him. He began to shout-sing a ditty to the tune of "La Bamba"—except the lyrics were about a girl named María whose exploits all rhymed with her name and gonorrhea. The girl kept saying "Oh, Daddy" and looking at me with pleading eyes. She wanted me to laugh along with the others. My companion and I stood silently waiting for the man to end his offensive song. When he finished, I looked not at him but at his daughter. I advised her calmly never to ask her father what he had done in the army. Then I walked between them and to my room. My friend complimented me on my cool handling of the situation. I confessed to her that I really had wanted to push the jerk into the swimming pool. I knew that this same man—probably a corporate executive, well educated, even worldly by most standards—would not have been likely to regale a white woman with a dirty song in public. He would perhaps have checked his impulse by assuming that she could be somebody's wife or mother, or at least *somebody* who might take offense. But to him, I was just an Evita or a María: merely a character in his cartoon-populated universe.

11   Because of my education and my proficiency with the English language, I have acquired many mechanisms for dealing with the anger I experience. This was not true for my parents, nor is it true for the many Latin women working at menial jobs who must put up with stereotypes about our ethnic group such as: "They make good domestics." This is another facet of the myth of the Latin woman in the United States. Its origin is simple to deduce. Work as domestics, waitressing, and factory jobs are all that's available to women with little English and few skills. The myth of the Hispanic menial has been sustained by the same media phenomenon that made "Mammy" from *Gone with the Wind* America's idea of the black woman for generations; María, the housemaid or counter girl,

is now indelibly etched into the national psyche. The big and the little screens have presented us with the picture of the funny Hispanic maid, mispronouncing words and cooking up a spicy storm in a shiny California kitchen.

12   This media-engendered image of the Latina in the United States has been documented by feminist Hispanic scholars, who claim that such portrayals are partially responsible for the denial of opportunities for upward mobility among Latinas in the professions. I have a Chicana friend working on a Ph.D. in philosophy at a major university. She says her doctor still shakes his head in puzzled amazement at all the "big words" she uses. Since I do not wear my diplomas around my neck for all to see, I too have on occasion been sent to that "kitchen," where some think I obviously belong.

13   One such incident that has stayed with me, though I recognize it as a minor offense, happened on the day of my first public poetry reading. It took place in Miami in a boat-restaurant where we were having lunch before the event. I was nervous and excited as I walked in with my notebook in my hand. An older woman motioned me to her table. Thinking (foolish me) that she wanted me to autograph a copy of my brand new slender volume of verse, I went over. She ordered a cup of coffee from me, assuming that I was the waitress. Easy enough to mistake my poems for menus, I suppose. I know that it wasn't an intentional act of cruelty, yet of all the good things that happened that day, I remember that scene most clearly, because it reminded me of what I had to overcome before anyone would take me seriously. In retrospect I understand that my anger gave my reading fire, that I have almost always taken doubts in my abilities as a challenge—and that the result is, most times, a feeling of satisfaction at having won a convert when I see the cold, appraising eyes warm to my words, the body language change, the smile that indicates that I have opened some avenue for communication. That day I read to that woman and her lowered eyes told me that she was embarrassed at her little faux pas, and when I willed her to look up at me, it was my victory, and she graciously allowed me to punish her with my full attention. We shook hands at the end of the reading, and I never saw her again. She has probably forgotten the whole thing but maybe not.

14   Yet I am one of the lucky ones. My parents made it possible for me to acquire a stronger footing in the mainstream culture by giving me the chance at an education. And, books and art have saved me from the harsher forms of ethnic and racial prejudice that many of my Hispanic *compañeras* have had to endure. I travel a lot around the United States, reading from my books of poetry and my novel, and the reception I most often receive is one of positive interest by people who want to know more about my culture. There are, however, thousands of Latinas without the privilege of an education or the entrée into society that I have. For them life is a struggle against the misconceptions perpetuated by the myth of the Latina as whore, domestic or criminal. We cannot change this by legislating the way people look at us. The transformation, as I see it, has to occur at a much more individual level. My personal goal in my public life is to try to replace the old pervasive stereotypes and myths about Latinas with a

much more interesting set of realities. Every time I give a reading, I hope the stories I tell, the dreams and fears I examine in my work, can achieve some universal truth which will get my audience past the particulars of my skin color, my accent, or my clothes.

15   I once wrote a poem in which I called us Latinas "God's brown daughters." This poem is really a prayer of sorts, offered upward, but also, through the human-to-human channel of art, outward. It is a prayer for communication, and for respect. In it, Latin women pray "in Spanish to an Anglo God / with a Jewish heritage," and they are "fervently hoping / that if not omnipotent, / at least He be bilingual."

EXERCISES

Some of the Issues

1. How does Cofer react to the young man's serenade in paragraph 1?
2. In paragraphs 2 through 5, Cofer talks about her childhood in New Jersey where she received different cultural signals from her Puerto Rican family than from the Anglo world outside. What were these signals? How were they confusing to her?
3. What are the stereotypes of Latin women that the American media perpetuate (paragraph 6)? Can you think of others besides the ones Cofer mentions?
4. According to Cofer, what behaviors or customs are interpreted differently in Puerto Rico than in the United States? Why? Can you give other examples of behaviors that have different meanings in different cultures?
5. What role do stereotypes play in explaining the behavior of the man in the tuxedo (paragraphs 9–10) and the woman at the poetry reading (paragraph 13)? What is your own opinion of how stereotypes are formed in our culture?
*6. Cofer says that she is "one of the lucky ones" (paragraph 14). What does she believe her privileges allow her to do? You may want to compare her viewpoint with that expressed in Aurora Levins Morales's "Class Poem."
7. To what extent is the stereotyping Cofer experiences based on her being a woman? How are stereotypes about Latin men different? How are stereotypes about women in other cultures the same or different?

The Way We Are Told

8. Like many writers, Cofer begins with a story. How does this narrative help illustrate her point?
9. Cofer uses references to Latina and black women in popular culture (María, Evita, and Mammy in *Gone with the Wind*) to indicate stereotypical roles that mainstream culture assigns to minority women. Were you familiar with the references? If not, was it easy for you to associate Cofer's ideas with other stereotypical images in the media?

Some Subjects for Writing

10. In "The Myth of the Latin Woman" Cofer explores how that myth prevents people from seeing her as who she is. Analyze common stereotypes that are applied to people belonging to a particular group. These stereotypes can be based on race, ethnicity, gender, or sexual orientation, but you can also use, for example, stereotypes about athletes, intellectuals, or lawyers.

11. What role do the media play in stereotyping? Find one or more examples of newspaper or magazine articles, television shows, or movies that you believe reinforce misconceptions about a particular group in American society. Explain in detail the nature of the misrepresentations.

*12. Gloria Naylor, in "The Meaning of a Word," writes about how the same word can be affectionate in the context of family but deeply hurtful when said by someone else. Cofer also talks about actions that can have different meanings in different contexts. Describe a situation in which your own behavior, or the behavior of someone toward you, was affected by context.

Hair

Malcolm X

Malcolm X, born in Omaha, Nebraska, in 1925, changed his name from Malcolm Little when he joined Elijah Muhammad's Black Muslims, in which he eventually moved up to become second in command. He broke with the Muslims because of major differences in policy and established an organization of his own. Soon after that he was assassinated at a public meeting, on February 21, 1965. The Autobiography of Malcolm X, written with Alex Haley (later more widely known as the author of Roots), was published in 1964. The selection reprinted here is from one of the early parts of the book and records an experience during Malcolm X's junior high school years in Michigan, in 1941. He gives the reader what amounts to a recipe, but a recipe on two levels: he describes in detail the painful process of "conking," straightening hair, that he as a boy subjected himself to. On a more fundamental level it was, as he says, a "big step toward self-degradation."

1   Shorty soon decided that my hair was finally long enough to be conked. He had promised to school me in how to beat the barbershop's three- and four-dollar price by making up congolene, and then conking ourselves.

2   I took the little list of ingredients he had printed out for me, and went to a grocery store, where I got a can of Red Devil lye, two eggs, and two medium-sized white potatoes. Then at a drugstore near the poolroom, I asked for a large jar of vaseline, a large bar of soap, a large-toothed comb and a fine-toothed comb, one of those rubber hoses with a metal spray-head, a rubber apron and a pair of gloves.

3   "Going to lay on that first conk?" the drugstore man asked me. I proudly told him, grinning, "Right!"

4   Shorty paid six dollars a week for a room in his cousin's shabby apartment. His cousin wasn't at home. "It's like the pad's mine, he spends so much time with his woman," Shorty said. "Now, you watch me—"

5   He peeled the potatoes and thin-sliced them into a quart-sized Mason fruit jar, then started stirring them with a wooden spoon as he gradually poured in a little over half the can of lye. "Never use a metal spoon; the lye will turn it black," he told me.

6   A jelly-like, starchy-looking glop resulted from the lye and potatoes, and Shorty broke in the two eggs, stirring real fast—his own conk and dark face bent down close. The congolene turned pale-yellowish. "Feel the jar," Shorty said. I cupped my hand against the outside, and snatched it away. "Damn right, it's hot, that's the lye," he said. "So you know it's going to burn when I comb it in—it burns *bad.* But the longer you can stand it, the straighter the hair."

7   He made me sit down, and he tied the string of the new rubber apron tightly around my neck, and combed up my bush of hair. Then, from the big vaseline jar, he took a handful and massaged it hard all through my hair and into the scalp. He also thickly vaselined my neck, ears and forehead. "When I get to washing out your head, be sure to tell me anywhere you feel any little stinging," Shorty warned me, washing his hands, then pulling on the rubber gloves, and tying on his own rubber apron. "You always got to remember that any congolene left in burns a sore into your head."

8   The congolene just felt warm when Shorty started combing it in. But then my head caught fire.

9   I gritted my teeth and tried to pull the sides of the kitchen table together. The comb felt as if it was raking my skin off.

10   My eyes watered, my nose was running. I couldn't stand it any longer; I bolted to the washbasin. I was cursing Shorty with every name I could think of when he got the spray going and started soap-lathering my head.

11   He lathered and spray-rinsed, lathered and spray-rinsed, maybe ten or twelve times, each time gradually closing the hot-water faucet, until the rinse was cold, and that helped some.

12   "You feel any stinging spots?"

13   "No," I managed to say. My knees were trembling.

14   "Sit back down, then. I think we got it all out okay."

15   The flame came back as Shorty, with a thick towel, started drying my head, rubbing hard. *"Easy, man, easy"* I kept shouting.

16   "The first time's always worst. You get used to it better before long. You took it real good, homeboy. You got a good conk."

17   When Shorty let me stand up and see in the mirror, my hair hung down in limp, damp strings. My scalp still flamed, but not as badly; I could bear it. He draped the towel around my shoulders, over my rubber apron, and began again vaselining my hair.

18   I could feel him combing, straight back, first the big comb, then the fine-tooth one.

19   Then, he was using a razor, very delicately, on the back of my neck. Then, finally, shaping the sideburns.

20   My first view in the mirror blotted out the hurting. I'd seen some pretty conks, but when it's the first time, on your *own* head, the transformation, after the lifetime of kinks, is staggering.

21   The mirror reflected Shorty behind me. We both were grinning and sweating. And on top of my head was this thick, smooth sheen of shining red hair— real red—as straight as any white man's.

22   How ridiculous I was! Stupid enough to stand there simply lost in admiration of my hair now looking "white," reflected in the mirror in Shorty's room. I vowed that I'd never again be without a conk, and I never was for many years.

23   This was my first really big step toward self-degradation: when I endured all of that pain, literally burning my flesh to have it look like a white man's hair.

I had joined that multitude of Negro men and women in America who are brainwashed into believing that the black people are "inferior"—and white people "superior"—that they will even violate and mutilate their God-created bodies to try to look "pretty" by white standards.

EXERCISES

Some of the Issues

1. What is a conk and why did Malcolm X want it?
2. Why does Malcolm X describe the process of buying the ingredients and of applying them in such detail?
3. What is the thesis of this short selection? With what arguments, information, or assertions does Malcolm X support his thesis?

The Way We Are Told

4. The selection divides into two very different parts. What are they? How do they differ?
5. The main part of the selection is a description of a process. How is it arranged? What qualities of instruction, even of a recipe, does it have? How and where does it differ from a recipe?

Some Subjects for Writing

6. Malcolm X describes a process that shows, among other things, that people will go to great lengths to conform. Develop a short essay describing, in a straightforward, neutral manner, some example of how people will subject themselves to pain, inconvenience, and embarrassment to conform to some fashion or idea.
7. Rewrite your previous essay, but take a strong stand indicating approval or disapproval of the process.
8. Write an essay examining the rewards American society offers for conforming, or the penalties for not conforming.

The College Dropout Boom

David Leonhardt

Journalist David Leonhardt has reported elsewhere that "At the most selective private universities across the country, more fathers of freshmen are doctors than are hourly workers, teachers, clergy members, farmers or members of the military—combined." In this essay he explores the many challenges students from working-class and lower-income families encounter not just in getting into college but in staying there through graduation. As Leonhardt shows us in this essay, while colleges have made great strides in recruiting and admitting students from diverse racial and ethnic backgrounds, they are only beginning to acknowledge and address the issues involved in recruiting and retaining students from diverse economic backgrounds.

Leonhardt, a graduate of Yale University, has been writing about economics for the New York Times *since 2000. He was one of the writers who produced "Class Matters," the paper's award-winning 2005 series on social class in the United States. "Class Matters" was a project in which a team of reporters spent more than a year exploring ways that class—defined as a combination of income, education, wealth, and occupation—influences destiny in a society that likes to think of itself as a land of unbounded opportunity. This essay originally appeared in the* Times *as part of that series.*

1   One of the biggest decisions Andy Blevins has ever made, and one of the few he now regrets, never seemed like much of a decision at all. It just felt like the natural thing to do.

2   In the summer of 1995, he was moving boxes of soup cans, paper towels, and dog food across the floor of a supermarket warehouse, one of the biggest buildings in the area of southwest Virginia surrounding the town of Chilhowie. The heat was brutal. The job had sounded impossible when he arrived fresh off his first year of college, looking to make some summer money, still a skinny teenager with sandy blond hair and a narrow, freckled face.

3   But hard work done well was something he understood, even if he was the first college boy in his family. Soon he was making bonuses on top of his $6.75 an hour, more money than either of his parents made. His girlfriend was around, and so were his hometown buddies. Andy acted more outgoing with them, more relaxed. People in Chilhowie noticed that.

4   It was just about the perfect summer. So the thought crossed his mind: maybe it did not have to end. Maybe he would take a break from college and keep working. He had been getting Cs and Ds, and college never felt like home, anyway.

5   "I enjoyed working hard, getting the job done, getting a paycheck," Blevins recalled. "I just knew I didn't want to quit."

6   So he quit college instead, and with that, Andy Blevins joined one of the largest and fastest-growing groups of young adults in America. He became a college dropout, though nongraduate may be the more precise term.

7   Many people like him plan to return to get their degrees, even if few actually do. Almost one in three Americans in their mid-twenties now fall into this group, up from one in five in the late 1960s, when the Census Bureau began keeping such data. Most come from poor and working-class families.

8   The phenomenon has been largely overlooked in the glare of positive news about the country's gains in education. Going to college has become the norm throughout most of the United States, even in many places where college was once considered an exotic destination—places like Chilhowie, an Appalachian hamlet with a simple brick downtown. At elite universities, classrooms are filled with women, blacks, Jews, and Latinos, groups largely excluded two generations ago. The American system of higher learning seems to have become a great equalizer.

9   In fact, though, colleges have come to reinforce many of the advantages of birth. On campuses that enroll poorer students, graduation rates are often low. And at institutions where nearly everyone graduates—small colleges like Colgate, major state institutions like the University of Colorado, and elite private universities like Stanford—more students today come from the top of the nation's income ladder than they did two decades ago.

10   Only 41 percent of low-income students entering a four-year college managed to graduate within five years, the U.S. Department of Education found in a 2004 study, but 66 percent of high-income students did. That gap had grown over recent years.

11   "We need to recognize that the most serious domestic problem in the United States today is the widening gap between the children of the rich and the children of the poor," Lawrence H. Summers, the president of Harvard, said when announcing in 2004 that Harvard would give full scholarships to all its lowest-income students. "And education is the most powerful weapon we have to address that problem."

12   There is certainly much to celebrate about higher education today. Many more students from all classes are getting four-year degrees and reaping their benefits. But those broad gains mask the fact that poor and working-class students have nevertheless been falling behind; for them, not having a degree remains the norm.

13   That loss of ground is all the more significant because a college education matters much more now than it once did. A bachelor's degree, not a year or two

of courses, tends to determine a person's place in today's globalized, computerized economy. College graduates have received steady pay increases over the past two decades, while the pay of everyone else has risen little more than the rate of inflation.

14   As a result, despite one of the great education explosions in modern history, economic mobility—moving from one income group to another over the course of a lifetime—has stopped rising, researchers say. Some recent studies suggest that it has declined over the last generation.

15   Put another way, children seem to be following the paths of their parents more than they once did. Grades and test scores, rather than privilege, determine success today, but that success is largely being passed down from one generation to the next. A nation that believes that everyone should have a fair shake finds itself with a kind of inherited meritocracy.

16   In this system, the students at the best colleges may be diverse—male and female and of various colors, religions, and hometowns—but they tend to share an upper-middle-class upbringing. An old joke that Harvard's idea of diversity is putting a rich kid from California in the same room as a rich kid from New York is truer today than ever; Harvard has more students from California than it did in years past and just as big a share of upper-income students.

17   Students like these remain in college because they can hardly imagine doing otherwise. Their parents, understanding the importance of a bachelor's degree, spent hours reading to them, researching school districts, and making it clear to them that they simply must graduate from college.

18   Andy Blevins says that he too knows the importance of a degree, but that he did not while growing up, and not even in his year at Radford University, sixty-six miles up the interstate from Chilhowie. Ten years after trading college for the warehouse, Blevins, who is twenty-nine, spends his days at the same supermarket company. He has worked his way up to produce buyer, earning $35,000 a year with health benefits and a 401(k) plan. He is on a path typical for someone who attended college without getting a four-year degree. Men in their early forties in this category made an average of $42,000 in 2000. Those with a four-year degree made $65,000.

19   Still boyish-looking but no longer rail thin, Blevins says he has many reasons to be happy. He lives with his wife, Karla, and their son, Lucas, in a small blue-and-yellow house at the end of a cul-de-sac in the middle of a stunningly picturesque Appalachian valley. He plays golf with some of the same friends who made him want to stay around Chilhowie.

20   But he does think about what might have been, about what he could be doing if he had the degree. As it is, he always feels as if he is on thin ice. Were he to lose his job, he says, everything could slip away with it. What kind of job could a guy without a college degree get? One night, while talking to his wife about his life, he used the word "trapped."

21   "Looking back, I wish I had gotten that degree," Blevins said in his soft-spoken lilt. "Four years seemed like a thousand years then. But I wish I would have just put in my four years."

THE BARRIERS

22   Why so many low-income students fall from the college ranks is a question without a simple answer. Many high schools do a poor job of preparing teenagers for college. Many of the colleges where lower-income students tend to enroll have limited resources and offer a narrow range of majors, leaving some students disenchanted and unwilling to continue.

23   Then there is the cost. Tuition bills scare some students from even applying and leave others with years of debt. To Blevins, like many other students of limited means, every week of going to classes seemed like another week of losing money—money that might have been made at a job.

24   "The system makes a false promise to students," said John T. Casteen III, the president of the University of Virginia, himself the son of a Virginia shipyard worker.

25   Colleges, Casteen said, present themselves as meritocracies in which academic ability and hard work are always rewarded. In fact, he said, many working-class students face obstacles they cannot overcome on their own.

26   For much of his fifteen years as Virginia's president, Casteen has focused on raising money and expanding the university, the most prestigious in the state. In the meantime, students with backgrounds like his have become ever scarcer on campus. The university's genteel nickname, the Cavaliers, and its aristocratic sword-crossed coat of arms seem appropriate today. No flagship state university has a smaller proportion of low-income students than Virginia. Just 8 percent of undergraduates in 2004 came from families in the bottom half of the income distribution, down from 11 percent a decade earlier.

27   That change sneaked up on him, Casteen said, and he had spent a good part of the previous year trying to prevent it from becoming part of his legacy. Starting with the fall 2005 freshman class, the university will charge no tuition and require no loans for students whose parents make less than twice the poverty level, or about $37,700 a year for a family of four. The university has also increased financial aid to middle-income students.

28   To Casteen, these are steps to remove what he describes as "artificial barriers" to a college education placed in the way of otherwise deserving students. Doing so "is a fundamental obligation of a free culture," he said.

29   But the deterrents to a degree can also be homegrown. Many low-income teenagers know few people who have made it through college. A majority of the nongraduates are young men, and some come from towns where the factory work ethic, to get working as soon as possible, remains strong, even if the factories themselves are vanishing. Whatever the reasons, college just does not feel normal.

30   "You get there and you start to struggle," said Leanna Blevins, Andy's older sister, who did get a bachelor's degree and then went on to earn a Ph.D. at Virginia studying the college experiences of poor students. "And at home your parents are trying to be supportive and say, 'Well, if you're not happy, if it's not

right for you, come back home. It's okay.' And they think they're doing the right thing. But they don't know that maybe what the student needs is to hear them say, 'Stick it out just one semester. You can do it. Just stay there. Come home on the weekend, but stick it out.'"

31   Today, Leanna, petite and high-energy, is helping to start a new college a few hours' drive from Chilhowie for low-income students. Her brother said he had daydreamed about attending it and had talked to her about how he might return to college.

32   For her part, Leanna says, she has daydreamed about having a life that would seem as natural as her brother's, a life in which she would not feel like an outsider in her hometown. Once, when a high school teacher asked students to list their goals for the next decade, she wrote, "having a college degree" and "not being married."

33   "I think my family probably thinks I'm liberal," Leanna, who is now married, said with a laugh, "that I've just been educated too much and I'm gettin' above my raisin'."

34   Her brother said that he just wanted more control over his life, not a new one. At a time when many people complain of scattered lives, Andy Blevins can stand in one spot—his church parking lot, next to a graveyard—and take in much of his world. "That's my parents' house," he said one day, pointing to a sliver of roof visible over a hill. "That's my uncle's trailer. My grandfather is buried here. I'll probably be buried here."

TAKING CLASS INTO ACCOUNT

35   Opening up colleges to new kinds of students has generally meant one thing over the last generation: affirmative action. Intended to right the wrongs of years of exclusion, the programs have swelled the number of women, blacks, and Latinos on campuses. But affirmative action was never supposed to address broad economic inequities, just the ones that stem from specific kinds of discrimination.

36   That is now beginning to change. Like Virginia, a handful of other colleges are not only increasing financial aid but also promising to give weight to economic class in granting admissions. They say they want to make an effort to admit more low-income students, just as they now do for minorities and children of alumni.

37   "The great colleges and universities were designed to provide for mobility, to seek out talent," said Anthony W. Marx, president of Amherst College. "If we are blind to the educational disadvantages associated with need, we will simply replicate these disadvantages while appearing to make decisions based on merit."

38   With several populous states having already banned race-based preferences and the United States Supreme Court suggesting that it may outlaw such

programs in a couple of decades, the future of affirmative action may well re-
volve around economics. Polls consistently show that programs based on class
backgrounds have wider support than those based on race.

39   The explosion in the number of nongraduates has also begun to get the attention of policy makers. In 2005, New York became one of a small group of states
to tie college financing more closely to graduation rates, rewarding colleges more
for moving students along than for simply admitting them. Nowhere is the strati-
fication of education more vivid than in Virginia, where Thomas Jefferson once
tried, and failed, to set up the nation's first public high schools. At a modest high
school in the Tidewater city of Portsmouth, not far from John Casteen's boyhood
home, a guidance-office wall filled with college pennants does not include one
from rarefied Virginia. The colleges whose pennants are up—Old Dominion
University and others that seem in the realm of the possible—have far lower
graduation rates.

40   Across the country, the upper middle class so dominates elite universities
that high-income students, on average, actually get slightly more financial aid
from colleges than low-income students do. These elite colleges are so expensive that even many high-income students receive large grants. In the early
1990s, by contrast, poorer students got 50 percent more aid on average than the
wealthier ones, according to the College Board, the organization that runs the
SAT entrance exams.

41   At the other end of the spectrum are community colleges, the two-year institutions that are intended to be feeders for four-year colleges. In nearly every
one are tales of academic success against tremendous odds: a battered wife or a
combat veteran or a laid-off worker on the way to a better life. But overall, community colleges tend to be places where dreams are put on hold.

42   Most people who enroll say they plan to get a four-year degree eventually;
few actually do. Full-time jobs, commutes, and children or parents who need
care often get in the way. One recent national survey found that about 75 percent
of students enrolling in community colleges said they hoped to transfer to a
four-year institution. But only 17 percent of those who had entered in the mid-
1990s made the switch within five years, according to a separate study. The rest
were out working or still studying toward the two-year degree.

43   "We here in Virginia do a good job of getting them in," said Glenn Dubois,
chancellor of the Virginia Community College System and himself a community college graduate. "We have to get better in getting them out."

"I WEAR A TIE EVERY DAY"

44   College degree or not, Andy Blevins has the kind of life that many Americans
say they aspire to. He fills it with family, friends, church, and a five-handicap
golf game. He does not sit in traffic commuting to an office park. He does not

talk wistfully of a relocated brother or best friend he sees only twice a year. He does not worry about who will care for his son while he works and his wife attends community college to become a physical therapist. His grandparents down the street watch Lucas, just as they took care of Andy and his two sisters when they were children. When he comes home from work, it is his turn to play with Lucas, tossing him into the air and rolling around on the floor with him and a stuffed elephant.

45   Blevins also sings in a quartet called the Gospel Gentlemen. One member is his brother-in-law; another lives on his street. In the long white van the group owns, they wend their way along mountain roads on their way to singing dates at local church functions, sometimes harmonizing, sometimes ribbing one another or talking about where to buy golf equipment.

46   Inside the churches, the other singers often talk to the audience between songs, about God or a grandmother or what a song means to them. Blevins rarely does, but his shyness fades once he is back in the van with his friends.

47   At the warehouse, he is usually the first to arrive, around 6:30 in the morning. The grandson of a coal miner, he takes pride, he says, in having moved up to become a supermarket buyer. He decides which bananas, grapes, onions, and potatoes the company will sell and makes sure that there is always enough. Most people with his job have graduated from college.

48   "I'm pretty fortunate to not have a degree but have a job where I wear a tie every day," he said.

49   He worries about how long it will last, though, mindful of what happened to his father, Dwight, a decade ago. A high school graduate, Dwight Blevins was laid off from his own warehouse job and ended up with another one that paid less and offered a smaller pension.

50   "A lot of places, they're not looking that you're trained in something," Andy Blevins said one evening, sitting on his back porch. "They just want you to have a degree."

51   Figuring out how to get one is the core quandary facing the nation's college nongraduates. Many seem to want one. In a *New York Times* poll, 43 percent of them called it essential to success, while 42 percent of college graduates and 32 percent of high school dropouts did. This in itself is a change from the days when "college boy" was an insult in many working-class neighborhoods. But once students take a break—the phrase that many use instead of "drop out"— the ideal can quickly give way to reality. Family and work can make a return to school seem even harder than finishing it in the first place.

52   After dropping out of Radford, Andy Blevins enrolled part-time in a community college, trying to juggle work and studies. He lasted a year. From time to time in the decade since, he has thought about giving it another try. But then he has wondered if that would be crazy. He works every third Saturday, and his phone rings on Sundays when there is a problem with the supply of potatoes or apples. "It never ends," he said. "There's never a lull."

53   To spend more time with Lucas, Blevins has already cut back on his singing. If he took night classes, he said, when would he ever see his little boy? Anyway, he said, it would take years to get a degree part-time. To him, it is a tug-of-war between living in the present and sacrificing for the future.

FEW BREAKS FOR THE NEEDY

54   The college admissions system often seems ruthlessly meritocratic. Yes, children of alumni still have an advantage. But many other pillars of the old system—the polite rejections of women or blacks, the spots reserved for graduates of Choate and Exeter—have crumbled.

55   This was the meritocracy John Casteen described when he greeted the parents of freshmen in a University of Virginia lecture hall in the late summer of 2004. Hailing from all fifty states and fifty-two foreign countries, the students were more intelligent and better prepared than he and his classmates had been, he told the parents in his quiet, deep voice. The class included seventeen students with a perfect SAT score.

56   If anything, children of privilege think that the system has moved so far from its old-boy history that they are now at a disadvantage when they apply, because colleges are trying to diversify their student rolls. To get into a good college, the sons and daughters of the upper middle class often talk of needing a higher SAT score than, say, an applicant who grew up on a farm, in a ghetto, or in a factory town. Some state legislators from northern Virginia's affluent suburbs have argued that this is a form of geographic discrimination and have quixotically proposed bills to outlaw it.

57   But the conventional wisdom is not quite right. The elite colleges have not been giving much of a break to the low-income students who apply. When William G. Bowen, a former president of Princeton, looked at admissions records recently, he found that if test scores were equal a low-income student had no better chance than a high-income one of getting into a group of nineteen colleges, including Harvard, Yale, Princeton, Williams, and Virginia. Athletes, legacy applicants, and minority students all got in with lower scores on average. Poorer students did not.

58   The findings befuddled many administrators, who insist that admissions officers have tried to give poorer applicants a leg up. To emphasize the point, Virginia announced in the spring of 2005 that it was changing its admissions policy from "need blind"—a term long used to assure applicants that they would not be punished for seeking financial aid—to "need conscious." Administrators at Amherst and Harvard have also recently said that they would redouble their efforts to take into account the obstacles students have overcome.

59   "The same score reflects more ability when you come from a less fortunate background," Lawrence Summers, the president of Harvard, said. "You haven't had a chance to take the test-prep course. You went to a school that didn't do as

good a job coaching you for the test. You came from a home without the same opportunities for learning."

60   But it is probably not a coincidence that elite colleges have not yet turned this sentiment into action. Admitting large numbers of low-income students could bring clear complications. Too many in a freshman class would probably lower the college's average SAT score, thereby damaging its ranking by *U.S. News & World Report*, a leading arbiter of academic prestige. Some colleges, like Emory University in Atlanta, have climbed fast in the rankings over precisely the same period in which their percentage of low-income students has tumbled. The math is simple: when a college goes looking for applicants with high SAT scores, it is far more likely to find them among well-off teenagers.

61   More spots for low-income applicants might also mean fewer for the children of alumni, who make up the fund-raising base for universities. More generous financial aid policies will probably lead to higher tuition for those students who can afford the list price. Higher tuition, lower ranking, tougher admission requirements: these do not make for an easy marketing pitch to alumni clubs around the country. But Casteen and his colleagues are going ahead, saying the pendulum has swung too far in one direction.

62   That was the mission of John Blackburn, Virginia's easygoing admissions dean, when he rented a car and took to the road in the spring of 2005. Blackburn thought of the trip as a reprise of the drives Casteen took twenty-five years earlier, when he was the admissions dean, traveling to churches and community centers to persuade black parents that the university was finally interested in their children.

63   One Monday night, Blackburn came to Big Stone Gap, in a mostly poor corner of the state not far from Andy Blevins's town. A community college there was holding a college fair, and Blackburn set up a table in a hallway, draping it with the University of Virginia's blue and orange flag.

64   As students came by, Blackburn would explain Virginia's new admissions and financial aid policies. But he soon realized that the Virginia name might have been scaring off the very people his pitch was intended for. Most of the students who did approach the table showed little interest in the financial aid and expressed little need for it. One man walked up to Blackburn and introduced his son as an aspiring doctor. The father was an ophthalmologist. Other doctors came by, too. So did some lawyers.

65   "You can't just raise the UVA flag," Blackburn said, packing up his materials at the end of the night, "and expect a lot of low-income kids to come out."

66   When the applications started arriving in his office, there seemed to be no increase in those from low-income students. So Blackburn extended the deadline two weeks for everybody, and his colleagues also helped some applicants with the maze of financial aid forms. Of 3,100 incoming freshmen, it now seems that about 180 will qualify for the new financial aid program, up from 130 who would have done so the year before. It is not a huge number, but Virginia administrators call it a start.

A BIG DECISION

67   On a still-dark February morning, with the winter's heaviest snowfall on the ground, Andy Blevins scraped off his Jeep and began his daily drive to the supermarket warehouse. As he passed the home of Mike Nash, his neighbor and fellow gospel singer, he noticed that the car was still in the driveway. For Nash, a school counselor and the only college graduate in the singing group, this was a snow day.

68   Blevins later sat down with his calendar and counted to 280: the number of days he had worked last year. Two hundred and eighty days—six days a week most of the time—without ever really knowing what the future would hold.

69   "I just realized I'm going to have to do something about this," he said, "because it's never going to end."

70   In the weeks afterward, his daydreaming about college and his conversations about it with his sister Leanna turned into serious research. He requested his transcripts from Radford and from Virginia Highlands Community College and figured out that he had about a year's worth of credits. He also talked to Leanna about how he could become an elementary school teacher. He always felt that he could relate to children, he said. The job would take up 180 days, not 280. Teachers do not usually get laid off or lose their pensions or have to take a big pay cut to find new work.

71   So the decision was made. Andy Blevins says he will return to Virginia Highlands, taking classes at night; the Gospel Gentlemen are no longer booking performances. After a year, he plans to take classes by video and on the Web that are offered at the community college but run by Old Dominion, a Norfolk, Virginia, university with a big group of working-class students.

72   "I don't like classes, but I've gotten so motivated to go back to school," Blevins said. "I don't want to, but, then again, I do."

73   He thinks he can get his bachelor's degree in three years. If he gets it at all, he will have defied the odds.

EXERCISES

Some of the Issues

1. Why does Leonhardt write that Andy Blevins's decision didn't really seem like a decision, but rather it "just felt like that natural thing to do" (paragraph 1)?
2. In paragraph 6, Leonhardt states that Blevins is part of "one of the largest and fastest-growing groups of young adults in America." To what does he attribute this growing rate of college dropouts?
3. In what ways, according to Leonhardt, have "colleges come to reinforce many of the advantages of birth?" How has college become not necessarily the "great equalizer" it was once hoped to be (paragraphs 8–9)?

4. Leonhardt asserts that a "college education matters much more now than it once did" (paragraph 13). Based on your own experience and what others have told you (your parents, teachers, school counselors, or peers) do you find this to be true?
5. How does Leonhardt question American concepts of diversity?
6. What reasons does Leonhardt give for the disproportionate number of low-income students who drop out of college (paragraphs 22–23)?
7. What changes has John T. Casteen III, the president of the University of Virginia, implemented and why? Are other universities following his lead?
8. What are some of the ways policy makers are beginning to address issues of college retention (paragraph 39)? Do the policies, such as the one initiated in New York State, seem important to you?
9. What are Andy Blevins's concerns about his own life and future? How does his own family history contribute to his fears?
10. What is the difference between a "need blind" and a "need conscious" admissions policy (paragraph 58)?
11. What are some of the "problems" that could potentially be brought on by admitting low-income students (paragraph 60)?
12. Leonhardt's article first appeared in the *New York Times* in a series dedicated to examining the subject of class in the United States. To what extent do you feel Americans talk openly about class? Do you think this is a subject that needs more or less attention here in the United States?
*13. Kristin Kovacic's "'Proud to Work for the University'" raises some of the same issues as Leonhardt's article. Where do you see similarities between the points they make? Where do you see differences?

The Way We Are Told

14. What is the effect of Leonhardt's opening paragraphs? How do they set up the subject of the article?
15. Leonhardt interweaves information about college and class with Blevins's story. Is this an effective way to approach the subject? Would he have benefited from focusing on a number of examples in more detail?
16. How would you characterize the author's tone at the end of the essay? Is it consistent with his tone throughout?

Some Subjects for Writing

17. What factors led you to choose to go to college? What do you expect to get from your college experience? Did you, or do you still, have any reservations about your decision? Write a narrative in which you explain your own decision to attend college and analyze your reasons for doing so. If you do not want to write about your own experience, interview two or three peers who come from different backgrounds about their experience

(you do not have use their real names). You may also choose to use your own experience and compare it to that of your peers.

*18. What, in your opinion, can or should be done to encourage more low-income students to go to or stay in college? Drawing from your own experience, along with ideas from Leonhardt's article as well as other readings, such as Kristin Kovacic's "'Proud to Work for the University,'" write an essay in which you present two to four possible ways to address the issue. Be sure to use specific examples to back up your point.

19. With the help of your instructor, research the retention rates at your own college. How many students leave after their first or second year? How many eventually graduate? What factors, if any, appear to determine who stays and who leaves? Has your school done anything to raise the rates of retention? Using the information you find, along with your own experience and that of your peers, write a paper in which you analyze your school's success in retaining students and helping them finish college.

Time Stood Still Again

Pennie Holmes-Brinson

Primarily a poet, Pennie Holmes-Brinson has also written short stories, short plays and songs. She has published three poetry chapbooks and is currently writing a novel. She studied art at Harold Washington College in Chicago where she received an A.A. degree in liberal arts in 1993. Holmes-Brinson is also a freelance writer for Residents' Journal *and the* North Lawndale Community News, *both based in Chicago.*

This piece was originally printed in the Winter 2004 issue of Journal of Ordinary Thought (JOT). JOT *is published quarterly by the Neighborhood Writing Alliance and features the personal histories and everyday experiences of adults writing in ten Chicago neighborhoods. Holmes-Brinson has been attending a* JOT *writing workshop at the Mabel Manning Branch of the Chicago Public Library since 1999. In 2002 she received an Illinois Arts Council Award for her piece "Casey's Story."*

You caught my presence from across the room
And made all the gestures a man would make
When trying to impress a woman.
You flirted
5   Be it for right purposes
Or not.

You saw me smile approvingly.

You made your way over.

You liked my smile
10   You liked my way
You liked the body
That presented me.

You reached for my hand
To kiss it perhaps

15   And saw my hand

A crippled hand
Just like the other.

You kissed the one
Out of politeness
20   Since it was there in yours
And people were around.

You glanced at the other
Crippled hand.
And smiled politely
25   And eased away.

Caught up in the mode of the moment
You wondered how it must've made me feel.

The question is
How does it make you feel?
30   I've lived this way all my life.

EXERCISES

Some of the Issues

1. The narrator starts the poem by addressing her audience as "you." To whom is she speaking?
2. How does the man respond to the narrator's hand and why? What was your own reaction to his response?
3. What is the meaning of the final stanza?

Some Subjects for Writing

*4. At the end of her essay "Hearing the Sweetest Songs," Nicolette Toussaint writes that conversations about disability are "conversations we all should have." To what extent to you feel that, as a society, we talk openly about disability? Write an essay in which you explore the kinds of conversations we might have about disability and how those might or might not change people's attitudes.

PART VI

AMERICAN ENCOUNTERS

Our lives and identities are shaped by encounters with people, places, and cultures. For better or worse, our most formative experiences can come from the challenges posed by our interactions with and reactions to that which is unfamiliar to us. In this chapter, writers explore how specific encounters have shaped their lives and ideas. Their encounters force them to question their assumptions and to confront other people's assumptions about them.

For immigrants to America, their move to the United States can be one of their most transformative encounters. Two hundred years ago, Michel Guillaume St. Jean de Crèvecoeur asked. "What is an American?" Crèvecoeur came as a young man to the "New World" and settled in the French colony of Louisiane. In his *Letters from an American Farmer* (1782), he defines the new creature, the American, as different in any number of ways from his classbound, traditional European ancestors. In defining "What is an American?" Crèvecoeur celebrates the creation of what he views as an almost classless society, in which persons can reach whatever position in life their abilities allow.

We all know by the time we reach our teens, and sometimes much sooner, the different ways people define what it means to be an American can often be viewed as threatening. Through ignorance and fear of the unknown, our worst selves can emerge. Brent Staples, a tall African-American man, becomes a fearsome entity with whom pedestrians avoid making eye contact. Piri Thomas recalls being on "Alien Turf"—the new kid, a Puerto Rican—in an Italian neighborhood. Walter White describes how his family's house became a target of a mob during a race riot in Atlanta early in this century.

249

The next three essays examine American encounters through the topic of immigration. In "Black Like Them" Malcolm Gladwell compares the lives of African Americans and West Indian black immigrants to the United States. How does each group define itself? How are their encounters with the white majority different? In a complex essay, Gladwell uses his own family history and the work of scholars to reflect on the kinds of racism experienced by both groups. Bharati Mukherjee shows us "Two Ways of Belonging in America" by comparing and contrasting the different choices she and her sister made after moving to the United States from India as young adults. The author decides to put down roots by becoming a U.S. citizen. Her sister, who has lived in the United States for just as long, decides to remain an expatriate and maintain stronger ties to her native country. In "Amérka, Amérka," Anton Shammas illustrates how immigrants can live in this country and keep their native traditions—as they encounter new ones—if they so choose. "This country is big," he says, "it has room not only for the newcomers, but for their portable homelands." In the poem at the end of this section, Dwight Okita recalls the irrational fears foisted on other Americans to justify the Japanese-American relocation policy of World War II.

What Is an American?

Michel Guillaume St. Jean de Crèvecoeur

Michel Guillaume St. Jean de Crèvecoeur (1735–1813) came as a young man to the New World, settling at first in the French colony of Louisiana, which at that time stretched in a huge arc from the mouth of the St. Lawrence River in the north to the mouth of the Mississippi in the south. In the Seven Years War (1756–63), called the French and Indian Wars in America, he fought under Montcalm against the British. When the Colonies passed into British hands, he remained and settled as a farmer in Vermont. The Revolutionary War found him on the side of the loyalists. Crèvecoeur returned to France permanently in 1790. His Letters from an American Farmer, *written in French, was published in 1782 and is among the earliest descriptions of life in America.*

Crèvecoeur defines and describes what he sees as the virtues and advantages America possesses as compared to the Europe of his day. He sees a prosperous agricultural society, virtually classless, in which persons can reach whatever position in life their abilities allow. He contrasts this to the Old World with its ingrained class structure, where a man (or woman) is born to wealth and high status or to poverty and lifelong drudgery, with no way to escape. He sees America as a young, mobile society in contrast to the static world from which the new man, the American, has made his escape.

1 I wish I could be acquainted with the feelings and thoughts which must agitate the heart and present themselves to the mind of an enlightened Englishman, when he first lands on this continent. He must greatly rejoice, that he lived at a time to see this fair country discovered and settled; he must necessarily feel a share of national pride, when he views the chain of settlements which embellishes these extended shores. When he says to himself, this is the work of my countrymen, who, when convulsed by factions, afflicted by a variety of miseries and wants, restless and impatient, took refuge here. They brought along with them their national genius, to which they principally owe what liberty they enjoy, and what substance they possess. Here he sees the industry of his native country, displayed in a new manner, and traces in their works the embryos of all the arts, sciences, and ingenuity which flourish in Europe. Here he beholds fair cities, substantial villages, extensive fields, an immense country filled with decent houses, good roads, orchards, meadows, and bridges, where an hundred years ago all was wild, woody, and uncultivated!

2 What a train of pleasing ideas this fair spectacle must suggest! It is a prospect which must inspire a good citizen with the most heartfelt pleasure. The difficulty consists in the manner of viewing so extensive a scene. He is

arrived on a new continent; a modern society offers itself to his contemplation, different from what he had hitherto seen. It is not composed, as in Europe, of great lords who possess every thing, and of a herd of people who have nothing. Here are no aristocratical families, no courts, no kings, no bishops, no ecclesiastical dominion, no invisible power giving to a few a very visible one; no great manufacturers employing thousands, no great refinements of luxury. The rich and the poor are not so far removed from each other as they are in Europe.

3   Some few towns excepted, we are all tillers of the earth, from Nova Scotia to West Florida. We are a people of cultivators, scattered over an immense territory, communicating with each other by means of good roads and navigable rivers, united by the silken bands of mild government, all respecting the laws without dreading their power, because they are equitable. We are all animated with the spirit of industry, which is unfettered, and unrestrained, because each person works for himself. If he travels through our rural districts, he views not the hostile castle, and the haughty mansion, contrasted with the clay-built hut and miserable cabin, where cattle and men help to keep each other warm, and dwell in meanness, smoke, and indigence. A pleasing uniformity of decent competence appears throughout our habitations. The meanest of our log-houses is a dry and comfortable habitation. Lawyer or merchant are the fairest titles our towns afford; that of a farmer is the only appellation of the rural inhabitants of our country. It must take some time ere he can reconcile himself to our dictionary, which is but short in words of dignity, and names of honour. There, on a Sunday, he sees a congregation of respectable farmers and their wives, all clad in neat homespun, well mounted, or riding in their own humble waggons. There is not among them an esquire, saving the unlettered magistrate. There he sees a parson as simple as his flock, a farmer who does not riot on the labour of others. We have no princes, for whom we toil, starve, and bleed: we are the most perfect society now existing in the world. Here man is free as he ought to be; nor is this pleasing equality so transitory as many others are. Many ages will not see the shores of our great lakes replenished with inland nations, nor the unknown bounds of North America entirely peopled. Who can tell how far it extends? Who can tell the millions of men whom it will feed and contain? for no European foot has as yet travelled half the extent of this mighty continent?

4   The next wish of this traveller will be to know whence came all these people? They are a mixture of English, Scotch, Irish, Dutch, Germans, and Swedes. From this promiscuous breed, the race now called Americans have arisen. The eastern provinces must indeed be excepted, as being the unmixed descendants of Englishmen. I have heard many wish they had been more intermixed also: for my part, I am no wisher; and think it much better as it has happened. They exhibit a most conspicuous figure in this great and variegated picture; they too enter for a great share in the pleasing perspective displayed in these thirteen provinces. I know it is fashionable to reflect on them; but I respect them for what they have done; for the accuracy and wisdom with which they have settled their territory;

for the decency of their manners; for their early love of letters; their ancient college, the first in this hemisphere; for their industry, which to me, who am but a farmer, is the criterion of every thing. There never was a people, situated as they are, who, with so ungrateful a soil, have done more in so short a time. Do you think that the monarchical ingredients which are more prevalent in other governments, have purged them from all foul stains? Their histories assert the contrary.

5   In this great American asylum, the poor of Europe have by some means met together, and in consequence of various causes; to what purpose should they ask one another, what countrymen they are? Alas, two thirds of them had no country. Can a wretch who wanders about, who works and starves, whose life is a continual scene of sore affliction of pinching penury; can that man call England or any other kingdom his country? A country that had no bread for him, whose fields procured him no harvest, who met with nothing but the frowns of the rich, the severity of the laws, with jails and punishments; who owned not a single foot of the extensive surface of this planet? No! Urged by a variety of motives, here they came. Everything has tended to regenerate them; new laws, a new mode of living, a new social system; here they are become men: in Europe they were as so many useless plants, wanting vegetative mould, and refreshing showers; they withered, and were mowed down by want, hunger, and war: but now, by the power of transplantation, like all other plants, they have taken root and flourished! Formerly they were not numbered in any civil list of their country, except in those of the poor; here they rank as citizens. By what invisible power has this surprizing metamorphosis been performed? By that of the laws and that of their industry. The laws, the indulgent laws, protect them as they arrive, stamping on them the symbol of adoption; they receive ample rewards for their labours; these accumulated rewards procure them lands; those lands confer on them the title of freemen; and to that title every benefit is affixed which men can possibly require. This is the great operation daily performed by our laws. From whence proceed these laws? From our government. Whence that government? It is derived from the original genius and strong desire of the people, ratified and confirmed by government. This is the great chain which links us all, this is the picture which every province exhibits.

6   What attachment can a poor European emigrant have for a country where he had nothing? The knowledge of the language, the love of a few kindred as poor as himself, were the only cords that tied him: his country is now that which gives him land, bread, protection, and consequence: *Ubi panis ibi patria*, is the motto of all emigrants. What then is the American, this new man? He is either an European, or the descendant of an European; hence that strange mixture of blood, which you will find in no other country. I could point out to you a man, whose grandfather was an Englishman, whose wife was Dutch, whose son married a French woman, and whose present four sons have now four wives of different nations. *He* is an American, who, leaving behind him all his ancient

prejudices and manners, receives new ones from the new mode of life he has embraced, the new government he obeys, and the new rank he holds. He becomes an American by being received in the broad lap of our great *Alma Mater.*

7   Here individuals of all nations are melted into a new race of men, whose labours and posterity will one day cause great change in the world. Americans are the western pilgrims, who are carrying along with them that great mass of arts, sciences, vigour, and industry, which began long since in the east; they will finish the great circle. The Americans were once scattered all over Europe; here they are incorporated into one of the finest systems of population which has ever appeared, and which will hereafter become distinct by the power of the different climates they inhabit. The American ought, therefore, to love this country much better than that wherein either he or his forefathers were born. Here the rewards of his industry follow with equal steps the progress of his labour; his labour is founded on the basis of nature, *self-interest;* can it want a stronger allurement? Wives and children, who before in vain demanded of him a morsel of bread, now, fat and frolicsome, gladly help their father to clear those fields whence exuberant crops are to arise to feed and to clothe them all; without any part being claimed, either by a despotic prince, a rich abbot, or a mighty lord. Here religion demands but little of him; a small voluntary salary to the minister, and gratitude to God; can he refuse these? The American is a new man, who acts upon new principles; he must therefore entertain new ideas, and form new opinions. From involuntary idleness, servile dependence, penury, and useless labour, he has passed to toils of a very different nature, rewarded by ample subsistence.—This is an American.

EXERCISES

Some of the Issues

1. Why should the "enlightened Englishman" rejoice at landing in America?
2. What is the central idea of the second paragraph? How does it relate to the first? How does it carry Crèvecoeur's ideas beyond the first paragraph?
3. Consider the last sentence in paragraph 2 and explain how it is expanded on in paragraph 3.
4. Paragraph 3 makes its point by means of contrasts. What are they?
5. Paragraphs 4 and 5 classify the people who came to America, but in two different ways. Paragraph 4 discusses national origins. How are Americans described in paragraph 5?
6. In paragraphs 6 and 7 Crèvecoeur asserts that these diverse Europeans are "melted into a new race of men"—Americans. How does that process take place? (Note the word "melted.")
7. Make a list of the contrasts Crèvecoeur makes or clearly implies between Europe and America. Then attempt to organize and classify them into major groupings.

The Way We Are Told

8. Why does Crèvecoeur create the character of the "enlightened Englishman" to report on America in paragraph 1, instead of continuing to use the first person singular, as he does in the opening sentence?

9. Crèvecoeur tries to convince the reader of the superiority of Americans and their institutions. Who, would you say, are his readers? What are their likely beliefs? How does Crèvecoeur respond to these beliefs?

10. Crèvecoeur uses rhetorical questions, exclamations, and repetition of words and phrases to strengthen his case. Find examples of each.

Some Subjects for Writing

11. Write an essay in praise of some institution that you admire. Select those aspects that seem important to you, organize them in some logical order, and write your description, stressing the favorable facts rather than giving your opinions.

12. Crèvecoeur presents the American as an ideal "new man," free of the shackles of history imposed on him in Europe. In an essay examine the extent to which the American can still be described in Crèvecoeur's terms today.

13. Crèvecoeur may have been the first to use the word *melt* to describe the fusion of people of different nationalities into a new "race of men"—Americans. The term *melting pot* has become a cliché representing that process. More recently some observers have cast doubts on the extent of that process and preferred the analogy of the salad bowl or mosaic to the melting pot. What are the implications of each of these terms? Write an essay discussing what term you might use to describe America and why.

Night Walker

Brent Staples

Brent Staples was born in 1951 in Chester, Pennsylvania. He holds a Ph.D. degree in psychology from the University of Chicago and is a member of the editorial board of the New York Times *and the author of* Parallel Time: A Memoir *(1991). The selection reprinted here appeared originally in* Ms. *magazine in September 1986. In it Staples describes repeated experiences he had taking walks at night. A tall African-American man, he aroused the fear of other pedestrians as well as drivers who saw him as the stereotypical mugger.*

1   My first victim was a woman—white, well-dressed, probably in her early twenties. I came upon her late one evening on a deserted street in Hyde Park, a relatively affluent neighborhood in an otherwise mean, impoverished section of Chicago. As I swung onto the avenue behind her, there seemed to be a discreet, uninflammatory distance between us. Not so. She cast back a worried glance. To her, the youngish black man—a broad six feet two inches with a beard and billowing hair, both hands shoved into the pockets of a bulky military jacket—seemed menacingly close. After a few more quick glimpses, she picked up her pace and was soon running in earnest. Within seconds she disappeared into a cross street.

2   That was more than a decade ago. I was 22 years old, a graduate student newly arrived at the University of Chicago. It was in the echo of that terrified woman's footfalls that I first began to know the unwieldy inheritance I'd come into—the ability to alter public space in ugly ways. It was clear that she thought herself the quarry of a mugger, a rapist, or worse. Suffering a bout of insomnia, however, I was stalking sleep, not defenseless wayfarers. As a softy who is scarcely able to take a knife to a raw chicken—let alone hold it to a person's throat—I was surprised, embarrassed, and dismayed all at once. Her flight made me feel like an accomplice in tyranny. It also made it clear that I was indistinguishable from the muggers who occasionally seeped into the area from the surrounding ghetto. That first encounter, and those that followed, signified that a vast, unnerving gulf lay between nighttime pedestrians—particularly women—and me. And I soon gathered that being perceived as dangerous is a hazard in itself. I only needed to turn a corner into a dicey situation, or crowd some frightened, armed person in a foyer somewhere, or make an errant move after being pulled over by a policeman. Where fear and weapons meet—and they often do in urban America—there is always the possibility of death.

3   In that first year, my first away from my hometown, I was to become thoroughly familiar with the language of fear. At dark, shadowy intersections

in Chicago, I could cross in front of a car stopped at a traffic light and elicit the *thunk, thunk, thunk, thunk* of the driver—black, white, male, or female— hammering down the door locks. On less traveled streets after dark, I grew accustomed to but never comfortable with people who crossed to the other side of the street rather than pass me. Then there were the standard unpleas- antries with police, doormen, bouncers, cab drivers, and others whose busi- ness it is to screen out troublesome individuals *before* there is any nastiness.

4   I moved to New York nearly two years ago and I have remained an avid night walker. In central Manhattan, the near-constant crowd cover minimizes tense one-on-one street encounters. Elsewhere—visiting friends in SoHo, where sidewalks are narrow and tightly spaced buildings shut out the sky— things can get very taut indeed.

5   After dark on the warrenlike streets of Brooklyn where I live, women seem to set their faces on neutral and, with their purse straps strung across their chests bandolier style, they forge ahead as though bracing themselves against being tackled. I understand, of course, that the danger they perceive is not a hal- lucination. Women are particularly vulnerable to street violence, and young black males are drastically overrepresented among the perpetrators of that vio- lence. Yet these truths are no solace against the kind of alienation that comes of being ever the suspect, against being set apart, a fearsome entity with whom pedestrians avoid making eye contact.

6   It is not altogether clear to me how I reached the ripe old age of 22 without being conscious of the lethality nighttime pedestrians attributed to me. Perhaps it was because in Chester, Pennsylvania, the small, angry industrial town where I came of age in the 1960s, I was scarcely noticeable against a backdrop of gang warfare, street knifings, and murders. I grew up one of the good boys, had per- haps a half-dozen fist fights. In retrospect, my shyness of combat has clear sources.

7   Many things go into the making of a young thug. One of those things is the consummation of the male romance with the power to intimidate. An infant dis- covers that random flailings send the baby bottle flying out of the crib and crashing to the floor. Delighted, the joyful babe repeats those motions again and again, seeking to duplicate the feat. Just so, I recall the points at which some of my boyhood friends were finally seduced by the perception of themselves as tough guys. When a mark cowered and surrendered his money without resis- tance, myth and reality merged—and paid off. It is, after all, only manly to em- brace the power to frighten and intimidate. We, as men, are not supposed to give an inch of our lane on the highway; we are to seize the fighter's edge in work and in play and even in love; we are to be valiant in the face of hostile forces.

8   Unfortunately, poor and powerless young men seem to take all this non- sense literally. As a boy, I saw countless tough guys locked away; I have since buried several, too. They were babies, really—a teenage cousin, a brother of 22, a childhood friend in his mid-twenties—all gone down in episodes of bravado

played out in the streets. I came to doubt the virtues of intimidation early on. I chose, perhaps even unconsciously, to remain a shadow—timid, but a survivor.

9   The fearsomeness mistakenly attributed to me in public places often has a perilous flavor. The most frightening of these confusions occurred in the late 1970s and early 1980s when I worked as a journalist in Chicago. One day, rushing into the office of a magazine I was writing for with a deadline story in hand, I was mistaken for a burglar. The office manager called security and, with an ad hoc posse, pursued me through the labyrinthine halls, nearly to my editor's door. I had no way of proving who I was. I could only move briskly toward the company of someone who knew me.

10   Another time I was on assignment for a local paper and killing time before an interview. I entered a jewelry store on the city's affluent Near North Side. The proprietor excused herself and returned with an enormous red Doberman pinscher straining at the end of a leash. She stood, the dog extended toward me, silent to my questions, her eyes bulging nearly out of her head. I took a cursory look around, nodded, and bade her good night. Relatively speaking, however, I never fared as badly as another black male journalist. He went to nearby Waukegan, Illinois, a couple of summers ago to work on a story about a murderer who was born there. Mistaking the reporter for the killer, police hauled him from his car at gunpoint and but for his press credentials would probably have tried to book him. Such episodes are not uncommon. Black men trade tales like this all the time.

11   In "My Negro Problem—And Ours" Podhoretz writes that the hatred he feels for blacks makes itself known to him through a variety of avenues—one being his discomfort with that "special brand of paranoid touchiness" to which he says blacks are prone. No doubt he is speaking here of black men. In time, I learned to smother the rage I felt at so often being taken for a criminal. Not to do so would surely have led to madness—via that special "paranoid touchiness" that so annoyed Podhoretz at the time he wrote the essay.

12   I began to take precautions to make myself less threatening. I move about with care, particularly late in the evening. I give a wide berth to nervous people on subway platforms during the wee hours, particularly when I have exchanged business clothes for jeans. If I happen to be entering a building behind some people who appear skittish, I may walk by, letting them clear the lobby before I return, so as not to seem to be following them. I have been calm and extremely congenial on those rare occasions when I've been pulled over by the police.

13   And on late-evening constitutionals along streets less traveled by, I employ what has proved to be an excellent tension-reducing measure: I whistle melodies from Beethoven and Vivaldi and the more popular classical composers. Even steely New Yorkers hunching toward nighttime destinations seem to relax, and occasionally they even join in the tune. Virtually everybody seems to sense that a mugger wouldn't be warbling bright, sunny selections from Vivaldi's *Four Seasons*. It is my equivalent of the cowbell that hikers wear when they know they are in bear country.

EXERCISES

Some of the Issues

1. How does Staples first discover his "ability to alter public space" (paragraph 2)?
2. What is Staples's reaction to the way he is perceived by strangers on his nightly walks? Does he show that he understands the feelings of some of those who fear him? Does he also show anger? Where?
3. What does Staples tell us about himself? About his childhood? How does this knowledge emphasize the contrast between his real self and the way he is often perceived by strangers?
4. How does Staples respond to Norman Podhoretz's contention that black men have a "special brand of paranoid touchiness" (paragraph 11)?
5. What has Staples learned to do to reduce the tension of passersby? Why does he choose the music he does? Does it solve his problem?

The Way We Are Told

6. Staples starts with an anecdote. Why does he use the word "victim" in the first sentence? Is there really a "victim"?
7. Identify examples drawn from Staples's own experience. How are they used to support the generalizations he makes?

Some Subjects for Writing

8. Write about a time when someone misjudged you or something you did. What were the circumstances? How did you feel? What was the resolution? What did you learn from the experience?
9. Observe and reflect on your own neighborhood. Write an essay in which you examine to what extent "outsiders" are welcome in your community. You may want to focus on one incident or examine a particular public place in your area.
10. In 1903 W. E. B. DuBois, one of the most prominent African-American intellectuals, predicted that the "problem of the Twentieth Century is the problem of the color line." To what extent do you believe he was right? Do you believe his statement also applies to the twenty-first century, or do you feel that there are other essential problems for our current century?

Alien Turf

Piri Thomas

Piri Thomas was born Juan Pedro Tomás in Spanish Harlem of Puerto Rican and Cuban parents in 1928, and grew up in its world of gangs, drugs, and petty crime. In his teens he became an addict, was convicted of attempted armed robbery, and served six years of a fifteen-year sentence. After his release, he began to work for drug rehabilitation programs in New York and Puerto Rico and developed a career as a writer. The autobiographical Down These Mean Streets *(1967), from which the following selection is taken, was his first book. A sequel,* Savior, Savior, Hold My Hand, *was published in 1972. Thomas has been an influential member of the Nuyorican movement, an intellectual movement of New York–based poets, writers, artists, and musicians of Puerto Rican descent.*

Thomas tells the reader about an event in his childhood, one that many young people will have experienced: being the new kid on the block. But when the block is in a poor neighborhood and when, moreover, the new kid is from a background different from the prevailing culture, then the mix can turn explosive.

1 Sometimes you don't fit in. Like if you're a Puerto Rican on an Italian block. After my new baby brother, Ricardo, died of some kind of germs, Poppa moved us from 111th Street to Italian turf on 114th Street between Second and Third Avenue. I guess Poppa wanted to get Momma away from the hard memories of the old pad.

2 I sure missed 111th Street, where everybody acted, walked, and talked like me. But on 114th Street everything went all right for a while. There were a few dirty looks from the spaghetti-an'-sauce cats, but no big sweat. Till that one day I was on my way home from school and almost had reached my stoop when someone called: "Hey, you dirty fuckin' spic."

3 The words hit my ears and almost made me curse Poppa at the same time. I turned around real slow and found my face pushing in the finger of an Italian kid about my age. He had five or six of his friends with him.

4 "Hey, you," he said, "What nationality are ya?"

5 I looked at him and wondered which nationality to pick. And one of his friends said, "Ah, Rocky, he's black enuff to be a nigger. Ain't that what you is, kid?"

6 My voice was almost shy in its anger. "I'm Puerto Rican," I said. "I was born here." I wanted to shout it, but it came out like a whisper.

7 "Right here inna street?" Rocky sneered. "Ya mean right here inna middle of da street?"

8   They all laughed. I hated them. I shook my head slowly from side to side.

9   "Uh-uh," I said softly. "I was born inna hospital—inna bed."

10   "Umm, *paisan*—born inna bed," Rocky said.

11   I didn't like Rocky Italiano's voice. "Inna hospital," I whispered, and all the time my eyes were trying to cut down the long distance from this trouble to my stoop. But it was no good; I was hemmed in by Rocky's friends. I couldn't help thinking about kids getting wasted for moving into a block belonging to other people.

12   "What hospital, *paisan?*" Bad Rocky pushed.

13   "Harlem Hospital," I answered, wishing like all hell that it was 5 o'clock instead of just 3 o'clock, 'cause Poppa came home at 5. I looked around for some friendly faces belonging to grown-up people, but the elders were all busy yakking away in Italian. I couldn't help thinking how much like Spanish it sounded. Shit, that should make us something like relatives.

14   "Harlem Hospital?" said a voice. "I knew he was a nigger."

15   "Yeah," said another voice from an expert on color. "That's the hospital where all them black bastards get born at."

16   I dug three Italian elders looking at us from across the street and I felt saved. But that went out the window when they just smiled and went on talking. I couldn't decide whether they had smiled because this new whatever-he-was was gonna get his ass kicked or because they were pleased that their kids were welcoming a new kid to their country. An older man nodded his head at Rocky, who smiled back. I wondered if that was a signal for my funeral to begin.

17   "Ain't that right, kid?" Rocky pressed. "Ain't that where all black people get born?"

18   I dug some of Rocky's boys grinding and pushing and punching closed fists against open hands. I figured they were looking to shake me up, so I straightened up my humble voice and made like proud. "There's all kinds of people born there. Colored people, Puerto Ricans like me, an'—even spaghetti-benders like you."

19   "That's a dirty fuckin' lie"—*bash*, I felt Rocky's fist smack into my mouth—"You dirty fuckin' spic."

20   I got dizzy and then more dizzy when fists started to fly from everywhere and only toward me. I swung back, *splat*, *bish*—my fist hit some face and I wished I hadn't, 'cause then I started getting kicked.

21   I heard people yelling in Italian and English and I wondered if maybe it was 'cause I hadn't fought fair in having hit that one guy. But it wasn't. The voices were trying to help me.

22   "Whas'sa matta, you no-good kids, leeva da kid alone," a man said. I looked through a swelling eye and dug some Italians pushing their kids off me with slaps. One even kicked a kid in the ass. I could have loved them if I didn't hate them so fuckin' much.

23   "You all right, kiddo?" asked the man.

24   "Where you live, boy?" said another one.

25   "Is the *bambino* hurt?" asked a woman.

26   I didn't look at any of them. I felt dizzy. I didn't want to open my mouth to talk, 'cause I was fighting to keep from puking up. I just hoped my face was cool-looking. I walked away from the group of strangers. I reached my stoop and started to climb the steps.

27   "Hey, spic," came a shout from across the street. I started to turn to the voice and changed my mind. "Spic" wasn't my name. I knew that voice, though. It was Rocky's. "We'll see ya again, spic," he said.

28   I wanted to do something tough, like spitting in their direction. But you gotta have spit in your mouth in order to spit, and my mouth was hurt dry. I just stood there with my back to them.

29   "Hey, your old man just better be the janitor in that fuckin' building."

30   Another voice added, "Hey, you got any pretty sisters? We might let ya stay onna block."

31   Another voice mocked, "Aw, fer Chrissake, where ya ever hear of one of them black broads being pretty?"

32   I heard the laughter. I turned around and looked at them. Rocky made some kind of dirty sign by putting his left hand in the crook of his right arm while twisting his closed fist in the air.

33   Another voice said, "Fuck it, we'll just cover the bitch's face with the flag an' fuck'er for old glory."

34   All I could think of was how I'd like to kill each of them two or three times. I found some spit in my mouth and splattered it in their direction and went inside.

35   Momma was cooking, and the smell of rice and beans was beating the smell of Parmesan cheese from the other apartments. I let myself into our new pad. I tried to walk fast past Momma so I could wash up, but she saw me.

36   "My God, Piri, what happened?" she cried.

37   "Just a little fight in school, Momma. You know how it is, Momma, I'm new in school an' . . ." I made myself laugh. Then I made myself say, "But Moms, I whipped the living _____ outta two guys, an' one was bigger'n me."

38   "*Bendito*, Piri, I raise my family in Christian way. Not to fight. Christ says to turn the other cheek."

39   "Sure, Momma." I smiled and went and showered, feeling sore at Poppa for bringing us into spaghetti country. I felt my face with easy fingers and thought about all the running back and forth from school that was in store for me.

40   I sat down to dinner and listened to Momma talk about Christian living without really hearing her. All I could think of was that I hadda go out in that street again. I made up my mind to go out right after I finished eating. I had to, shook up or not; cats like me had to show heart.

41   "Be back, Moms," I said after dinner. "I'm going out on the stoop." I got halfway to the stoop and turned and went back to our apartment. I knocked.

42   "Who is it?" Momma asked.

43   "Me, Momma."

44   She opened the door. "*¿Qué pasa?*" she asked.

45   "Nothing, Momma, I just forgot something," I said. I went into the bedroom and fiddled around and finally copped a funny book and walked out the door again. But this time I made sure the switch on the lock was open, just in case I had to get back real quick. I walked out on that stoop as cool as could be, feeling braver with the lock open.

46   There was no sign of Rocky and his killers. After awhile I saw Poppa coming down the street. He walked like beat tired. Poppa hated his pick-and-shovel job with the WPA. He couldn't even hear the name WPA without getting a fever. *Funny, I thought, Poppa's the same like me, a stone Puerto Rican, and nobody in this block even pays him a mind. Maybe older people get along better'n us kids.*

47   Poppa was climbing the stoop. "Hi, Poppa," I said.

48   "How's it going, son? Hey, you sure look a little lumped up. What happened?"

49   I looked at Poppa and started to talk it outta me all at once and stopped, 'cause I heard my voice start to sound scared, and that was no good.

50   "Slow down, son," Poppa said. "Take it easy." He sat down on the stoop and made a motion for me to do the same. He listened and I talked. I gained confidence. I went from a tone of being shook up by the Italians to a tone of being a better fighter than Joe Louis and Pedro Montanez lumped together, with Kid Chocolate thrown in for extra.

51   "So that's what happened," I concluded. "And it looks like only the beginning. Man, I ain't scared, Poppa, but like there's nothin' but Italianos on this block and there's no me's like me except for me an' our family."

52   Poppa looked tight. He shook his head from side to side and mumbled something about another Puerto Rican family that lived a coupla doors down from us.

53   I thought, *What good would that do me, unless they prayed over my dead body in Spanish?* But I said, "Man! That's great. Before ya know it, there'll be a whole bunch of us moving in, huh?"

54   Poppa grunted something and got up. "Staying out here, son?"

55   "Yeah, Poppa, for a little while longer."

56   From that day on I grew eyes all over my head. Anytime I hit that street for anything, I looked straight ahead, behind me and from side to side all at the same time. Sometimes I ran into Rocky and his boys—the cat was never without his boys—but they never made a move to snag me. They just grinned at me like a bunch of hungry alley cats that could get to their mouse anytime they wanted. That's what they made me feel like—a mouse. Not like a smart house mouse but like a white house pet that ain't got no business in the middle of cat country but don't know better 'cause he grew thinking he was a cat—which wasn't far from wrong 'cause he'd end up as part of the inside of some cat.

57   Rocky and his fellas got to playing a way-out game with me called "One-finger-across-the-neck-inna-slicing-motion," followed by such gentle words as "It won't be long, spico." I just looked at them blank and made it to wherever I was going.

58   I kept wishing those cats went to the same school I went to, a school that was on the border between their country and mine, and I had *amigos* there—and there I could count on them. But I couldn't ask two or three *amigos* to break into Rocky's block and help me mess up his boys. I knew 'cause I had asked them already. They had turned me down fast, and I couldn't blame them. It would have been murder, and I guess they figured one murder would be better than four.

59   I got through the days trying to play it cool and walk on by Rocky and his boys like they weren't there. One day I passed them and nothing was said. I started to let out my breath. I felt great; I hadn't been seen. Then someone yelled in a high, girlish voice, "Yoo-hoo . . . Hey, *paisan* . . . we see yoo . . ." And right behind that voice came a can of evaporated milk—whoosh, clatter. I walked cool for ten steps then started running like mad.

60   This crap kept up for a month. They tried to shake me up. Every time they threw something at me, it was just to see me jump. I decided that the next fucking time they threw something at me I was gonna play bad-o and not run. That next time came about a week later. Momma sent me off the stoop to the Italian market on 115th Street and First Avenue, deep in Italian country. Man, that was stompin' territory. But I went, walking in the style which I had copped from the colored cats I had seen, a swinging and stepping down hard at every step. Those cats were so down and cool that just walking made a way-out sound.

61   Ten minutes later I was on my way back with Momma's stuff. I got to the corner of First Avenue and 114th Street and crushed myself right into Rocky and his fellas.

62   "Well-l, fellas," Rocky said, "Lookee who's here."

63   I didn't like the sounds coming out of Rocky's fat mouth. And I didn't like the sameness of the shitty grins spreading all over the boys' faces. But I thought, *No more! No more! I ain't gonna run no more.* Even so, I looked around, like for some kind of Jesus miracle to happen. I was always looking for miracles to happen.

64   "Say, *paisan*," one guy said, "you even buying from us *paisans*, eh? Man, you must wantta be Italian."

65   Before I could bite that dopey tongue of mine, I said, "I wouldn't be a guinea on a motherfucking bet."

66   "Wha-at?" said Rocky, really surprised. I didn't blame him; I was surprised myself. His finger began digging a hole in his ear, like he hadn't heard me right. "Wha-at? Say that again?"

67   I could feel a thin hot wetness cutting itself down my leg. I had been so ashamed of being so damned scared that I had peed on myself. And then I wasn't scared any more; I felt a fuck-it-all attitude. I looked real bad at Rocky and said, "Ya heard me. I wouldn't be a guinea on a bet."

68   "Ya little sonavabitch, we'll kick the shit outta ya," said one guy, Tony, who had made a habit of asking me if I had any sen-your-ritas for sisters.

69   "Kick the shit outta me yourself if you got any heart, you mother fuckin' fucker," I screamed at him. I felt kind of happy, the kind of feeling that you get only when you got heart.

70   Big-mouth Tony just swung out, and I swung back and heard all of Momma's stuff plopping all over the street. My fist hit Tony smack dead in the mouth. He was so mad he threw a fist at me from about three feet away. I faked and jabbed and did fancy dance steps. Big-mouth put a stop to all that with a punch in my mouth. I heard the home cheers of "Yea, yea, bust that spic wide open!" Then I bloodied Tony's nose. He blinked and sniffed without putting his hands to his nose, and I remembered Poppa telling me, "Son, if you're ever fighting somebody an' you punch him in the nose, and he just blinks an' sniffs without holding his nose, you can do one of two things: fight like hell or run like hell—'cause that cat's a fighter."

71   Big-mouth came at me and we grabbed each other and pushed and pulled and shoved. *Poppa*, I thought, *I ain't gonna cop out. I'm a fighter, too*. I pulled away from Tony and blew my fist into his belly. He puffed and butted my nose with his head. I sniffed back. *Poppa, I didn't put my hands to my nose*. I hit Tony again in that same weak spot. He bent over in the middle and went down to his knees.

72   Big-mouth got up as fast as he could, and I was thinking how much heart he had. But I ran toward him like my life depended on it; I wanted to cool him. Too late. I saw his hand grab a fistful of ground asphalt which had been piled nearby to fix a pothole in the street. I tried to duck; I should have closed my eyes instead. The shitty-gritty stuff hit my face, and I felt the scrappy pain make itself a part of my eyes. I screamed and grabbed for two eyes with one hand, while the other I beat some kind of helpless tune on air that just couldn't be hurt. I heard Rocky's voice shouting, "Ya scum bag, ya didn't have to fight the spic dirty; you could've fucked him up fair and square!" I couldn't see. I heard a fist hit a face, then Big-mouth's voice: "Whatta ya hittin' me for?" and then Rocky's voice: "*Putana!* I ought ta knock all your fuckin' teeth out."

73   I felt hands grabbing at me between my screams. I punched out. *I'm gonna get killed*, I thought. Then I heard many voices: "Hold it, kid." "We ain't gonna hurt ya." "Je-*sus*, don't rub your eyes." "Ooooohhhh, shit, his eyes is fulla that shit."

74   *You're fuckin' right*, I thought, *and it hurts like* coño.

75   I heard a woman's voice now: "Take him to a hospital." And an old man asked: "How did it happen?"

76   "Momma, Momma," I cried.

77   "Comon, kid," Rocky said, taking my hand. "Lemme take ya home." I fought for the right to rub my eyes. "Grab his other hand, Vincent," Rocky said. I tried to rub my eyes with my eyelids. I could feel hurt tears cutting down my cheeks. "Come on, kid, we ain't gonna hurt ya," Rocky tried to assure me. "Swear to our mudders. We just wanna take ya home."

78   I made myself believe him, and trying not to make pain noises, I let myself be led home. I wondered if I was gonna be blind like Mr. Silva, who went around from door to door selling dish towels and brooms, his son leading him around.

79   "You okay, kid?" Rocky asked.

80   "Yeah," what was left of me said.

81   "A-huh," mumbled Big-mouth.

82   "He got much heart for a nigger," somebody else said.

83   A *spic*, I thought.

84   "For anybody," Rocky said. "Here we are kid," he added. "Watch your step."

85   I was like carried up the steps. "What's your apartment number?" Rocky asked.

86   "One-B—inna back—ground floor," I said, and I was led there. Somebody knocked on Momma's door. Then I heard running feet and Rocky's voice yelling back, "Don't rat, huh, kid?" And I was alone.

87   I heard the door open and Momma say, "*Bueno*, Piri, come in." I didn't move. I couldn't. There was a long pause; I could hear Momma's fright. "My God," she said finally "What's happened?" Then she took a closer look. "Aieeee," she screamed. "*¡Dios mío!*"

88   "I was playing with some kids, Momma," I said, "an' I got some dirt in my eyes." I tried to make my voice come out without the pain, like a man.

89   "*Dios eterno*—your eyes!"

90   "What's the matter? What's the matter?" Poppa called from the bedroom.

91   "*¡Está ciego!*"Momma screamed. "He is blind!"

92   I heard Poppa knocking things over as he came running. Sis began to cry. Blind, hurting tears were jumping out of my eyes. "Whattya mean, he's blind?" Poppa said as he stormed into the kitchen. "What happened?" Poppa's voice was both scared and mad.

93   "Playing, Poppa."

94   "Whatta ya mean, 'playing'?" Poppa's English sounded different when he got warm.

95   "Just playing, Poppa."

96   "Playing? Playing got all that dirt in your eyes? I bet my ass. Them damn Ee-ta-liano kids ganged up on you again." Poppa squeezed my head between the fingers of one hand. "That settles it—we're moving outta this damn section, outta this damn block, outta this damn shit."

97   *Shit*, I thought, *Poppa's sure cursin' up a storm*. I could hear him slapping the side of his leg, like he always did when he got real mad.

98   "Son," he said, "you're gonna point them out to me."
99   "Point who out, Poppa? I was playin' an'—"

100   "Stop talkin' to him and take him to the hospital!" Momma screamed.

101   "*Pobrecito*, poor Piri," cooed my little sister.

102   "You sure, son?" Poppa asked. "You was only playing?"

103   "Shit, Poppa, I said I was."

104   *Smack*—Poppa was so scared and mad, he let it out in the slap to the side of my face.

105   "*¡Bestia!* ani-*mul!*" Momma cried. "He's blind, and you hit him!"

106   "I'm sorry, son, I'm sorry," Poppa said in a voice like almost crying. I heard him running back into the bedroom yelling, "Where's my pants?"

107　　Momma grabbed away fingers that were trying to wipe away the hurt in my eyes. "*Caramba*, no rub, no rub," she said, kissing me. She told Sis to get a rag and wet it with cold water.

108　　Poppa came running back into the kitchen. "Let's go, son, let's go. Jesus! I didn't mean to smack ya, I really didn't," he said, his big hand rubbing and grabbing my hair gently.

109　　"Here's the rag, Momma," said Sis.

110　　"What's that for?" asked Poppa.

111　　"To put on his eyes," Momma said.

112　　I heard the smack of a wet rag, *blapt*, against the kitchen wall. "We can't put nothing on his eyes. It might make them worse. Come on, son," Poppa said nervously, lifting me up in his big arms. I felt like a little baby, like I didn't hurt so bad. I wanted to stay there, but I said, "Let me down, Poppa, I ain't no kid."

113　　"Shut up," Poppa said softly. "I know you ain't but it's faster this way."

114　　"Which hospeetal are you taking him to?" Momma asked.

115　　"Nearest one," Poppa answered as we went out the door. He carried me through the hall and out into the street, where the bright sunlight made a red hurting color through the crap in my eyes. I heard voices on the stoop and on the sidewalk: "Is that the boy?"

116　　"A-huh. He's probably blinded."

117　　"We'll get a cab, son," Poppa said. His voice loved me. I heard Rocky yelling from across the street, "We're pulling for ya, kid. Remember what we . . ." The rest was lost to Poppa's long legs running down to the corner of Third Avenue. He hailed a taxi and we zoomed off toward Harlem Hospital. I felt the cab make all kinds of sudden stops and turns.

118　　"How do you feel, *hijo?*" Poppa asked.

119　　"It burns like hell."

120　　"You'll be okay," he said, and as an afterthought added, "Don't curse, son."

121　　I heard cars honking and the Third Avenue el roaring above us. I knew we were in Puerto Rican turf, 'cause I could hear our language.

122　　"Son."

123　　"Yeah, Poppa."

124　　"Don't rub your eyes, fer Christ sake." He held my skinny wrists in his one hand, and everything got quiet between us.

125　　The cab got to Harlem Hospital. I heard change being handled and the door opening and Poppa thanking the cabbie for getting here fast. "Hope the kid'll be okay," the driver said.

126　　*I will be*, I thought, *I ain't gonna be like Mr. Silva.*

127　　Poppa took me in his arms again and started running. "Where's emergency mister?" he asked someone.

128　　"To your left and straight away," said a voice.

129　　"Thanks a lot," Poppa said, and we were running again.

130　　"Emergency?" Poppa said when we stopped.

131　　"Yes, sir," said a girl's voice. "What's the matter?"

132   "My boy's got his eyes full of ground-up tar an'—"

133   "What's the matter?" said a man's voice.

134   "Youngster with ground tar in his eyes, doctor."

135   "We'll take him, mister. You just put him down here and go with the nurse. She'll take down the information. Uh, you the father?"

136   "That's right, doctor."

137   "Okay, just put him down here."

138   "Poppa, don't leave me," I cried.

139   "Sh, son, I ain't leaving you. I'm just going to fill out some papers, an' I'll be right back."

140   I nodded my head up and down and was wheeled away. When the rolling stretcher stopped, somebody stuck a needle in me and I got sleepy and started thinking about Rocky and his boys, and Poppa's slap, and how great Poppa was, and how my eyes didn't hurt no more . . .

141   I woke up in a room blind with darkness. The only lights were the ones inside my head. I put my fingers to my eyes and felt bandages. "Let them be, sonny," said a woman's voice.

142   I wanted to ask the voice if they had taken my eyes out, but I didn't. I was afraid the voice would say yes.

143   "Let them be, sonny," the nurse said, pulling my hand away from the bandages. "You're all right. The doctor put the bandages on to keep the light out. They'll be off real soon. Don't you worry none, sonny."

144   I wished she would stop calling me sonny. "Where's Poppa?" I asked cool like.

145   "He's outside, sonny. Would you like me to send him in?"

146   I nodded. "Yeah." I heard walking-away shoes, a door opening, a whisper, and shoes walking back toward me. "How do you feel, *hijo?*" Poppa asked.

147   "It hurts like shit, Poppa."

148   "It's just for awhile, son, and then off come the bandages. Everything's gonna be all right."

149   I thought, *Poppa didn't tell me to stop cursing.*

150   "And son, I thought I told you to stop cursing," he added.

151   I smiled. Poppa hadn't forgotten. Suddenly I realized that all I had on was a hospital gown. "Poppa, where's my clothes?" I asked.

152   "I got them. I'm taking them home an'—"

153   "Whatta ya mean, Poppa?" I said, like scared. "You ain't leavin' me here? I'll be damned if I stay." I was already sitting up and feeling my way outta bed. Poppa grabbed me and pushed me back. His voice wasn't mad or scared any more. It was happy and soft, like Momma's.

154   "Hey," he said, "get your ass back in bed or they'll have to put a bandage there too."

155   "Poppa," I pleaded. "I don't care, wallop me as much as you want, just take me home."

156   "Hey, I thought you said you wasn't no kid. Hell, you ain't scared of being alone?"

157   Inside my head there was a running of *Yeah, yeah, yeah,* but I answered, "Naw, Poppa, it's just that Momma's gonna worry and she'll get sick an' everything, and—"

158   "Won't work, son," Poppa broke in with a laugh.

159   I kept quiet.

160   "It's only for a couple days. We'll come and see you an' everybody'll bring you things."

161   I got interested but played it smooth. "What kinda things, Poppa?"

162   Poppa shrugged his shoulders and spread his big arms apart and answered me like he was surprised that I should ask. "Uh . . . fruits and . . . candy and ice cream. And Momma will probably bring you chicken soup."

163   I shook my head sadly, "Poppa, you know I don't like chicken soup."

164   "So we won't bring chicken soup. We'll bring what you like. Goddammit, whatta ya like?"

165   "I'd like the first things you talked about, Poppa," I said softly. "But instead of soup I'd like"—I held my breath back, then shot it out—"some roller skates!"

166   Poppa let out a whistle. Roller skates were about $1.50, and that was rice and beans for more than a few days. Then he said, "All right, son, soon as you get home, you got 'em."

167   But he had agreed too quickly. I shook my head from side to side. Shit, I was gonna push all the way for the roller skates. It wasn't every day you'd get hurt bad enough to ask for something so little like a pair of roller skates. I wanted them right away.

168   "Fer Christ sakes," Poppa protested, "you can't use 'em in here. Why, some kid will probably steal 'em on you." But Poppa's voice died out slowly in a "you win" tone as I just kept shaking my head from side to side. "Bring 'em tomorrow," he finally mumbled, "but that's it."

169   "Thanks, Poppa."

170   "Don't ask for no more."

171   My eyes were starting to hurt like mad again. The fun was starting to go outta the game between Poppa and me. I made a face.

172   "Does it hurt, son?"

173   "Naw, Poppa. I can take it." I thought how I was like a cat in a movie about Indians, taking it like a champ, tied to a stake and getting like burned toast.

174   Poppa sounded relieved. "Yeah, it's only at first it hurts." His hand touched my foot. "Well, I'll be going now . . ." Poppa rubbed my foot gently and then slapped me the same gentle way on the side of my leg. "Be good, son," he said and walked away. I heard the door open and the nurse telling him about how they were gonna move me to the ward 'cause I was out of danger. "Son," Poppa called back, "you're *un hombre.*"

175   I felt proud as hell.

176   "Poppa."
177   "Yeah, son?"
178   "You won't forget to bring the roller skates, huh?"
179   Poppa laughed, "Yeah, son."
180   I heard the door close.

EXERCISES

Some of the Issues

1. How do the first two sentences set the scene?
2. Piri wants to project a certain self-image in front of the gang. Characterize it.
3. Until the climactic fight, the cat-and-mouse game that Rocky's gang plays goes through several stages. Determine what these stages are and how Piri reacts to them.
4. How do the adults (those in the street as well as Piri's parents) react to the situation at the various stages? How does Piri deal with his parents' reactions in particular?
5. How does Rocky's attitude toward Piri change after one of the gang members throws the asphalt? What causes the change?
6. What is the significance of Thomas calling himself a "spic" in paragraph 83?
7. Explain Piri's reaction to "spic" and "nigger." Is Piri's desire to be identified as a Puerto Rican a matter of pride or practicality?
8. What is the importance of being "*un hombre*," of having "heart"? How does Piri prove himself a man? By whose standards?

The Way We Are Told

9. There is almost no description in this selection; it is all action and dialogue. Thomas nevertheless manages to convey some strong impressions of individuals and their attitudes. How does he do it? Cite some examples.
*10. Both Maya Angelou ("Graduation") and Thomas tell their stories from an adolescent's point of view. Apart from the content, how do the two stories differ? Use specific examples.

Some Subjects for Writing

11. Write about a conflict that you have had. Set the scene and then use mostly dialog to tell your story. See if you can make the voices authentic.

*12. The term *rite of passage* is usually used to indicate the ceremony marking the formal change of a young person from childhood to adulthood, such as a confirmation or bar mitzvah, though it is not always a religious ceremony. Write an essay arguing that Angelou's graduation and Thomas's big fight (or one or the other) were such rites of passage.

I Learn What I Am

Walter White

Walter White was born in Atlanta, Georgia, in 1893. He joined the NAACP early in its development and served as its head from 1931 until his death in 1955. The following excerpt is taken from his autobiography, A Man Called White (1948).

The events White describes took place in his childhood, at the beginning of the twentieth century. The year was 1906 and he was living in Atlanta with his large family, near the line that separated the white community from his own. His father, an employee of the U.S. Postal Service, kept the house in immaculate repair, its white picket fence symbolizing the American Dream. When a race riot erupted in Atlanta, their house became a target of the mob. White tells the dramatic story of those two days.

1   There were nine light-skinned Negroes in my family: mother, father, five sisters, an older brother, George, and myself. The house in which I discovered what it meant to be a Negro was located on Houston Street, three blocks from the Candler Building, Atlanta's first skyscraper, which bore the name of the ex-drug clerk who had become a millionaire from the sale of Coca-Cola. Below us lived none but Negroes; toward town all but a very few were white. Ours was an eight room, two-story frame house which stood out in its surroundings not because of its opulence but by contrast with the drabness and unpaintedness of the other dwellings in a deteriorating neighborhood.

2   Only Father kept his house painted, the picket fence repaired, the board fence separating our place from those on either side whitewashed, the grass neatly trimmed, and flower beds abloom. Mother's passion for neatness was even more pronounced and it seemed to me that I was always the victim of her determination to see no single blade of grass longer than the others or any one of the pickets in the front fence less shiny with paint than its mates. This spic-and-spanness became increasingly apparent as the rest of the neighborhood became more down-at-heel, and resulted, as we were to learn, in sullen envy among some of our white neighbors. It was the violent expression of that resentment against a Negro family neater than themselves which set the pattern of our lives.

3   On a day in September 1906, when I was thirteen, we were taught that there is no isolation from life. The unseasonably oppressive heat of an Indian summer day hung like a steaming blanket over Atlanta. My sisters and I had casually commented upon the unusual quietness. It seemed to stay Mother's volubility and reduced Father, who was more taciturn, to monosyllables. But,

as I remember it, no other sense of impending trouble impinged upon our consciousness.

4   I had read the inflammatory headlines in the *Atlanta News* and the more re-strained ones in the *Atlanta Constitution* which reported alleged rapes and other crimes committed by Negroes. But these were so standard and familiar that they made—as I look back on it now—little impression. The stories were more fre-quent, however, and consisted of eight-column streamers instead of the usual two- or four-column ones.

5   Father was a mail collector. His tour of duty was from three to eleven P.M. He made his rounds in a little cart into which one climbed from a step in the rear. I used to drive the cart for him from two until seven, leaving him at the point nearest our home on Houston Street, to return home either for study or sleep. That day Father decided that I should not go with him. I appealed to Mother, who thought it might be all right, provided Father sent me home be-fore dark because, she said, "I don't think they would dare start anything before nightfall." Father told me as we made the rounds that ominous rumors of a race riot that night were sweeping the town. But I was too young that morning to understand the background of the riot. I became much older during the next thirty-six hours, under circumstances which I now recognize as the inevitable outcome of what had preceded. . . .

6   During the afternoon preceding the riot little bands of sullen, evil-looking men talked excitedly on street corners all over downtown Atlanta. Around seven o'clock my father and I were driving toward a mail box at the corner of Peachtree and Houston Streets when there came from near-by Pryor Street a roar the like of which I had never heard before, but which sent a sensation of mingled fear and excitement coursing through my body. I asked permission of Father to go and see what the trouble was. He bluntly ordered me to stay in the cart. A little later we drove down Atlanta's main business thoroughfare, Peachtree Street. Again we heard the terrifying cries, this time near at hand and coming toward us. We saw a lame Negro bootblack from Herndon's barber shop pathetically trying to outrun a mob of whites. Less than a hundred yards from us the chase ended. We saw clubs and fists descending to the accompani-ment of savage shouting and cursing. Suddenly a voice cried, "There goes an-other nigger!" Its work done, the mob went after the new prey. The body with the withered foot lay dead in a pool of blood on the street.

7   Father's apprehension and mine steadily increased during the evening, al-though the fact that our skins were white kept us from attack. Another circum-stance favored us—the mob had not yet grown violent enough to attack United States government property. But I could see Father's relief when he punched the time clock at eleven P.M. and got into the cart to go home. He wanted to go the back way down Forsyth Street, but I begged him, in my childish excitement and ignorance, to drive down Marietta to Five Points, the heart of Atlanta's business district, where the crowds were densest and the yells loudest. No sooner had we turned into Marietta Street, however, than we saw careening toward us an

undertaker's barouche. Crouched in the rear of the vehicle were three Negroes clinging to the sides of the carriage as it lunged and swerved. On the driver's seat crouched a white man, the reins held taut in his left hand. A huge whip was gripped in his right. Alternately he lashed the horses and, without looking backward, swung the whip in savage swoops in the faces of members of the mob as they lunged at the carriage determined to seize the three Negroes.

8   There was no time for us to get out of its path, so sudden and swift was the appearance of the vehicle. The hub cap of the right rear wheel of the barouche hit the right side of our much lighter wagon. Father and I instinctively threw our weight and kept the cart from turning completely over. Our mare was a Texas mustang which, frightened by the sudden blow, lunged in the air as Father clung to the reins. Good fortune was with us. The cart settled back on its four wheels as Father said in a voice which brooked no dissent, "We are going home the back way and not down Marietta."

9   But again on Pryor Street we heard the cry of the mob. Close to us and in our direction ran a stout and elderly woman who cooked at a downtown white hotel. Fifty yards behind, a mob which filled the street from curb to curb was closing in. Father handed the reins to me and, though he was of slight stature, reached down and lifted the woman into the cart. I did not need to be told to lash the mare to the fastest speed she could muster.

10   The church bells tolled the next morning for Sunday service. But no one in Atlanta believed for a moment that the hatred and lust for blood had been appeased. Like skulls on a cannibal's hut the hats and caps of victims of the mob of the night before had been hung on the iron hooks of telegraph poles. None could tell whether each hat represented a dead Negro. But we knew that some of those who had worn the hats would never again wear any.

11   Late in the afternoon friends of my father's came to warn of more trouble that night. They told us that plans had been perfected for a mob to form on Peachtree Street just after nightfall to march down Houston Street to what the white people called "Darktown," three blocks or so below our house, "to clean out the niggers." There had never been a firearm in our house before that day. Father was reluctant even in those circumstances to violate the law, but he at last gave in at Mother's insistence.

12   We turned out the lights early, as did all our neighbors. No one removed his clothes or thought of sleep. Apprehension was tangible. We could almost touch its cold and clammy surface. Toward midnight the unnatural quiet was broken by a roar that grew steadily in volume. Even today I grow tense in remembering it.

13   Father told mother to take my sisters, the youngest of them only six, to the rear of the house, which offered more protection from stones and bullets. My brother George was away, so Father and I, the only males in the house, took our places at the front windows of the parlor. The windows opened on a porch along the front side of the house, which in turn gave onto a narrow lawn that sloped down to the street and a picket fence. There was a crash as Negroes

smashed the street lamp at the corner of Houston and Piedmont Avenue down the street. In a very few minutes the vanguard of the mob, some of them bearing torches, appeared. A voice which we recognized as that of the son of the grocer with whom we had traded for many years yelled, "That's where that nigger mail carrier lives! Let's burn it down! It's too nice for a nigger to live in!" In the eerie light Father turned his drawn face toward me. In a voice as quiet as though he were asking me to pass him the sugar at the breakfast table, he said, "Son, don't shoot until the first man puts his foot on the lawn and then—don't you miss!"

14   In the flickering light the mob swayed, paused, and began to flow toward us. In that instant there opened up within me a great awareness; I knew then who I was. I was a Negro, a human being with an invisible pigmentation which marked me a person to be hunted, hanged, abused, discriminated against, kept in poverty and ignorance, in order that those whose skin was white would have readily at hand a proof of their superiority, a proof patent and inclusive, accessible to the moron and the idiot as well as to the wise man and the genius. No matter how low a white man fell, he could always hold fast to the smug conviction that he was superior to two-thirds of the world's population, for those two-thirds were not white.

15   It made no difference how intelligent or talented my millions of brothers and I were, or how virtuously we lived. A curse like that of Judas was upon us, a mark of degradation fashioned with heavenly authority. There were white men who said Negroes had no souls, and who proved it by the Bible. Some of these now were approaching us, intent upon burning our house.

16   Theirs was a world of contrasts in values: superior and inferior, profit and loss, cooperative and noncooperative, civilized and aboriginal, white and black. If you were on the wrong end of the comparison, if you were inferior, if you were noncooperative, if you were aboriginal, if you were black, then you were marked for excision, expulsion, or extinction. I was a Negro; I was therefore that part of history which opposed the good, the just, and the enlightened. I was a Persian, falling before the hordes of Alexander. I was a Carthaginian, extinguished by the Legions of Rome. I was a Frenchman at Waterloo, an Anglo-Saxon at Hastings, a Confederate at Vicksburg. I was the defeated, wherever and whenever there was a defeat.

17   Yet as a boy there in the darkness amid the tightening fright, I knew the inexplicable thing—that my skin was as white as the skin of those who were coming at me.

18   The mob moved toward the lawn. I tried to aim my gun, wondering what it would feel like to kill a man. Suddenly there was a volley of shots. The mob hesitated, stopped. Some friends of my father's had barricaded themselves in a two-story brick building just below our house. It was they who had fired. Some of the mobsmen, still blood-thirsty, shouted, "Let's go get the nigger." Others, afraid now for their safety, held back. Our friends, noting the hesitation, fired another volley. The mob broke and retreated up Houston Street.

19   In the quiet that followed I put my gun aside and tried to relax. But a tension different from anything I had ever known possessed me. I was gripped by the knowledge of my identity, and in the depths of my soul I was vaguely aware that I was glad of it. I was sick with loathing for the hatred which had flared before me that night and come so close to making me a killer; but I was glad I was not one of those who hated; I was glad I was not one of those made sick and murderous by pride. I was glad I was not one of those whose story is in the history of the world, a record of bloodshed, rapine, and pillage. I was glad my mind and spirit were part of the races that had not fully awakened, and who therefore had still before them the opportunity to write a record of virtue as a memorandum to Armageddon.

20   It was all just a feeling then, inarticulate and melancholy, yet reassuring in the way that death and sleep are reassuring, and I have clung to it now for nearly half a century.

EXERCISES

Some of the Issues

1. In paragraph 1 White explains the location of his house in Atlanta. What is most important about the location?
2. In paragraph 2 White describes the appearance of the house and yard. Why is it important for him to stress the difference between it and its surroundings?
3. What does White mean when he says in paragraph 3, "we were taught that there is no isolation from life"?
4. In paragraph 4 White describes the headlines in the newspapers. How do they change in the days before the riot? Does he imply that his family believed what the papers said or not?
5. In paragraphs 5 through 13 there are indications that the riots are neither new nor isolated, unique occasions. Find and list these indicators.
6. In what ways do the actions of the mob differ between the first and second day of the rioting?
7. Where are the police?
8. In paragraphs 14 through 17 White interrupts his account of the mob's actions to describe his thoughts and feelings of bitterness. Contrast them to his thoughts in paragraphs 19 and 20, after the mob had fled and the danger was—temporarily—past.

The Way We Are Told

9. White gives his description of home and neighborhood in two separate paragraphs (1 and 2). How do the paragraphs differ?

10. How does White begin to build suspense in paragraph 3? How do paragraphs 4 and 5 also prepare the reader for what is to come?
11. Paragraph 6 gives the first description of a specific event, using several words and phrases that have emotional impact. Cite four or five of these.
12. In paragraph 9 White describes another episode of rescue. See if there are any words here, like those in paragraph 6, that have emotional connotations.
13. How does White heighten the suspense in the final paragraphs of the essay?

Some Subjects for Writing

14. Have you ever felt yourself in real danger? If so, try to describe the circumstances in two ways: give an objective description of the events and then rewrite your essay, trying to heighten the effect by the careful use of emotionally effective words and phrases. (You will find that the overuse of emotional words diminishes rather than enhances the effect.)
15. White describes his experience in the Atlanta riots as a turning point in his life. Describe an experience in your own life that profoundly changed your values.

Two Ways to Belong in America

Bharati Mukherjee

Born in 1940 in Calcutta, India, Bharati Mukherjee came to the United States in 1961 to study writing at the University of Iowa after attending college at the University of Calcutta. She has lived in many places across the United States and Canada and has taught at several universities, including Columbia University and the University of California at Berkeley. She is the author of many books of fiction and nonfiction, including most recently the novels The Holder of the World *(1993),* Leave It To Me *(1997), and* The Tree Bride *(2004). Much of her work portrays the experiences of Indian and other immigrants in North American Culture. Mukherjee became a Canadian citizen in 1972 and a United States citizen in 1988.*

This essay, Mukherjee's "tale of two sisters," originally appeared in the New York Times *in 1996. The "current debate over the status of immigrants" she mentions in the first paragraph of her essay refers to legislation being debated at the time that called for new restrictions on immigration. The Illegal Immigration Reform and Immigrant Responsibility Act, which became law in 1996, toughened border enforcement and made it more difficult for refugees to gain asylum. It also greatly expanded the grounds for deporting even long-resident immigrants and created harsh penalties for resident aliens who return to their country without U.S. permission, even in circumstances such as serious illness or death of a family member. Immigration law continues to be a hotly contested issue in the United States, especially since the events of September 11, 2001.*

1   This is a tale of two sisters from Calcutta, Mira and Bharati, who have lived in the United States for some 35 years, but who find themselves on different sides in the current debate over the status of immigrants. I am an American citizen and she is not. I am moved that thousands of long-term residents are finally taking the oath of citizenship. She is not.

2   Mira arrived in Detroit in 1960 to study child psychology and pre-school education. I followed her a year later to study creative writing at the University of Iowa. When we left India, we were almost identical in appearance and attitude. We dressed alike, in saris; we expressed identical views on politics, social issues, love, and marriage in the same Calcutta convent-school accent. We would endure our two years in America, secure our degrees, then return to India to marry the grooms of our father's choosing.

3   Instead, Mira married an Indian student in 1962 who was getting his business administration degree at Wayne State University. They soon acquired the labor certifications necessary for the green card of hassle-free residence and employment.

4   Mira still lives in Detroit, works in the Southfield, Mich., school system, and has become nationally recognized for her contributions in the fields of pre-school education and parent-teacher relationships. After 36 years as a legal immigrant in this country, she clings passionately to her Indian citizenship and hopes to go home to India when she retires.

5   In Iowa City in 1963, I married a fellow student, an American of Canadian parentage. Because of the accident of his North Dakota birth, I bypassed labor-certification requirements and the race-related "quota" system that favored the applicant's country of origin over his or her merit. I was prepared for (and even welcomed) the emotional strain that came with marrying outside my ethnic community. In 33 years of marriage, we have lived in every part of North America. By choosing a husband who was not my father's selection, I was opting for fluidity, self-invention, blue jeans and T-shirts, and renouncing 3,000 years (at least) of caste-observant, "pure culture" marriage in the Mukherjee family. My books have often been read as unapologetic (and in some quarters overenthusiastic) texts for cultural and psychological "mongrelization." It's a word I celebrate.

6   Mira and I have stayed sisterly close by phone. In our regular Sunday morning conversations, we are unguardedly affectionate. I am her only blood relative on this continent. We expect to see each other through the looming crises of aging and ill health without being asked. Long before Vice President Gore's "Citizenship U.S.A." drive, we'd had our polite arguments over the ethics of retaining an overseas citizenship while expecting the permanent protection and economic benefits that come with living and working in America.

7   Like well-raised sisters, we never said what was really on our minds, but we probably pitied one another. She, for the lack of structure in my life, the erasure of Indianness, the absence of an unvarying daily core. I, for the narrowness of her perspective, her uninvolvement with the mythic depths or the superficial pop culture of this society. But, now, with the scapegoatings of "aliens" (documented or illegal) on the increase, and the targeting of long-term legal immigrants like Mira for new scrutiny and new self-consciousness, she and I find ourselves unable to maintain the same polite discretion. We were always unacknowledged adversaries, and we are now, more than ever, sisters.

8   "I feel used," Mira raged on the phone the other night. "I feel manipulated and discarded. This is such an unfair way to treat a person who was invited to stay and work here because of her talent. My employer went to the I.N.S. and petitioned for the labor certification. For over 30 years, I've invested my creativity and professional skills into the improvement of *this* country's pre-school system. I've obeyed all the rules, I've paid my taxes, I love my work, I love my students, I love the friends I've made. How dare America now change its rules

in midstream? If America wants to make new rules curtailing benefits of legal immigrants, they should apply only to immigrants who arrive after those rules are already in place."

9   To my ears, it sounded like the description of a long-enduring, comfortable yet loveless marriage, without risk or recklessness. Have we the right to demand, and to expect, that we be loved? (That, to me, is the subtext of the arguments by immigration advocates.) My sister is an expatriate, professionally generous and creative, socially courteous and gracious, and that's as far as her Americanization can go. She is here to maintain an identity, not to transform it.

10   I asked her if she would follow the example of others who have decided to become citizens because of the anti-immigration bills in Congress. And here, she surprised me. "If America wants to play the manipulative game, I'll play it, too," she snapped. "I'll become a U.S. citizen for now, then change back to India when I'm ready to go home. I feel some kind of irrational attachment to India that I don't to America. Until all this hysteria against legal immigrants, I was totally happy. Having my green card meant I could visit any place in the world I wanted to and then come back to a job that's satisfying and that I do very well."

11   In one family, from two sisters alike as peas in a pod, there could not be a wider divergence of immigrant experience. America spoke to me—I married it—I embraced the demotion from expatriate aristocrat to immigrant nobody, surrendering those thousands of years of "pure culture," the saris, the delightfully accented English. She retained them all. Which of us is the freak?

12   Mira's voice, I realized, is the voice not just of the immigrant South Asian community but of an immigrant community of the millions who have stayed rooted in one job, one city, one house, one ancestral culture, one cuisine, for the entirety of their productive years. She speaks for greater numbers than I possibly can. Only the fluency of her English and the anger, rather than fear, born of confidence from her education, differentiate her from the seamstresses, the domestics, the technicians, the shop owners, the millions of hard-working but effectively silenced documented immigrants as well as their less fortunate "illegal" bothers and sisters.

13   Nearly 20 years ago, when I was living in my husband's ancestral homeland of Canada, I was always well-employed but never allowed to feel part of the local Quebec or larger Canadian society. Then, through a Green Paper that invited a national referendum on the unwanted side effects of "nontraditional" immigration, the Government officially turned against its immigrant communities, particularly those from South Asia.

14   I felt then the same sense of betrayal that Mira feels now. I will never forget the pain of that sudden turning, and the casual racist outbursts the Green Paper elicited. That sense of betrayal had its desired effect and drove me, and thousands like me, from the country.

15   Mira and I differ, however, in the ways in which we hope to interact with the country that we have chosen to live in. She is happier to live in America

as expatriate Indian than as an immigrant American. I need to feel like a part of the community I have adopted (as I tried to feel in Canada as well). I need to put roots down, to vote and make the difference that I can. The price that the immigrant willingly pays, and that the exile avoids, is the trauma of self-transformation.

EXERCISES

Some of the Issues

1. In what ways were Mukherjee and her sister the same when they left India? How did their choices and perspectives eventually differ? In what ways did they remain similar?
2. How does Mukherjee feel about having married someone who is not from her own ethnic community? How does she describe her life in paragraph 5?
3. For what does Mukherjee feel she and her sister probably pity each other (paragraph 7)? Why does she admit this now?
4. What argument does Mira make in paragraph 8? How does Mukherjee respond to it?
5. Who does Mukherjee feel Mira's voice represents (paragraph 12)?
6. To what extent does Mukherjee sympathize with Mira? Why?

The Way We Are Told

7. Mukherjee begins her piece in the third person then reveals that she is actually referring to herself and her sister. Why do you think she does this?
8. Why does Mukherjee put the words "pure culture" in quotation marks (paragraph 11)?
9. Consider the title. Why does Mukherjee use the word "belong" as opposed to "live" or "reside"? What does the word "belong" imply?
10. Mukherjee uses a personal story to make a more general point. What is she arguing for?

Some Subjects for Writing

11. Mukherjee tells the story of two sisters who were "alike as peas in a pod" but ended up taking different paths when they came to the United States. Write a narrative about two people you know (this could include yourself) who were close but who had very different experiences when they entered a new context or setting. Your narrative should not only recount what happened; it should also analyze what might account for those differences in experiences. Like Mukherjee, you might write about moving to a different country, city,

or state, or you might write about another move such as the transition from grammar school to high school or from high school to college.

12. "Two Ways to Belong in America" was written in response to a congressional proposal to deny government benefits to resident aliens. Consider a piece of legislation that you feel has had or might have a personal impact on your life or the life of someone close to you. Write an essay in which, like Mukherjee, you explore the complicated ways in which changes in laws and regulations can impact people's everyday lives.

Amérka, Amérka: A Palestinian Abroad in the Land of the Free

Anton Shammas

Anton Shammas is a Palestinian born in Israel in 1950. He attended Hebrew University in Jerusalem and came to the United States in 1987 as a Rockefeller Fellow at the University of Michigan. He is the author of the novel Arabesques *(1989) and has published numerous essays. Shammas teaches in the Department of Near Eastern Studies at the University of Michigan.*

Historic Palestine, on the eastern coast of the Mediterranean, is sacred land to three major religions—Judaism, Christianity, and Islam—and, throughout history, ownership of this land has been often and bitterly contested. After the Second World War, the part of Palestine known as the West Bank was administered by Jordan and known as West Jordan. After the Israeli victory in the war of 1967, it was occupied by Israel. The majority of inhabitants of the West Bank are Palestinian Arabs, though there are Israeli settlements in several communities.

In this essay published in Harper's *magazine in 1991, Shammas speaks of Arab immigrants who, although physically separated from their home in the Middle East, carry with them the spiritual and cultural heritage of their "lost Palestine.'*

1   Some years ago, in San Francisco, I heard the following tale from a young, American-educated Palestinian engineer. We had found a rustic, trendy place and managed to find a quiet table. Over lukewarm beers, rather than small cups of lukewarm cardamomed coffee, we talked about his family, which had wandered adrift in the Arab world for some time before finding its moorings on the West Coast, and in particular of a relative of his living to the south of San Francisco whom we were planning to visit the following day. We never did make that visit—that is a story, too—but the story about this man has fluttered inside my head ever since.

2   We will call him Abu-Khalil. Imagine him as a fortysomething Palestinian (he is now past sixty) whose West Bank homeland was, once again in his life-time, caving in on him in June 1967 after what the Arabs call the Defeat of Hazieran 5 and the Israelis and Americans call the Six-Day War. Where was he to spend the occupation years of his life? Where could he get as far away from the Israeli "benign" presence as his captive mind could go? The choices were essentially two: He could cross the Allenby Bridge to His Majesty's Jordan or he could take an unhijackable flight west, from Ben-Gurion Airport. He chose the latter, a plane that would carry him to the faraway U.S.A.—to those mem-bers of his large family (Arabs always seem to have *large* families) who had dis-covered the New World centuries after Columbus. (They had discovered the New World, as they would tell him later, in a sort of belated westbound re-venge for the eastbound expulsion of their great ancestors from Andalusia/Spain the same year that Columbus's Spanish ships arrived on the shores of his imaginary India.)

3   To continue our tale: Abu-Khalil lands in San Francisco one warm Septem-ber afternoon, clad in a heavy black coat that does not astonish his waiting rela-tives a bit, since they are familiar with the man's eccentricities. But what about the security guys at Ben-Gurion Airport? Didn't the out-of-season coat merit suspicion and a frisking? Apparently not. Abu-Khalil is, as far as I can tell, the only Palestinian to have seeped out through the thick security screenings at Ben-Gurion Airport—née Lydda—unsearched. How else to account for the fact that he had managed to carry on board with him a veritable Little Palestine—flora, fauna, and all?

4   His bags were heavy with small plants and seeds that went undetected by Is-raeli security. (It should be said, of course, that flora poised to explode is not what they look for in a Palestinian's luggage at Ben-Gurion Airport.) As for U.S. Customs Form 6059B, which inbound foreigners are graciously asked to fill out before they land—it prohibits passengers from importing "fruits, vegetables, plants, plant products, soil, meats, meat products, birds, snails, and other live animals and animal products"—our passenger, to the best of the storyteller's au-thorial knowledge (and mine), could not read English, and no American officer, lawful or otherwise, bothered to verify his declarations—albeit not made—through questioning, much less through physical search, these being two proce-dures that Palestinians are much accustomed to in their comings and goings in the Middle East.

5   So that's how Abu-Khalil managed to bring to California some representa-tive plants of Palestine, many still rooted in their original, fecund soil. It seems, however, that he took pride mainly—think of it as a feather in his kaffiyeh—in his having managed to smuggle out of the West Bank, through Israel, and into the United States seven representative birds of his homeland. The duri, the hassoun, the sununu, the shahrur, the bulbul, the summan, and the hudhud, small-talk companion to King Solomon himself—they all surrounded him now

in California, re-chirping Palestine away in his ears from inside their unlocked American cages. "They will not leave their open cages," Abu- Khalil would say, or so the story went, "till I leave mine."

6   Abu-Khalil's was a cage of his own making; he has not left it to this very day. But I was mainly interested in the birds, in their mute, wondrous migration. In the years that followed, I asked the storyteller, did they forget their mother chirp? Did they eventually adopt the mellow sounds of California? And how, I asked, did he manage to smuggle in these birds in the first place? "Well," said my friend, "he had a coat of many pockets, you see."

7   I found the story hard to believe at the time; but one has to trust the storyteller, even a Palestinian. After all, where else could the birds of Palestine go "after the last sky," in the words of the poet Mahmoud Darwish, but to the Land of the Free.

8   My storyteller and I belong to a different generation from Abu-Khalil's. We, and others like us, are too young to think of smuggling roots and soil, though not young enough to forget all about the birds we left behind. We travel light, empty-pocketed, with the vanity of those who think home is a portable idea, something that dwells mainly in the mind or within a text. Celebrating the modern powers of imagination and of fiction, we have lost faith in our old idols— memory, storytelling. We are not even sure anymore whether there ever was a home out there, a territory, a homeland. We owe allegiance to no memory; and we have adopted as our anthem Derek Walcott's perhaps too-often-quoted line: "I had no nation now but the imagination." Our language, Arabic, was de-territorialized by another, and only later did we realize that Arabic does not even have a word for "territory." The act of de-territorialization, then, took place outside our language, so we could not talk, much less write, about our plight in our mother tongue. Now we need the language of the Other for that, the language that can categorize the new reality and sort it out for us in upper and lower cases; the language that can re-territorialize us, as imaginary as that might be, giving us some allegedly solid ground. It is English for my San Francisco storyteller-friend, French for others, Hebrew for me: the unlocked cages of our own choices. In short, we are Palestine's post-Abu-Khalilians, if you like.

9   Many Middle Eastern Abu-Khalils have immigrated to the U.S.A. over the years, driven out of their respective homelands by wars, greedy foreigners, and pangs of poverty. At the turn of the century, when the Ottomans—who had been ruling the Middle East since 1517—were practicing some refined forms of their famine policy, Arabs left their homes and families and sailed to the Americas. Brazil and Argentina had their charm; Michigan, too. Today, Michigan is home to the largest Arab-American community in North America. If you were to take a stroll through the streets of Dearborn, a south-by-southwest suburb of Detroit, the signs and names might remind you of some ancient legend.

10   Bereft of names and deeds, these Arabs came to Michigan to make names for themselves as a twentieth-century self-mocking variation on the old

Mesopotamian tradition of the *shuma shakanu*, the preservation of one's name and deeds. That also was the original aim of those who followed Nimrod the Hunter in his biblical endeavor to reach heaven and said, "Let us make us a name for ourselves" (Gen. 11:4). An American heaven of sorts and, in this case, an American name; no concealed Nimrods.

11   Hoping for a happier ending than the biblical one, they have come from places whose names Mark Twain, the great American nomenclator, traveling with "the innocents abroad" some 123 years ago, found impossible to pronounce. "One of the great drawbacks to this country," he wrote in September 1867, from Palestine, "is its distressing names that nobody can get the hang of . . . . You may make a stagger of pronouncing these names, but they will bring any Christian to grief that tries to spell them. I have an idea that if I can only simplify the nomenclature of this country, it will be of the greatest service to Americans who may travel here in the future."

12   This may account for the notorious Hollywood tradition, many years after tongue-in-cheek Twain, of assuming that all men Middle Eastern—if fortunate enough to actually have names of their own in the films—should be called Abdul. (In fact, Abdul is but the first half of a common Middle Eastern compound.) So all these anonymous Abduls are here now, trying, so far away from home, to complete their names, in a new world that has been practicing the renaming of things now for five centuries and counting.

* * * * *

13   From Fassuta, my small village in the Galilee, émigrés went mainly to Brazil and Argentina. My grandfather and his brothers and brother-in-law left for Argentina in 1896, only to return home, empty-handed, a year later. Then, on the eve of the First World War, my grandfather tried his luck again, this time on his own, heading once more to Argentina (at least that's what he told my grandmother the night before he took off), where he vanished for about ten years, leaving behind three daughters and three sons, all of them hungry. His youngest son, my uncle Jiryes, followed in his footsteps in 1928, leaving his wife and child behind, never to come back.

14   One of my childhood heroes, an old villager whom we, the children of Fassuta, always blamed for having invented school, had actually been to Salt Lake City. I don't have the foggiest idea what he did there for three years before the Depression; his deeds remain a sealed and, I suspect, quite salty book, but he certainly did not betray the Catholic faith, no sir. I still remember him in the late 1950s, breathing down my neck during Mass at the village's church. He used to wear impeccable white American shirts under his Arab *abaya*, even some thirty years after he had returned to the village. But that was the only American fingerprint on him; the rest was Middle Eastern.

15   The most famous American immigrant from my village, though, was M., my aunt Najeebeh's brother-in-law, Najeebeh being my father's sister. I hate to be finicky about the exact relationship, but that is simply the way it is in Arabic:

There are different words to refer to the father's and the mother's side of the family. At any rate, M. left the village in the early 1920s and came back to visit his brothers some forty years later, with his non-Arabic-speaking sons. As a matter of fact, he was the only one of a long, winding line of immigrants who had really made it, or "had it fixed," as the Galileans would say. He came to own a chain of fast-food restaurants, quite famous in the Midwest. Before I myself left the Mideast for these parts, I went to see his nephews—my cousins—in the village and promised them, under oath, that I would certainly look M. up one day and introduce myself, or at least pop into one of his restaurants and, naturally, ask for a free meal. I have not yet done the former and am still keeping the latter for a rainy Michigan day. However, whenever I come across his chain's emblem, a plump plastic boy holding a plate high above his plumply combed head, I remember my late aunt Najeebeh and think how disconcerted she would be had she known what kind of a mnemonic-device-in-the-form-of-a-cultural-shock she had become for her nephew, in faraway Amérka, as it is called in my part of the world.

16   Upon first arriving in Amérka, one of my first cultural shocks was the otherwise trivial American fact that shirts had not only a neck size but also a sleeve size. Fassuta's Salt Lake City visitor and I, we both come from a culture where, insofar as shirts are concerned, one's arm length doesn't matter much. People in the Middle East are still immersed in figuring out the length of their postcolonial borders, personal and otherwise, and all indications show that a long time will elapse before they start paying attention to the lonely business of their sleeve size.

17   Which may or may not have something to do with the fact that in a culture with an oral background of storytelling, where choices continue, even in postcolonial times, to be made for you (be they by God, fate, nature, or the ruler), you don't enjoy the luxuries of the novel's world, where characters make their own choices and have to live, subsequently, with the consequences, sleeve size and all. The storyteller's world revolves around memory; the novelist's, around imagination. And what people in places like the Middle East are struggling to do, I think, is to shrug off the bondage of their memory and decolonize their imagination. So, in this regard, for a Middle Easterner to have a sleeve size would be a sign of such a decolonization.

18   My first stroll ever on American soil took place in a park along the Iowa River, in Iowa City. I was thirty years old, and there were so many things I had not seen before. On that day I saw my first squirrel. There are many jittery, frail creatures in the Middle East, but, to the best of my zoological knowledge, there are no squirrels. However, people do talk of the *sinjabi*, the squirrelish color. I remember thinking, during my walk, that if there were no squirrels in the Middle East, how come the Arabs use the word *sinjabi*?

19   Not long after the day I took my walk, I found out, as I had expected, that there were *sinjabs* in Iran and that the word *sinjabi* was derived from the Persian, a language that had given Arabic, long before the Koran, so many beautiful

words. Some 1,300 years later, at the very time of my stay in Iowa, the Ayatollah Khomeini was busy squirreling away some ideas about a new order, about the Mesopotamian tradition of the *shuma shakanu*. A half-world away, Salman Rushdie was, apparently, squirreling away some counter-ideas of his own. It was not hard to imagine, later, who would play the Crackers, and who—or on whose—Nuts.

20   My Galilean friend J., not to be confused with the biblical author, came to America some sixteen years ago. We'd met at the Hebrew University in Jerusalem, in the early Seventies. He was my instructor in the Introduction to Arabic literature course, and I'm still indebted to him for teaching me the first steps of academic research and, most importantly, for being so decent a friend as to have unabashedly explained to me how I would never have the proper discipline.

21   At that time he was mulling over the idea that he should perhaps come to this country to work on a Ph.D. in modern Arabic literature. Once he had made up his mind, he started frantically looking for a wife with whom to share the burden of American self-exile. I asked him once whether it wouldn't be wiser to find himself an already naturalized American lady, to which he replied: "I'm looking for a woman that when I put my weary head against her arm, I want to hear her blood murmuring in Arabic." He did eventually find one, and they both immigrated to Amérka and have been happily listening to each other's blood ever since.

22   J. was looking for the blood tongue, for the primordial language, wherein the names of things, long before the confusion of tongues, were so deeply lodged in the things they designated that no human eye could decipher the sign. Had he been a Cabalist, he would have believed that what God introduced into the world was written words, not murmurings of blood. But J. came from the oral Middle East to the literate West, and he knew upon arriving in Amérka that he would be expected to trade in his mother tongue and keep the secret language circulating only in his veins.

23   I saw the already "naturalized" J. again, in Jerusalem, some ten years after he'd left. At the end of a very long night of catching up, he picked up a Hebrew literary magazine from my desk and browsed through it. Something caught his eye; he paused for a moment. "What is *this* doing here?" "This" turned out to be an ad for a famous Israeli brand of women's underwear. I wasn't sure what he meant. It was a full-page ad, an exact replica of the famous photograph of Marilyn Monroe standing on a grate in the street, her dress blowing above her waist. "You know what the reference is to, right?" I asked. No, he did not. And I thought, How could a bright guy like J. live for so long in the U.S.A., be an *American citizen*, and not be familiar with what I thought were the basics of American iconography?

24   I had been settled for a year in Ann Arbor when I went to visit J. and his wife in Ohio. Having just returned from a short visit to our Galilee home,

I brought J., who has a green thumb, what he had asked me to: some local lubia peas for his thriving backyard garden. We were reminiscing late at night, with Fayruz, the famous Lebanese singer, on the stereo in the background and some Middle Eastern munchies on the coffee table, when I suddenly remembered that night in Jerusalem years before and the ad with the Marilyn knockoff. It would be nice if you did recognize the American icon, I thought to myself, but it is nice too that you can live in this country for decades without being forced to go native. You can always pick up your own fold of the huge map and chart yourself into it.

25 Now it is my fourth year in Ann Arbor. I moved in early in September of 1987, and for three months my relationship with the squirrels outside my window was quite good. "Quite good," as my English professor at the Hebrew University in Jerusalem used to say, means "yes, good, but there's no need to be so excited about it." So I was developing an unexciting relationship with these creatures, especially with one of them, whom I told myself I was able to tell from the others, although they all did look alike, if I may say so without prejudice. Anyway, I would open the door early in the morning to pick up the *New York Times* from the doorstep, and he would be goofing around its blue, transparent wrap (that's how the paper is home-delivered in Michigan), unalarmed by my invasion of *his* kingdom.

26 But one morning, as I reached down for the paper, he froze, all of a sudden, in the middle of one of his silly gesticulations, gaping at me in utter terror, and then fled away as if I were about to—well, throw a stone at him. Maybe it was a morning in December 1987, and he had peeked at the *Times*. Maybe I will never cease to look east for my images and metaphors.

27 For J., for my friend in San Francisco, for me, the Old World will never cease to hold us hostage in this way. Sometimes I think that no matter how deep I have traveled *into* the American life, I still carry my own miniature Abu-Khalils in my pockets and a miniature Middle East in my mind. There is little space for Amérka in the most private of my maps.

28 And speaking of maps, how many adult Americans know where the "heartbroken piece of territory" Mark Twain was talking about actually is?

29 Still, would it matter if they did?

30 I don't think it would. After all, modern colonialism (sometimes euphemistically referred to as "our American interests"), unlike its old-fashioned, European counterpart, is not geographically oriented. Geographical literacy is defunct; its demise was caused by the invention of the remote control. And if you happen to live in this vast country, your sense of geography is necessarily numbed by what Aldous Huxley would have called one's "local validity." Paradoxically, the vastness of the land provides Americans with a continental alibi. A look at the map of the U.S.A. from, say, a Palestinian point of view would psychologically suffice to make a clear-cut distinction between the American people and their government's policy. Unlike England, for instance, where every

Brit seems to be living in London and has something or another to do with the business of running the rather rusty machinery of a worn-out colonialism, there is an utter distinction when it comes to the United States between the Americans on Capitol Hill and the *real* Americans who, on a good day, want absolutely nothing to do with Washington's follies.

31   Maybe that's why Abu-Khalil can feel at home in California, surrounded by the artifacts of his lost Palestine. This country is *big*; it has enough room not only for the newcomers but also for their portable homelands. Among other achievements, Amérka has made homesickness obsolete.

EXERCISES

Some of the Issues

1. What is the significance of Abu-Khalil's smuggling seven birds out of Palestine to the United States? What do these birds represent?
2. How is Shammas's concept of home different from Abu-Khalil's? What historical events have shaped younger Arabs' views?
3. Explain what Shammas means by "unlocked cages of our own choices" in paragraph 8.
4. How does Shammas distinguish the storyteller from the novelist in paragraphs 8 and 17?
5. In paragraph 17, Shammas asserts that many Middle Easterners are struggling to cast off "the bondage of their memory and decolonize their imagination." What are the political implications of this statement?
6. Shammas's friend J. married an Arab woman before coming to America. Why is it important for him to keep "the secret language circulating only in his veins" (paragraph 22)?
7. In paragraph 23, what is the source of his friend J.'s confusion over the underwear ad in the Hebrew literary magazine? How does his friend's ignorance strike Shammas?
8. How do you understand the last line, "Amérka has made homesickness obsolete?"

The Way We Are Told

9. How does the squirrel metaphor in paragraphs 18 and 19 and 25–27 relate to the Middle Eastern experience?
10. Shammas uses part of Mark Twain's description of Palestine as that "most hopeless, dreary, heartbroken piece of territory out of Arizona" to underscore the fact that many Americans are geographically illiterate. He cites this American characteristic as a possible advantage. Why?
11. Find several examples of the author's humorous or sarcastic tone.
12. In paragraph 23, why is the word *naturalized* in quotation marks?

Some Subjects for Writing

13. If you were forced to leave home, what objects would you take with you? Write an essay in which you describe the objects and explain your choices.

*14. ". . . Home is a portable idea, something that dwells mainly in the mind or within a text" (paragraph 8). In an essay, consider what home means to you and develop a personal definition of "home." Illustrate your idea with your experience and, if appropriate, the experiences of Shammas and other authors in *Crossing Cultures*.

Black Like Them

Malcolm Gladwell

Malcolm Gladwell was born in 1963 in England, grew up in Canada, and graduated from the University of Toronto in 1984. "Black Like Them" originally appeared in the New Yorker in 1996, where Gladwell is a staff writer. He is also the author of two books, The Tipping Point: How Little Things Can Make A Big Difference (2000), and Blink: The Power of Thinking Without Thinking (2005).

Gladwell begins his essay by telling the story of his cousins Rosie and Noel, immigrants from Jamaica who have settled in New York City. Gladwell explores the question of why West Indians and American blacks are treated differently in the United States, and why they perceive themselves as fitting into American society in a different way. Drawing from family experience, historical information, and sociological studies, Gladwell uses the experience of West Indian blacks to investigate both the roots and the pervasiveness of racism in the United States.

1   My cousin Rosie and her husband, Noel, live in a two-bedroom bungalow on Argyle Avenue, in Uniondale, on the west end of Long Island. When they came to America, twelve years ago, they lived in a basement apartment a dozen or so blocks away, next to their church. At the time, they were both taking classes at the New York Institute of Technology, which was right nearby. But after they graduated, and Rosie got a job managing a fast-food place and Noel got a job in asbestos removal, they managed to save a little money and bought the house on Argyle Avenue.

2   From the outside, their home looks fairly plain. It's in a part of Uniondale that has a lot of tract housing from just after the war, and most of the houses are alike—squat and square, with aluminum siding, maybe a dormer window in the attic, and a small patch of lawn out front. But there is a beautiful park down the street, the public schools are supposed to be good, and Rosie and Noel have built a new garage and renovated the basement. Now that Noel has started his own business, as an environmental engineer, he has his office down there—Suite 2B, it says on his stationery—and every morning he puts on his tie and goes down the stairs to make calls and work on the computer. If Noel's business takes off, Rosie says, she would like to move to a bigger house, in Garden City, which is one town over. She says this even though Garden City is mostly white. In fact, when she told one of her girlfriends, a black American, about this idea, her friend said that she was crazy—that Garden City was no place for a black person. But that is just the point. Rosie and Noel are from Jamaica. They don't consider themselves black at all.

3   This doesn't mean that my cousins haven't sometimes been lumped together with American blacks. Noel had a job once removing asbestos at Kennedy Airport, and his boss there called him "nigger" and cut his hours. But Noel didn't take it personally. That boss, he says, didn't like women or Jews, either, or people with college degrees—or even himself, for that matter. Another time, Noel found out that a white guy working next to him in the same job and with the same qualifications was making ten thousand dollars a year more than he was. He quit the next day. Noel knows that racism is out there. It's just that he doesn't quite understand—or accept—the categories on which it depends.

4   To a West Indian, black is a literal description: you are black if your skin is black. Noel's father, for example, is black. But his mother had a white father, and she herself was fair-skinned and could pass. As for Rosie, her mother and my mother, who are twins, thought of themselves while they were growing up as "middle-class brown," which is to say that they are about the same shade as Colin Powell. That's because our maternal grandfather was part Jewish, in addition to all kinds of other things, and Grandma, though she was a good deal darker than he was, had enough Scottish blood in her to have been born with straight hair. Rosie's mother married another brown Jamaican, and that makes Rosie a light chocolate. As for my mother, she married an Englishman, making everything that much more complicated, since by the racial categories of my own heritage I am one thing and by the racial categories of America I am another. Once, when Rosie and Noel came to visit me while I was living in Washington, D.C., Noel asked me to show him "where the black people lived," and I was confused for a moment until I realized that he was using "black" in the American sense, and so was asking in the same way that someone visiting Manhattan might ask where Chinatown was. That the people he wanted to see were in many cases racially indistinguishable from him didn't matter. The facts of his genealogy, of his nationality, of his status as an immigrant made him, in his own eyes, different.

5   This question of who West Indians are and how they define themselves may seem trivial, like racial hairsplitting. But it is not trivial. In the past twenty years, the number of West Indians in America has exploded. There are now half a million in the New York area alone and, despite their recent arrival, they make substantially more money than American blacks. They live in better neighborhoods. Their families are stronger. In the New York area, in fact, West Indians fare about as well as Chinese and Korean immigrants. That is why the Caribbean invasion and the issue of West Indian identity have become such controversial issues. What does it say about the nature of racism that another group of blacks, who have the same legacy of slavery as their American counterparts and are physically indistinguishable from them, can come here and succeed as well as the Chinese and the Koreans do? Is overcoming racism as simple as doing what Noel does, which is to dismiss it, to hold himself above it, to brave it and move on?

6   These are difficult questions, not merely for what they imply about American blacks but for the ways in which they appear to contradict conventional views of

what prejudice is. Racism, after all, is supposed to be indiscriminate. For example, sociologists have observed that the more blacks there are in a community the more negative the whites' attitudes will be. Blacks in Denver have a far easier time than blacks in, say, Cleveland. Lynchings in the South at the turn of this century, to give another example, were far more common in counties where there was a large black population than in areas where whites were in the majority. Prejudice is the crudest of weapons, a reaction against blacks in the aggregate that grows as the perception of black threat grows. If that is the case, however, the addition of hundreds of thousands of new black immigrants to the New York area should have made things worse for people like Rosie and Noel, not better. And, if racism is so indiscriminate in its application, why is one group of blacks flourishing and the other not?

7   The implication of West Indian success is that racism does not really exist at all—at least, not in the form that we have assumed it does. The implication is that the key factor in understanding racial prejudice is not the behavior and attitudes of whites but the behavior and attitudes of blacks—not white discrimination but black culture. It implies that when the conservatives in Congress say the responsibility for ending urban poverty lies not with collective action but with the poor themselves they are right.

8   I think of this sometimes when I go with Rosie and Noel to their church, which is in Hempstead, just a mile away. It was once a white church, but in the past decade or so it has been taken over by immigrants from the Caribbean. They have so swelled its membership that the church has bought much of the surrounding property and is about to add a hundred seats to its sanctuary. The pastor, though, is white, and when the band up front is playing and the congregation is in full West Indian form the pastor sometimes seems out of place, as if he cannot move in time with the music. I always wonder how long the white minister at Rosie and Noel's church will last—whether there won't be some kind of groundswell among the congregation to replace him with one of their own. But Noel tells me the issue has never really come up. Noel says, in fact, that he's happier with a white minister, for the same reasons that he's happy with his neighborhood, where the people across the way are Polish and another neighbor is Hispanic and still another is a black American. He doesn't want to be shut off from everyone else, isolated within the narrow confines of his race. He wants to be part of the world, and when he says these things it is awfully tempting to credit that attitude with what he and Rosie have accomplished.

9   Is this confidence, this optimism, this equanimity all that separates the poorest of American blacks from a house on Argyle Avenue?

10   In 1994, Philip Kasinitz, a sociologist at Manhattan's Hunter College, and Jan Rosenberg, who teaches at Long Island University, conducted a study of the Red Hook area of Brooklyn, a neighborhood of around thirteen or fourteen thousand which lies between the waterfront and the Gowanus Expressway. Red Hook has a large public-housing project at its center, and around the project, in

the streets that line the waterfront, are several hundred thriving blue-collar businesses—warehouses, shipping companies, small manufacturers, and contractors. The object of the study was to resolve what Kasinitz and Rosenberg saw as the paradox of Red Hook: despite Red Hooks seemingly fortuitous conjunction of unskilled labor and blue-collar jobs, very few of the Puerto Ricans and African-Americans from the neighborhood ever found work in the bustling economy of their own back yard.

11   After dozens of interviews with local employers, the two researchers uncovered a persistent pattern of what they call positive discrimination. It was not that the employers did not like blacks and Hispanics. It was that they had developed an elaborate mechanism for distinguishing between those they felt were "good" blacks and those they felt were "bad" blacks, between those they judged to be "good" Hispanics and those they considered "bad" Hispanics. "Good" meant that you came from outside the neighborhood, because employers identified locals with the crime and dissipation they saw on the streets around them. "Good" also meant that you were an immigrant, because employers felt that being an immigrant implied a loyalty and a willingness to work and learn not found among the native-born. In Red Hook, the good Hispanics are Mexican and South American, not Puerto Rican. And the good blacks are West Indian.

12   The Harvard sociologist Mary C. Waters conducted a similar study, in 1993, which looked at a food-service company in Manhattan where West Indian workers have steadily displaced African-Americans in the past few years. The transcripts of her interviews with the company managers make fascinating reading, providing an intimate view of the perceptions that govern the urban workplace. Listen to one forty-year-old white male manager on the subject of West Indians:

> They tend more to shy away from doing all of the illegal things because they have such strict rules down in their countries and jails. And they're nothing like here. So like, they're like really paranoid to do something wrong. They seem to be very, very self-conscious of it. No matter what they have to do, if they have to try and work three jobs, they do. They won't go into drugs or anything like that.

13   Or listen to this, from a fifty-three-year-old white female manager:

> I work closely with this one girl who's from Trinidad. And she told me when she first came here to live with her sister and cousin, she had two children. And she said I'm here four years and we've reached our goals. And what was your goal? For her two children to each have their own bedroom. Now she has a three bedroom apartment and she said that's one of the goals she was shooting for. . . . If that was an American, they would say, I reached my goal. I bought a Cadillac.

14   This idea of the West Indian as a kind of superior black is not a new one. When the first wave of Caribbean immigrants came to New York and Boston,

in the early nineteen-hundreds, other blacks dubbed them Jewmaicans, in derisive reference to the emphasis they placed on hard work and education. In the nineteen-eighties, the economist Thomas Sowell gave the idea a serious intellectual imprimatur by arguing that the West Indian advantage was a historical legacy of Caribbean slave culture. According to Sowell, in the American South slaveowners tended to hire managers who were married, in order to limit the problems created by sexual relations between overseers and slave women. But the West Indies were a hardship post, without a large and settled white population. There the overseers tended to be bachelors, and, with white women scarce, there was far more commingling of the races. The resulting large group of coloreds soon formed a kind of proto-middle class, performing various kinds of skilled and sophisticated tasks that there were not enough whites around to do, as there were in the American South. They were carpenters, masons, plumbers, and small businessmen, many years in advance of their American counterparts, developing skills that required education and initiative.

15   My mother and Rosie's mother came from this colored class. Their parents were schoolteachers in a tiny village buried in the hills of central Jamaica. My grandmother's and grandfather's salaries combined put them, at best, on the lower rungs of the middle class. But their expectations went well beyond that. In my grandfather's library were Dickens and Maupassant. My mother and her sister were pushed to win scholarships to a proper English-style boarding school at the other end of the island; and later, when my mother graduated, it was taken for granted that she would attend university in England, even though the cost of tuition and passage meant that my grandmother had to borrow a small fortune from the Chinese grocer down the road.

16   My grandparents had ambitions for their children, but it was a special kind of ambition, born of a certainty that American blacks did not have—that their values were the same as those of society as a whole, and that hard work and talent could actually be rewarded. In my mother's first year at boarding school, she looked up "Negro" in the eleventh edition of the Encyclopedia Britannica. "In certain . . . characteristics . . . the negro would appear to stand on a lower evolutionary plane than the white man," she read. And the entry continued:

> The mental constitution of the negro is very similar to that of a child, normally good-natured and cheerful, but subject to sudden fits of emotion and passion during which he is capable of performing acts of singular atrocity, impressionable, vain, but often exhibiting in the capacity of servant a dog-like fidelity which has stood the supreme test.

17   All black people of my mother's generation—and of generations before and since—have necessarily faced a moment like this, when they are confronted for the first time with the allegation of their inferiority. But, at least in my mother's case, her school was integrated, and that meant she knew black girls who were more intelligent than white girls, and she knew how she measured against the

world around her. At least she lived in a country that had blacks and browns in every position of authority, so her personal experience gave the lie to what she read in the encyclopedia. This, I think, is what Noel means when he says that he cannot quite appreciate what it is that weighs black Americans down, because he encountered the debilitating effects of racism late, when he was much stronger. He came of age in a country where he belonged to the majority.

18   When I was growing up, my mother sometimes read to my brothers and me from the work of Louise Bennett, the great Jamaican poet of my mother's generation. The poem I remember best is about two women—one black and one white—in a hair salon, the black woman getting her hair straightened and, next to her, the white woman getting her hair curled:

> same time me mind start 'tink
> 'bout me and de white woman
> how me tek out me natural perm
> and she put in false one

19   There is no anger or resentment here, only irony and playfulness—the two races captured in a shared moment of absurdity. Then comes the twist. The black woman is paying less to look white than the white woman is to look black:

> de two a we da tek a risk
> what rain or shine will bring
> but fe har risk is t're poun'
> fi me onle five shillin'

20   In the nineteen-twenties, the garment trade in New York was first integrated by West Indian women, because, the legend goes, they would see the sign on the door saying "No blacks need apply" and simply walk on in. When I look back on Bennett's poem, I think I understand how they found the courage to do that.

21   It is tempting to use the West Indian story as evidence that discrimination doesn't really exist—as proof that the only thing inner-city African-Americans have to do to be welcomed as warmly as West Indians in places like Red Hook is to make the necessary cultural adjustments. If West Indians are different, as they clearly are, then it is easy to imagine that those differences are the reason for their success—that their refusal to be bowed is what lets them walk on by the signs that prohibit them or move to neighborhoods that black Americans would shy away from. It also seems hard to see how the West Indian story is in any way consistent with the idea of racism as an indiscriminate, pernicious threat aimed at all black people.

22   But here is where things become more difficult, and where what seems obvious about West Indian achievement turns out not to be obvious at all. One of

the striking things in the Red Hook study, for example, is the emphasis that the employers appeared to place on hiring outsiders—Irish or Russian or Mexican or West Indian immigrants from places far from Red Hook. The reason for this was not, the researchers argue, that the employers had any great familiarity with the cultures of those immigrants. They had none, and that was the point. They were drawn to the unfamiliar because what was familiar to them—the projects of Red Hook—was anathema. The Columbia University anthropologist Katherine Newman makes the same observation in a recent study of two fast-food restaurants in Harlem. She compared the hundreds of people who applied for jobs at those restaurants with the few people who were actually hired, and found, among other things, that how far an applicant lived from the job site made a huge difference. Of those applicants who lived less than two miles from the restaurant, ten per cent were hired. Of those who lived more than two miles from the restaurant, nearly forty per cent were hired. As Newman puts it, employers preferred the ghetto they didn't know to the ghetto they did.

23   Neither study describes a workplace where individual attitudes make a big difference, or where the clunky and impersonal prejudices that characterize traditional racism have been discarded. They sound like places where old-style racism and appreciation of immigrant values are somehow bound up together. Listen to another white manager who was interviewed by Mary Waters:

> Island blacks who come over, they're immigrant. They may not have such a good life where they are so they gonna try to strive to better themselves and I think there's a lot of American blacks out there who feel we owe them. And enough is enough already. You know, this is something that happened to their ancestors, not now. I mean, we've done so much for the black people in America now that it's time that they got off their butts.

24   Here, then, are the two competing ideas about racism side by side: the manager issues a blanket condemnation of American blacks even as he holds West Indians up as a cultural ideal. The example of West Indians as "good" blacks makes the old blanket prejudice against American blacks all the easier to express. The manager can tell black Americans to get off their butts without fear of sounding, in his own ears, like a racist, because he has simultaneously celebrated island blacks for their work ethic. The success of West Indians is not proof that discrimination against American blacks does not exist. Rather, it is the means by which discrimination against American blacks is given one last, vicious twist: I am not so shallow as to despise you for the color of your skin, because I have found people your color that I like. Now I can despise you for who you are.

25   This is racism's newest mutation—multicultural racism, where one ethnic group can be played off against another. But it is wrong to call West Indians the victors in this competition, in anything but the narrowest sense. In American history, immigrants have always profited from assimilation: as they have

adopted the language and customs of this country, they have sped their passage into the mainstream. The new racism means that West Indians are the first group of people for whom that has not been true. Their advantage depends on their remaining outsiders, on remaining unfamiliar, on being distinct by custom, culture, and language from the American blacks they would otherwise resemble. There is already some evidence that the considerable economic and social advantages that West Indians hold over American blacks begin to dissipate by the second generation, when the island accent has faded, and those in positions of power who draw distinctions between good blacks and bad blacks begin to lump West Indians with everyone else. For West Indians, assimilation is tantamount to suicide. This is a cruel fate for any immigrant group, but it is especially so for West Indians, whose history and literature are already redolent with the themes of dispossession and loss, with the long search for identity and belonging. In the nineteen-twenties, Marcus Garvey sought community in the idea of Africa. Bob Marley, the Jamaican reggae singer, yearned for Zion. In "Rites of Passage" the Barbadian poet Edward Kamau Brathwaite writes:

> Where, then, is the nigger's
> home?

> In Paris Brixton Kingston
> Rome?

> Here?
> Or in Heaven?

26   America might have been home. But it is not: not Red Hook, anyway; not Harlem; not even Argyle Avenue.

27   There is also no small measure of guilt here, for West Indians cannot escape the fact that their success has come, to some extent, at the expense of American blacks, and that as they have noisily differentiated themselves from African-Americans—promoting the stereotype of themselves as the good blacks—they have made it easier for whites to join in. It does not help matters that the same kinds of distinctions between good and bad blacks which govern the immigrant experience here have always lurked just below the surface of life in the West Indies as well. It was the infusion of white blood that gave the colored class its status in the Caribbean, and the members of this class have never forgotten that, nor have they failed, in a thousand subtle ways, to distance themselves from those around them who experienced a darker and less privileged past.

28   In my mother's house, in Harewood, the family often passed around a penciled drawing of two of my great-grandparents; she was part Jewish, and he was part Scottish. The other side—the African side—was never mentioned. My grandmother was the ringleader in this. She prized my grandfather's light skin, but she also suffered as a result of this standard. "She's nice, you know, but she's

too dark," her mother-in-law would say of her. The most telling story of all, though, is the story of one of my mother's relatives, whom I'll call Aunt Joan, who was as fair as my great-grandmother was. Aunt Joan married what in Jamaica is called an Injun—a man with a dark complexion that is redeemed from pure Africanness by straight, fine black hair. She had two daughters by him—handsome girls with dark complexions. But he died young, and one day, while she was travelling on a train to visit her daughter, she met and took an interest in a light-skinned man in the same railway car. What happened next is something that Aunt Joan told only my mother, years later, with the greatest of shame. When she got off the train, she walked right by her daughter, disowning her own flesh and blood, because she did not want a man so light-skinned and desirable to know that she had borne a daughter so dark.

29   My mother, in the nineteen-sixties, wrote a book about her experiences. It was entitled *Brown Face, Big Master,* the brown face referring to her and the big master, in the Jamaican dialect, referring to God. Sons, of course, are hardly objective on the achievements of their mothers, but there is one passage in the book that I find unforgettable, because it is such an eloquent testimony to the moral precariousness of the Jamaican colored class—to the mixture of confusion and guilt that attends its position as beneficiary of racism's distinctions. The passage describes a time just after my mother and father were married, when they were living in London and my eldest brother was still a baby. They were looking for an apartment, and after a long search my father found one in a London suburb. On the day after they moved in, however, the landlady ordered them out. "You didn't tell me your wife was colored," she told my father, in a rage.

30   In her book my mother describes her long struggle to make sense of this humiliation, to reconcile her experience with her faith. In the end, she was forced to acknowledge that anger was not an option—that as a Jamaican "middle-class brown," and a descendant of Aunt Joan, she could hardly reproach another for the impulse to divide good black from bad black:

> I complained to God in so many words: "Here I was, the wounded representative of the negro race in our struggle to be accounted free and equal with the dominating whites!" And God was amused; my prayer did not ring true with Him. I would try again. And then God said, "Have you not done the same thing? Remember this one and that one, people whom you have slighted or avoided or treated less considerately than others because they were different superficially, and you were ashamed to be identified with them. Have you not been glad that you are not more colored than you are? Grateful that you are not black?" My anger and hate against the landlady melted. I was no better than she was, nor worse for that matter. . . . We were both guilty of the sin of self-regard, the pride and the exclusiveness by which we cut some people off from ourselves.

31   I grew up in Canada, in a little farming town an hour and a half outside of Toronto. My father teaches mathematics at a nearby university, and my mother

is a therapist. For many years, she was the only black person in town, but I cannot remember wondering or worrying, or even thinking, about this fact. Back then, color meant only good things. It meant my cousins in Jamaica. It meant the graduate students from Africa and India my father would bring home from the university. My own color was not something I ever thought much about, either, because it seemed such a stray fact. Blacks knew what I was. They could discern the hint of Africa beneath my fair skin. But it was a kind of secret—something that they would ask me about quietly when no one else was around. ("Where you from?" an older black man once asked me. "Ontario," I said, not thinking. "No," he replied. "Where you *from?*" And then I understood and told him, and he nodded as if he had already known. "We was speculatin' about your heritage," he said.) But whites never guessed, and even after I informed them it never seemed to make a difference. Why would it? In a town that is ninety-nine per cent white, one modest alleged splash of color hardly amounts to a threat.

32   But things changed when I left for Toronto to attend college. This was during the early nineteen-eighties, when West Indians were immigrating to Canada in droves, and Toronto had become second only to New York as the Jamaican expatriates' capital in North America. At school, in the dining hall, I was served by Jamaicans. The infamous Jane-Finch projects, in northern Toronto, were considered the Jamaican projects. The drug trade then taking off was said to be the Jamaican drug trade. In the popular imagination, Jamaicans were—and are—welfare queens and gun-toting gangsters and dissolute youths. In Ontario, blacks accused of crimes are released by the police eighteen per cent of the time; whites are released twenty-nine per cent of the time. In drug-trafficking and importing cases, blacks are twenty-seven times as likely as whites to be jailed before their trial takes place, and twenty times as likely to be imprisoned on drug-possession charges.

33   After I had moved to the United States, I puzzled over this seeming contradiction—how West Indians celebrated in New York for their industry and drive could represent, just five hundred miles northwest, crime and dissipation. Didn't Torontonians see what was special and different in West Indian culture? But that was a naïve question. The West Indians were the first significant brush with blackness that white, smug, comfortable Torontonians had ever had. They had no bad blacks to contrast with the newcomers, no African-Americans to serve as a safety valve for their prejudices, no way to perform America's crude racial triage.

34   Not long ago, I sat in a coffee shop with someone I knew vaguely from college, who, like me, had moved to New York from Toronto. He began to speak of the threat that he felt Toronto now faced. It was the Jamaicans, he said. They were a bad seed. He was, of course, oblivious of my background. I said nothing, though, and he launched into a long explanation of how, in slave times, Jamaica was the island where all the most troublesome and obstreperous slaves were sent, and how that accounted for their particularly nasty disposition today.

35   I have told that story many times since, usually as a joke, because it was funny in an appalling way—particularly when I informed him much, much later that my mother was Jamaican. I tell the story that way because otherwise it is too painful. There must be people in Toronto just like Rosie and Noel, with the same attitudes and aspirations, who want to live in a neighborhood as nice as Argyle Avenue, who want to build a new garage and renovate their basement and set up their own business downstairs. But it is not completely up to them, is it? What has happened to Jamaicans in Toronto is proof that what has happened to Jamaicans here is not the end of racism, or even the beginning of the end of racism, but an accident of history and geography. In America, there is someone else to despise. In Canada, there is not. In the new racism, as in the old, somebody always has to be the nigger.

EXERCISES

Some of the Issues

1. Examine the description of Rosie and Noel's house and office in paragraph 2. What is your image of Rosie and Noel? How do the beginning paragraphs serve as an introduction to the ideas presented in the article?

2. According to the author, what are some of the reasons behind Noel's response to racism (paragraph 3)?

3. Summarize the differences the author describes between the West Indian definition of black and the American definition (paragraph 4).

4. Reread paragraphs 5 through 7. What are some of the other immigrant groups to which the author compares West Indians? Why are some of the questions raised by Gladwell "difficult"?

5. What are the conclusions of each of the studies Gladwell discusses in paragraphs 10 through 13 and 22 through 24? How does he use these conclusions to support his ideas?

6. What are the differences between the history and culture of American blacks and those of West Indians, particularly Gladwell's family (paragraphs 14–15)?

7. What happened when Gladwell's mother looked up the word "Negro" in the encyclopedia? How did her personal experience give "the lie to what she read" (paragraph 17)?

8. In paragraph 21, the author writes, "It is tempting to use the West Indian story as evidence that discrimination doesn't really exist." How does the author go on to question this "evidence"?

9. How does the author define "multicultural racism" in paragraph 25? Why are West Indians not "the victims in this competition, in anything but the narrowest sense"?

10. In paragraphs 31 through 35, Gladwell compares the history and treatment of Canadian West Indians to those of American West Indians. What is Gladwell trying to point out through these comparisons?

The Way We Are Told

11. The author waits until the end of paragraph 2 to tell us that Rosie and Noel are from Jamaica. What is the effect of doing so?
12. How does Gladwell combine the use of personal and family history with more objective sources? Do you find the mixture effective?
13. Gladwell concludes his essay with a strong statement. How does he build his evidence for this statement throughout the essay? Why might he have chosen not to make this statement toward the beginning?
14. We are not absolutely sure of Gladwell's point until the middle or even the end of his essay. In fact, we might initially suspect that Gladwell is making an opposite point to the one he finally makes. What might he gain from structuring the essay this way?

Some Subjects for Writing

15. Interview two or more relatives or friends who either immigrated to the United States or identify with a specific ethnic or racial group. Keeping in mind some of the issues Gladwell raises, focus on both their self-image and identity as well as how they perceive themselves to be treated by others. Make sure you develop a series of questions beforehand and, as you are interviewing, ask follow-up questions that might help your subjects elaborate on, explain, or analyze their experience. Write an essay in which you recount their stories and compare their experiences.

In Response to Executive Order 9066: All Americans of Japanese Descent Must Report to Relocation Centers

Dwight Okita

*Dwight Okita was born in Chicago in 1958. A poet and playwright, he has had three plays—*The Salad Bowl Dance, The Rainy Season, *and* Richard Speck—*produced. In 1992, he published a collection of poetry,* Crossing with the Light.

Okita's mother was among the thousands of Japanese Americans who were interned shortly after the United States entered World War II. This poem is written in his mother's voice.

Dear Sirs:
Of course I'll come. I've packed my galoshes
and three packets of tomato seeds. Janet calls them
"love apples." My father says where we're going
5   they won't grow.

I am a fourteen-year-old girl with bad spelling
and a messy room. If it helps any, I will tell you
I have always felt funny using chopsticks
and my favorite food is hot dogs.
10   My best friend is a white girl named Denise—
we look at boys together. She sat in front of me
all through grade school because of our names:
O'Connor, Ozawa. I know the back of Denise's head very well.
I tell her she's going bald. She tells me I copy on tests.

15   We are best friends.
        I saw Denise today in Geography class.
        She was sitting on the other side of the room.
        "You're trying to start a war," she said, "giving secrets away
        to the Enemy, Why can't you keep your big mouth shut?"
20   I didn't know what to say.
        I gave her a packet of tomato seeds
        and asked her to plant them for me, told her
        when the first tomato ripened
        she'd miss me.

EXERCISES

Some of the Issues

1. How do the tone and contents of the letter contrast with the title?
2. Okita's poem is written in the voice of a fourteen-year-old girl. What indications do we have that she sees the world as a "typical" American teenager? Why is this important to the ideas presented in the poem?
3. What does Denise say in lines 18 through 19? Does she make any sense? How do her comments reflect the government's policy toward Japanese Americans?
4. What is the tone set by the opening lines of the letter? Does that tone change by the end of the poem?
5. What is the significance of the tomato seeds?

Some Subjects for Writing

6. Imagine yourself as a child or adolescent who is suddenly placed into a new and unfriendly environment. Write an imaginary journal entry for either the day before, or the day of, your arrival. Make sure your entry includes some direct or indirect indication of your age and your life before.

PART VII

HOME AND AWAY

We travel for many reasons. We may take a trip to discover someplace unfamiliar—whether it be a new continent or a new neighborhood. We may revisit a place we used to live, or visit the homeland of our ancestors to learn more about ourselves. We may also travel just to escape our everyday routine. In any case, transplanting ourselves into another context can sharpen our awareness and appreciation of cultural differences, and give us insight into our own culture. Though "home" and "away" are of often thought of in opposition to each other, they are in fact integrally related. It is difficult to go someplace else without taking our own ideas of home—including our ideas of community, neighborhood, and family—with us. When we go away, we carry with us a sense of our history, and our home.

The first piece in this section explores the shifting meaning of home in a society that has become increasingly transitory and globalized. In "Home Is Every Place," Pico Iyer describes his life as a member of a new breed of "transcontinental warriors," people for whom every place is equally familiar and strange. For Iyer, who sees himself living in an increasingly small and interconnected world, home can no longer be defined through our connection to place and nationality.

The next three pieces take us to other places as two Americans—one of immigrant parents—recount experiences abroad. In "My Lai, Thirty Years After," Rachel Louise Snyder visits the site of the My Lai massacre, one of the Vietnam War's most brutal and controversial atrocities. Snyder questions what it means to be an American visiting Vietnam, and what responsibility we as

Americans—even those of us born long afterward—bear for understanding, confronting, and attempting to heal the damage caused by the United States' actions. Uzodinma Iweala writes of "A Close Encounter" in his parents' homeland of Nigeria, where a young boy gives him a lesson in inequality and reciprocity. David Sedaris, in "Picka Pocketoni" humorously gives his take on Americans in Paris and describes an encounter that, for him, captures the spirit of what others have called the Ugly American.

In the poem that ends the section, Gloria Anzaldúa explores living with several different and perhaps warring identities, crossing categories of race, ethnicity, and gender roles that others consider fixed. To live in the borderlands between cultures is to live in a dangerous place, but it is the only place that Anzaldúa feels she can be free.

Home Is Every Place

Pico Iyer

Pico Iyer was born in Oxford, England, in 1957 to Indian parents. The son of two college professors, he was educated in the elite British public school system and at Oxford and Harvard universities. He later became an American citizen.

Iyer works as a freelance journalist, and has contributed to such publications as Time, Harper's *and* The New York Review of Books. *He is the author of more than a dozen books, most recently* Sun After Dark: Flights into the Foreign *(2004).*

Iyer has said of his work, "Writing should be an act of communication more than of mere self-expression—a telling of a story rather than a flourishing of skills. The less conscious one is of being 'a writer,' the better the writing. . . . Writing, in fact, should ideally be as spontaneous and urgent as a letter to a lover, or a message to a friend who has just lost a parent. And because of the ways a writer is obliged to tap the private selves that even those closest to him never see, writing is, in the end, the oddest of anomalies; an intimate letter to a stranger."

This essay originally appeared in Homeground *(1996), an anthology of writings about the concept of "home." Iyer uses terms such as "Transit Loungers" and "privileged homeless" to describe a group of people, himself included, for whom the idea of home is not tied to a particular place, and who feel equally at home (or not at home) in many places. Iyer asserts that the modern world, with its blending of cultures and its distances shortened by fax, phone, and airplane, is increasingly made for people like him: "resident aliens of the world, impermanent residents of nowhere." By describing himself as a member of this tribe of nomads who supposedly lack a specific national or cultural identity, Iyer, in a sense, claims a home for himself.*

1   By the time I was nine, I was already used to going to school by trans-Atlantic plane, to sleeping in airports, to shuttling back and forth, three times a year, between my parents' (Indian) home in California and my boarding school in England. Throughout the time I was growing up, I was never within 6,000 miles of the nearest relative—and came, therefore, to learn how to define relations in non-familial ways. From the time I was a teenager, I took it for granted that I could take my budget vacations (as I did) in Bolivia and Tibet, China and Morocco. It never seemed strange to me that a girlfriend might be on the other side of a continent or sea.

2   It was only recently that I realized that all these habits of mind and life would scarcely have been imaginable in my parents' youth; the very facts and

facilities that shape my world are all distinctly new developments, and mark me as a modern type.

3   It was only recently, in fact, that I realized that I am an example, perhaps, of an entirely new breed of people, a transcontinental tribe of wanderers that is multiplying as fast as international phone lines and Frequent Flyer programs. We are the Transit Loungers, forever heading to the Departure Gate, forever orbiting the world. We buy our interests duty-free, we eat our food on plastic plates, we watch the world through borrowed headphones. We pass through countries as through revolving doors, resident aliens of the world, impermanent residents of nowhere. Nothing is strange to us, and nowhere is foreign. We are visitors even in our own homes.

4   This is not, I think, a function of affluence so much as of simple circumstance. I am not, that is, a jet-setter pursuing vacations from Marbella to Phuket; I am simply a fairly typical product of a movable sensibility, living and working in a world that is itself increasingly small and increasingly mongrel. I am a multinational soul on a multicultural globe where more and more countries are as polyglot and restless as airports. Taking planes seems as natural to me as picking up the phone, or going to school; I fold up my self and carry it around with me as if it were an overnight case.

5   The modern world seems increasingly made for people like me. I can plop myself down anywhere and find myself in the same relation of familiarity and strangeness: Lusaka, after all, is scarcely more strange to me than the foreigners' England in which I was born; the America where I am registered as an "alien"; and the almost unvisited India that people tell me is my home. I can fly from London to San Francisco to Osaka and feel myself no more a foreigner in one place than another; all of them are just locations—pavilions in some intercontinental Expo—and I can work or live or love in any one of them. All have Holiday Inns, direct-dial phones, CNN, and DHL. All have sushi and Thai restaurants, Kentucky Fried Chicken and Coke. My office is as close as the nearest fax machine or modem. Roppongi is West Hollywood is Leblon.

6   This kind of life offers an unprecedented sense of freedom and mobility: tied down to nowhere, we can pick and choose among locations. Ours is the first generation that can go off to visit Tibet for a week, or meet Tibetans down the street; ours is the first generation to be able to go to Nigeria for a holiday to find our roots or to find they are not there. At the lowest level, this new internationalism also means that I can get on a plane in Los Angeles, get off a few hours later in Jakarta, check into a Hilton, order a cheeseburger in English, and pay for it all with an American Express card. At the next level, it means that I can meet, in the Hilton coffee shop, an Indonesian businessman who is as conversant as I am with Michael Kinsley and Magic Johnson and Madonna. At a deeper level, it means that I need never feel estranged. If all the world is alien to us, all the world is home.

7   I have learned, in fact, to love foreignness. In any place I visit, I have the privileges of an outsider: I am an object of interest, and even fascination; I am a

person set apart, able to enjoy the benefits of the place without paying the taxes. And the places themselves seem glamorous to me, romantic, as seen through foreign eyes: distance on both sides lends enchantment. Policemen let me off speeding tickets, girls want to hear the stories of my life, pedestrians will gladly point me to the nearest Golden Arches. Perpetual foreigners in the transit lounge, we enjoy a kind of diplomatic immunity; and, living off room service in our hotel rooms, we are never obliged to grow up, or even, really, to be ourselves.

8   Thus, many of us learn to exult in the blessings of belonging to what feels like a whole new race. It is a race, as Salman Rushdie says, of "people who root themselves in ideas rather than places, in memories as much as in material things; people who have been obliged to define themselves—because they are so defined by others—by their otherness; people in whose deepest selves strange fusions occur, unprecedented unions between what they were and where they find themselves." And when people argue that our very notion of wonder is eroded, that alienness itself is as seriously endangered as the wilderness, that more and more of the world is turning into a single synthetic monoculture, I am not worried: a Japanese version of a French fashion is something new, I say, not quite Japanese and not truly French. Comme des Garcons hybrids are the art form of the time.

9   And yet, sometimes, I stop myself and think. What kind of heart is being produced by these new changes? And must I always be a None of the Above? When the stewardess comes down the aisle with disembarkation forms, what do I fill in? My passport says one thing, my face another; my accent contradicts my eyes. Place of Residence, Final Destination, even Marital Status are not much easier to fill in; usually I just tick "Other."

10   And beneath all the boxes, where do we place ourselves? How does one fix a moving object on a map? I am not an exile, really, nor an immigrant; not deracinated, I think, any more than I am rooted. I have not fled the oppression of war, nor found ostracism in the places where I do alight; I can scarcely feel severed from a home I have barely known. Yet is "citizen of the world" enough to comfort me? And does taking my home as every place make it easier to sleep at night?

11   Alienation, we are taught from kindergarten, is the condition of the time. This is the century of exiles and refugees, of boat people and statelessness; the time when traditions have been abolished, and men become closer to machines. This is the century of estrangement: more than a third of all Afghans live outside Afghanistan; the second city of the Khmers is a refugee camp; the second tongue of Beverly Hills is Farsi. The very notion of nation-states is outdated; many of us are as crosshatched within as Beirut.

12   We airport-hoppers can, in fact, go through the world as through a house of wonders, picking up something at every stop, and taking the whole globe as our playpen, or our supermarket (and even if we don't go to the world, the

world will increasingly come to us: just down the street, almost wherever we are, are nori and salsa, tiramisu and *naan*). We don't have a home, we have a hundred homes. And we can mix and match as the situation demands. "Nobody's history is my history," Kazuo Ishiguro, a great spokesman for the privileged homeless, once said to me, and then went on, "Whenever it was convenient for me to become very Japanese, I could become very Japanese, and then, when I wanted to drop it, I would just become this ordinary Englishman." Instantly, I felt a shock of recognition: I have a wardrobe of selves from which to choose. And I savor the luxury of being able to be an Indian in Cuba (where people are starving for yoga and Tagore), or an American in Thailand, to be an Englishman in New York.

13   And so we go on circling the world, six miles above the ground, displaced from time, above the clouds, with all our needs attended to. We listen to announcements given in three languages. We confirm our reservations at every stop. We disembark at airports that are self-sufficient communities, with hotels, gymnasia, and places of worship. At customs we have nothing to declare but ourselves.

14   But what is the price we pay for all of this? I sometimes think that this mobile way of life is as novel as high-rises, or the video monitors that are rewiring our consciousness. And even as we fret about the changes our progress wreaks in the air and on the airwaves, in forests and on streets, we hardly worry about the changes it is working in ourselves, the new kind of soul that is being born out of a new kind of life. Yet this could be the most dangerous development of all, and not only because it is the least examined.

15   For us in the Transit Lounge, disorientation is as alien as affiliation. We become professional observers, able to see the merits and deficiencies of anywhere, to balance our parents' viewpoints with their enemies' position. Yes, we say, of course it's terrible, but look at the situation from Saddam's point of view. I understand how you feel, but the Chinese had their own cultural reasons for Tiananmen Square. Fervor comes to seem to us the most foreign place of all.

16   Seasoned experts at dispassion, we are less good at involvement, or suspensions of disbelief; at, in fact, the abolition of distance. We are masters of the aerial perspective, but touching down becomes more difficult. Unable to get stirred by the raising of a flag, we are sometimes unable to see how anyone could be stirred. I sometimes think that this is how Rushdie, the great analyst of this condition, somehow became its victim. He had juggled homes for so long, so adroitly, that he forgot how the world looks to someone who is rooted, in country or belief. He had chosen to live so far from affiliation that he could no longer see why people choose affiliation in the first place. Besides, being part of no society means one is accountable to no one, and need respect no laws outside one's own. If single-nation people can be fanatical as terrorists, we can end up ineffectual as peacekeepers.

17   We become, in fact, strangers to belief itself, unable to comprehend many of the rages and dogmas that animate (and unite) people. Conflict itself seems

inexplicable to us sometimes, simply because partisanship is; we have the agnostic's inability to retrace the steps of faith. I could not begin to fathom why some Moslems would think of murder after hearing about *The Satanic Verses;* yet sometimes I force myself to recall that it is we, in our floating skepticism, who are the exceptions, that in China or Iran, in Korea or Peru, it is not so strange to give up one's life for a cause.

18   We end up, then, a little like nonaligned nations, confirming our reservations at every step. We tell ourselves, self-servingly, that nationalism breeds monsters, and choose to ignore the fact that internationalism breeds them too. Ours is the culpability not of the assassin, but of the bystander who takes a snapshot of the murder. Or, when the revolution catches fire, hops on the next plane out.

19   In any case, the issues in the Transit Lounge are passing; a few hours from now, they'll be a thousand miles away. Besides, this is a foreign country, we have no interests here. The only thing we have to fear are hijackers—passionate people with beliefs.

20   Sometimes, though, just sometimes, I am brought up short by symptoms of my condition. They are not major things, but they are peculiar ones, and ones that would not have been so common 50 years ago. I have never bought a house of any kind, and my ideal domestic environment, I sometimes tell my friends, is a hotel-room. I have never voted, or ever wanted to vote, and I eat in restaurants three times a day. I have never supported a nation (in the Olympic Games, say), or represented "my country" in anything. Even my name is weirdly international, because my "real name" is one that makes sense only in the home where I have never lived.

21   I choose to live in America in part, I think, because it feels more alien the longer I stay there. I love being in Japan because it reminds me, at every turn, of my foreignness. When I want to see if any place is home, I must subject the candidates to a battery of tests. Home is the place of which one has memories but no expectations.

22   If I have any deeper home, it is, I suppose, in English. My language is the house I carry round with me as a snail his shell; and in my lesser moments I try to forget that mine is not the language spoken in America, or even, really, by any member of my family.

23   Yet even here, I find, I cannot place my accent, or reproduce it as I can the tones of others. And I am so used to modifying my English inflections according to whom I am talking to—an American, an Englishman, a villager in Nepal, a receptionist in Paris—that I scarcely know what kind of voice I have.

24   I wonder, sometimes, if this new kind of non-affiliation may not be alien to something fundamental in the human state. The refugee at least harbors passionate feelings about the world he has left—and generally seeks to return there; the exile at least is propelled by some kind of strong emotion away from the old country and towards the new—indifference is not an exile emotion. But what

does the Transit Lounger feel? What are the issues that we would die for? What are the passions that we would live for?

25   Airports are among the only sites in public life where emotions are hugely sanctioned, in block capitals. We see people weep, shout, kiss in airports; we see them at the furthest edges of excitement and exhaustion. Airports are privileged spaces where we can see the primal states writ large—fear, recognition, hope. But there are some of us, perhaps, sitting at the Departure Gate, boarding passes in hand, watching the destinations ticking over, who feel neither the pain of separation nor the exultation of wonder; who alight with the same emotions with which we embarked; who go down to the baggage carousel and watch our lives circling, circling, circling, waiting to be claimed.

EXERCISES

Some of the Issues

1. How does Iyer describe his life in paragraph 1?
2. In paragraph 3, Iyer defines himself as part of a new "breed" of people that he calls a "transcontinental tribe of wanderers"? Why does he use these terms? What other terms does he use to describe himself and others like him?
3. Iyer speculates that his situation is not "a function of affluence" (paragraph 4). To what extent do you agree with him?
4. Looking at paragraph 5, consider the extent to which chains, franchises, and modern technology affect the "smallness" of the world.
5. How does the perspective of the essay change in paragraph 9?
6. Viewing the essay as a whole, what does Iyer mean when he describes himself and those like him as "seasoned experts at dispassion" (paragraph 16)?
7. Looking at the whole essay, summarize what Iyer describes as both the benefits and drawbacks of being a "Transit Lounger."
8. How does Iyer define home throughout the essay? What role does language play in Iyer's conception of home?
*9. Read Anton Shammas's "Amérka, Amérka." What is the difference between Shammas's idea of a "portable" home (Shammas, paragraph 8) and Iyer's?
10. Working in small groups, use an atlas or the Internet to find all the places Iyer mentions in his essay. On a map of the world, mark all of the places you find. Discuss what you know about these places or the images you have of them.

The Way We Are Told

11. Consider the title. How well does it describe the ideas discussed in the essay? What are some other titles Iyer might have used?
12. Paragraphs 9 and 10 offer a series of questions. What purpose do they serve? How do they help guide the reader?

13. The author uses descriptive language, but never describes one place in detail. Why is this appropriate to the essay?
14. What metaphor does Iyer use in his concluding paragraph? How does this metaphor help summarize his ideas?

Some Subjects for Writing

15. In paragraph 12, Iyer writes, "Even if we don't go to the world, the world will increasingly come to us." How true is this of the place you live now? Describe your city or town by painting a vivid picture of the various cultures and nationalities represented.
16. Reflecting on your relationship to your family, culture, nationality, and the place you were born, write an essay in which you provide your own definition of home.

My Lai, Thirty Years After

Rachel Louise Snyder

Rachel Louise Snyder is a freelance journalist and writer who has written for the New York Times, Travel & Leisure, Rolling Stone, Glamour, *and the online magazines* Salon *and* Slate, *among many other publications. Her radio essays have also appeared on National Public Radio's* All Things Considered *and* This American Life.

My Lai, the Vietnamese village Snyder visits in this essay, was the site of one of the most brutal and controversial atrocities of the Vietnam War. On the morning of March 16, 1968, U.S. soldiers ambushed and destroyed the village of My Lai, killing approximately 500 unarmed civilian men, women, children, and babies, some of whom were also raped or tortured. The attack, which seemingly had no military strategic purpose, prompted widespread outrage around the world and drastically reduced American support at home for the war in Vietnam.

This essay is excerpted from an anthology of travel writing entitled A Women's Passion for Travel: True Stories of World Wanderlust. *Snyder currently lives and writes in Cambodia.*

1 The sun scorches through the metal of the car, baking the black, vinyl seats. They feel pliable as new tar. Tank top and shorts—the uniform of choice— offers no respite and my bandanna is soaked in minutes. Sweat dribbles down my forehead, stings my eyes. The wind, through the car's open windows, feels like steady air from a torrid oven—relentless, constant, unbearable. This is Vietnam, mid-July.

2 I am on my way to visit the site of the 1968 My Lai Massacre during the Vietnam/American War. On that March day, soldiers from Charlie Company fired for four hours on the village of My Lai 4, near Pinkville in the Quang Ngai province. The result: 504 villagers dead, 6 survivors. I am an American traveling with an Australian couple three hours by car from Hoi An south to My Lai. I'd met them days before on a boat trip in Nha Trang and, as often happens with travelers, our paths had crossed again the night before in Hoi An. After telling them of my plans for the following day, they asked if they could split the cost and accompany me on my journey. We booked a car for 7 A.M. the following morning, hoping to drive before the worst of the midday heat began. We were assured an English-speaking driver.

3 "Hello," he said, when we climbed in the car. We'd arranged to be picked up outside of Hoi An, in an alley where authorities wouldn't see foreigners

climbing in a car that wasn't government authorized. If caught, the driver would be heavily fined.

4   I greeted him, then asked how far it was to My Lai.

5   "Yes, My Lai," he said.

6   "How far?"

7   "Hello," he said.

8   I hadn't specified how many English words were required.

9   For three weeks, I had been in Vietnam—partly because I had wander-lust, but mostly because I had taught Vietnam War literature for nearly three years. I researched the topic in graduate school; the romance had appealed to me—innocent men following the orders of a wrong government, men losing their lives in a futile fight. But gradually, the romance slipped away, and my interest became academic. And personal. I wanted to experience a Vietnam outside of books. A Vietnam before capitalism changed the country's face en-tirely. Here was something, a war, our country couldn't seem to get past. I wanted to know why.

10   The mood in the car is somber; no one talks most of the way. Together, the Australians and I watch a motorbike buried under more than a hundred dead ducks tied together and slung behind, over top, and in front of the driver as he pulls beside, then passes our car. The ducks' eyes and beaks are open, flapping with the bumps in the road as if startled to be caught so suddenly by death. One of the Australians asks me how I feel.

11   "Hot," I tell her. "Sweaty. My water bottle is boiling."

12   This is not the answer she is looking for, I know. What does she want to hear? I feel guilty that American soldiers killed innocent Vietnamese? Remorse over the incident? Embarrassed by the actions of my country's citizens? A yearning to unravel the world and manipulate the past so that it wouldn't have happened?

13   I feel all these things.

14   I also feel nothing.

15   In March of 1968, when Charlie Company opened fire on the civilians of My Lai, I was barely even a fetus. When Lt. William Calley was tried and found guilty, I was learning to wave good-bye. When he was released from house arrest, I was learning to count to three. I never protested. I never personally knew any-one who died in the war. I barely remember the tanks crashing through the gate at Saigon in 1975. The Vietnam veterans I have happened to meet are middle-aged men now, some bitter, some angry, some indifferent, and all with other lives. Why does any of this matter to me?

16   "How do Americans feel about England now?" one of the Australians asks me.

17   England? I am silent for a moment, wondering if I've missed some impor-tant news event, some skirmish between the U.S. and Great Britain.

18   "You know," she says, "the war?"

19   "The Revolutionary War?"

20   "Yes."

21   "I don't think Americans think of it at all." I am amazed to be asked this question; I nearly burst out laughing. Does anyone have the Revolutionary War even in the farthest recesses of his conscious mind? England? I think fish and chips, dark beer, castles, and scandalous royalty. It occurs to me she is looking for a connection to My Lai. It also occurs to me that 100 years from now the Vietnam/American War will be little more than a tiny phase of history taught in progressive colleges throughout the U.S. It's almost there now.

22   I explain to her that the circumstances between the two wars are different, not comparable, though I know her question stems from never having heard anything of My Lai until last night when I told her the story. I ask about the connection she's attempting to make, and she mumbles vaguely about imperialism and war. She has seen too much propaganda, I think. In Vietnam, Americans are referred to as the Imperialist Aggressors.

23   We are close to My Lai, and I feel my stomach muscles start to tighten. What will I find there? Will I be cursed? Hated? Spit on? Will I face what many U.S. soldiers faced upon their arrival home? Or am I blanketed by time, gender, age? The Australians in back have begun to lather themselves with suntan lotion—here, the sun can blister through sunblock in minutes. I am hoping the couple does not hate me by the end of the day.

24   Am I to blame?

25   Of course not. I was barely alive. But should future generations not strive to eradicate the mistakes of the past? Certainly. But the My Lai Massacre, to be seen objectively, must be seen in the context of war. That war, in particular. But 500 innocent people are dead. And I am a citizen from the country that killed them.

26   The car pulls in to a long driveway and parks under the shade of a tree. We are charged 20,000 dong each to enter the My Lai monument site—just under two dollars. To say that the Vietnamese have learned to market the American war sounds cynical and defensive. But you can buy Zippo lighters and flak jackets at Saigon's war surplus market. You can buy helicopter and B-52 bomber replicas made of bullets at the War Remnants Museum. You can buy compasses and rusting dog tags in every town along the coast from Ho Chi Minh City to Hanoi. The trick is not thinking about where they've come from.

27   "I wait," our driver says, urging us forward. A long sidewalk leads into an enormous concrete sculpture, though it is so far away I can't quite make it out. I look away, unprepared to discover exactly what it is yet. My palms are clammy and I know heat is not the cause. I grin stupidly at the Australians, feel like my skin is too loose for my bones. They are waiting for me to proceed. I am the expert here. I'd planned on coming here alone, but last night they'd insisted, and sharing the cost was a bonus for me. Now, I waver between elation and embarrassment, glad they are here and wishing them gone, all at once.

28   To my left is the grave of Mrs. Thong, her children, and two relatives. The marker is etched in stone. I read and reread the names, calculate each age of the victims had they lived, compare them to my own twenty-nine years. We

walk forward. How long should one look at a stranger's grave? There is a fine line between remorse and obsession. I am all jumbled up; a curious mixture of emotion and numbness. Several stone statues line up along the sidewalk. These sculptures were done by a group of artists in Hanoi—all but the huge one in the distance.

29   One stone woman falls forward, her hand clutching her stomach—a replica of the photo by Ronald Herberle. Another woman kneels, her hair blowing in the wind as she falls sideways, one arm outstretched. Opposite her, down a thin sidewalk bordered by yellow wildflowers, is the temporary museum. A woman leans in the doorway, arms crossed, waiting for us. She wears long brown pants, a pink long-sleeved blouse. I am amazed at how the Vietnamese withstand the heat. Women ride bicycles covered head to toe, saving their skin from the sun, complete in elbow-high gloves and hats. In the mountains of Da Lat, where it may get down to seventy-eight degrees Fahrenheit at night, people wear winter coats, sweaters, scarves, knit caps.

30   The woman greets us in flawless English. Like most Vietnamese, she speaks quietly, gently. She welcomes us to My Lai, tells us she is a guide and will show us around. No other visitors are here, and the silence is loud, oppressive as the heat. The museum is maybe ten by twenty feet. She asks where we are from.

31   "Australia," my companions say together, maybe a little proudly.

32   "America," I say, shifting my weight, "the States."

33   She smiles at us, looks at me a second longer than the Australians, though this may be my imagination. First she explains that we need to look at a map of the area to understand how the Americans planned the attack.

34   "Planned?" I ask her.

35   She nods. "Yes, the massacre was planned."

36   I hear the Australians gasp, slightly, under their breath. The woman continues to smile.

37   Planned? How could it have been planned? A recon patrol, perhaps, was planned, maybe even a search-and-destroy mission; burn the hamlets, interrogate the villagers, and all that. But a full-scale massacre? Strategies are planned. Brutalities just happen. My heart is thumping. She shows us how My Lai is actually a series of villages: My Lai 1, 2, 3, 4, 5, 6. She points to the hill near My Lai 4 where the Americans were based. She explains how the Americans knew the people of My Lai 4, how the soldiers would come down and play with the children.

38   "So you can see," she says softly, "how this wasn't an accident."

39   No, I want to tell her, I don't see. I don't see what you see at all. I see men who obeyed the leaders of their country, then lost themselves. The Australians are nodding, horrified. Clearly, they believe her. I want to tell them she is wrong, that this wasn't planned, but I cannot be sure, and anyway, the three of them have moved on to other displays. I stumble, follow, stand behind them.

40   The woman walks us around the room. On the walls there are pictures of people: Lieutenant Calley, who was the First Platoon leader, Captain Ernest

Medina, the company commander, Oran Henderson, the brigade commander. Of them all, soldiers and commanders, Calley was the sole man tried and found guilty. He served three years house arrest. There are others, Ron Ridenhour, the soldier whose letters spurred the initial investigation in Washington, Ron Herberle, the American photographer whose photos told the story of My Lai 4, and two South Vietnamese interpreters who testified to the massacre in 1978. You see, the pictures seem to suggest, how even many Americans knew what had happened was wrong? The people at this museum have done their homework. They do not blame all Americans, I think; they blame one group of American soldiers. Perhaps it is not in the Vietnamese where we will find our forgiveness.

41   There are pictures of helicopters landing, soldiers walking with guns drawn or M16s blasting away, hamlets burning to the ground. The black-and-white photos have been blown up so that the details are blurry, everything a little less focused like the world that day was trapped in shadow.

42   Glass cases hold items from the villagers: one woman's conical hat and betel nut spittoon, a young girl's shoe, a bullet-riddled cooking pot, marbles, and a little boy's school notebooks. There are the 1978 testimonies from the ARVN interpreters encased, along with blown-up news clips from papers all over the world. The woman points to the photo of a wounded American soldier after he'd shot himself in the foot because he refused to participate.

43   "He killed himself a few years ago," the woman tells us, then adds, "he was unable to live with the memories of the massacre."

44   Does she know how many men and women are unable to live with the memories? Or how many are forced to? Does she know how many men were following orders that day, and how few were giving them? Yes, men from my country did a horrible thing; they were wrong. But men from my country also brought this horrible thing to light. Men from my country fed Vietnamese citizens, played with Vietnamese children, were led to believe they fought for something worthwhile.

45   It occurs to me that the nationality—American—doesn't matter, not to this woman, anyway. What matters is that innocent people from her village were lost. The monument is not put here simply to remember American sins, it is put here to honor lost lives.

46   Our guide shows us the graves of entire families killed. Next to each grave is the foundation that was once the family's hamlet. Though they were all burned down, the foundations remain, a foot higher than ground level and covered with grass, weeds, flowers. There are two replicas of bomb shelters, which we crawl inside; the darkness is remarkably cool. There is a monument next to an irrigation ditch where over 100 bodies were found. There is a wall of tiny colored tiles constructed to depict the horror and suffering of that day. Flames shoot up and around people running, falling, screaming. It is mostly red. There is a heated stillness to everything here. Not a sound. Not even the construction on the new museum is audible, like the horror of that day was the final voice, the village now enshrined in silence.

47   The woman leads us to a tiny room next to the temporary museum where we are offered hot tea and given a large, red book to record our thoughts and feelings. She leaves for a few minutes then returns, places a box on the table for donations. I do not remind her that we already paid entrance fees. The Australians and I leave the box untouched. I am glad to see, on this small measure, they feel as I do.

48   The guest book is passed to me, and I suddenly feel the pressure to write something profound and remorseful. I thumb through the hundreds of entries. A few from U.S. soldiers catch my eye; they all write their rank and years for their tours of duty. Many apologize. There are foreigners: Germans, Australians, Dutch, Japanese. Some write about war in general, how wrong and evil it is. Others are more personal. "The Americans should pay retribution," one German writes, ironically. "How can the Americans commit such atrocities?" a Japanese woman questions.

49   I write something general in the book, something about wanting better actions in the future, something about learning from our mistakes, about learning to have the character to admit our blunders. What I really want to write, though, is how strangely proud I am, at that moment, for that one hour, and on that one day in the relentless heat of a wounded village, to be an American confronting her nation's ugly past, to see how no one, no history, no country, is free from its dark moments, and it is this human frailty, in these imperfections that we can find unity, that we can build a future where My Lai 4s will never happen again.

EXERCISES

Some of the Issues

1. What does Snyder tell us about the My Lai Massacre in paragraph 2? What, if anything, had you known about My Lai or about the Vietnam War prior to reading Snyder's essay?
2. What was your response to Snyder's interactions with the driver? Why do you think she includes this dialogue?
3. What appealed to Snyder about Vietnam before traveling there (paragraph 9)? How and why did her views change? What did you think of her motivation for going there?
4. Why does the Australian ask Snyder how she feels (paragraph 10)? How does Snyder respond? Why does she say to herself "I fell all of these things. I also feel nothing"?
5. What was your response to the Australian's question about England in paragraph 19? What did you think of Snyder's response to the question (paragraphs 21–22)?
6. What are the various thoughts that race through Snyder's head in paragraph 25?

7. What is Snyder's response to the idea that the massacre was "planned"? What explanation does she give for her response and what does it say about her view of the American soldiers who served in Vietnam?
8. Why does Snyder say, "Perhaps it is not in the Vietnamese where we will find our forgiveness"?
9. Why does Snyder point out specifically what the German and Japanese tourists have written in the guest book (paragraph 48)?
10. Look at some of the points in the essay when what Snyder says differs from, or is less complex than, what she thinks. What do you think accounts for these differences? Do you think she should have been more forthcoming in her responses?

The Way We Are Told

11. What is the effect of Snyder's opening paragraph? How does it set the tone for the piece?
12. Snyder writes primarily in the present tense. What is the effect?
13. How would you describe Snyder's tone throughout the piece? Does her tone change at any point or points?

Some Subject for Writing

14. How much of our country's history—or our family, town, or city's history—are we responsible for as individuals? To what extent are we responsible for confronting our histories? Using Snyder's text as a starting point, write an essay in which you reflect on people's connection to and their responsibility for actions committed by previous generations or people not connected to them.
15. Write an essay in which you examine the idea of disaster sites as tourist attractions. How should the history of the event be presented? Should other goods be sold at the site and if so what kinds of goods? If you have visited such a site or know someone who has, draw examples from those experiences.

A Close Encounter

Uzodinma Iweala

Uzodinma Iweala was born in 1982. He has lived part of his life in Nigeria, where his mother is currently minister of finance, but grew up with his parents in Washington, DC. He entered Harvard University as a premed student but eventually moved to the English department and creative writing program, where he received a number of prizes for his work. He was also co-president of the African Students Association.

Iweala's first book started as a short sketch he wrote in his senior year of high school, after reading a Newsweek *article about child soldiers in Sierra Leone. He later expanded that sketch into a 50-page short story that became his senior thesis at Harvard, and, in 2005, the critically acclaimed novel* Beasts of No Nation. *Iweala has said that it was his unease with his own privilege that in part motivated him to write that story, an unease which is also reflected in this selection, originally published in* The New York Times Magazine *in 2005.*

1 I return to Nigeria, after graduating from college. I have been to Abuja, the capital, a couple of times, but that was before my mother was appointed minister of finance.

2 Two weeks into my stay, on a rare occasion when my mother has time to chat, I tell her that I'm bored. Her response: "Here are the car keys. Go and buy some fruit." Overjoyed, I jump into the car, salute the heavily armed security at the gate and speed off in search of—fruit.

3 The young boy sees me, or rather he sees the car first—a silver BMW— and quickly springs up from his spot under a small tree, eager to sell his bunches of bananas and bottles of roasted peanuts. His dingy shirt hangs low over too-short shorts. His sucked-in cheeks and puckered lips suggest that although he appears to be about 12, he already knows the sourness of life. By the time I stop the car, he is at the passenger door, grunting: "Banana 300 naira (roughly $2). Groundnut 200 naira. Sah!" I look skeptically at his black-striped bananas and bargain him down to 200 total for the fruit and nuts. When he agrees, I reach for my wallet and hand him a crisp 500 naira note. He doesn't have change, so I tell him not to worry. He is grateful and smiles a row of perfect teeth.

4 When, two weeks later, I see this same boy, I am more aware of my position in Nigerian society. Security people at the house have told me: "You are the son of a minister! Kai! You should enjoy this country!" But it's hard to find enjoyment in a place where it's not that rare to see a little boy who should be in school standing on the corner selling fruit in the intense heat.

My parents have raised me and my three siblings to be aware of the privilege we have been afforded and the responsibility it brings. "To whom much is given. . . ." my grandfather always says. And I have been given much, from education at the best schools in the United States to this car and its 12 speakers, which have changed the way I listen to music. But I worry about what is expected of me.

5   I pull over and wind down my window. He wears the same shirt and shorts and has a bunch of bananas and a bottle of peanuts ready. I wave them away. "What's up?" I ask him. He answers in broken English: "I dey oh. But I no get money to buy book for school." I reach into my wallet and pull out two fresh 500 naira notes. "Will this help?" I ask. He looks around nervously before sticking his hand into the car to take the bills. One thousand naira is a lot of money to someone whose family probably makes about 50,000 naira ($380) or less each year. "Thank you, sah," he says. "Thank you very much, oh!"

6   Later, I say to my mother: "That's the way it works? He doesn't have any money so I dash him some. Trickle-down economics, right?" My mother winces when anyone speaks of the slow progress of the economic reforms. "No, I'm trying to better his situation first," she says. The next morning the Secret Service officers caution me, "Sometimes in this place, when you give a little, people think you're a fountain of opportunity."

7   It's true that people will take advantage of you in Nigeria, but this happens everywhere in the world. I wonder if my little friend actually used the money for schoolbooks. What if he's a fraud? And then I wonder about my own motives. Did I give to alleviate my own guilt? Am I using him? Later, I realize that I don't know his name or the least bit about him nor did I think to ask.

8   Over the next six months, I am busy working in a refugee camp in northern Nigeria, biking across France and Spain and writing. Sometime after I return, I go for a drive, and I see the boy standing on the road next to a man who sells exotic birds. He jumps up and down to get my attention and has a big smile ready when I roll down the window.

9   "Oga sah!" he says. "Long time."

10   "Are you in school now?" I ask.

11   He nods.

12   "That's good," I say. A silence falls as we look at each other, and then I realize what he wants. "Here," I hold out a 500 naira note. "Take this."

13   He shakes his head vigorously and steps back as if offended. "What's wrong?" I ask. "It's a gift."

14   He shakes his head again and brings his hand from behind his back. His face glistens with sweat. He drops a bunch of bananas and a bottle of peanuts in the front seat before he says, "I've been waiting to give these to you."

EXERCISES

Some of the Issues

1. What do we know about Iweala's background from the first few paragraphs?
2. Why do you think Iweala bargains the boy down to 200 naira and then hands him 500, allowing the boy to keep the change?
3. Why do you think Iweala worries about what is expected of him? How does he seem to feel about his own position in Nigeria?
4. How do Iweala's views of money and inequality differ from those of his mother and those of the Secret Service (paragraph 6)? In your opinion, what do these differences say about him? Why does he question his own motives?
5. Why does the boy give Iweala the bananas and peanuts six months later? How does his gesture potentially change Iweala's view of the relationship?

The Way We Are Told

6. Iweala's essay is written in the present as opposed to the past tense. Why do you suppose he chose to write it this way? What is the effect?
7. Why does Iweala never tell us the name of the boy?
8. Examine Iweala's use of dialogue and quotations throughout the piece. Where does he use them and to what effect?

Some Subjects for Writing

9. How should Iweala feel about his own position in Nigeria? What responsibilities does he have to the country and its people? Write a short essay explaining your views.
10. Write a narrative of an encounter with an individual or a group of people that changed your perspective in a significant way. Using Iweala's essay as a model, think carefully about your use of dialogue and detailed description.
*11. Read Rasma Haidri's "Urdu, My Love Song" and "Saying Something in African" by Emiene Shija Wright. How are their relationships to their home countries or their parents' countries both similar to and different from Iweala's? What do these pieces tell us about the complicated relationships immigrant children often have with their parents' home countries? Write an essay in which you analyze some of these differences and similarities, and attempt to examine some of the reasons for them.

Picka Pocketoni

David Sedaris

David Sedaris was born in 1956 in Binghamton, New York, and raised in Raleigh, North Carolina. In his teens and twenties, he dabbled in visual and performance art. After working a string of odd jobs across Raleigh, Chicago, and New York City, Sedaris achieved prominence with the NPR radio essay "The SantaLand Diaries," which described his experiences working as a department store elf during Christmas time in New York. Sedaris went on to become known as a frequent contributor to the radio program "This American Life." He has since published several books of humorous essays including Naked *(1996),* Me Talk Pretty One Day *(2000), from which this essay is excerpted, and most recently* Dress Your Family in Corduroy and Denim *(2004).*

Sedaris's style is sardonic, incisive, and often deadpan, and his humor is mostly autobiographical, concerning his large and eccentric family, various jobs, education, and relationships. At what was perhaps the height of his fame he moved with his longtime boyfriend Hugh from New York City to a relatively reclusive life in France, where he still lives. Several of his recent essays, including "Picka Pocketoni," have dealt with his experiences as an American living abroad.

1   It was July, and Hugh and I were taking the Paris Métro from our neighborhood to a store where we hoped to buy a good deal of burlap. The store was located on the other side of town, and the trip involved taking one train and then switching to another. During the summer months a great number of American vacationers can be found riding the Métro, and their voices tend to carry. It's something I hadn't noticed until leaving home, but we are a loud people. The trumpeting elephants of the human race. Questions, observations, the locations of blisters and rashes—everything is delivered as though it were an announcement.

2   On the first of our two trains I listened to a quartet of college-age Texans who sat beneath a sign instructing passengers to surrender their folding seats and stand should the foyer of the train become too crowded. The foyer of the train quickly became too crowded, and while the others stood to make more room, the young Texans remained seated and raised their voices in order to continue their debate, the topic being "Which is a better city, Houston or Paris?" It was a hot afternoon, and the subject of air-conditioning came into play. Houston had it, Paris did not. Houston also had ice cubes, tacos, plenty of free parking, and something called a Sonic Burger. Things were not looking good for

Paris, which lost valuable points every time the train stopped to accept more passengers. The crowds packed in, surrounding the seated Texans and reducing them to four disembodied voices. From the far corner of the car, one of them shouted that they were tired and dirty and ready to catch the next plane home. The voice was weary and hopeless, and I identified completely. It was the same way I'd felt on my last visit to Houston.

3   Hugh and I disembarked to the strains of "Texas, Our Texas" and boarded our second train, where an American couple in their late forties stood hugging the floor-to-ceiling support pole. There's no sign saying so, but such poles are not considered private. They're put there for everyone's use. You don't treat it like a fireman's pole; rather, you grasp it with one hand and stand back at a respectable distance. It's not all that difficult to figure out, even if you come from a town without any public transportation.

4   The train left the station, and needing something to hold on to, I wedged my hand between the American couple and grabbed the pole at waist level. The man turned to the woman, saying, "Peeeeew, can you smell that? That is pure French, baby." He removed one of his hands from the pole and waved it back and forth in front of his face. "Yes indeed," he said. "This little froggy is ripe."

5   It took a moment to realize he was talking about me.

6   The woman wrinkled her nose. "Golly Pete!" she said, "Do they all smell this bad?"

7   "It's pretty typical," the man said. "I'm willing to bet that our little friend here hasn't had a bath in a good two weeks. I mean, Jesus Christ, someone should hang a deodorizer around this guy's neck."

8   The woman laughed, saying, "You crack me up, Martin. I swear you do."

9   It's a common mistake for vacationing Americans to assume that everyone around them is French and therefore speaks no English whatsoever. These two didn't seem like exceptionally mean people. Back home they probably would have had the decency to whisper, but here they felt free to say whatever they wanted, face-to-face and in a normal tone of voice. It was the same way someone might talk in front of a building or a painting they found particularly unpleasant. An experienced traveler could have told by looking at my shoes that I wasn't French. And even if I were French, it's not as if English is some mysterious tribal dialect spoken only by anthropologists and a small population of cannibals. They happen to teach English in schools all over the world. There are no eligibility requirements. Anyone can learn it. Even people who reportedly smell bad despite the fact that they've just taken a bath and are wearing clean clothes.

10   Because they had used the tiresome word *froggy* and complained about my odor, I was now licensed to hate this couple as much as I wanted. This made me happy, as I'd wanted to hate them from the moment I'd entered the subway car and seen them hugging the pole. Unleashed by their insults, I was now free to criticize Martin's clothing: the pleated denim shorts, the baseball cap, the T-shirt advertising a San Diego pizza restaurant. Sunglasses hung

from his neck on a fluorescent cable, and the couple's bright new his-and-her sneakers suggested that they might be headed somewhere dressy for dinner. Comfort has its place, but it seems rude to visit another country dressed as if you've come to mow its lawns.

11   The man named Martin was in the process of showing the woman what he referred to as "my Paris." He looked at the subway map and announced that at some point during their stay, he'd maybe take her to the Louvre, which he pronounced as having two distinct syllables. *Loov-rah*. I'm hardly qualified to belittle anyone else's pronunciation, but he was setting himself up by acting like such an expert. "Yeah," he said, letting out a breath, "I thought we might head over there some day this week and do some nosing around. It's not for everyone, but something tells me you might like it."

12   People are often frightened of Parisians, but an American in Paris will find no harsher critic than another American. France isn't even my country, but there I was, deciding that these people needed to be sent back home, preferably in chains. In disliking them, I was forced to recognize my own pretension, and that made me hate them even more. The train took a curve, and when I moved my hand farther up the pole, the man turned to the woman, saying, "Carol— hey, Carol, watch out. That guy's going after your wallet."

13   "What?"

14   "Your wallet," Martin said. "That joker's trying to steal your wallet. Move your pocketbook to the front where he can't get at it."

15   She froze, and he repeated himself, barking, "The front. Move your pocketbook around to the front. Do it now. The guy's a pickpocket."

16   The woman named Carol grabbed for the strap on her shoulder and moved her pocketbook so that it now rested on her stomach. "Wow," she said. "I sure didn't see *that* coming."

17   "Well, you've never been to Paris before, but let that be a lesson to you." Martin glared at me, his eyes narrowed to slits. "This city is full of stinkpots like our little friend here. Let your guard down, and they'll take you for everything you've got."

18   Now I was a stinkpot *and* a thief. It occurred to me to say something, but I thought it might be better to wait and see what he came up with next. Another few minutes, and he might have decided I was a crack dealer or a white slaver. Besides, if I said something at this point, he probably would have apologized, and I wasn't interested in that. His embarrassment would have pleased me, but once he recovered, there would be that awkward period that sometimes culminates in a handshake. I didn't want to touch these people's hands or see things from their point of view, I just wanted to continue hating them. So I kept my mouth shut and stared off into space.

19   The train stopped at the next station. Passengers got off, and Carol and Martin moved to occupy two folding seats located beside the door. I thought they might ease on to another topic, but Martin was on a roll now, and there was no stopping him. "It was some shithead like him that stole my wallet on my

last trip to Paris," he said, nodding his head in my direction. "He got me on the subway—came up from behind, and I never felt a thing. Cash, credit cards, driver's license: *poof*—all of it gone, just like that."

20   I pictured a scoreboard reading MARTY 0 STINKPOTS 1, and clenched my fist in support of the home team.

21   "What you've got to understand is that these creeps are practiced professionals," he said. "I mean, they've really got it down to an art, if you can call that an art form."

22   "I wouldn't call it an art form," Carol said. "Art is beautiful, but taking people's wallets . . . that stinks, in my opinion."

23   "You've got that right," Martin said. "The thing is that these jokers usually work in pairs." He squinted toward the opposite end of the train. "Odds are that he's probably got a partner somewhere on this subway car."

24   "You think so?"

25   "I know so," he said. "They usually time it so that one of them clips your wallet just as the train pulls into the station. The other guy's job is to run interference and trip you up once you catch wind of what's going on. Then the train stops, the doors open, and they disappear into the crowd. If Stinky there had gotten his way, he'd probably be halfway to Timbuktu by now. I mean, make no mistake, these guys are fast."

26   I'm not the sort of person normally mistaken for being fast and well-coordinated, and because of this, I found Martin's assumption to be oddly flattering. Stealing wallets was nothing to be proud of, but I like being thought of as cunning and professional. I'd been up until 4 A.M. the night before, reading a book about recluse spiders, but to him the circles beneath my eyes likely reflected a long evening spent snatching flies out of the air, or whatever it is that pickpockets do for practice.

27   "The meatball," he said. "Look at him, just standing there waiting for his next victim. If I had my way, he'd be picking pockets with his teeth. An eye for an eye, that's what I say. Someone ought to chop the guy's hands off and feed them to the dogs."

28   *Oh*, I thought, *but first you'll have to catch me.*

29   "It just gets my goat," he said, "I mean, where's a *policioni* when you need one?"

30   *Policioni?* Where did he think he was? I tried to imagine Martin's conversation with a French policeman and pictured him waving his arms, shouting, "That man tried to picka my frienda's pocketoni!" I wanted very much to hear such a conversation and decided I would take the wallet from Hugh's back pocket as we left the train. Martin would watch me steal from a supposed stranger and most likely would intercede. He'd put me in a headlock or yell for help, and when a crowd gathered, I'd say, "What's the problem? Is it against the law to borrow money from my boyfriend?" If the police came, Hugh would explain the situation in his perfect French while I'd toss in a few of my most polished phrases. "That guy's crazy," I'd say, pointing at Martin. "I think he's

drunk. Look at how his face is swollen." I was practicing these lines to myself when Hugh came up from behind and tapped me on the shoulder, signaling that the next stop was ours.

31   "There you go," Martin said. "That's him, that's the partner. Didn't I tell you he was around here somewhere? They always work in pairs. It's the oldest trick in the book."

32   Hugh had been reading the paper and had no idea what had been going on. It was too late now to pretend to pick his pocket, and I was stuck without a decent backup plan. As we pulled into the station, I recalled an afternoon ten years earlier. I'd been riding the Chicago el with my sister Amy, who was getting off three or four stops ahead of me. The doors opened, and as she stepped out of the crowded car, she turned around to yell, "So long, David. Good luck beating that rape charge." Everyone onboard had turned to stare at me. Some seemed curious, some seemed frightened, but the overwhelming majority appeared to hate me with a passion I had never before encountered. "That's my sister," I'd said. "She likes to joke around." I laughed and smiled, but it did no good. Every gesture made me appear more guilty, and I wound up getting off at the next stop rather than continue riding alongside people who thought of me as a rapist. I wanted to say something that good to Martin, but I can't think as fast as Amy. In the end this man would go home warning his friends to watch out for pickpockets in Paris. He'd be the same old Martin, but at least for the next few seconds, I still had the opportunity to be somebody different, somebody quick and dangerous.

33   The dangerous me noticed how Martin tightened his fists when the train pulled to a stop. Carol held her pocketbook close against her chest and sucked in her breath as Hugh and I stepped out of the car, no longer finicky little boyfriends on their overseas experiment, but rogues, accomplices, halfway to Timbuktu.

EXERCISES

Some of the Issues

1. How does Sedaris characterize American tourists in Paris in the opening paragraphs? What was your response to his characterization?
2. Why does Sedaris enjoy the license to hate the American couple on the subway (paragraph 10)? What did you think of them based on his description? What did you think of Sedaris?
3. Why does Sedaris say, "In disliking them, I was forced to recognize my own pretension, and that made me hate them even more" (paragraph 12)?
4. Why doesn't Sedaris tell the couple that he is from the United States (paragraph 18)?
5. Who do you suppose the "home team" is in paragraph 20? Why?

The Way We Are Told

6. How does Sedaris set the scene in the opening paragraphs?
7. What is the purpose of the line: "It was the same way I'd felt on my last visit to Houston" (paragraph 2)?
8. How would you characterize Sedaris's use of humor? Did you find it funny? Why or why not?

Some Subjects for Writing

9. Write a narrative about a time when you had to adapt to other people's customs. You might write about a trip you took to another country or another part of the country, or you might write about a time when you visited someone whose family or household had very different rules or customs than your own.
10. Though Sedaris's piece is meant to be humorous, one could also read it as having more serious implications. Using specific evidence from the text, write a short response to Sedaris in which you interpret what he might be saying about American tourists. Based on your own interpretation, do you agree or disagree? Why or why not? Feel free to include examples from your own experience or from other texts you've read.

To live in
the Borderlands
means you . . .

Gloria Anzaldúa

*Gloria Anzaldúa (1942–2004) was a self-described "Chicana tejana les-
bian-feminist poet and fiction writer." She taught Chicana studies, feminist
studies, and creative writing at various universities, and her award-winning
work was published widely.*

She was editor of Making Face Making Soul/Haciendo Caras: Creative and Critical Perspectives by Women of Color *(1990) and coeditor of*
This Bridge Called My Back: Writings by Radical Women of Color
(1981). She also authored a novel, La Prieta ("The Dark One") *published in
1997. This poem is taken from* Borderlands/La Frontera: The New Mestiza *(1987), a collection of prose and poetry that describes the author's childhood along the Texas–Mexico border, growing up between two cultures, Anglo
and Mexican, equally at home and alien in both. Anzaldúa speaks of an actual
physical border, but expands her metaphor to include the psychological "borderlands" that occur whenever two or more cultures coexist together.*

To live in the Borderlands means you . . .

are neither *hispana india negra española*
ni gabacha, eres mestiza, mulata, half-breed
caught in the crossfire between camps
5   while carrying all five races on your back
not knowing which side to turn to, run from;

To live in the Borderlands means knowing
that the *india* in you, betrayed for 500 years,
is no longer speaking to you,
10   that *mexicanas* call you *rajetas,*
that denying the Anglo inside you
is as bad as having denied the Indian or Black;

Cuando vives en la frontera
people walk through you, the wind steals your voice,

15 you're a *burra, buey,* scapegoat,
    forerunner of a new race,
    half and half—both woman and man, neither—
    a new gender;

    To live in the Borderlands means to
20 put *chile* in the borscht,
    eat whole wheat *tortillas,*
    speak Tex-Mex with a Brooklyn accent;
    be stopped by *la migra* at the border checkpoints;

    Living in the Borderlands means you fight hard to
25 resist the gold elixir beckoning from the bottle,
    the pull of the gun barrel,
    the rope crushing the hollow of your throat;

    In the Borderlands
    you are the battleground
30 where enemies are kin to each other;
    you are at home, a stranger,
    the border disputes have been settled
    the volley of shots have shattered the truce
    you are wounded, lost in action
35 dead, fighting back;

    To live in the Borderlands means
    the mill with the razor white teeth wants to shred off
    your olive-red skin, crush out the kernel, your heart
    pound you pinch you roll you out
40 smelling like white bread but dead;

    To survive the Borderlands
    you must live *sin fronteras*
    be a crossroads.

EXERCISES

Some of the Issues

1. The title of Anzaldúa's poem is also its beginning line and is repeated, with some variation, again and again. What is the effect of the near repetition and of the changes?
2. What might Anzaldúa gain by her use of Spanish words?

3. Throughout the poem, Anzaldúa speaks of borders within herself, and borders imposed by the outside world. What are these? Why is it sometimes difficult to tell the difference?

4. Anzaldúa often uses contradictory images in her poem. For example, in the third stanza she is both "a scapegoat" and the "forerunner of a new race." Find other pairs of opposing images. What is their effect?

5. What is "the mill with the razor white teeth" (line 37) and what is its danger?

6. What is Anzaldúa's suggestion for survival? What does she mean by it?

7. Although the author speaks of the difficulty of living in the borderlands, there are also indications of optimism. Which do you see as the principal message of the poem?

*8. Read Aurora Levins Morales's "Class Poem." Like Anzaldúa, she writes about her various heritages and their relationship to her current identity. What similarities and differences do you see between the two authors' points of view?

*9. Read Pico Iyer's "Home Is Every Place." Both authors talk about borders and use geography as a symbol of their own identity. Compare and contrast their views.

Some Subjects for Writing

10. Although not all of us are of mixed or battling heritages, most of us have felt split—*rajetas*—at some point in our lives. For example, we may feel both allegiance to and conflict with the identities prescribed by our family's traditions, our religion, our social class, or our society's ideas about appropriate gender roles. In an essay, describe a way in which you see yourself on the border of any of these identities or others important to you.

11. Do you think society is becoming more or less accepting of people who cross conventional roles of race, ethnicity, or gender? Why or why not? Write an essay giving evidence to support your views.

PART VIII
COMMUNICATING

How do we communicate? The first answer to come to most people's minds is through language: we speak, we listen, we read, we write. When we think further, we become increasingly aware that we also communicate in nonverbal ways, through gestures and other visual images. Increasingly, advances in technology—videos, faxes, e-mail, cell phones, voice mail, etc.—have in some ways decreased the necessity of personal, physical contact and have changed the ways in which our messages are relayed. On the other hand, the Internet and e-mail can allow us to share intimate details of our lives almost instantaneously with people we would otherwise never interact with in real life. These changes in communication also raise questions about the influence of technology on culture itself. Do changes in communication bring us closer to understanding each other or do they threaten to erode our unique cultural differences? Or both?

In general, communication is rarely a simple or straightforward endeavor. An obvious example might be if you speak only English and the person you wish to talk to speaks only Japanese. Communication will be limited—although you might be able to understand each other to some extent by means of gestures. But often the complexities are more subtle. Between speakers of the same language, problems may be the result of dialectal or intracultural differences, that is, language distinctions between subgroups. Gloria Naylor, in the first selection, alerts the reader to one such example concerning the use of an incendiary word that takes on different meanings within the African-American community.

The next two pieces deal with the intricate relationship between language and family. Amy Tan, in "Mother Tongue," talks about the effect of growing up in a world of mixed languages, including her mother's ungrammatical but richly expressive Chinese-influenced English. Tan's first attempts as a fiction writer used a stiff and formal style completely unlike the speech she had heard around her as she grew up. Her real career as a novelist begins when she takes advantage of all the Englishes she grew up with and writes with her mother as the imagined audience. In "Urdu, My Love Song," Rasma Haidri reflects on her relationship with her father using the metaphor of his mother tongue, Urdu. Her struggle with the language becomes symbolic of her complex and often conflicted view of her father—both he and Urdu are at once soothing and difficult to grasp.

The next four essays turn our eyes toward the media. Geraldine Brooks focuses on her town of Waterford, Virginia, and, using both irony and humor, recounts the story of how the townspeople fought back against the local cable company. In "Unplugged" she demonstrates that we, as individuals and communities, can make decisions that allow us to shape our environments regardless of larger changes in technology and communication. Alexis Bloom explores what happens when foreign television comes to Bhutan, a country that has prided itself on its isolation from the rest of the world. She looks not only at television's impact on people's interests and attitudes in Bhutan, but also proposes that it might influence how the Bhutanese communicate with one another through stories. She points out that as "sitcoms and action films become more popular, this transmission [of stories] becomes more fragile." Rob Walker explores the phenomenon of "The Hidden (In Plain Sight) Persuaders," everyday people who take part in word-of-mouth marketing campaigns. He questions not only how much this method has the potential to change advertising, but also the impact it could have on our everyday interactions with others.

In the poem that ends the book, Lisel Mueller shows us how the words we use and the stories we tell shape our lives.

The Meaning of a Word

Gloria Naylor

Gloria Naylor, a native of New York City, was born in 1950 and educated at Brooklyn College and Yale. She has taught at George Washington, New York, and Boston universities. Her first novel, The Women of Brewster Place *(1982), won an American Book Award. Her newest book, published in 2005, is a fictionalized memoir entitled* 1996. *The essay included here appeared in the* New York Times *on February 20, 1986.*

The word whose meaning Naylor learned was nigger. *She explains that she had heard it used quite comfortably by friends and relatives, but the way it was uttered to her by a white child in school was so different that she at first did not realize that it was the same word.*

1 Language is the subject. It is the written form with which I've managed to keep the wolf away from the door and, in diaries, to keep my sanity. In spite of this, I consider the written word inferior to the spoken, and much of the frustration experienced by novelists is the awareness that whatever we manage to capture in even the most transcendent passages falls far short of the richness of life. Dialogue achieves its power in the dynamics of a fleeting moment of sight, sound, smell and touch.

2 I'm not going to enter the debate here about whether it is language that shapes reality or vice versa. That battle is doomed to be waged whenever we seek intermittent reprieve from the chicken and egg dispute. I will simply take the position that the spoken word, like the written word, amounts to a nonsensical arrangement of sounds or letters without a consensus that assigns "meaning." And building from the meanings of what we hear, we order reality. Words themselves are innocuous; it is the consensus that gives them true power.

3 I remember the first time I heard the word nigger. In my third-grade class, our math tests were being passed down the rows, and as I handed the papers to a little boy in back of me, I remarked that once again he had received a much lower mark than I did. He snatched his test from me and spit out that word. Had he called me a nymphomaniac or a necrophiliac, I couldn't have been more puzzled. I didn't know what a nigger was, but I knew that whatever it meant, it was something he shouldn't have called me. This was verified when I raised my hand, and in a loud voice repeated what he had said and watched the teacher scold him for using a "bad" word. I was later to go home and ask the inevitable question that every black parent must face—"Mommy, what does 'nigger' mean?"

4   And what exactly did it mean? Thinking back, I realize that this could not have been the first time the word was used in my presence. I was part of a large extended family that had migrated from the rural South after World War II and formed a close-knit network that gravitated around my maternal grandparents. Their ground-floor apartment in one of the buildings they owned in Harlem was a weekend mecca for my immediate family, along with countless aunts, uncles and cousins who brought along assorted friends. It was a bustling and open house with assorted neighbors and tenants popping in and out to exchange bits of gossip, pick up an old quarrel or referee the ongoing checkers game in which my grandmother cheated shamelessly. They were all there to let down their hair and put up their feet after a week of labor in the factories, laundries and shipyards of New York.

5   Amid the clamor, which could reach deafening proportions—two or three conversations going on simultaneously, punctuated by the sound of a baby's crying somewhere in the back rooms or out on the street—there was still a rigid set of rules about what was said and how. Older children were sent out of the living room when it was time to get into the juicy details about "you-know-who" up on the third floor who had gone and gotten herself "p-r-e-g-n-a-n-t!" But my parents, knowing that I could spell well beyond my years, always demanded that I follow the others out to play. Beyond sexual misconduct and death, everything else was considered harmless for our young ears. And so among the anecdotes of the triumphs and disappointments in the various workings of their lives, the word nigger was used in my presence, but it was set within contexts and inflections that caused it to register in my mind as something else.

6   In the singular, the word was always applied to a man who had distinguished himself in some situation that brought their approval for his strength, intelligence or drive:

7   "Did Johnny *really* do that?"

8   "I'm telling you, that nigger pulled in $6,000 of overtime last year. Said he got enough for a down payment on a house."

9   When used with a possessive adjective by a woman—"my nigger"—it became a term of endearment for husband or boyfriend. But it could be more than just a term applied to a man. In their mouths it became the pure essence of manhood—a disembodied force that channeled their past history of struggle and present survival against the odds into a victorious statement of being: "Yeah, that old foreman found out quick enough—you don't mess with a nigger."

10   In the plural, it became a description of some group within the community that have overstepped the bounds of decency as my family defined it: Parents who neglected their children, a drunken couple who fought in public, people who simply refused to look for work, those with excessively dirty mouths or unkempt households were all "trifling niggers." This particular circle could forgive hard times, unemployment, the occasional bout of depression—they had gone through all of that themselves—but the unforgivable sin was a lack of self-respect.

11   A woman could never be a "nigger" in the singular, with its connotation of confirming worth. The noun girl was its closest equivalent in that sense, but only when used in direct address and regardless of the gender doing the addressing. "Girl" was a token of respect for a woman. The one-syllable word was drawn out to sound like three in recognition of the extra ounce of wit, nerve or daring that the woman had shown in the situation under discussion.

12   "G-i-r-l, stop. You mean you said that to his face?"

13   But if the word was used in a third-person reference or shortened so that it almost snapped out of my mouth, it always involved some element of communal disapproval. And age became an important factor in these exchanges. It was only between individuals of the same generation, or from an older person to a younger (but never the other way around), that "girl" would be considered a compliment.

14   I don't agree with the argument that use of the word nigger at this social stratum of the black community was an internalization of racism. The dynamics were the exact opposite: the people in my grandmother's living room took a word that whites used to signify worthlessness or degradation and rendered it impotent. Gathering there together, they transformed "nigger" to signify the varied and complex human beings they knew themselves to be. If the word was to disappear totally from the mouths of even the most liberal of white society, no one in that room was naïve enough to believe it would disappear from white minds. Meeting the word head-on, they proved it had absolutely nothing to do with the way they were determined to live their lives.

15   So there must have been dozens of times that the word "nigger" was spoken in front of me before I reached the third grade. But I didn't "hear" it until it was said by a small pair of lips that had already learned it could be a way to humiliate me. That was the word I went home and asked my mother about. And since she knew that I had to grow up in America, she took me in her lap and explained.

EXERCISES

Some of the Issues

1. What reasons does Naylor give for considering the spoken word superior to the written? Do you agree or disagree?
2. Reread paragraph 2. What, according to Naylor, gives meaning to words? Do you agree or disagree?
3. In paragraph 3 the author tells a story from her experience as a child. How does it relate to the general statement on language that she made in the first two paragraphs? What is it that made Naylor think that she had been called a "bad" word?

4. At the end of paragraph 5 and in the examples that follow, Naylor demonstrates that she had heard the word "nigger" before the boy in her class used it. Why did the previous uses register with her as something different?

The Way We Are Told

5. Naylor starts with a general statement—"Language is the subject"—which she then expands on in paragraphs 1 and 2. What focus does this beginning give her essay? How would the focus differ if she started with the anecdote in paragraph 3?
6. Naylor asserts that "the written word is inferior to the spoken." What devices does she use to help the reader *hear* the dialogue?
7. The essay consists of three parts: paragraphs 1 and 2, 3–13, and 14 and 15. The first is a general statement and the second an anecdote followed by records of conversations. How does the third part relate to the preceding two?

Some Subjects for Writing

8. Many words differ in their meaning depending on the circumstances in which they are used. Write a brief essay on the different words applied to a particular nationality or ethnic group and explain their impact.
*9. "Sticks and stones may break my bones but words can never hurt me." Do you have any experiences that would either confirm or deny the truth of that saying? You may also want to read Countee Cullen's poem "Incident."
10. Do you think teachers should set limits on language permitted in the classroom? Why or why not?

Mother Tongue

Amy Tan

Amy Tan was born in Oakland, California, in 1952, two years after her parents came to the United States from China.

Amy Tan's literary career was not planned—she first began writing fiction as a form of self-therapy. Considered a workaholic by her friends, Tan had been working 90 hours a week as a freelance technical writer; she hoped to eradicate her tendency to overwork by instead immersing herself in fiction writing. Her first efforts were stories, one of which secured her a place in a fiction writers' workshop. Tan's first novel, the semi-autobiographical The Joy Luck Club, *was published in 1989 and made into a very successful film. It tells the story of the lives of four Chinese women and their American daughters in California.*

Amy Tan's writing focuses on the lives of Chinese-American women; her novels introduce characters who are ambivalent, as she once was, about their Chinese background. Tan remarked in an interview that though she once tried to distance herself from her ethnicity, writing The Joy Luck Club *helped her discover "how very Chinese I was. And how much had stayed with me that I had tried to deny."*

Tan has since written four other novels, The Kitchen God's Wife *(1991),* The Hundred Secret Senses *(1996),* The Bonesetter's Daughter *(2001), and* Saving Fish From Drowning *(2005). She has also published a book of essays entitled* The Opposite of Fate *(2003).*

1   I am not a scholar of English or literature. I cannot give you much more than personal opinions on the English language and its variations in this country or others.

2   I am a writer. And by that definition, I am someone who has always loved language. I am fascinated by language in daily life. I spend a great deal of my time thinking about the power of language—the way it can evoke an emotion, a visual image, a complex idea, or a simple truth. Language is the tool of my trade. And I use them all—all the Englishes I grew up with.

3   Recently, I was made keenly aware of the different Englishes I do use. I was giving a talk to a large group of people, the same talk I had already given to half a dozen other groups. The nature of the talk was about my writing, my life, and my book, *The Joy Luck Club.* The talk was going along well enough, until I remembered one major difference that made the whole talk sound wrong. My mother was in the room. And it was perhaps the first time she had heard me give a lengthy speech, using the kind of English I have never used with her. I was

saying things like, "The intersection of memory upon imagination" and "There is an aspect of my fiction that relates to thus-and-thus"—a speech filled with carefully wrought grammatical phrases, burdened, it suddenly seemed to me, with nominalized forms, past perfect tenses, conditional phrases, all the forms of standard English that I had learned in school and through books, the forms of English I did not use at home with my mother.

4   Just last week, I was walking down the street with my mother, and I again found myself conscious of the English I was using, the English I do use with her. We were talking about the price of new and used furniture and I heard myself saying this: "Not waste money that way." My husband was with us as well, and he didn't notice any switch in my English. And then I realized why. It's because over the twenty years we've been together I've often used that same kind of English with him, and sometimes he even uses it with me. It has become our language of intimacy, a different sort of English that relates to family talk, the language I grew up with.

5   So you'll have some idea of what this family talk I heard sounds like, I'll quote what my mother said during a recent conversation which I videotaped and then transcribed. During this conversation, my mother was talking about a political gangster in Shanghai who had the same last name as her family's, Du, and how the gangster in his early years wanted to be adopted by her family, which was rich by comparison. Later, the gangster became more powerful, far richer than my mother's family, and one day showed up at my mother's wedding to pay his respects. Here's what she said in part:

6   "Du Yusong having business like fruit stand. Like off the street kind. He is Du like Du Zong—but not Tsung-ming Island people. The local people call putong, the river east side, he belong to that side local people. That man want to ask Du Zong father take him in like become own family. Du Zong father wasn't look down on him, but didn't take seriously, until that man big like become a mafia. Now important person, very hard to inviting him. Chinese way, came only to show respect, don't stay for dinner. Respect for making big celebration, he shows up. Mean gives lots of respect. Chinese custom. Chinese social life that way. If too important won't have to stay too long. He come to my wedding. I didn't see, I heard it. I gone to boy's side, they have YMCA dinner. Chinese age I was nineteen."

7   You should know that my mother's expressive command of English belies how much she actually understands. She reads the *Forbes* report, listens to *Wall Street Week*, converses daily with her stockbroker, reads all of Shirley MacLaine's books with ease—all kinds of things I can't begin to understand. Yet some of my friends tell me they understand 50 percent of what my mother says. Some say they understand 80 to 90 percent. Some say they understand none of it, as if she were speaking pure Chinese. But to me, my mother's English is perfectly clear, perfectly natural. It's my mother tongue. Her language, as I hear it, is vivid, direct, full of observation and imagery. That was the language that helped shape the way I saw things, expressed things, made sense of the world.

8   Lately, I've been giving more thought to the kind of English my mother speaks. Like others, I have described it to people as "broken" or "fractured" English. But I wince when I say that. It has always bothered me that I can think of no way to describe it other than "broken," as if it were damaged and needed to be fixed, as if it lacked a certain wholeness and soundness. I've heard other terms used, "limited English," for example. But they seem just as bad, as if everything is limited, including people's perceptions of the limited English speaker.

9   I know this for a fact, because when I was growing up, my mother's "limited" English limited my perception of her. I was ashamed of her English. I believed that her English reflected the quality of what she had to say. That is, because she expressed them imperfectly her thoughts were imperfect. And I had plenty of empirical evidence to support me: the fact that people in department stores, at banks, and at restaurants did not take her seriously, did not give her good service, pretended not to understand her, or even acted as if they did not hear her.

10   My mother has long realized the limitations of her English as well. When I was fifteen, she used to have me call people on the phone to pretend I was she. In this guise, I was forced to ask for information or even to complain and yell at people who had been rude to her. One time it was a call to her stockbroker in New York. She had cashed out her small portfolio and it just so happened we were going to go to New York the next week, our very first trip outside California. I had to get on the phone and say in an adolescent voice that was not very convincing, "This is Mrs. Tan."

11   And my mother was standing in the back whispering loudly, "Why he don't send me check, already two weeks late. So mad he lie to me, losing me money."

12   And then I said in perfect English, "Yes, I'm getting rather concerned. You had agreed to send the check two weeks ago, but it hasn't arrived."

13   Then she began to talk more loudly. "What he want, I come to New York tell him front of his boss, you cheating me?" And I was trying to calm her down, make her be quiet, while telling the stockbroker, "I can't tolerate any more excuses. If I don't receive the check immediately, I am going to have to speak to your manager when I'm in New York next week." And sure enough, the following week there we were in front of this astonished stockbroker, and I was sitting there red-faced and quiet, and my mother, the real Mrs. Tan, was shouting at his boss in her impeccable broken English.

14   We used a similar routine just five days ago, for a situation that was far less humorous. My mother had gone to the hospital for an appointment, to find out about a benign brain tumor a CAT scan had revealed a month ago. She said she had spoken very good English, her best English, no mistakes. Still, she said, the hospital did not apologize when they said they had lost the CAT scan and she had come for nothing. She said they did not seem to have any sympathy when she told them she was anxious to know the exact diagnosis, since her husband and son had both died of brain tumors. She said they would not give her any

more information until the next time and she would have to make another appointment for that. So she said she would not leave until the doctor called her daughter. She wouldn't budge. And when the doctor finally called her daughter, me, who spoke in perfect English—lo and behold—we had assurances the CAT scan would be found, promises that a conference call on Monday would be held, and apologies for any suffering my mother had gone through for a most regrettable mistake.

15   I think my mother's English almost had an effect on limiting my possibilities in life as well. Sociologists and linguists probably will tell you that a person's developing language skills are more influenced by peers. But I do think that the language spoken in the family, especially in immigrant families which are more insular, plays a large role in shaping the language of the child. And I believe that it affected my results on achievement tests, IQ tests, and the SAT. While my English skills were never judged as poor, compared to math, English could not be considered my strong suit. In grade school I did moderately well, getting perhaps B's, sometimes B-pluses, in English and scoring perhaps in the sixtieth or seventieth percentile on achievement tests. But those scores were not good enough to override the opinion that my true abilities lay in math and science, because in those areas I achieved A's and scored in the ninetieth percentile or higher.

16   This was understandable. Math is precise; there is only one correct answer. Whereas, for me at least, the answers on English tests were always a judgment call, a matter of opinion and personal experience. Those tests were constructed around items like fill-in-the-blank sentence completion, such as, "Even though Tom was _____, Mary thought he was _____." And the correct answer always seemed to be the most bland combinations of thoughts, for example, "Even though Tom was shy, Mary thought he was charming," with the grammatical structure "even though" limiting the correct answer to some sort of semantic opposites, so you wouldn't get answers like, "Even though Tom was foolish, Mary thought he was ridiculous." Well, according to my mother, there were very few limitations as to what Tom could have been and what Mary might have thought of him. So I never did well on tests like that.

17   The same was true with word analogies, pairs of words in which you were supposed to find some sort of logical, semantic relationship—for example, "*Sunset* is to *nightfall* as _____ is to _____." And here you would be presented with a list of four possible pairs, one of which showed the same kind of relationship: *red* is to *stoplight, bus* is to *arrival, chills* is to *fever, yawn* is to *boring.* Well, I could never think that way. I knew what the tests were asking, but I could not block out of my mind the images already created by the first pair, "*sunset* is to *nightfall*"—and I would see a burst of colors against a darkening sky, the moon rising, the lowering of a curtain of stars. And all the other pairs of words—red, bus, stoplight, boring—just threw up a mass of confusing images, making it impossible for me to sort out something as logical as saying: "A sunset precedes nightfall" is the same as "a chill precedes a fever." The only way I would have

gotten that answer right would have been to imagine an associative situation, for example, my being disobedient and staying out past sunset, catching a chill at night, which turns into feverish pneumonia as punishment, which indeed did happen to me.

18   I have been thinking about all this lately, about my mother's English, about achievement tests. Because lately I've been asked, as a writer, why there are not more Asian Americans represented in American literature. Why are there few Asian Americans enrolled in creative writing programs? Why do so many Chinese students go into engineering? Well, these are broad sociological questions I can't begin to answer. But I have noticed in surveys—in fact, just last week—that Asian students, as a whole, always do significantly better on math achievement tests than in English. And this makes me think that there are other Asian-American students whose English spoken in the home might also be described as "broken" or "limited." And perhaps they also have teachers who are steering them away from writing and into math and science, which is what happened to me.

19   Fortunately, I happen to be rebellious in nature and enjoy the challenge of disproving assumptions made about me. I became an English major my first year in college, after being enrolled as pre-med. I started writing nonfiction as a freelancer the week after I was told by my former boss that writing was my worst skill and I should hone my talents toward account management.

20   But it wasn't until 1985 that I finally began to write fiction. And at first I wrote using what I thought to be wittily crafted sentences, sentences that would finally prove I had mastery over the English language. Here's an example from the first draft of a story that later made its way into *The Joy Luck Club*, but without this line: "That was my mental quandary in its nascent state." A terrible line, which I can barely pronounce.

21   Fortunately, for reasons I won't get into today, I later decided I should envision a reader for the stories I would write. And the reader I decided upon was my mother, because these were stories about mothers. So with this reader in mind—and in fact she did read my early drafts—I began to write stories using all the Englishes I grew up with: the English I spoke to my mother, which for lack of a better term might be described as "simple"; the English she used with me, which for lack of a better term might be described as "broken"; my translation of her Chinese, which could certainly be described as "watered down"; and what I imagined to be her translation of her Chinese if she could speak in perfect English, her internal language, and for that I sought to preserve the essence, but neither an English nor a Chinese structure. I wanted to capture what language ability tests can never reveal: her intent, her passion, her imagery, the rhythms of her speech and the nature of her thoughts.

22   Apart from what any critic had to say about my writing, I knew I had succeeded where it counted when my mother finished reading my book and gave me her verdict: "So easy to read."

EXERCISES

Some of the Issues

1. What are some possible meanings of the title of Tan's essay?
2. In paragraph 3, how does Tan describe the language used in the speech she made?
3. In paragraph 6, Tan gives us a sample of her mother's speech transcribed from a videotape. Rewrite the paragraph in a more standard from of English. What changes did you need to make? Did you have any difficulty understanding what her mother meant?
4. Why, in paragraphs 8 and 9, does Tan object to the terms "broken" or "fractured" or "limited" English?
5. As a child, how did Tan view her mother's "limited" English (paragraph 9)? What evidence does Tan present that her childhood perception was false?
6. On two occasions, Tan's mother asks her daughter to speak on her behalf— the incident with the stockbroker (paragraphs 10–13) and the more recent incident at the hospital (paragraph 14). Describe each incident. Why are they significant?
7. In paragraphs 15 through 17 Tan talks about how growing up in a family that did not have complete control of English may have affected her ability to do well on standardized English tests. What are the examples she cites of typical questions on those tests? Do you think other imaginative people, even if they did not grow up in an immigrant family, might have trouble with such questions?
8. In paragraph 18, Tan states that she and many other Asian-Americans select, or are guided toward, careers in which mastery of language is less important than skills in math or science. What, according to Tan, are the consequences of this?
9. What were the steps in Tan's own development as a writer (paragraphs 19–22)?

The Way We Are Told

10. Tan begins her essay by telling you about herself—her limitations and her interests. What does she gain by doing this?
11. Tan uses quotations at several points in the essay to illustrate both her mother's language and her own. Find several of these quotations and explain how they help support Tan's ideas about the different Englishes she understands and uses.
12. Why does Amy Tan's mother have the last word in the essay?
13. Writing teachers have probably talked to you about the importance of imagining a reader or an audience when you write. Who does Tan say was the imagined audience for her novel? Who is the audience for this essay?

Some Subjects for Writing

14. Describe an experience in which you felt either very limited or particularly effective when speaking or writing. For example, you could describe a time you took a test and forgot everything you studied because of nervousness or a time in which you managed to explain your ideas or feelings particularly well to a friend.

15. Tan talks about the challenge of disproving early negative assumptions about her abilities as a writer. Write an essay explaining a time in which you, or someone you know, managed to succeed despite others' predictions of failure.

16. Tan tells in paragraphs 2 and 21 of her attempts to use "all the Englishes [she] grew up with." Even if we do not grow up in a bilingual family, as Tan did, we all use several versions of English, depending on audience and situations. For example, we probably use a more relaxed vocabulary and more incomplete sentences when talking with friends about a subject we know well than when we are giving a presentation in class.

    Spend some time listening to your own speech and that of others in various settings. Keep a small notebook with you to jot down what you hear as accurately as possible, or use a tape recorder. Then write up your observations in a short paper.

17. Tan cites evidence that Asian-American students often major in math, science, or engineering, even when they have talents in other areas. Find out if this is the case at your university and, if possible, interview several students about their choices of majors. You could also study sources in the library that would give you information about choice of professions by different ethnic groups. Write the results of what you have found out in a short paper, citing the sources of your information.

Urdu, My Love Song

Rasma Haidri

Rasma Haidri grew up in Oak Ridge, Tennessee, the daughter of an Indian father and a Wisconsin-born Norwegian mother. Her writing has appeared in literary journals including Nimrod, Prairie Schooner, Fourth Genre, Ice Floe, *and* Kalliope. *"Urdu, My Love Song," for which she received the Southern Women Writers Conference Emerging Writer Award in creative nonfiction, was published in the anthology* Waking Up American: Coming of Age Biculturally *(2005). Haidri has taught French, English, remedial reading, poetry, and creative writing. She currently lives with her daughter on the arctic coast of Norway.*

Urdu is the native language of Haidri's father, and though she herself never learns to speak more than a few words of it, it plays a role of great importance in her sense of family and identity. It also provides a framework for her attempts to understand and unravel the complexities of her relationship with her father.

1   In a restaurant called Gandhi, a sari-clad woman brings rice to my table and I want to say *shukria*. The word rolls down my tongue, then stops before my dread of being wrong. It is one of the few Urdu words I know, and I think it means "thank you." Or does it mean "please"? On the other hand, *shukria* may have something to do with sugar. I'm unsure. All I know is I learned the word from my father in India during my first visit to his homeland. He most likely explained the word to me in his Dr. S. Zafar Ali Haidri manner of learned professor instructing pupil.

2   "So you see, honey, the word *shukria*, when pronounced in the Hindi, *shoo-KRI-ah*, in this region of India means 'thank you, kindly.' However, when pronounced in the Urdu of the Punjab as *SHU-kri-ah*, it means most simply 'please.' "

3   Probably none of this is accurate. At age twenty I was too sure of myself to take notes, so now, twenty years later, I'm too unsure of the meaning of *shukria* to try it out on the waitress.

4   My confusion around *shukria* and the overlapping meanings of "please" and "thank you" is confounded by the fact that my father used these words differently than anyone else I knew growing up in the South in the 1960s. He was a biochemist, a Fulbright scholar from the Indian Subcontinent whose work in pharmaceutical research had brought us to Oak Ridge, Tennessee, Atomic City U.S.A. True to his image as an upper-class Indian, my father always wore a three-piece suit. To my chagrin, he even attended my Girl Scout father-daughter picnic in this attire, and further embarrassed me by saying

"please" (meaning "yes") when offered a slab of Jell-O, and "thank you" (meaning "no, of course not, you filthy infidel!") when someone made the faux pas of offering him a hunk of ham.

5   We lived in Wiltshire Estates, a settlement of farmettes within the Oak Ridge city limits. Our neighbor Mr. McNabb, in stark contrast to my father, was a true Southerner. The McNabb yard was a mess of tractor tires, odd pieces of metal, and a gaggle of kids and dogs named Mickey, Mackey, Marty, Mitsy, Mindy, and Misery. Mr. McNabb, being neighborly, would lean over our oak-rail fence, remove the chaw-straw from his mouth, and offer, "Howbow summadose toon'p gweens?" I accepted the turnip greens and brought them to my mother, a Wisconsin-born Norwegian, who giggled as I imitated Mr. McNabb's hillbilly talk, and then shoved the greens into the growl of the garbage disposal. She had no idea how to cook them. If my father were around, he would hack them up in a curry and serve them alongside rice and mango chilies. And if he heard me and my brothers mocking Mr. McNabb's vernacular, he would yelp, "Nyaap! Bad manners!" and send us out of the room with a wave of his cuff-linked, manicured hand.

6   My brothers and I grew up in a linguistic no-man's-land between our well-educated Asian father and our hillbilly neighbor. To us, the word "please" (followed by the obligatory-and-punishable-by-hellfire-if-omitted "ma'am" or "sir") preceded requests such as, "May I have another helping of that bodacious marshmallow salad?" "Thank you (ma'am or sir)" was what we said before stabbing the sticky mess with a fork. Unlike my father or Mr. McNabb, we spoke "normal" English.

7   My father's English included other oddities, such as "up-a-stairs," which sent us rolling on the floor in convulsions every time we heard it. There were stories from our parents' early years, when my dad thought a baby sitter was a kind of chair they were going to leave one of us in, or that fried chicken wings were called "flies." My father understood the comic value of his lingo and exercised it to the fullest. His regular deadpan reference to my friend Peggy Mead as "Meggy Peed" never failed to send my mother into a fit of red-faced laughter. I didn't laugh. My father's feigned inability to learn my own best friend's name was an annoying reminder that he was different, and therefore the rest of us had to be, too.

8   My father's outsider language and peculiar accent were just part of his overall eccentricity. It was impossible to figure him out. His formal dress and fasting at Christmas were oddly juxtaposed with his applying his background in physical science to our dog, who had been hit by a car. He set the creature's broken leg with a stick and bandaging tape, and stitched up the wounds with mercerized cotton thread. One afternoon I came home to find him butchering one of our sheep in the storeroom. At times he worked for several drug companies at once and would disappear for months on business to places like New Brunswick and Grosse Pointe Woods, whose very names connoted illusions of grandeur. For the longest time I believed that "Miami" was his "Ami." For the most part,

his absences were a welcome reprieve from the intensity of his presence. When he was home, I could be snagged into one of his somnolent lectures on an endless array of scholarly topics, ranging from the history of Islam to the workings of the carburetor engine. I wondered what life was like for kids with normal dads who spoke normal English and, for example, knew something about baseball.

9   I enjoyed some of my father's quirks. He brought home RC Cola, which no one else seemed to know about. He filled glass jars with a perfect mixture of salty cashews and moist yellow raisins. He could create a delicious meal from whatever he found around the kitchen, and for breakfast he served strong creamy tea and a one-egg omelet folded neatly in the center of my plate like a good-news letter. He told us an Indian folk tale that included a banana leaf SO BIG that his wide arms pushed us helter-skelter off the bed. When he sang to us in Urdu, the words themselves were pure music. As much as I was vexed by his English, I was entranced by the exotic and mysterious tones of his native tongue.

10   When I was nine, the ladies from the Baptist Outreach Mission offered to take us kids to church on Sundays. When they came to the door my mom decided I was of age and offered me up like a little lamb. As an agnostic Lutheran, she reckoned that some religion was better for me than none. And my father, who was away most of the time anyway, knew the Bible Belt provided no Muslim alternative. He was content to let us kids grow up to be regular Christian Americans.

11   If only it had been that easy.

12   I sat in the golden oak pew in Robertsville Baptist Church on my first Sunday, rubbing my thumb over a pearly white pin with blue letters that spelled VISITOR. "No thank you, ma'am," I said to the flowery-smelling ladies from the Outreach who asked if I wanted to Go Forward at the Call and Be Saved. I liked being a visitor. I liked my smooth white button with the blue letters. I wasn't at all sure I liked what was going on up front where the preacher was waving his arms and shouting, and people were sobbing into their hands.

13   Down in the Sunday school classroom, pretty Miss Thomas smiled at us and talked, but I wasn't paying attention to her words. I wondered if she knew there was a color difference between her face and her neck where the makeup ended. I decided that when I grew up I'd rub the makeup all the way down my neck so it wouldn't show. I'd rub it all the way into my blouse. As I stared at Miss Thomas's white pillar neck between her pale lemon suit and black flipped-out hair, I noticed that she was talking about other religions. I raised my hand and said that my father was a Muslim, we were raised like Muslims and didn't eat pork, not even ham at Christmas. Once my mom hid bacon in the freezer because she was a Lutheran, I said, but we had to make sure it was gone before my dad came home so we ate the whole package before his plane landed and I got a headache. And one time our mom gave our dad a leather notepad with his name stamped on it in gold, but he yelled and she cried because on the back it

said GENUINE PIGSKIN, and what was she thinking? Our hot dogs were called "beef franks" and our language was Urdu. I could read it and write it, and, yes, next Sunday I'd bring some in to show the class.

14   I left the church sickened by the gravity of my deception. Days passed in fear and dread until I was engulfed in an all-encompassing existential numbness. I spent Saturday afternoon crouched on the carpet slowly fashioning curlicues on a square of paper with a fat lead pencil. This was Urdu. At least this was sort of what Urdu looked like in the exotic books next to the *Physicians' Desk Reference* behind the glass doors of my father's mahogany bookcase.

15   My father wasn't home that week, but I would not have approached him with my problem if he had been. I had told the Sunday school class that I could read, write, and speak Urdu, and the enormity of the lie made me unable to admit the deception even to myself, not to mention my father. Even pretty Miss Thomas's smile couldn't pierce the wall of self-delusion that insulated me from the fact that my language resembled Mr. McNabb's more than my own father's. The truth was that Urdu, along with banana leaves, elephants, tigers, and the buttery ghee that made Little Black Sambo's pancakes so delicious, was not really part of my life. I wanted it to be, but it wasn't. I was just a skinny brown girl running barefoot in the hills of Tennessee, scooped up by Baptists and dressed in Sunday clothes with a nickel in the palm of my white glove for the collection basket.

16   Sunday again. I sat stiff and wordless in my pew as the throng sang "Softly and Tenderly Jesus Is Calling!" and the Saved Went Forward at the Call. Instead of a white VISITOR button, I held the piece of Urdu writing I had promised Miss Thomas. Down in the Sunday school classroom I unfolded the small page for all to see. Then, ignoring the look of concern on Miss Thomas's face, I read my Islamic scripture to the class.

17   "*Nnngha-chokri goo dal!*" I began, imitating the sounds that flowed like song from my father's throat when he talked on the phone to Karachi. "*Chaa-beep hoori gangani? Gung challee lohr reena!*" and so on. I continued for minutes. When I finished, Miss Thomas's eyes were wide open and her skin above the jawline a deeper shade than usual. She cracked out a small "thank you." I sat down and stuffed the paper deep inside my zippered black leather King James Bible.

18   That's all I remember of Sunday school at Robertsville Baptist Church. I never did go Forward to Be Saved and I must have been a great disappointment to Miss Thomas and the ladies of the Outreach Mission. My disappointment with myself was too grave to register. At home, I ripped up the piece of hateful scribbling, tearing it over and over, driven by confusion, self-loathing, and a fearful panic that someone would find it.

19   When I was twelve I was introduced to the secrets of the sari. We were in Manhattan, where we often spent summers since my father kept an apartment there for work. A Hindi business associate of his took it upon herself to teach me how to fold, tuck, and drape the long cloth over my still boyish body. Then

she gave me a sari to keep. It was yellow chiffon with silver embroidery and had an orange midriff-baring top. All summer I practiced folding the long sheer cloth, and wore the sari over jeans in case of accidental unfurling.

20   One afternoon my father double-parked the car to run an errand, leaving me in charge of my little brother. I felt important in the driver's seat, traffic grinding past my window. Suddenly my brother opened the back door and started to get out, right into the street. The scene is frozen in my memory: my brother in a striped polo shirt, Beatles haircut, one leg still in the car; me, exiting through the open driver's window, my long brown arm trailing yellow chiffon; the avenue, resounding with Manhattan's symphony—horns, motors, brakes, shouts; and then the clean, clear snap of a newspaper being opened by a man jaywalking toward our car. I noticed the man at the moment I grabbed my brother and started scolding him at the top of my lungs in something resembling primeval screams:

21   "*Djeepchok kali sin heh nodra! Guldoobi kahan fedrani!*"

22   As my fake Urdu poured forth, the man looked up from his newspaper and met my eyes. For an instant I wondered if he knew that I was not really a fascinating foreign national speaking an exotic tongue. Did he see the blue jeans under my sari? My brother staggered stunned and pale back into the car, and I opened the door to resume my place in the driver's seat. There was something awful happening here, something deceitful and unbearably pathetic, but I let it go. I tried neither to understand nor explain it. I knew my brother was too little to be able to relate this scene to my father, or worse, to the woman whose yellow sari I wore. I let myself believe that I had pulled it off and that the man with the newspaper had been duly impressed by my exotic dress and speech. He saw that I was no ordinary American. But deep down I knew. I knew that this strange outburst just showed how lost I was, cut off from the land of my birthright and the elusive mysteries of my glorious ancestral tongue.

23   When I was twenty-one I got married. We gave my parents three days' notice of the wedding. My mother immediately fell to worrying, while my father announced he would make the cake. The night before the wedding, he stayed up baking cakes of descending sizes from whatever we had on hand of assorted mixes. He formed these into a pyramid, which he inscribed with pink Arabic script like the marble detail embedded in the Taj Mahal. I never thanked my father for that cake. We were young, caught up in our ultra-nontraditional wedding, and didn't think we even needed a cake. Now I see it was the most generous gift. How my father must have innovated in our poorly equipped kitchen to make different-sized layers, two colors of frosting, and something with which to write. The inscription was Urdu love poetry or marriage verses from the Koran. He told us, but I don't remember. In one photograph, my husband and I are standing with my parents behind the cake. My mother looks distressed. My father is smiling behind dark sunglasses. There might have been a joke on the order of "Meggy Peed" written on that cake, but only he would have known.

24   The winter after I got married, I wrote to my father asking about a song he used to sing when we were little. *May-rahah-salam-alay-ajum.* It was, and

remains, the most tender memory of my childhood. I missed that song. I longed for it. I asked him to record it for me. Perhaps I could learn it and someday sing it for my own children. At Christmas it arrived: a homemade cassette with "Urdu Wedding Songs" written on it in both Urdu and English. For weeks I played the tape and attempted to sing along, but the bell-like tone of my father singing Urdu was a music my voice could not make. After a while I packed the tape away, worried it would break with wear and I would lose the song forever.

25   When my daughter was five, her Montessori preschool introduced the children to Indian culture. I suggested she write and tell my father about it. "Ask Nano to teach you the Urdu alphabet," I said. She called him "Nano" instead of "Grandfather," just as at her age I called him "Abba" instead of "Daddy." A short while later her study packet arrived: homemade flash cards of the Urdu alphabet scripted in Arabic with phonetic English renditions and a cassette tape for pronunciation. It was a full-blown Dr. S. Zafar Ali production—each letter was an artistic composition, and the tape included a short history of the etymology of Urdu as well as pronunciation exercises. We admired the cards and listened to my father's sonorous voice on the scratchy tape. But neither my daughter nor I learned the Urdu alphabet.

26   Each time we moved, I worried about the cards being lost. "Where are those flash cards Nano made you?" I would ask, and my daughter would dutifully produce them. I would take out the cards and examine the letters that still resembled art more than language, then tuck them back into the Chase Manhattan check box my father had sent them in. Having the cards seemed proof that Urdu was still part of my life. Someday my daughter would learn the alphabet. Maybe I would, too. But that conviction was as transparent as the yellow sari I kept carefully wrapped up in a box. Even after visits with my Karachi cousins and traveling across India, *shukria* (meaning "please" or "thank you" or "sugar") and *challo* (meaning "get a move on" to a rickshaw driver) is all the Urdu I know how to say.

27   I did learn how to write my name. "Rasma" is Latvian, but my father chose the name for its resonance with his language. "So you see, honey, *RAHZ-ma* in Arabic means 'my flower.' However, *Rah-ZI-ma*, in Persian, from which we have derived Urdu, means 'my secret' or 'our secret' in the manner in which you are your mother's and my secret." I even attempted a semester of Urdu in college, but my name remains the one word I know how to write in my father's language. *Rasma.* My secret.

28   When my father died, his younger brother ordered a Muslim burial. My mother and I knew my father would want to be cremated, but my uncle said this was abhorrent. Without a proper Muslim burial my father's soul would roam the earth disconsolate. *Hindus* were cremated. I wondered if this had been my father's intent, a sly last jab at his brothers whom he loved to provoke with religious arguments. Nonetheless, my mother and I agreed to let the Islamic Center take care of everything.

29   At the funeral, my mother and my daughter and I were relegated to the women's section. It was a vast room with mirrors covering the length of one wall

and not a stick of furniture in it. My uncle had instructed us to wear head scarves. We shuffled around, avoiding ourselves in the mirrors and not daring to speak as rhythmic chanting rose from the men's section on the other side of the wall. I searched in vain for peepholes to get a glimpse of what was going on. When my uncle came in, I asked to see my father's body. He said it was not possible, that women could not enter the prayer hall. When I insisted, he consulted with the mullah, who allowed me to come in for just a moment. I wasn't a Muslim woman anyway.

30   My father, wrapped in a white shroud, was lying on a straw mat on the floor with all his teeth removed and the blue-ink tattoo on his right bicep clearly visible. It startled me. I hadn't seen that tattoo for years, not since I was little enough to call him Abba. He would lie on the floor in his undershirt, lifting me on his feet to guess my weight. The tattoo had been given to my father by the Royal Indian Army to signify his status as a Muslim. It was the name of God, and to me it looked like a single harmonious letter from the Urdu card pack. I loved that tattoo. I wanted to possess it. A scheme of cutting it out of his arm rushed madly through my head. I longed for that tattoo as much as I had longed for my father's song the first winter of my adulthood. But now I was being ushered out. I looked up over the sea of men bending and bowing over a myriad of small prayer rugs. My brothers looked as helpless as I felt. They couldn't even mouth these prayers for our father. Who were all these strangers? Where was my father's prayer rug and his blue-cloth Koran? How could we save his tattoo? Then, from some recess in my being, or from the air just above my right ear, I heard the peculiar voice that as a child had sometimes made me cringe and sometimes dream of dappled jungle leaves and elephants. "Oh honey," my father said, "it does not matter."

31   I felt a weight lift from my shoulders. I looked around and saw how, to my father, this could all be quite amusing. His women trying to be demure while fighting off scarves that wanted to slip over our noses; his sons mute and awkward in three-piece suits and sanctified bare feet; himself, our only translator, dead on the floor.

32   "Oh honey, it does not matter."

33   It was true. I smiled to myself, and took one last look at the beautiful sky-blue tattoo. This was Urdu. It had come to me, and was leaving, with my father. Its mysterious curves were inextricable from him, indelibly marked on his skin. But all my life I had heard its love song. It didn't matter that it could never be mine.

EXERCISES

Some of the Issues

1. What does the opening paragraph tell us about the author? How does it highlight the theme of her narrative?

2. What impression do you have of Haidri's father? What details give you that impression?

3. How does Haidri set up the contrast between her family and her neighbors in Oak Ridge, Tennessee (paragraphs 4–6)? How did you feel about Haidri's portrayal of Mr. McNabb?

4. What was your response to the sentence: "My father's feigned inability to learn my own best friend's name was an annoying reminder that he was different, and therefore the rest of us had to be, too"?

5. What are some of Haidri's conflicted feelings toward her father? To what extent are these conflicts rooted in language?

6. What prompts Haidri to deceive her Sunday school class?

7. How did you read Miss Thomas's reaction to Haidri's Urdu (paragraph 17)?

8. Why do you suppose the flash cards her father sends her daughter are so important to Haidri, even though she never learns the Urdu alphabet (paragraphs 25–26)?

9. Describe Haidri's feelings at her father's funeral. What accounts for those feelings? What finally comforts her?

10. What does Haidri ultimately seem to learn from her father?

11. Why does Haidri view language as such an important part of personal identity? How important do you think it is?

The Way We Are Told

12. How old is Haidri when she writes this narrative? Does she always seem to be writing from an adult perspective? How does her perspective change as she grows older?

13. How does Haidri use humor throughout her narrative? Provide specific examples from the text.

Some Issues for Writing

14. Write a narrative about a situation or a circumstance that you see differently now than you did as a child. You might, for example, focus on a relative who you now view differently; your changed attitudes toward the place you grew up or your family home; or your perception of elementary or middle school both now and then. Like Haidri, use details to give the reader a clear sense of how you saw things at the time and try to convey a clear sense of the motivations behind those perceptions.

*15. Read Amy Tan's "Mother Tongue." Using examples from both Tan and Haidri's essays, as well as from your own experience, write an essay in which you analyze the ways our parents' language can influence our own sense of language and identity. How does language work to connect or disconnect us to family members? Can language influence the complicated power relationships between parents and children?

Unplugged

Geraldine Brooks

Geraldine Brooks is a native of Australia and a graduate of Sydney University and the Columbia University School of Journalism. She has spent extensive time in the Middle East, is a former foreign correspondent for the Wall Street Journal. She is the author of Nine Parts of Desire *(1995), a book about Arab women, a memoir,* Foreign Correspondence: A Pen Pal's Journey From Down Under to All Over *(1998), and two novels,* Year of Wonders: A Novel of the Plague *(2001), and* March *(2005), which won the Pulitzer Prize for fiction.*

In "Unplugged," Brooks reflects on the question of whether to bring cable television to Waterford, the small town in Virginia where she lives. The residents of Waterford are seen as eccentric because they choose to reject "more than seventy channels of the finest programming available" and question whether the information and entertainment brought to us by mass media expands our horizons or compromises our individuality.

1   Jake came to dinner a few weeks ago. We talked about the nine muses, and why tragedy is important in human storytelling. Jake has been reading a lot of Greek mythology lately. He's eight. A few nights later, Jake's dad, Mike, and I walked up the hill to the old schoolhouse for a Citizens' Association meeting about bringing cable TV to Waterford, a town of 250 people in the foothills of Virginia's Blue Ridge Mountains. The hills do terrible things to TV reception.

2   The president of the cable company had come to tell us that it probably wasn't a moneymaker for him to string the cable all the way out to our eighty-some houses, but he felt it was only right to give us the chance to partake of the rich offerings of his service. He passed around the latest full-color guide describing what we were missing that month. The cover featured Melanie Griffith. If we had cable, we would have been able to watch her in the movie *Milk Money.*

3   Mike's house on Main Street doesn't have a TV. But like most houses here, it has broad views of farmland rolling away to the wooded hillside, and big, old maples in the garden. From the high meadow behind town you can look at the Catoctin Creek as it wends through the valley, and see why the young Pennsylvania Quaker, Amos Janney, figured back in 1733 that this would be a fine place to build a mill.

4   The mill is still there, and like most buildings in town, it has American history written into the horsehair mortar holding up its walls. Just opposite, there's a stone house whose Quaker inhabitant found slaves a worse evil than war, even though fighting for the Union caused him to be read out of Meeting for violating pacifist principles. The Baptist church on the High Street still has bullet

holes in the bricks from the skirmish that took place there between the Confederates and Waterford's Loudoun Rangers, the only regiment raised in Virginia that fought on the Union side.

5   There aren't many Quakers here now, but they left behind a tradition of stubborn singularity. The townspeople—farmers and carpenters who've always lived here, artists and software designers who've arrived more recently—like the fact that this place is different: always has been, always will.

6   At the Citizens' Association meeting, the cable guy brags about how his service offers "more than seventy channels of the finest programming available." Mike, beside me, fidgets on his chair. Suddenly, he's speaking, softly and diffidently, as he always does.

7   "People here have time to talk to each other. I'm proud of our bad TV reception because it gets us out of our houses, and I'd kind of hate that to change because there's nine different football games to watch. Personally, I'd rather go fishing than watch the fishing channel."

8   The cable man doesn't realize that this is one of those Martin Luther moments, and that Mike has just nailed the theses to the door. His tone, when he replies, is unctuously patronizing.

9   "Well, that's your opinion and you're certainly entitled to it. But do you have a child?" Mike nods. "Then you should think about his future. He's going to be at a disadvantage when he gets to college and has to compete with young people who've been exposed to all the marvelous information that cable can bring them."

10   People who know Mike's boy Jake burst into loud guffaws. "That's bullshit!" shouts our neighbor Phil, sitting in back. And suddenly the tone of the meeting has changed, changed utterly. If Waterford could stand up to the Confederate States of America, it certainly can stand up to Cablevision of Loudoun County.

11   Someone who has just moved out here from a suburb that has Cablevision is on her feet, saying what a bunch of crap the programs are, and how she had canceled her subscription after a couple of months.

12   "Haven't you ever heard of books?" someone else shouts. "There's more 'marvelous information' in the local library than's on seven hundred cable channels!" Last year, the county decided that Waterford was too small to warrant visits from the Bookmobile. We had a meeting about that, too. Our neighbors Casey and Jeff donated the front room of their house—a bay-windowed storefront that used to be the village milliner—so we'd have a place to put a cooperative library.

13   That meeting wasn't nearly as loud as this one. The decibels don't come down until someone gets us off on a discussion of the life of Thomas Jefferson, and whether one could say it was impoverished for lack of television.

14   People barely notice when the cable man melts away. The next speaker is our neighbor Mary, who wants to tell us about laying rumble strips to slow the traffic through town. "Well," she says, raising an eyebrow, "I'm not sure I want to get up in front of *this* crowd!"

15   The next morning, when we meet up at the post office to pick up our mail, a few of us allow that we feel a bit sheepish about more or less running the cable man out of town. But then we look up at the ugly tangle of power lines—one of the few twentieth-century intrusions in town—and consider how one more big thick cable running along up there would make it even more unsightly, and less likely that we'll ever realize the village's long-standing dream of getting the things buried.

16   Marie, who lives right across from the post office, grows a morning glory vine every spring. She trains it up the power pole in front of her balcony, and lets the wires become a trellis for a cascade of royal blue blooms. In summer, a team from the power company came out intending to chop the vine down. Marie gave them each a cup of tea and a fresh-baked scone, then put them on the phone with the local agricultural extension agent, who explained that morning glory is a tender annual that will be gone with the first frost. The team finished their tea, and decided they'd leave the flowers be.

17   In less than a week, word of the Waterford Cable Rebellion filtered to the outside world. It seems we're the first town in the United States to resist it. Reporters from the *Washington Post*, CBS news, Fox network, and even South Korean TV showed up and filed bemused, "can-you-believe-it" features about the bunch of oddball hayseeds who don't want cable.

18   It's become eccentric not to want every place to be just like every other place. It isn't just the cable. Waterford is battling a new law that says the eighty buildings here, which have done just fine for 250 years without addresses, must now post three-inch-high, light-reflecting, five-digit street numbers to fit in with a county-wide grid system. One tiny lane has all of three cottages. But the first house will have to post a number that makes it 15545 Butchers Row.

19   Perhaps we'd have a better chance of holding on to what's here if the history it represented was linked with the museum-like grand estate of some long-ago rich man. But what's here isn't grand. These cottages and ice houses and root cellars are the templates of ordinary lives.

20   The old rooms have a way of slowly shaping you to fit them. You arrive here thinking you simply must have more built-in closets, but instead find yourself shedding your excess wardrobe. You open up the old stone-lined, hand-dug well so your arms can feel the effort of hauling a full water-bucket up thirty feet. I suppose, if we had cable, I could be watching *Body by Jake* on the Family Channel instead.

21   Down on Main Street, my neighbor Jake is toning his biceps by helping his dad stack the woodpile. I think I'll amble down there and have a word with him about a Corinthian king named Sisyphus.

EXERCISES

Some of the Issues

1. Brooks briefly describes two scenarios in her opening paragraph. How do they serve as an introduction to her essay?
2. What historical events or moments does Brooks recount? How does she use this history to help her make her point?
3. Why is it ironic that the cable representative refers specifically to Mike's child in paragraph 9?
*4. Consider Brooks's statement: "It's become eccentric not to want every place to be just like every other place" (paragraph 18). For a different point of view, read Pico Iyer's "Home Is Every Place." What are the perspectives presented by each author? What are your own views on the subject?
5. Brooks presents a very positive view of Waterford. Some might see her as nostalgic or overly resistant to change. What do you think?

The Way We Are Told

6. Why do you suppose Brooks chose this title for the essay?
7. What tone does Brooks use to portray the cable representative in paragraph 2? Where else in the essay do you notice a similar tone?
8. Brooks's thesis is implied rather than directly stated. If you were to develop a thesis statement for her essay, what might it be?

Some Subjects for Writing

9. Brooks presents two different views of cable television: those of the cable representative and those of the townspeople and herself. Whose views come closest to your own? Write an essay in which you defend or criticize the role television plays in our society. Although you should present a strong defense of your opinion, make sure to consider other viewpoints.
*10. In Pico Iyer's "Home Is Every Place," the author's sense of attachment to place clearly differs from Brooks's. Consider your own attachment to a place, or various places. How has it helped to shape your identity? Do you feel that the media in any way influence your attachment to (or detachment from) place?

Switch on Bhutan

Alexis Bloom

Born in Johannesburg, South Africa, in 1975, Alexis Bloom is a journalist who received her B.A. and M.A. from Cambridge University in England and a master's degree in journalism from the University of California at Berkeley. She has written for British publications the Observer *and the* Sunday Independent, *as well as the* New York Times, *where this essay originally appeared.*

Bloom is also a documentary filmmaker and has been traveling to Asia since she was a teenager. She was intrigued when she heard in 1999 that television was coming to Bhutan, a small landlocked South Asian country that prided itself on its isolation from the cultures of most of the rest of the world, and went there to film a documentary on the phenomenon. She wrote this article based on her impressions after a four-week shoot that resulted in a short film called Switch on Bhutan.

Bhutan is a monarchy of about two million people. Roughly half the size of Indiana, it is bordered on the north and northwest by Tibet and India on the remainder. Bhutan is overwhelmingly rural: virtually the entire country is mountainous and about three-quarters of it is forested land.

Buddhism is Bhutan's official religion, and most aspects of life there are guided by Buddhist ethics and principles. For centuries, Bhutan followed a policy of self-imposed isolation and controlled development, with a particular focus on the preservation of its unique ancient culture, and paid little atten-tion to the world around it. Bhutan's king, Jigme Singye Wangchuck, holds among his ideals what he has nicknamed "gross national happiness," the idea that the peaceful well-being of the people is as important to a country as any economic development would be. In a speech quoted in the article, he warns the citizens of Bhutan that television can be both beneficial and harmful and cautions them to "use your good sense and judgment."

1   The impish conspirators huddle in a side street of Bhutan's capital, tearing cardboard boxes into strips. Once the strips are trimmed to size, the boys proudly hold them against their waists, like little grooms adjusting cummer-bunds. With varying degrees of accuracy, they scrawl "W.W.F. Championship" across the makeshift belts.

2   "I am the Rock!" screams a child in a yellow T-shirt, grasping a pint-size opponent by the neck. "I am the champion!"

3   "I am Triple H!" his opponent squawks in reply before he's knocked to the ground.

4   Less than a mile away, boys the same age chant prayers inside a Buddhist temple. Drawing their wine-colored robes close, the monks, some as young as 5, nod and bow as the wind rattles the prayer wheels outside.

5   This is still a country where rural areas look as they did in ancient times, and where, for every television antenna, a thousand prayer flags flutter. But in the villages children peer through doorways, craning to catch sight of flickering televisions. And when the young monks walk past a set, they, too, stop and stare.

6   In June 1999, from a golden podium in Bhutan's only stadium, King Jigme Singye Wangchuck welcomed the arrival of modern communications technology to his remote Buddhist kingdom, the last country in the world to legalize television. But he cautioned his citizens: "Use your good sense and judgment. Television and the Internet can be both beneficial and harmful to the individual and to society." Two years later, young Bhutanese girls learn dance steps from MTV, and the extravagant, theatrical violence of the World Wrestling Federation has unexpectedly gained a devoted audience of Buddhists.

7   "We've always been this exotic, hidden, mystical land," said Kinley Dorji, editor of the weekly Kuensel, Bhutan's only newspaper. "We've been the last Shangri-La. And suddenly you have an electronic invasion. Suddenly you have TV. And not just TV, you have 25, 30 channels. We've been pried open quite dramatically."

8   Unlike most Bhutanese, Mr. Dorji, a graduate of the Columbia School of Journalism, has ventured beyond the Himalayas. He's deeply concerned about the impact of television on what he calls "a pristine society." "We've been getting letters to the newspaper," he said. "These were letters from children who were brought up in very benign, Buddhist families. They specifically asked us about this World Wrestling Federation program. 'Why are these big men standing there hitting each other? What is the purpose of it?' The children don't understand."

9   Television is a service that just about everyone here can afford. Rinzy Dorji, Bhutan's most successful cable operator, provides 45 channels for just $5 a month—the price of a bag of dried red chilies. "We have sweepers, plumbers and people at the lowest rung of society connected to our cable line," said Rinzy Dorji (who is not related to Kinley), sitting at his desk in the office of Sigma Cable. "Even if they live in a hut or a temporary shed, they can all watch the same programs for an affordable price."

10   Customers call Mr. Dorji at home night and day; Sherub, his 15-year-old daughter, unplugs the telephones when they ring cacophonously. Demand always outstrips supply, but because of the initial cost of laying cable, Sigma Cable still runs at a loss. Mr. Dorji is one of about a half-dozen surviving cable operators; many companies, unable to make a profit, have already gone out of business.

11   Sigma's 45 channels, mostly Indian and American, include three or four Hindi movie channels, CNN, the Indian and American versions of MTV, sports

channels, Discovery, the BBC and a Chinese channel. Also included is Bhutan's only home-grown broadcast station: The Bhutan Broadcasting Society (BBS). Television was launched on the condition that the BBS provide the country with content of its own, but limited technical experience means that the BBS produces just one hour of programming a day, mostly news.

12   Surveys in Bhutan are a haphazard affair, and nobody knows exactly how many people are hooked up to cable or have satellite dishes. But owning a television set is certainly a social priority, and Rinzy Dorji estimates that within a year or so, everyone in Thimphu with a telephone connection—about 6,000 people—will also have cable television.

13   "I'm making a social contribution," Mr. Dorji said. "Children who used to do undesirable things now stay at home. Vandalism, fighting, drinking; we curb such social nuisance because most children are now glued to the TV. They don't go out as they used to."

14   Bhutan, with its policy of placing "Gross National Happiness" ahead of gross national product, is also a country where the police detain or fine adults for not wearing traditional Bhutanese dress—the knee-length gho for men, the apronlike kira for women—in public.

15   "But we'd like to wear the clothes they wear on MTV," Sherub Dorji said. "At parties we used to wear the kira, but now everybody is wearing pants. Pants and miniskirts."

16   Fortunately for Sherub's generation, the fashion police don't frequent Club X, the more long-standing of Bhutan's two discos. Young people hunch over the bar, order up Red Panda beers and potent Bhutanese gin. The sale of tobacco is prohibited in most Bhutanese provinces, but you'd never guess it from the locomotive puffing of boys with seal-slick hair. Not one person in this basement hideaway is wearing traditional clothing: leather jackets shine, halter tops are clean and pressed. And they're dancing to rock 'n' roll.

17   This is a change that Kinley Dorji laments.

18   "We have always dressed like this," he said, rubbing the heavy cloth of his robe. "But now the young people want to dress like their new heroes on television, like their favorite movie stars. A generation gap is emerging with great contrast."

19   Across the Wong Chu river, at the Center for Bhutan Studies, the only sounds are the calling of crows and the occasional rattling of a passing car. Karma Ura, the center's Oxford-educated director, studies contemporary Bhutanese culture in a traditional wooden building with a view of the Thimphu valley; it's more Swiss chalet than research center. Mr. Ura is impeccably dressed in a white-cuffed, charcoal-grey gho. Visitors to this self-styled home of Bhutanese sociology are invited to take off their shoes and don slippers sewn of local fabric.

20   "Some of us thought it was too early to introduce television into Bhutan," he said, "but we were a small minority. People argued that TV could be used to positive effect, but I don't see much evidence of that. There is a case to be made

for widening people's environment, but I see commercial television as a tool for marketing."

21   Television has undoubtedly given Bhutanese a greater understanding of the outside world: before cable, international media was limited to two-day-old newspapers from India. But with news of earthquakes and elections comes advertising. International access has a cost, Mr. Ura said, and young girls now want cosmetics. Not just any cosmetics, but the brand names they have seen on television.

22   Kinley Dorji has interviewed children about their changing habits. "They said that before they didn't know that Signal was better than Colgate," he said. "But now they do, because the television said so."

23   Mr. Ura points to the arrival of a Hallmark shop on Thimphu's main street as evidence of dramatic social change. With indignation, he says that birthdays— and the associated cards, cakes and presents—were, until now, unheard of in Bhutan. This celebration of individualism, he said, has taken root as a result of Westernization.

24   "They must reflect people's changing patterns of marking social relationships," he said. "The advent of modernization is now reinforced quite powerfully by television. And very soon you will have Christmas celebrations."

25   Bhutan strictly controls tourism: fewer than 8,000 people were granted visas to enter the country last year (still an all-time high), and each paid a fee of at least $200 a day. Officials, who use the phrase "Quality Not Quantity," fear the intrusion of foreigners. But the on-screen invaders are more ill-mannered than the trekkers. "Slowly the language of violence that's heard on TV has been introduced into everyday language," Mr. Ura said. "Language here has changed. In traditional Bhutanese society, we don't use language of violence too often— our language is highly moderated. But, that's in sharp contrast to what's available on television."

26   The Bhutanese rely heavily on spoken stories; in the style of Aesop's fables, family tales serve as vehicles for instruction in cultural values. And though they include intrigue, romance and tragedy, Mr. Ura said, very few are told for sheer entertainment. "Stories are our way of transmitting social values," he said. "Our way of showing the idealized way of living." As sitcoms and action films become more popular, this transmission becomes more fragile. "This is a society where the family depended on the grandfather's stories," Kinley Dorji said. "Suddenly this family has multiple channels to watch. I think the implication of what could happen to such a society is quite clear."

27   It's not only young people who are entranced by "Baywatch" and Hollywood films: through her pebble-thick spectacles, the wizened mother-in-law of Rinzy Dorji watches hours of television each day. Danchoe Dema says she likes the Cartoon Network, which she watches with her grandchildren. And though she doesn't understand the rules of the games shown on Rupert Murdoch's Star Sports, she says, "I see them playing, running, wrestling, having fun, and this is entertaining." Ms. Dema confesses that amid all the excitement, she sometimes forgets to say her prayers.

EXERCISES

Some of the Issues

1. What do you think accounts for the popularity of wrestling shows in Bhutan? Does this surprise you? Why or why not?
2. Why was television illegal until 1999? Do you think there was a good reason for it? Why or why not?
3. How much programming is the local television network able to produce and why? Why is this significant?
4. Why does Rinzy Dorji see himself as making a "social contribution" (paragraph 13)? Given the current critique of television in the United States, does his statement seem strange or ironic to you?
5. How does Bloom describe the youth who frequent Club X? What do their dress and social habits indicate about changes in Bhutanese culture?
6. What do Karma Ura and Kinley Dorji see as the primary role of television? What evidence do they point to?
7. Summarize the debate between those for and against television in Bhutan.
8. How has television influenced the language of the people of Bhutan, according to Karma Ura?

The Way We Are Told

9. In paragraphs 1 through 4 Bloom contrasts two images. What implications do these contrasting images have? How do they relate to the rest of the article?
10. Bloom relies on fairly detailed descriptions. How might these descriptions help support her claims?
11. Does Bloom make a specific argument for or against having television in Bhutan? What technique does she use to present different perspectives?
12. Look at Bloom's last paragraph. Do you find it to be an effective conclusion? Why or why not?

Some Subjects for Writing

13. As an experiment, avoid watching television for five to seven days. Write a paper in which you document your experiences over these days, paying particular attention to both your changes in habits and your changes in attitude or perspectives on the world. Do you feel more or less in touch with what is going on around you?
*14. In "Unplugged," Geraldine Brooks defends her town's decision to ban the cable company. Bhutan went from having no TV to having up to 45 channels. Using these two readings along with other sources (including your

own experience), write an essay in which you make a claim about one possible impact of television, particularly cable television. How might television enhance or detract from people's local culture and their everyday interactions in their communities?

15. How do you interpret the policy of "placing 'Gross National Happiness' ahead of gross national product" (paragraph 14)? What implications does this policy have for Bhutan? What might it mean for such a policy to be carried out in your country? Write an essay in which you explore that possibility.

The Hidden (In Plain Sight) Persuaders

Rob Walker

A friend or a coworker raves over a new restaurant or a cool pair of sneakers. Are they simply expressing honest enthusiasm about a new discovery, or are you both part of a new phenomenon called "word of mouth" marketing? According to journalist Rob Walker, it could be a little bit of both. In this essay, Walker explores how, in an attempt to cut through the clutter of commercials on TV and radio, marketing companies have begun to enlist the help of "agents"—cadres of enthusiastic volunteers who, in exchange for free merchandise and other perks, enthusiastically spread the word about new products to their friends, families, and even strangers.

Rob Walker is a freelance journalist who contributes regularly to Inc., Slate, *and many other publications. He is the author of the book* Letters from New Orleans *(2005), and writes the "Consumed" column for* The New York Times Magazine. *This article originally appeared there in 2004.*

1   Over the July 4 weekend last summer, at cookouts up and down the East Coast and into the Midwest, guests arrived with packages of Al Fresco chicken sausage for their hosts to throw on the grill. At a family gathering in Kingsley, Mich. At a small barbecue in Sag Harbor, N.Y. At a 60-guest picnic in Philadelphia.

2   We know that this happened, and we even know how various party guests reacted to their first exposure to Al Fresco, because the Great Sausage Fanout of 2004 did not happen by chance. The sausage-bearers were not official representatives of Al Fresco, showing up in uniforms to hand out samples. They were invited guests, friends or relatives of whoever organized the get-togethers, but they were also—unknown to most all the other attendees—"agents," and they filed reports. "People could not believe they weren't pork!" one agent related. "I told everyone that they were low in fat and so much better than pork sausages." Another wrote, "I handed out discount coupons to several people and made sure they knew which grocery stores carried them." Another noted that "my dad will most likely buy the garlic" flavor, before closing, "I'll keep you posted."

3   These reports went back to the company that Al Fresco's owner, Kayem Foods, had hired to execute a "word of mouth" marketing campaign. And while the Fourth of July weekend was busy, it was only a couple of days in an effort

that went on for three months and involved not just a handful of agents but 2,000 of them. The agents were sent coupons for free sausage and a set of instructions for the best ways to talk the stuff up, but they did not confine themselves to those ideas, or to obvious events like barbecues. Consider a few scenes from the life of just one agent, named Gabriella.

4   At one grocery store, Gabriella asked a manager why there was no Al Fresco sausage available. At a second store, she dropped a card touting the product into the suggestion box. At a third, she talked a stranger into buying a package. She suggested that the organizers of a neighborhood picnic serve Al Fresco. She took some to a friend's house for dinner and (she reported back) "explained to her how the sausage comes in six delicious flavors." Talking to another friend whom she had already converted into an Al Fresco customer, she noted that the product is "not just for barbecues" and would be good at breakfast too. She even wrote to a local priest known for his interest in Italian food, suggesting a recipe for Tuscan white-bean soup that included Al Fresco sausage. The priest wrote back to say he'd give it a try. Gabriella asked me not to use her last name. The Al Fresco campaign is over—having notably boosted sales, by 100 percent in some stores—but she is still spreading word of mouth about a variety of other products, and revealing her identity, she said, would undermine her effectiveness as an agent.

5   The sausage campaign was organized by a small, three-year-old company in Boston called BzzAgent, but that firm is hardly the only entity to have concluded that the most powerful forum for consumer seduction is not TV ads or billboards but rather the conversations we have in our everyday lives. The thinking is that in a media universe that keeps fracturing into ever-finer segments, consumers are harder and harder to reach; some can use TiVo to block out ads or the TV's remote control to click away from them, and the rest are simply too saturated with brand messages to absorb another pitch. So corporations frustrated at the apparent limits of "traditional" marketing are increasingly open to word-of-mouth marketing. One result is a growing number of marketers organizing veritable armies of hired "trendsetters" or "influencers" or "street teams" to execute "seeding programs," "viral marketing," "guerrilla marketing." What were once fringe tactics are now increasingly mainstream; there is even a Word of Mouth Marketing Association.

6   Marketers bicker among themselves about how these approaches differ, but to those of us on the receiving end, the distinctions might seem a little academic. They are all attempts, in one way or another, to break the fourth wall that used to separate the theater of commerce, persuasion and salesmanship from our actual day-to-day life. To take what may be the most infamous example, Sony Ericsson in 2002 hired 60 actors in 10 cities to accost strangers and ask them: Would you mind taking my picture? Those who obliged were handed, of course, a Sony Ericsson camera-phone to take the shot, at which point the actor would remark on what a cool gadget it was. And thus an act of civility was converted into a branding event.

7   This idea—the commercialization of chitchat—resembles a scenario from a paranoid science-fiction novel about a future in which corporations have become so powerful that they can bribe whole armies of flunkies to infiltrate the family barbecue. That level of corporate influence sounds sure to spark outrage—another episode in the long history of mainstream distrust of commercial coercion and marketing trickery. Fear of unchecked corporate reach is what made people believe in the power of subliminal advertising and turn Vance Packard's book "The Hidden Persuaders" into a best seller in the 1950's; it is what gave birth to the consumer-rights movement of the 1970's; and it is what alarms people about neuroscientists supposedly locating the "buy button" in our brains today. Quite naturally, many of us are wary of being manipulated by a big, scary, Orwellian "them."

8   In this case, however, it is not just "them." It turns out that Gabriella and the rest of the sausage agents are not paid flunkies trying to manipulate Main Street Americans; they are Main Street Americans. Unlike the Sony Ericsson shills, Gabriella is not an actress. She is an accountant, with full-time work and a 12-year-old daughter, living in Bayonne, N.J. Aside from free samples, she gets no remuneration. She and her many fellow agents have essentially volunteered to create "buzz" about Al Fresco sausage and dozens of other products, from books to shoes to beer to perfume. BzzAgent currently has more than 60,000 volunteer agents in its network. Tremor, a word-of-mouth operation that is a division of Procter & Gamble (maker of Crest, Tide and Pampers) has an astonishing 240,000 volunteer teenagers spreading the word about everything from toothbrushes to TV shows. A spinoff, Tremor Moms, is in the works. Other marketers, particularly youth-oriented firms, have put up Web sites recruiting teenagers to serve as "secret agents."

9   Given that we are a nation of busy, overworked people who in poll after poll claim to be sick of advertisers jumping out at us from all directions, the number of people willing to help market products they had previously never heard of, for no money at all, is puzzling to say the least. BzzAgent, which has a particularly intense relationship with its fast-growing legions of volunteers, offers a rare and revealing case study of what happens when word-of-mouth theory meets consumer psychology in the real world. In finding thousands of takers, perfectly willing to use their own creativity and contacts to spread the good news about, for instance, Al Fresco sausage, it has turned commercial influence into an open-source project. It could be thought of as not just a marketing experiment but also a social experiment. The existence of tens of thousands of volunteer marketing "agents" raises a surprising possibility—that we have already met the new hidden persuaders, and they are us.

10   Dave Balter, the 33-year-old founder of BzzAgent, is a smart guy, but he would be poorly cast as a slick, Madison Avenue mastermind. He's fresh-faced, good-humored, almost goofy. And he will cheerfully tell you that he has no definitive explanation for the number of average citizens who want to be, in company parlance, BzzAgents. In the beginning, he had a theory about what would

motivate average citizens to generate word of mouth for his clients, but that theory was full of holes. It assumed, for instance, that agents would require some kind of quasi-financial motivation to do legwork for consumer companies.

11　　Dave Balter's background was in loyalty marketing—those frequent-flier-style programs that give rewards to dedicated users of a particular product, service or credit card. He read up on word-of-mouth marketing theory, raised some money, hired a right-hand man and put the word out among family and friends that he was looking for "agents." The idea was to build a network of people who would get points for spreading "honest word of mouth" and could cash in the points for cool products. "The whole concept," he said, "was rewards, rewards, rewards."

12　　The first full-fledged Bzz campaign was for a book called *The Frog King*. It lasted one month and focused on New York City. Balter persuaded Penguin Publishing to let him do it by charging the publisher nothing.

13　　*The Frog King* was a quirky, comic first novel by a young writer named Adam Davies. Davies had some connections in New York publishing (including Liz Smith, the gossip columnist), but he wasn't exactly going to get a giant publicity blitz. "We didn't expect much" from the buzz campaign, recalled Rick Pascocello, a Penguin vice president.

14　　The guide for the agents, a no-frills seven-page document in those early days, welcomed them as members of "an elite group" of word-of-mouth spreaders and listed the contact information for "your BzzLeader," BzzAgent JonO. (That was Jon O'Toole, Balter's right-hand man.) It summarized some of the novel's highlights, noting a few passages in particular that might be useful "conversation points," and suggested tactics like reading the book on mass transit with the cover clearly visible, posting a review on Amazon.com and calling up bookstores and chatting with the clerk about this great new book about New York publishing with lots of sex and drinking whose title you can't quite recall. JonO signed the cover letter assuring agents that the folks back at the hive found the book laugh-out-loud funny.

15　　Local events for *The Frog King* drew larger-than-expected crowds of 100 or 150 people, according to Pascocello, who said that thanks to the word-of-mouth campaign, the book sold in three months what he had hoped it would sell in a year. There are now more than 50,000 copies of *The Frog King* in print, and it's still selling. BzzAgent has had a steady flow of paying clients ever since (including Penguin, which has used BzzAgent to promote other books, like the novel *The Quality of Life Report*). The fee it charges varies according to the size and nature of the campaign, but Balter said a 12-week campaign involving 1,000 agents would now cost $95,000.

16　　BzzAgent has fewer than two dozen paid employees, though it is growing and recently moved to a larger office. These people are mostly young, without backgrounds in traditional marketing. When the company takes on a new client, they huddle to figure out whatever is most buzzable about the product at hand. This summer, for instance, they handed around and discussed a new line of

Johnston & Murphy dress shoes, which feature a fiberglass shank, rather than a traditional metal one, so they won't set off metal detectors at airports. A whiteboard was filled with suggested conversation starters and likely sites for word-of-mouth opportunities, which later was transferred to a slick "Bzz Guide" for the agents.

17   As the number of agents has grown, the company can meet increasingly specific requests for, say, agents of a certain age or income level, or who live in certain parts of the country. It has done campaigns for a wide array of goods, and for major companies and brands like Anheuser-Busch, Lee Jeans, Ralph Lauren, even DuPont. Recently the company has also begun working with clients to begin converting existing loyal customers into private, well-organized, word-of-mouth missionaries.

18   Although Balter says he was pleased with his agents' efforts from the start, he did worry early on that the system could not be sustained. The problem was that while agents were spreading buzz and thus earning and piling up points, most were not cashing them in. That is, they weren't bothering to collect their rewards. "We've built a broken model," Balter remembers thinking. He asked his colleagues from his loyalty-marketing days: Is it that the rewards aren't good enough? Are they too hard to get? After many hours of listening to the conflicting analyses of experts, he and O'Toole decided to ask the agents themselves about the points. "We didn't realize the agents would want to talk to us," Balter said. This was another miscalculation; many of the agents very much did want to talk. In essence, they told Balter that there was nothing wrong with the rewards; it was just that the rewards weren't really the point. Even now, only about a quarter of the agents collect rewards, and hardly any take all they have earned.

19   Karen Bollaert, who is 32 and lives in the Bay Ridge section of Brooklyn, was among the firm's earliest agents, and became one of its most effective. When she signed up for her first BzzAgent campaign—*The Frog King*, in fact—she was working with a pharmaceutical researcher, mostly doing paperwork, and thinking about finding a more fulfilling way to spend her days. Like everyone who signs up at the BzzAgent site, she was accepted.

20   During active stretches, Bollaert puts in between 5 and 10 hours a week talking up products and writing reports about her activities. (She has signed up for many campaigns, including a perfume called Ralph Lauren Blue, a line of jeans for Lee and something called No Puffery, a gel to soothe skin below the eyes.) What, I asked her, if not the potential to get some free prizes for effort, made her bother to volunteer with BzzAgent? First, she told me, she gets the chance to sample new products shortly before they hit the stores, so she gets to feel a bit like an insider. Second, she has always liked to give people her opinion about what she's reading or what products she's using, and BzzAgent gives her more to talk about. Third, if she does like something, then telling other people is helpful to them. So participating is both a chance to weigh in and be heard, and also something close to an act of altruism.

21   What Balter said he learned from his agents is that lots of people like to tell others what they are reading and what restaurant they've discovered and what

gizmo they just bought. In his view, BzzAgent is simply harnessing, channeling and organizing that consumer enthusiasm. This is presumably why it's so easy, so natural, for someone like Karen Bollaert to work word-of-mouth efforts into daily life. When, for example, a friend mentioned to Bollaert that she would have to get up early after a late night out on the town, she brought up No Puffery. When a pharmaceutical representative visiting her office worried about looking lousy at a meeting she had to fly to, Bollaert mentioned No Puffery. At her grandfather's wake, "a relative told me how well I was looking," she wrote in one report back to the BzzAgent hive, "and I mentioned that No Puffery helped to keep me looking calm instead of puffy-eyed and as horrible as I felt."

22   The endless chatter of American consumer life that BzzAgent has infiltrated is not simply a formless cacophony; it has its structures and hierarchies, which have been studied exhaustively for decades. Tremor, the Procter & Gamble word-of-mouth unit, which also does work for a variety of non-P.&G. clients, was founded four years ago with those structures in mind. A key Tremor premise is that the most effective way for a message to travel is through networks of real people communicating directly with one another. "We set out to see if we could do that in some systematic way," Steve Knox, Tremor's C.E.O., said recently. He added a second, closely related premise: "There is a group of people who are responsible for all word of mouth in the marketplace." In other words, some friends are more influential than others, and those are the ones who are chosen to join Tremor.

23   Who are they? Check out the word-of-mouth industry's favorite graph. The graph is meant to show the pattern by which ideas or products or behaviors are adopted, and it looks like a hill: on the left are the early adopters; then the trend-spreaders; the mainstream population is the big bulge in the middle; then come the laggards, represented by the right-hand slope. This is not new stuff—Knox himself cites research from the 1930's, as well as the 1962 academic book *Diffusion of Innovation*, by Everett Rogers—but it has become extremely popular over the past five years or so. Seth Godin, who wrote *Permission Marketing, Unleashing the Ideavirus* and other popular marketing books (and whose ideas partly inspired BzzAgent), uses it, as do dozens of other marketing experts. Malcolm Gladwell's *The Tipping Point* made an argument about these ideas that was simultaneously more textured and easier to digest than most of what had come before (or since), and it became a best seller. But whatever the intentions and caveats of the various approaches to the subject, the most typical response to the graph is to zero in on the segment that forms the bridge over which certain ideas or products travel into the mainstream—influentials, trend-translators, connectors, alphas, hubs, sneezers, bees, etc. Let's just call them Magic People.

24   Knox said that Tremor's approach to finding the Magic People is intensively researched. The company tries to isolate the psychological characteristics of the subset of influential teenagers, and has developed a screening process to identify them. The details of this are a secret, but as an example, Knox noted that most teenagers have 25 or 30 names on their instant-messaging "buddy list,"

whereas a Tremor member might have 150. Tremor recruits volunteers mostly through online advertisements and accepts only 10 or 15 percent of those who apply. The important thing, Knox said, is they are the right kind of kids—the connected, influential trend-spreading kind. Knox mentioned a focus group of Tremor kids in Los Angeles, where several teenagers showed up with business cards. Magic.

25   Janet Onyenucheya was chosen by Tremor, and she is pretty much what you picture when you picture a trend-influencer. She is 18, African-American, beautiful, smart and, on the day I met her, was wearing a really cool pair of sneakers. An intern at an independent music publishing company in Manhattan, she is preparing to enter the Berklee College of Music in Boston in the spring. She got involved with Tremor a couple of years ago, while attending LaGuardia High School.

26   Onyenucheya gets free stuff from Tremor, and sometimes even a small check for taking surveys and participating in focus groups. She got to vote on the design for a T-shirt for the 10th anniversary of the Vans Warped Tour and for the design of a Crest toothbrush. This past July, she was invited to an advance viewing of two television shows, *Lost* and *Complete Savages*, at the Millennium screening room in downtown Manhattan. There were about 70 teenagers there, and pizza and sodas for everybody. Onyenucheya particularly loved *Lost*. "When I came home," she said, "I immediately told my five closest friends, like: 'Oh, my God, you just missed the greatest shows. I got to go down to the Millennium and saw a show called *Lost* and it was so good, and we have to watch it when it comes out.' And I felt like I had the upper hand. Like, 'You don't know what I know.' "

27   By and large, the word-of-mouth literature tends to describe our influence and degree of connectedness as something hard-wired. Magic People like Onyenucheya are born, not made, is the idea, which is why companies spend so much effort developing psychological profiles to find them. But the BzzAgent experiment largely discards that premise. Its agents are not screened. They are not chosen. They simply sign up. They are all kinds of people, all over the country: a 50-something bookstore owner in suburban Chicago, a young housewife near Mobile, Ala., a college student in Kansas. Many are teenagers, or even younger. At least one is 86 years old. And yet, it seems, they are able to persuade.

28   Jason Desjardins is a regular guy, a good guy, accommodating and polite. Twenty-eight, slim, clean-shaven, with close-cropped hair, he is the dairy manager at a supermarket in rural New Hampshire, part of the same supermarket chain he has worked for since high school. While he was wearing a Brooklyn T-shirt when we met, the truth is he bought it at the Old Navy in the Concord Mall, and has never been on an airplane or even traveled outside of New England. Jason Desjardins is sweet and guileless, but he is not, by any expert definition, a Magic Person.

29   Desjardins stumbled across a reference to BzzAgent online, and he was interested. How could this thing work? He signed up, and soon after, they sent

him *Purple Cow: Transform Your Business by Being Remarkable*—Seth Godin's most recent book at the time, which was written with a BzzAgent marketing plan in mind—and his life changed. It's hard to overstate how enthusiastic Desjardins is about BzzAgent. He joined campaigns for several other books, as well as for a beer called Bare Knuckle Stout, a spam-blocking service called Mail-Block and, yes, Al Fresco sausage. He figures he spends about 10 hours a week either buzzing or writing reports about buzzing. I visited him at his apartment in Bradford, N.H. We were joined by his wife, Melissa, a pretty woman with a stylish haircut and a big smile, and their 2-year-old daughter. I wondered how Melissa felt about her husband spending so much time on a no-money hobby. In fact, she was thrilled. She said she thought it had made him more open to other people. He used to be the kind of guy who just hated to call a mechanic about a noise the car was making; he would wait until the car actually broke down and he had no choice but to bother someone about it. He was in a shell. But that has changed—partly because of Melissa, Jason wisely interjected—but also partly because of his involvement in BzzAgent.

30   For starters, Desjardins said, BzzAgent "turned me on to reading." And having enjoyed *Purple Cow*, he wanted to do his best to spread the word. The Bzz guide suggested he call a bookstore. For a while, he put it off. He would look at the phone and tell himself, I can do this, and he would try to rehearse what he would say, and this would go on for 15 or 20 minutes. "I thought: What have I got to lose?" he said. "I'm never going to see this person." And finally he called and pretended he did not know the name of Seth Godin's new book. "He'll call anybody now," Melissa said, smiling.

31   He printed slogans from *Purple Cow* ("Be Remarkable or Be Invisible") onto card stock and hung them where his fellow employees could see them. He posted reviews on Amazon. He started conversations with co-workers, customers, strangers. He submitted a rave review for a fantasy novel he was buzzing called *Across the Nightingale Floor* to the *Concord Monitor*, and it was published; there's a laminated copy of the review on the fridge. He wrote to the governor touting Mail-Block. At the grocery store, when a co-worker moaned about not liking her job, Desjardins practically turned into a motivational speaker, waving his hands and quoting from another book called *Five Patterns of Extraordinary Careers*, telling her that if she wasn't happy she needed to take control of the situation. "She did end up finding another job after that," he observed. Desjardins is ranked the 45th most effective BzzAgent, out of 60,000 nationwide, and proud of it. He has learned to influence.

32   This was all good for Desjardins, but it complicates what we thought we knew about word-of-mouth influence. The whole premise of the Magic People is that the rest of us take our cues from them because they have some special credibility, in the form of reputation or expertise or connections. In April 2003, that premise was put to the test when BzzAgent began a 13-week campaign for a restaurant chain called Rock Bottom Restaurant and Brewery, which has about 30 locations around the country. This particular campaign was studied by two academics: David Godes, an assistant professor at Harvard Business School, and

Dina Mayzlin, an assistant professor at Yale's School of Management. The experiment involved more than 1,000 subjects; some were devoted Rock Bottom customers, and the rest were BzzAgents—none of them Rock Bottom loyalists, and only a few had even heard of the chain. Rock Bottom wasn't running any other significant marketing program at the time.

33   Sales increased markedly. Godes and Mayzlin found that, consistent with past research, word-of-mouth traveled more effectively when it was spread not through close friends but through acquaintances (meaning that networkers— the people with the big Buddy Lists—are more valuable). But curiously, it turned out that the agents—the "nonloyals"—were more effective spreaders of word of mouth than the chain's own fans. Godes and Mayzlin hypothesize that the Rock Bottom's most devoted customers had probably already talked up the restaurant to all the friends and acquaintances that they were likely to tell.

34   The researchers also looked at the tendency of marketing efforts to focus on "opinion leaders," who often gain that social status by way of expertise. The results here were somewhat mixed, in an interesting way. A loyal opinion leader— someone who was seen by her social network as an expert on restaurants and who was also a Rock Bottom fan—was pretty effective; if that restaurant expert was ambivalent about Rock Bottom, she was of little use. In contrast, it didn't really matter if the nonloyal agents knew much about restaurants. What mattered was that they told a lot of people (and presumably that they were enthusiastic). The implication is that it doesn't matter if you know what you're talking about, as long as you are willing to talk a lot.

35   Godes offered some caveats to that particular conclusion. He pointed out that expertise may be much more important to real-world word of mouth—the kind that occurs absent an orchestrated effort to create buzz from scratch. He also emphasized that willingness to talk doesn't mean much if you have no one to talk to. Maybe so. But when Dave Balter saw the results, it provided strong evidence for a position he had been coming to for a while: he doesn't quite believe in Magic People anymore. BzzAgent's system does, of course, try to identify who has a large network of friends, who is an expert, who is outspoken, just as Tremor does in its screening. (Actually, several BzzAgents are Tremor members, as well.) "But we also know that sometimes those people aren't the best at spreading word of mouth," Balter said. "We all get information from people around us who don't fit any type of profile that would make them more intelligent or more focused on products than someone else." And the information we share changes, too. "We might go from influential to noninfluential, from trendsetter to nontrendsetter all year long," he suggested, "because we have continued interactions that change our opinions."

36   On some level, then, participating in a voluntary marketing army serves as a kind of consumer-status enabler. You weren't the first on your block with Moon Boots; at least you can be the one to tell your friends about Al Fresco sausage. The more people you can persuade that Al Fresco sausage is good, the better you'll feel about your discovery. BzzAgent, in turn, will help you be a

better persuader. Pretty much everyone likes the feeling of having "the upper hand," as Janet Onyenucheya put it. Even in the small orbit of your own social circle, knowing about something first—telling a friend about a new CD, or discovering a restaurant before anyone else in the office—is satisfying. Maybe it's altruism, maybe it's a power trip, but influencing other people feels good. As an example of how powerful the desire to have the upper hand can be, consider that some participants in a campaign for a new scent called Ralph Cool simply could not wait for their free sample to arrive and rushed out to buy the $40 product so they could start buzzing. Word-of-mouth marketing leverages not simply the power of the trendsetter but also, as Balter puts it, "the power of wanting to be a trendsetter."

37   BzzAgents are under no obligation to push a product they don't like. In fact, if they think it's awful, they're encouraged to say so. Yet, of all the agents I spoke to, and the hundreds of reports I read, there were hardly any examples of outright dissatisfaction with a product. Most of the agents seemed genuinely excited about most of what they were buzzing.

38   Part of the reason is that people tend to join campaigns for things that interest them. Perhaps just as important is that the volunteers, hearing that BzzAgent turns down 80 percent of potential clients, seem to believe that the folks at BzzAgent spend their days sorting through the morass of consumer culture, choosing only the best of the best. BzzAgent does want to keep lousy products out of the system, of course, but it also wants to make money. It's a business. And its ability to keep the system relatively free of awful products probably has much less to do with acting as a consumer-culture curator than with the simple fact that there are probably more perfectly good products being sold in America now than at any time in history.

39   Barry Schwartz, a psychology professor at Swarthmore, is the author of *The Paradox of Choice*, a book that addresses the incredible (and at times paralyzing) abundance of options available to the contemporary consumer. In the past, Schwartz notes, the challenge for the consumer was navigating a world of faulty, shoddy or unsafe products. That's not much of an issue anymore. Now, Schwartz told me, *Consumer Reports* might test 40 stoves, find that 38 of them are pretty good and then resort to sifting among increasingly minor differences to decide which one is the very best value of all, by however narrow a margin. The "Pretty Good" Problem complicates our lives as consumers and makes it increasingly difficult for one of those 38 stoves to stand out. But it gives BzzAgent plenty of work.

40   Still, people's tastes differ, and it seems remarkable that agents are so rarely disappointed. One oddity that Schwartz notes in his book is the "endowment effect." This is one of the many discoveries of the behavioral economists Daniel Kahneman and Amos Tversky. They found that when two items of equal value are handed out randomly to a group of people and those people are given the opportunity to trade, hardly anyone does. It's very unlikely that all the participants were randomly handed the objects they would have preferred had they

been asked in advance, so the economists concluded that once something has been given to us, we value it more. In another experiment, conducted in the early 1990's by a psychology professor at the University of Louisville, two groups of subjects were given nine similarly valued objects and asked to rate the desirability of each. The group that was informed in advance it would get to keep one of the items (one of those insulating tubes that keeps canned drinks cold, as it happens) gave that item a more desirable rating than the other objects. The group that didn't get to keep anything rated them all the same. A follow-up experiment found that this "mere ownership effect" was essentially instantaneous. Other studies have shown that we like things more simply by virtue of repeated or prolonged exposure to them. (Which could explain why, during the course of that Johnston & Murphy meeting, I gradually went from being indifferent to the shoes to wishing I could get a pair.)

41   This research on how we value—or irrationally overvalue—things that are given to us might help explain why BzzAgents and other word-of-mouth volunteers get excited about whatever they are asked to push. (And if you're curious why, in light of this, you're not crazy about every product you've ever bought, the answer may be adaptation—our tendency to get used to our possessions and, in effect, fall out of love with them. For the word-of-mouth volunteer this hardly matters, since by the time it happens the campaign is over.) But it doesn't address another mystery: Why would the volunteers work so hard to get other people excited about these products? Another line of research suggests a possible answer. This school of thought would characterize word-of-mouth volunteers as operating not in a traditional money-in-exchange-for-effort "monetary market," but rather in a "social market." A social market is what we engage in when we ask our friends to help us load up the moving van in exchange for pizza. The research suggests that we are likely to get a better effort out of our friends under the social-market scenario than by offering the cash equivalent of the pizza. (A recent article in the journal *Psychological Science* finds that "monetizing" a gift, like the pizza, by announcing how much it is worth, effectively shifts the whole situation from social market to monetary market.) Under some circumstances, we will expend more effort for social rewards than we will for monetary rewards. This suggests that the agents may do more to spread word of mouth precisely because they are not being paid.

42   Add to all of this the idea that they have been granted status as "agents" in an "elite group" that most of the world doesn't even know about, and have received a free sample of a brand-new product from a source that they trust, and they are almost certain to expend some kind of effort, unless the product is truly awful.

43   There is another advantage to the social market. Since the agents are not being paid, and have the option to ignore any Bzz object they don't like, they tend to see themselves as not being involved in marketing at all. Almost all of the BzzAgents I interviewed made this point. "In marketing, obviously, those people are paid to pump a product, whereas I'm not really getting paid to do this,"

Bollaert, the agent from Brooklyn, explained. "I don't talk about a product if I don't feel strongly about it. I'll give my honest opinion."

44 The notion of the "honest opinion" came up again and again in conversations with the agents and with Balter. Seth Godin, the writer and speaker on marketing whose ideas partly inspired BzzAgent, agrees that the agents' honesty is crucial. Paying people to promote products, hiring supermodels to show up in a bar and request a particular vodka, is "disingenuous, dishonest and almost unethical," and it represents a subversion of honest peer-to-peer communication. And honest peer-to-peer communication, he maintains, is the future of marketing.

45 Godin is not just a BzzAgent fan—he's also a client. *Purple Cow* was marketed through BzzAgent, and Godin quietly plugs the company at the end of the book. He describes BzzAgent as a company at the center of a conversation between its corporate clients and thousands of agents who serve as a kind of guild of consumers. "I think this is a new kind of media," he said. Specifically, this new kind of media is people like Gabriella, or Desjardins, or Bollaert, chatting with friends and strangers.

46 This argument requires you to accept that a conversation can be honest even if one participant has a hidden agenda. Whether that's possible is something I asked several agents, and Balter himself several times. Of course the agents believe in their own integrity, but that's the easy part. Do we really want a world where every conversation about a product might be secretly tied to a word-of-mouth "campaign"? Doesn't that kind of undermine, you know, the fabric of social discourse?

47 "The key is," Balter said, "people already talk about this stuff. They already talk about things they love." Manufactured word of mouth is indeed a bad and scary thing, he maintains, but that's not what his company is doing. "For whatever reason, we have this natural instinct to tell a friend about a product—and to get them to believe what you believe. We're not trying to change that. All we're trying to do is put some form around it, so it can be measured and understood. That's not changing the social fabric."

48 It is certainly easier to defend the voluntary buzz-spreaders as less devious than the paid model pretending to like a product in public—but the honesty and openness come with an asterisk or two. Those suggestions in the Bzz guides to call bookstores and pretend you don't know the exact title or author you're looking for are pretty hard to define as "honest." Similarly, it's most unlikely that Amazon.com (let alone the *Concord Monitor*) would consider the reviews of a BzzAgent quite as unbiased and helpful to readers as a review from someone who hadn't consulted talking points compiled with input from the publisher. The whole tone of the Bzz guides—which read like a cross between a brochure and a training manual—is a bit difficult to square with the idea of genuineness.

49 Finally, while BzzAgent tells its volunteers that they are under no obligation to hide their association with the company and its campaigns, the reality is

that most of them do hide it most of the time. They don't tell the people they are "bzzing," that they really found out about the sausage, or the perfume, or the shoes, or the book, from some company in Boston that charges six-figure fees to corporations. "It just seems more natural, when I talk about something, if people don't think I'm trying to push a product," Karen Bollaert explained to me. Other agents said the same. Gabriella, for instance, insisted that she really does think Al Fresco makes the best sausage around. Basically, they trust BzzAgent, and they trust themselves, so they don't see a problem.

50   Nevertheless, Jason Desjardins has told a few people about his efforts for BzzAgent, with mixed results. Some people thought it sounded exciting. Others, however, said they felt "used." One friend he tried to recruit now responds with suspicion when Desjardins talks up something he has done: "Are you buzzing me?" the friend will ask. Desjardins shrugs. "I've been honest about everything."

51   One reward Bollaert did collect from BzzAgent was, of all things, the William Gibson novel *Pattern Recognition*—an actual paranoid science-fiction novel about a future in which corporations have become so powerful they can bribe flunkies to infiltrate your life and talk up products. "It made me think, when somebody says something about a product—I wonder. That gave me a little pause," she said. Earlier in our conversation, I touted my iPod. Wouldn't she feel differently about my comments, I asked, if it turned out that I'd gotten it from Apple or a BzzAgent equivalent? "That's true," she said. "But you know what? If you start questioning everyone's motives, then you'll be in a home with tinfoil on your head."

52   The motives of chattering consumers can, of course, be biased in all kinds of ways. If your friend is bragging about his great new cellphone, he may not be a buzz agent, but he may not be the purely rational information source you assume. He says it's the best phone around, and maybe he even believes it—but the truth may be that he bought it because it looks cool and he read that Jake Gyllenhaal has one just like it. It may be true that we trust our friends more than TV ads, but that doesn't actually mean they've become more reliable.

53   "I think we all do this naturally anyway," Bollaert concluded. "If you find something you like and somebody asks your advice and you have a product, good or bad, you'll say don't get it or do get it. We're a consumer society."

54   Crucial to the BzzAgent system is the small team of young people in Boston who read and answer every single Bzz report. They offer encouragement, tips on how to improve word-of-mouth strategies. Every report is rated and every agent ranked according to a complicated formula, one that is constantly being tweaked, taking into account everything from how often the agent reports to how many people they tend to buzz to the quality of their summaries—plus intangibles like originality. (This system is part of BzzAgent's defense against people signing up for free stuff and simply making up fake reports about their buzz activities; the home office is trained to spot such things.)

Along with the feedback, they almost always throw in a joke or a comment so it's clear that they have actually read the report.

55 No doubt because of this, many agent reports are full of personality. Some are almost confessional; others are revealing perhaps without intending to be. Casual mentions of boyfriend or girlfriend problems come up, as do complaints about bosses, friends, strangers. One of the most memorable was from a young BzzAgent who reported that a man she met in a bar complimented her on her Ralph Cool perfume, one thing led to another and they spent the night together. The next morning he asked about the perfume again and said he liked it so much he might have to buy some for his wife. (These reports are ultimately handed over to the client—a trove of anecdotal research from the front lines of consumption.)

56 Along the way, Agent JonO has become a kind of celebrity, or at least a figure of mystery. There are more calls and e-mail messages and instant messages to "JonO" than Jon O'Toole himself can possibly deal with, so lately JonO has become more of a construct than a person. Jason Desjardins sounds honored to have had a chance to meet the real JonO not long ago: O'Toole lined up a dinner in Cambridge with several BzzAgent volunteers, to meet them and hear their thoughts and ideas. Desjardins was so excited about this that at first he overlooked the fact that it was on the same night as his wedding anniversary. (Melissa encouraged him to go anyway. "But we'll see if JonO is still there for you 10 years from now," she said.)

57 Balter did not count on the agents taking BzzAgent so seriously. He still doesn't seem to know quite what to make of it. He has met only a handful of agents, and while he said he intends to meet more, he sounded almost nervous about it. A number of those he has met have been almost apologetic about not doing more—about not buzzing enough on this or that campaign. The biggest complaints come from people who say they have not been invited to join enough campaigns. One agent resigned because he said he was unsure whether he could live up to BzzAgent's ethical standards.

58 This might be the most peculiar thing about BzzAgent: not only are its volunteer agents willing to become shock troops in the marketing revolution, but many of them are flat-out excited about it. At his apartment, Desjardins told me about another book he had read because of BzzAgent. Called *Join Me*, it's about a guy who decides he wants to start some sort of voluntary group—a commune, a cult, whatever you want to call it. He puts an ad in the paper that just says, "Join me," and to his surprise, people are interested. They didn't know what they were joining, or why, but they joined anyway. The guy, whose name is Danny Wallace, decided to turn his followers into a good-deeds army, basically on the "Pay It Forward" method. The book is nonfiction.

59 Why, I asked Desjardins, did people join a group without even knowing what it was? Well, he explained, Wallace's theory was that they just wanted to be part of something. That made sense to me. After all, some people are lucky

enough to find meaning and fulfillment through their work, family or spirituality. But many people don't. Many people have boring jobs and indifferent bosses. They feel ignored by politicians. They send e-mail to customer service and no one responds. They get no feedback. It's easy to feel helpless, uncounted, disconnected. Do you think, I asked Desjardins, that there's some element of that going on with BzzAgent?

60   "I think for some people it probably is," he answered. "For me, it's being part of something big. I think it's such a big thing that's going to shape marketing. To actually be one of the people involved in shaping that is, to me, big." That made sense to me too. After all, there is one thing that is even more powerful than the upper hand, more seductive than persuading: believing.

EXERCISES

Some of the Issues

1. What was the Great Sausage Fanout of 2004? How do you respond to the word "fanout"?
2. Why are the people who do the word-of-mouth marketing called "agents"? What does that word imply to you?
3. What is your response to Gabriella's tactics in paragraph 4?
4. Do you agree that "the most powerful form of consumer seduction is not TV ads or billboards but rather the conversations we have in our everyday lives" (paragraph 5)? Why or why not? What is BzzAgent's reason for thinking this is the case?
5. What does Walker mean by the "fourth wall" in paragraph 6?
6. What makes the use of the "agents" Walker discusses different from earlier forms of advertising? What does Walker mean when he writes: "we have already met the new hidden persuaders, and they are us" (paragraph 9)?
7. What are people's motivations for wanting to become agents?
8. What did David Godes and Dina Mayzlin's study demonstrate (paragraphs 31–35)? What, in your opinion, does their study imply?
9. What other studies does Walker cite and why?
10. Why don't many of the agents see themselves as "being involved in marketing" (paragraph 43)? Do you agree with their belief that they are not marketing the products they "buzz"?
11. Why is it ironic that Karen Bollaert has read William Gibson's *Pattern Recognition* (paragraph 51), and Jason Desjardins has read *Join Me* (paragraph 58)?
12. Would you, or have you ever, considered working as an "agent" for a marketing campaign? What factors would make you consider doing or not doing it? Do you ever find yourself working as a kind of unofficial "agent" for products you like?
13. What factors influence your decisions as a consumer? How do you make decisions about what to buy? Has your way of making decisions changed in any way over the years?

The Way We Are Told

14. What is the effect of the opening paragraphs? What do you think the author is trying to do?

15. Look closely at the examples Walker uses to elaborate on his claims. What kinds of details does he provide? How do these details help him back up his claims?

16. At what points in the article does Walker refer to himself in the first person "I"? Why does he do so? What, in the end, do you think his perspective toward word-of-mouth marketing is? Why?

Some Subjects for Writing

17. How much do you think marketing campaigns have influenced not only the way we think but also the way we talk about products and communicate with our friends? After taking notes and reflecting on the conversations you have with your friends over the next several days, write a paper in which you analyze the degree to which the way you talk about the things you like (or don't like) has been influenced by the language of marketing. You might also consider the amount of time you talk about products versus the amount of time you discuss other aspects of your life (friends, family, relationships).

18. To what extent do you think that the form of marketing Walker describes is tied to this particular historical moment? Using both Walker's article and ideas and examples you've gathered from your own experience, write an essay in which you analyze why buzz advertising is, or isn't, an appropriate form of advertising for the early 21st century. How does it fit in to our current lifestyles? Why have marketers come to see it as potentially more effective than traditional forms of marketing?

19. Imagine that you are making a pitch to a client and create your own buzz marketing campaign for a product you like or find particularly interesting. Include details such as: Who would make the best marketers? Where would they try to "pitch" the product and to whom? What kinds of tactics might they use in order to pitch it and what might they say? Organize your pitch in the way you think would be most effective—for example, you might use images alongside your writing, or create a PowerPoint presentation.

Why We Tell Stories

Lisel Mueller

Lisel Mueller, who came to the United States from Germany at the age of fif-teen, is the author of several collections of poetry, as well as a volume of es-says. Her poetry collection, Alive Together: New and Selected Poems *(1996), won the Pulitzer Prize.* The Need to Hold Still *(1980), from which this poem is taken, received the National Book Award.*

For Linda Nemec Foster

1
Because we used to have leaves
and on damp days
our muscles feel a tug,
painful now, from when roots
5   pulled us into the ground

and because our children believe
they can fly, an instinct retained
from when the bones in our arms
were shaped like zithers and broke
10   neatly under their feathers

and because before we had lungs
we know how far it was to the bottom
as we floated open-eyed
like painted scarves through the scenery
15   of dreams, and because we awakened

and learned to speak

2
We sat by the fire in our caves,
and because we were poor, we made up a tale
about a treasure mountain
20   that would open only for us

and because we were always defeated,
we invented impossible riddles
only we could solve,

25 monsters only we could kill,
women who could love no one else

and because we had survived
sisters and brothers, daughters and sons,
we discovered bones that rose
from the dark earth and sang
30 as white birds in the trees

3
Because the story of our life
becomes our life

Because each of us tells
the same story
35 but tells it differently

and none of us tells it
the same way twice

Because grandmothers looking like spiders
want to enchant the children
and grandfathers need to convince us
40 what happened happened because of them

and though we listen only
haphazardly, with one ear,
we will begin our story
with the word *and*

EXERCISES

Some of the Issues

1. Part 1 of Mueller's poem tells us how we are, at least in our imaginations, connected to earlier forms of life before "we awakened / and learned to speak." Imagine that you were without language. How would that fact shape your ability to think, feel, and communicate with others?
2. Part 2 of the poem deals with the time when humans first began to talk and tell stories. Why, according to Mueller, did we invent stories? What function did they serve then? What function do they serve now?
3. Why will we "begin our story with the word *and*"?

4. What is your own answer to the question, "Why do we tell stories?" Do you agree with Mueller that the way we talk about our lives shapes the way we lead our lives? Why or why not?

*5. Read Maxine Hong Kingston's "Girlhood Among Ghosts." In that selection, the author remembers a story her mother told her in which the mother cuts a section from under Kingston's tongue. The incident may never have happened, yet it appears to have deep significance in Kingston's life. How does Mueller's idea "that the story of our life becomes our life" apply to Kingston?

Some Subjects for Writing

6. Most of us remember stories our families have told again and again about our childhood. Sometimes these stories are about a funny incident, sometimes they carry a moral. Often, the repetition of the story helps to establish the family's view of that child and may shape the child's own self image. Recount a story told about you and explain its influence then and now.

Credits

Alexie, Sherman. "Indian Education" from *The Lone Ranger and Tonto Fistfight in Heaven* by Sherman Alexie. Copyright © 1993 by Sherman Alexie. Used by permission of Grove/Atlantic, Inc.

Angelou, Maya. From *I Know Why the Caged Bird Sings* by Maya Angelou, copyright © 1969 and renewed 1997 by Maya Angelou. Used by permission of Random House, Inc.

Anzaldúa, Gloria. From *Borderlands/La Frontera: The New Mestiza*. Copyright © 1987, 1999 by Gloria Anzaldúa. Reprinted by permission of Aunt Lute Books.

Bellafante, Ginia. "Courtship Ideas of South Asians Get a U.S. Touch" by Ginia Bellafante from *New York Times*, August 23, 2005. Copyright © 2005 by The New York Times Co. Reprinted with permission.

Bloom, Alexis. "Switch on Bhutan" by Alexis Bloom from *New York Times*, May 13, 2001. Copyright © 2001 by The New York Times Co. Reprinted with permission.

Brandt, Barbara. "Less Is More: A Call for Shorter Work Hours" by Barbara Brandt from *Utne Reader*, July/August 1991. Used by permission of the author.

Brooks, Geraldine. "Unplugged" by Geraldine Brooks, former foreign correspondent for *Wall Street Journal* and author of *Nine Parts of Desire: The Hidden World of Islamic Women*. Used with permission of the author.

Cofer, Judith Ortiz. "The Myth of the Latin Woman: I Just Met a Girl Named María" from *The Latin Deli: Prose and Poetry* by Judith Ortiz Cofer, the University of Georgia Press. Reprinted by permission.

Coontz, Stephanie. "Where Are the Good Old Days?" Used by permission of the author.

Cullen, Countee. "Incident" from *Color* by Countee Cullen. Copyright 1925 by Harper & Brothers; copyright renewed 1953 by Ida M. Cullen. Reprinted by permission of GRM Associates, Inc., agents for the Estate of Ida M. Cullen.

Delpit, Lisa. "No Kinda Sense" Copyright © 2001 *The Skin That We Speak: Thoughts on Language and Culture in the Classroom* by Lisa Delpit and Joanne Kilgour Dowdy, Eds. Reprinted by permission of The New Press, www.thenewpress.com.

Eighner, Lars. From *Travels With Lizbeth* by Lars Eighner. Copyright © 1993 by the author and reprinted by permission of St. Martin's Press LLC.

Espada, Martín. "Who Burns for the Perfection of Paper," from *City of Coughing and Dead Radiators* by Martín Espada. Used by permission of W. W. Norton & Company, Inc.

Farmanfarmaian, Roxane. From *Half and Half* edited by Claudine Chiawei O'Hearn, copyright © 1998 by Claudine Chiawei O'Hearn. Used by permission of Pantheon Books, a division of Random House, Inc.

Gladwell, Malcolm. "Black Like Them" by Malcolm Gladwell in *The New Yorker*, April 29–May 6, 1996. Used by permission of the author.

Grossman, Elizabeth. "High-Tech Wasteland" by Elizabeth Grossman. Originally appeared in the July/August 2004 issue of *Orion*. 187 Main Street, Great Barrington, MA 01230. 888-909-6568. www.oriononline.org. Used by permission of the author.

Haidri, Rasma "Urdu, My Love Song" by Rasma Haidri from *Waking Up American: Coming of Age Biculturally*. Copyright © 2005 by Rasma Haidri. Reprinted by permission of Seal Press.

Harmon, Amy. "Love You, K2a2a, Whoever You Are" by Amy Harmon from *New York Times*, January 22, 2006. Copyright © 2006 by The New York Times Co. Reprinted with permission.

Holmes-Brinson, Pennie. "Time Stood Still Again" by Pennie Holmes-Brinson. Originally published in the *Journal of Ordinary Thought*, Winter 2004. Used by permission of the author.

Iweala, Uzodinma. "A Close Encounter" by Uzodinma Iweala first published in *The New York Times Magazine*. Copyright © 2005 by Uzodinma Iweala, permission of The Wylie Agency.

Iyer, Pico. "Home Is Every Place" by Pico Iyer from *Homeground* (Blue Heron Publishing, Hillsboro, OR, 1996). Used by permission of the author.

Jen, Gish. "An Ethnic Trump" by Gish Jen from *The New York Times Magazine*, July 7, 1996. Copyright © 1996 by The New York Times Co. Reprinted by permission.

Kazin, Alfred. Excerpt from *A Walker in the City*, copyright 1951 and renewed 1979 by Alfred Kazin, reprinted by permission of Harcourt, Inc.

Kelley, Robin D. G. "The People in Me" from *ColorLines Magazine*, Winter 1999, www.colorlines.com. Used by permission of *ColorLines*.

Kingston, Maxine Hong. From *The Woman Warrior* by Maxine Hong Kingston, copyright © 1975, 1976 by Maxine Hong Kingston. Used by permission of Alfred A. Knopf, a division of Random House, Inc.

Kovacic, Kristin. "'Proud to Work for the University'" from *Women's Studies Quarterly* (Spring/Summer 1995). Copyright © 1995 by the Feminist Press at the City University of New York. Reprinted with permission of the publishers, www.feministpress.org. All rights reserved.

Laurino, Maria. "Scents" from *Were You Always an Italian? Ancestors and Other Icons of Life in Italian America* by Maria Laurino. Copyright © 2000 by Maria Laurino. Used by permission of W. W. Norton & Company, Inc.

Leonhardt, David. "The College Dropout Boom" by David Leonhardt from *New York Times*, May 24, 2005. Copyright © 2005 by The New York Times Co. Reprinted with permission.

Mabry, Marcus. "Living in Two Worlds" from *Newsweek on Campus*, April 1988. Used by permission of the author.

Malcolm X and Alex Haley. "Hair" from *The Autobiography of Malcolm X* by Malcolm X and Alex Haley, copyright © 1964 by Alex Haley and Malcolm X. Copyright © 1965 by Alex Haley and Betty Shabazz. Used by permission of Random House, Inc.

Meier, Daniel. "One Man's Kids" by Daniel Meier from *The New York Times Magazine*, November 1, 1987. Copyright © 1987 by The New York Times Co. Reprinted by permission.

Morales, Aurora Levins. "Class Poem" from *Getting Home Alive* by Aurora Levins Morales, 1986. Copyright © 1986 by Aurora Levins Morales and Rosario Morales. Used by permission of Firebrand Books.

Mueller, Lisel. "Why We Tell Stories" from *The Need to Hold Still* by Lisel Mueller. Copyright © 1980 by Lisel Mueller. Reprinted by permission of Louisiana State University Press.

Mukherjee, Bharati. "Two Ways to Belong in America" from *The New York Times Magazine*, September 22, 1996. Copyright © 1996 by The New York Times Co. Reprinted by permission.

Naylor, Gloria. "The Meaning of the Word" by Gloria Naylor. Copyright © 1986 by Gloria Naylor. Reprinted by permission of SLL/Sterling Lord Literistic, Inc.

Okita, Dwight. "In Response to Executive Order 9066: All Americans of Japanese Descent Must Report to Relocation Centers" from *Crossing with the Light* by Dwight Okita (Tia Chucha Press, Chicago). Copyright © 1992 by Dwight Okita. Used by permission of the author.

Petrakis, Harry Mark. "Barba Nikos" from *Reflections: A Writer's Life—A Writer's Work* (Lake View Press Chicago, Illinois). Copyright © 1983 by Harry Mark Petrakis. Used by permission of the author.

Register, Cheri. "The Field Trip" from *Packinghouse Daughter: A Memoir*. Copyright © 2000 by Cheri Register. (Minnesota Historical Society Press, 2000.) Used with permission.

Roethke, Theodore. "My Papa's Waltz," copyright 1942 by Hearst Magazines, Inc., from *The Collected Poems of Theodore Roethke* by Theodore Roethke. Used by permission of Doubleday, a division of Random House, Inc.

Rose, Mike. "I Just Wanna Be Average" reprinted and abridged with the permission of The Free Press, a Division of Simon & Schuster Adult Publishing Group, from *Lives on the Boundary: The Struggles and Achievements of America's Underprepared* by Mike Rose. Copyright © 1989 by Mike Rose. All rights reserved.

Savage, Dan. "Role Reversal" by Dan Savage. Copyright © 2001 by Dan Savage. Used by permission of the author.

Sedaris, David. "Picka Pocketoni" from *Me Talk Pretty One Day* by David Sedaris. Copyright © 2000 by David Sedaris. By permission of Little, Brown and Co., Inc.

Shammas, Anton. "Amérka, Amérka" by Anton Shammas from *Harper's Magazine*, February 1991. Copyright © 1991 by Harper's Magazine. All rights reserved. Reproduced from the February issue by special permission.

Snyder, Rachel Louise. "My Lai, Thirty Years After" by Rachel Louise Snyder. Copyright © 1999 by Rachel Louise Snyder. Used by permission of the author.

Soto, Gary. "The Jacket." Copyright © 1986 by Gary Soto. Used by permission of the author and BookStop Literary Agency. All rights reserved.

Staples, Brent. "Night Walker" by Brent Staples from *Ms.* Magazine, September 1986. Used by permission of the author.

Tan, Amy. "Mother Tongue" by Amy Tan. Copyright © 1990 by Amy Tan. First appeared in *The Threepenny Review*. Reprinted by permission of the author and the Sandra Dijkstra Literary Agency.

Thomas, Piri. "Alien Turf" from *Down These Mean Streets* by Piri Thomas, copyright © 1967 by Piri Thomas. Used by permission of Alfred A. Knopf, a division of Random House, Inc.

Thompson, Clive. "Meet the Life Hackers" by Clive Thompson from *The New York Times Magazine*, October 16, 2005. Used by permission of Featurewell.com.

Toussaint, Nicolette. "Hearing the Sweetest Songs" by Nicolette Toussaint from *Newsweek*, May 23, 1994.

Vida, Vendela. "Bikinis and Tiaras: Quinceañeras" from *Girls on the Verge* by Vendela Vida, Copyright © 2000 by Vendela Vida and reprinted by permission of St. Martin's Press, LLC.

Walker, Rob. "The Hidden (In Plain Sight) Persuaders" by Rob Walker from *The New York Times Magazine*, December 5, 2004. Copyright © 2004 by The New York Times Co. Reprinted by permission.

White, Walter. "I Learn What I Am" from *A Man Called White* by Walter White (Arno Press, 1948). Used by permission of Jane White Viazzi.

Wright, Emiene Shija. "Saying Something in African" by Emiene Shija Wright from *Waking Up American: Coming of Age Biculturally*. Copyright © 2005 by Emiene Shija Wright. Reprinted by permission of Seal Press.

Author/Title Index